THE LIMITS OF THE

Felicity Nussbaum examines literary and culⁱ human difference in England and its empire eenth century. With a special focus on women's writing, she analyzes canonical and lesser-known novels and plays from the Restoration to abolition. She considers a range of anomalies (defects, disease, and disability) as they intermingle with ideas of a racial femininity and masculinity to define "normalcy" as national identity. Incorporating writings by Behn, Burney, and the Bluestockings – as well as Southerne, Shaftesbury, Johnson, Sterne, and Equiano – Nussbaum treats a range of disabilities – being mute, blind, lame – and physical oddities such as eunuchism and giantism. She shows that these corporeal features, perceived as aberrant and extraordinary, combine in the popular imagination to reveal a repertory of differences located between the extremes of splendid and horrid novelty.

FELICITY NUSSBAUM is Professor of English at the University of California, Los Angeles. She is the author of *Torrid Zones: Maternity, Sexuality and Empire in Eighteenth-Century English Narratives* (1995), *The Autobiographical Subject: Gender and Ideology in Eighteenth-Century England* (1989), and editor of *The Global Eighteenth Century* (2003).

THE LIMITS OF THE HUMAN

Fictions of Anomaly, Race, and Gender in the Long
Eighteenth Century

FELICITY A. NUSSBAUM

CAMBRIDGE
UNIVERSITY PRESS

PUBLISHED BY THE PRESS SYNDICATE OF THE UNIVERSITY OF CAMBRIDGE
The Pitt Building, Trumpington Street, Cambridge CB2 IRP, United Kingdom

CAMBRIDGE UNIVERSITY PRESS
The Edinburgh Building, Cambridge, CB2 2RU, UK
40 West 20th Street, New York, NY 10011-4211, USA
477 Williamstown Road, Port Melbourne, VIC 3207, Australia
Ruiz de Alarcón 13, 28014 Madrid, Spain
Dock House, The Waterfront, Cape Town 8001, South Africa

http://www.cambridge.org

First published 2003

Printed in the United Kingdom at the University Press, Cambridge

Typeface Adobe Garamond 11/12.5 pt   *System* LATEX 2$_\varepsilon$ [TB]

A catalogue record for this book is available from the British Library

ISBN 0 521 81167 8 hardback
ISBN 0 521 01642 8 paperback

For Nicole

Contents

Illustrations

Acknowledgments

This book was conceived and written after my move to the welcoming climes of California in 1996. I could not imagine a more congenial environment in which to pursue eighteenth-century studies, located as it is near the extraordinary resources of the William Andrews Clark Memorial Library, the Henry E. Huntington Library, and of course the University of California, Los Angeles. I am especially grateful to Peter Reill, Director of the Clark, to Roy Ritchie, Director of the Huntington, and to Thomas Wortham, Chair of the Department of English at the University of California, Los Angeles. All three of these institutions provided research support for this project over the past few years, as well as the National Endowment for the Humanities. In addition, the scholars gathered at the many extraordinarily rich conferences at these institutions fomented my ideas. I am also indebted to the many audiences in the United States and Britain who prodded me toward new conclusions.

The friends and colleagues I list here comprise only a small portion of those who contributed in multiple ways to the book. I am deeply grateful to my graduate students at UCLA, and my former students at Syracuse University, who continually challenge and inspire me. Most especially I thank Jean Howard for her astute intellectual advice and enduring support. Laura Brown remains an unfailingly generous colleague; closer to home Carole Fabricant, Donna Guy, and Alice Wexler regularly offer their intelligent and witty perspectives on work and life. Helen Deutsch early on helpfully discussed issues of defect and disability with me, and stimulated my thinking. Other colleagues at UCLA offered thoughtful critique including Ali Behdad, Joseph Bristow, Lynn Hunt, Margaret Jacob, Rachel Lee, Jayne Lewis, Anne Mellor, Maximillian Novak, and Jenny Sharpe. Friends and colleagues elsewhere including John Bender, Dympna Callaghan, Jill Campbell, Vincent Carretta, Harriet Guest, Kim Hall, Margo Hendricks, Cora Kaplan, Judith Fossett Jackson, Nicholas Mirzoeff, Angela Rosenthal, Roxann Wheeler, and Kathleen Wilson generously shared their ideas and work-in-progress. K. Dian Kriz patiently and willingly guided me through art historical puzzles. Anne Sheehan and Carol Wald expertly assisted with the bibliography and many other research matters.

Special thanks are directed to Jonathan Lamb at Princeton and Joseph Roach at Yale who invited me to speak at conferences on related issues that helped my ideas to take shape. Margaret Powell at the Lewis Walpole Library speedily forwarded prints. I also thank Linda Bree, the editor at Cambridge University Press and herself a knowledgeable eighteenth-century scholar, for her interest and assistance, as well as the particularly perceptive anonymous readers for the Press whose suggestions I have sometimes silently adapted.

Portions of chapter 1 were published previously in *"Defects": Engendering the Modern Body*, co-edited with Helen Deutsch (University of Michigan Press 2000) and *The Passionate Fictions of Eliza Haywood: Essays on her Life and Work*, ed. Rebecca Bocchicchio and Kirsten Saxton (University Press of Kentucky 2000). Part of chapter 2 was first published as "Effeminacy and Femininity: Domestic Prose Satire and Fielding's *David Simple*," *Eighteenth-Century Fiction*, 11.4 (July 1999), 194–216. An earlier version of chapter 5 appeared as "Women and Race: 'A Difference of Complexion,'" in *Women and Literature in Britain, 1700–1800*, ed. Vivien Jones (Cambridge University Press 2000). Sections of chapter 7 appeared as "Being a Man: Olaudah Equiano and Ignatius Sancho," *Genius in Bondage: Literature of the Early Black Atlantic*, ed. Vincent Carretta and Philip Gould (University of Kentucky Press 2001).

Finally, Chris Contreras, Alexandria Currin, Rebecca Petit, and Aaron Steele cheerfully and skillfully provided essential assistance at home. John Agnew, a steady source of wisdom and encouragement, has been my most acute critic and kindest friend. My family, as always, buoys my spirits, even as they wonder at my devotion to a century. The inspiration for this project, my son Marc, continues to defy definitions of human limitation. Finally, I dedicate this book to my daughter, Nicole, whose passionate commitments and dedicated activism I admire, and whose strength and love I treasure.

Introduction: monstrous tales

> Monsters and monster lands were never more in request, and we may
> often see a philosopher or a wit run a tale-gathering in those "idle
> deserts" as familiarly as the silliest woman or merest boy.
> Shaftesbury, *Characteristics of Men, Manners, Opinions, Times*

I

This book considers categories of the human during a period when sexual
and racial differences evolve into their modern shapes within emergent notions of national identity. It focuses on recurring fictions and performances
in England from Aphra Behn's novellas and plays in the late seventeenth
century until the decades of abolition in the early nineteenth century. The
crosshatched representations of race, gender, and anomaly in literary texts
make these differences from the ordinary, at least in the eighteenth century,
at once very easy and very difficult to locate. It is not simply that each of
these differences transmogrifies into one or the other clearly identifiable
form, but rather that the various kinds of difference interrelate to complicate prevailing ideas about the cultural meanings of normalcy and of
humankind.

Here I hope to build on the important work that has invigorated
eighteenth-century studies in the past several decades to bring together
more comprehensively the interplay among these categories and in particular adding *anomaly* to the mix. While *race* and *gender* are terms frequently
investigated in this historical period, the third term *anomaly* requires a bit
of explanation. I am using the word here to describe a variety of irregularities or deviations from that which is presumed to be the natural order of
things. The applications include a range of disabilities (for example, being
mute, blind, lame) and of physical and mental oddities (for example, dark
skin, pock-marked complexion, eunuchism, giantism) occurring naturally
or caused by accident. I have also included the deaf among the anomalous,

I

though they are now defined by many in the non-hearing world as forming a linguistic minority rather than possessing a deficiency; but in the
eighteenth century deafness is most often perceived as a curious flaw. All
three categories – race, gender, and anomaly – are represented at times as
nominal, but at other times as fundamental, or in some cases as a perplex-
ing combination of both. The emerging standards of what it means to be
human in the eighteenth century are increasingly articulated, clarified, and
located within a system of classification which needed to be flexible enough
to incorporate the world's variety within it.

The body, marked or unmarked, is an unstable variable always engaged
with its particular social environment. Recent theories of disability combine
the social model of disability, of an oppressed population in which society
disables the physically and mentally impaired and restricts their activity,
with an older medical model that emphasizes the biological aspects of
difference. This newer formulation, similar in approach to recent feminist
and racialist studies in their retreat from completely denying difference to
complicate instead its relation to historical and cultural contingencies, treats
disability as "both a biological condition *and* a social construct"[1] to offer
alternative models of interaction and accommodation. Just as the legitimacy
of essentialist racial and sexual identity politics has been questioned and
sometimes abandoned, disability "cannot be reduced to a singular identity"
and contests the idea of pure essence.[2] Rather, an "impaired" body and its
restrictive environment have come to be regarded as mutually constitutive
and historically variable. It is one aim of this book to include the anomalous
as critical to the formation of racially and sexually designated normalized
modern subjects. By the end of the eighteenth century gendered identity
is deeply bonded to imagining a normative identity.

A central subject of this book is also the characterization of a defective
and racialized femininity that paradoxically energizes an imperial England
as it struggles to demarcate the limits of the human through women.
Near the beginning of the century Anthony Ashley Cooper, the third
Earl of Shaftesbury (1671–1713), published *Characteristics of Men, Manners,
Opinions, Times* (1711) of which *Soliloquy, or Advice to an Author* is an important part. This text integrates gender issues, race, and monstrosity in
ways that seem especially pertinent to the issues at hand and helps demonstrate the way they often cluster together. Travel narratives, Shaftesbury
categorically asserts in his motley collection of ideas in *Characteristics*, are
merely modern versions of ancient romance. In his rendering, the country
enthralled with monsters and prodigies attempts to expel anomaly from
the home territory in part by attaching the residue of the uncivilized to a

racialized femininity. Natural anomalies, man-made monsters, and imaginary beings often serve as the test cases for the racial and sexual limits of the human as national identity takes shape.

The *Soliloquy* is a conversation between men designed to educate masculine taste to evidence a moral authority that would extend beyond the flawed but tempting aesthetic pleasures afforded by the grotesque or the effeminate, typified in exotica such as "the Indian figures, the Japan work, [or] the enamel."[3] Each of these disturbingly superficial enticements distracts the English from more appropriate pursuits, according to Shaftesbury. Without knowing and recognizing the more enduring beauty exemplified in the classical Venus, a truly refined gentleman cannot "on these [trivial] terms, represent merit and virtue or mark deformity and blemish" (150). Recommending appropriate choices for a gentleman's reading material, the narrator criticizes as soft and flaccid those who delight in the strange and remote: "We care not how Gothic or barbarous our models are, what ill-designed or monstrous figures we view or what false proportions we trace or see described in history, romance or fiction. And thus our eye and ear is lost. Our relish or taste must of necessity grow barbarous while barbarian customs, savage manners, Indian wars and wonders of the *terra incognita* employ our leisure hours and are the chief materials to furnish out a library" (153). Thus it would seem that Shaftesbury entangles the nation's barbarity and its fascination with the marginal and unusual with effeminate tastes and locates them on the world's margins. The appeal of the wondrous tale marks an inadequacy in attaining an achieved masculinity that he assumes to be necessary to a civil society. Even the prototypical romance hero Don Quixote, chides Clara Reeve in *The Progress of Romance* (1785), is "more respectable and more amiable, than a human being, wholly immersed in low, groveling, effeminate, or mercenary pursuits, without one grain of private virtue, or public spirit; whose only thoughts, wishes, and desires, are absorbed in a worthless self."[4] The self-interested aspect of effeminacy in its amplified and inauthentic version of femininity mocks the ideal and runs counter to the best instincts of a truly civilized society. Effeminate beings reflect a society's most vulnerable core and are, like the status of women, a significant measure of the progress of civil society. Shaftesbury, then, in connecting monstrosity to effeminacy and to a perverse femininity, delimits the parameters of sexual difference through its purported excesses.

Taste according to Shaftesbury ought to be home-grown, familiar, and plausible rather than following the current trend which prefers "hearing the monstrous accounts of monstrous men and manners [to] the politest and best narrations of the affairs, the governments and lives of the wisest and most polished people" (154). These writers, seeking to appeal to women's monstrous taste, ought to craft instead a polite, urbane masculinity that is oblivious to fantastic indigenous peoples and to improbable tales of piracy and adventure. Travel tales which recount spellbinding stories arouse and sustain the passion for the unusual in effeminate men and impressionable women readers:

Yet so enchanted we are with the travelling memoirs of any casual adventurer that, be his character or genius what it will, we have no sooner turned over a page or two, than we begin to interest ourselves highly in his affairs... And thus, full of desire and hope, we accompany him, till he enters on his great scene of action, and begins by the description of some enormous fish, or beast. From monstrous brutes he proceeds to yet more monstrous men. For in this race of authors he is ever compleatest and of the first rank who is able to speak of things the most unnatural and monstrous. (154–55)

It was a commonplace, of course, in the eighteenth century that women most favored reading "a wild, extravagant, fabulous Story," as Clara Reeve characterizes romance later in the century.[5] A private habit that wreaks public difficulties when its "high imaginations, florid desires and specious sentiment" penetrate the public affectation of modesty that the English population should cultivate, reading the genre should give way to "polite reading, and converse with mankind of the better sort" (162) to supplant these romances that are located elsewhere in an earlier stage of civilization. According to Shaftesbury's account, what most attracts vulnerable English readers of both sexes to these contagious influences is the appeal of the physiologically and anatomically dissimilar. These irresistably erotic narratives threaten conventional gender difference, since women and effeminate men, the willing auditors of monstrous tales, come to embody that very monstrosity themselves. Reading travel narratives threatens to make monsters of them all.

For the eighteenth-century audience, it seems that Othello embodies the racialized monstrousness that undermines the nation. Believing that Shakespeare especially catered to readers' passionate desire for fantastic tales, Shaftesbury tells his readers that Othello is just such a tale weaver, a "Moorish hero, full-fraught with prodigy, a wondrous story-teller!" who seduced his "fair lady" Desdemona with his invented histories. Superstitious, passionate, and above all womanish, all eighteenth-century readers of wondrous stories resemble Desdemona's succumbing to Othello's "round unvarnish'd tale," later echoed by travel writers including Mungo Park who claims to write "a plain unvarnished tale, without pretentions of any kind," in his enormously popular *Travels in the Interior Districts of Africa* (1799). Shaftesbury quotes Othello's affectation of truthtelling:

> Of antres vast and deserts idle...
> It was my hint to speak...
> And of the cannibals that each other eat,
> The anthropophagi, and men whose heads
> Do grow beneath their shoulders. These [things] to hear
> Would Desdemona seriously incline.
> (*Othello.* Act 1.iii, 155)

One might think, Shaftesbury intones, that such tales would terrify young English ladies. But instead "the fair sex of this island [are], by other monstrous tales, ... so seduced as to turn their favour chiefly on the persons of the taletellers and change their natural inclination for fair, candid and courteous knights into a passion for a mysterious race of black enchanters, such as of old were said to 'creep into houses' and 'lead captive silly women' " (155). These unruly elements, best personified in Othello, undo the proper taste that men of rank should possess, just as women's passion for these elements occasions their sexual fall. England's insatiable lust for the marvellous effeminates the country, corrupts its innocent women, and threatens national integrity.

A powerful cultural image throughout the eighteenth century, then, is that of the woman in love with African tales, Desdemona, whose "Moorish fancy" for Othello and the illicit, miscegenous desire he represents typifies England's desire: "The tender virgins, losing their natural softness, assume this tragic passion, of which they are highly susceptible, especially when a suitable kind of eloquence and action attends the character of the narrator. A thousand Desdemonas are then ready to present themselves and would frankly resign fathers, relations, countrymen and country itself to follow the fortunes of a hero of the black tribe" (156). Caught in earlier stages of civilization, irrational and sentimental women like Desdemona also resemble "native" peoples who are captivated by the mysterious unknown. In short, reading travel narratives deforms, pollutes, effeminates, and even blackens the English imagination. These imaginative geographies taint and seduce the population of England which is eager, like Desdemona, to gobble up travel tales.

The pages that follow return repeatedly to the connections articulated so forcefully by Shaftesbury between domestic and imperial romance which is countered by the increased demand for facticity in England's expanding

The D—of   playing at Foils with her favorite Lap Dog Mungo after Expending
near 10000 to make him a——

1 William Austin, "The Eccentric Duchess of Queensbury fencing with her protégé the
Creole Soubise (otherwise 'Mungo')" (1773). The book Soubise has cast aside burlesques
his master Angelo's illustrated folio on fencing, while "vol 5th Mungo Bill," lies at the
Duchess's feet as a telling record of her support for his aristocratic tastes.

terrain. Displaced from its former prominence to become conclusively the
bailiwick of silly women readers and writers,[6] the apparent rejection of
romance parallels the crucial shift away from speculative geography which
tolerated and even welcomed inventive descriptions, to a more modern form
that claimed to present a transparent image of the world and reproducible
maps of territory that had formerly been *terra incognita* to Europeans.[7]

Contributing to this shift was the fact that small but increasing numbers
of freed slaves entered England later in the eighteenth century making
the threat of real-life Othellos less speculative and more real. The perils to
femininity posed by fascination with the racial monstrous cluster also within
the caricature of "The Eccentric Duchess of Queensbury fencing with her
protégé the Creole Soubise (otherwise 'Mungo')," a print which appears in
the memoirs of Soubise's fencing and riding master, Domenico Angelo, later
in the century (illustration 1). The cartoon portrays Catherine Hyde, Third
Duchess of Queensberry (Matthew Prior's "Kitty") with her black servant.

The beautiful and well-connected Duchess, "Sa Singularité," friend to Gay, Swift, Congreve, Pope, and Pitt, was known as a mad eccentric for preferring unfashionably short hair to modish headdresses, dressing in pink lutestring in defiance of her advanced age, boldly staging plays at a small theatre in Queensberry House (including Young's *Revenge*), perversely giving a party in honor of someone she refused to invite, and hosting numerous dances and masquerades where "her odd freaks strained the forbearance of her friends."[8] The spirited Duchess championed John Gay's sequel to *The Beggar's Opera, Polly* (written in 1728 but not performed until 1777), in which Macheath appears in blackface throughout. Perhaps imagining herself as the crossdressed Polly to Morano (Macheath), she sang the ballad opera airs along with the actors from the audience at the late eighteenth-century performance.

The engraving, printed nine years after Soubise's arrival in England, caricatures the genre of more stately portraiture showing aristocratic white women with their slaves, lapdogs, and other pets. In fact, a different title in some versions makes the association explicit: "The Duchess of Queensberry playing at folio with her favorite Lap Dog Mungo after expending near £10,000 to make him a —." In addition, the picture also resonates with the many illustrations of Thomas Southerne's play *Oroonoko* (1695) that featured a black hero and a white heroine, in which the white woman encourages her African husband to murder her with a dagger. Their passion results in death.[9] The aristocratic Queensberry, superior in color, rank, and stature to her black opponent in the cartoon, is represented as compromised during the potentially mortal contest because of her near fatal attraction to her alleged lover.

Arriving in England on 2 April 1764 at the age of ten, Julius Soubise (taken on board the Royal Naval vessel *Richmond* under the name Othello) was born on St. Kitts of a free white father and enslaved mother. His presence stirred interest among philanthropic women of rank. Stair Douglas, the captain of Soubise's ship, awarded him to the Duchess who renamed him for a hero of the Seven Years' War who was later a courtier in the court of Louis XV and Madame de Pompadour, Charles de Rohan, prince de Soubise (1715–87). Soubise's elegant clothing and extravagant lifestyle seemed to mime the French stereotype associated with his name, and stories of his sexual conquests circulated. In spite of the fact that the Duchess, reputed to be strikingly attractive even in her later years, was more than half a century older that Soubise, the pair were rumored to be lovers. Horace Walpole snidely comments about her, "One should sooner take her for a young beauty of an old-fashioned century than for an antiquated goddess of this age" (and adds roguishly, "I mean by twilight") and she was styled as "most bewitching, most perverse and provoking."[10] Accused of raping another woman, Soubise eventually absconded to Calcutta shortly after his mistress's death (from a surfeit of cherries) in order to escape prosecution. There he successfully managed a riding school for women and men.

Soubise's education in accomplishments usually reserved for the privileged (fencing, riding, playing the violin) afforded him a sanctioned entry into the homes of the wealthy (something Lady Mary Coke and other aristocratic ladies thought would give him inappropriate expectations), and he troubled those who wished to keep blacks within their station. In the picture the combat portrayed between the Duchess and her servant becomes a metaphor for a sexual encounter as well. In their fencing bout, Soubise pins her with his dueling instrument in a winning thrust between the shoulders and the groin. By scoring a touch (touché), Soubise earns a point to best her at the game the fencing master has taught him at her expense. In fact, he touches her at the heart. The Duchess conjures up ideas of manliness, and she had on occasion been compared to the famously hermaphroditic Chevalier D'Eon. Until very recently women were allowed to compete only in foil competitions, not in épée and sabre, and it was unusual for an eighteenth-century woman of any rank to engage in fencing. The Duchess wears a metallic mask suggesting that her head as well as her heart might also be at risk as a target area. The satire directed at both of them registers a variety of levels of grotesqueness.

In the balloon emanating from Soubise's mouth are the words, "Mungo here Mungo dere, Mungo Ev'ry where, above, & below Hah! Vat your Gracy tink of me Now." These lines are drawn directly from a scene in the popular play (which I discuss in chapter 8), Isaac Bickerstaffe's *The Padlock* (1768) when the central character, Mungo, a much-maligned black servant, outfoxes his master Don Diego. The audience would have been well aware of this parallel. A demeaning generic name for a black in the later eighteenth century, the Scots origin of "Mungo" draws implicit connections between the barbarian internal to Great Britain, the Scotsman stuck in an early stage of primitivism, and the foreign "savage"; Soubise was also very likely the subject of a caricature of a black effeminate, "A Mungo Macaroni." Both versions of the cartoon toy with making the former slave a sign of multiple alterities – French and Scots, foppish and primitive, black and aristocratic. Soubise's fashionable dress – "a large nosegay . . . with his laced hat, tasselled cane"[11] – paints him as at once effeminate, the epitome of luxurious display, and bestial.

Was this pairing, then, meant to suggest a cross between different species as well as sexes and races? The black man is complicated by insinuated affinities to the savage, the bestial, *and* the luxurious effete, while the white man-woman is similarly linked both to the lowest of creatures and to the most advanced stages of a corrupt aristocracy weakened by excess. There is even a visual hint that the couple resemble each other in the way the Duchess's mask mirrors Soubise's blackness, and the extent to which the outline of the back of the Duchess's head approximates his simian facial features. His diminutive size, protruding stomach, exaggerated lips and nose recall Edward Tyson's pictures of human-like apes in his notorious *Orang-Outang, sive Homo Sylvestris: or, the Anatomy of a Pygmie* (1699), as well as Edward Long's claim that the Negroes who mated with the orang-outang shared the beast's limited intellectual capacity, and Lord Monboddo's links between the simian and the human. In short, the picture displays two ends of the human spectrum from the black African to the white woman as two contrasting, but congruent, extremes; these sexually and racially equivocal images depend upon each other for the meanings ascribed to them. The unstable and nuanced oppositions I have described in this picture are testimony to the ferment swirling around definitions of difference in the eighteenth century, and to the clusters of such meanings in cultural texts central to this book.

II

Beyond being an index to the level of civilization a society has achieved, an English femininity is predicated on competing assumptions about sexual difference that intersect with other definitions of the human in the New World, India, the Levant, and the South Pacific. As I have suggested in the discussion of Shaftesbury's *Soliloquy*, travel accounts to other parts of the globe make possible and necessary the conceptualization not only of a racially marked femininity, but also a racial masculinity and effeminacy, and a reconciliation of other anomalous beings to definitions of a gendered humankind. As with femininity, the degree of effeminacy within both sexes was regarded, perhaps less obviously, to reflect the state of civilization in England and elsewhere. Most suspect are European men who actually embody masculine loss such as eunuchs and the castrati but also those disappointingly unmanly figures who boast intact genitals but still elicit fears of national weakness through excessive foppishness, exaggerated femininity, and the enervation that results from commercial corruption.

In the midst of observing extensive variation around the newly "discovered" world, the European dilemma is to determine how to provide a satisfactory explanation for human kinship with the most alien of beings while remaining untainted by their incivility and degeneracy. In his account of the Society Islands, Johann Forster in *Observations Made during a Voyage Round the World*, notes the conventional distinctions between animal and beast including common sense, reason, and the ability to speak, as well as the capacity for moral sentiment, the need to suckle the young, and the ability to walk erect. Yet Forster insists on the integrity of the whole species: "Indeed, if we are at once to make a sudden transition from the contemplation of the fairest beauty of Europe to that of a deformed negro; the difference is so great, and the contrast so strong, that we might be tempted to think them of a distinct species: but if we examine the insensible gradations, in the form, habit, size, colour, and some external differences, we shall find that they are by no means so widely remote from each other in the scale of beings, as to form separate species"[12]. In the spectrum that extends from the fairest beauty to the most deformed negro, the woman – explicitly a European woman in spite of Eve's more likely African roots – is the fulcrum and the pinnacle; yet she is also part of the same species with the most degenerate Terra Fuegian. Forster concludes *"that all mankind, though ever so much varied, are, however, but of one species"* (175).

An image equally powerful to that of Desdemona, the Duchess of Queensbury, and others who long for black men is the "fair defect" Eve who personifies a racialized femininity in its most ideal form. In the long and wide eighteenth century, prototypical woman – and in particular the first and fairest of them all – is central to monogenetic claims that human beings are uniformly distinct from the animal species. Exemplary of a perfect femininity, the "lovely fair," a standard of humanity, exhibits a modest but pleasing sexuality that infuses sweetness into men who desire her: "I cannot... enter into any serious argumentation with the patrons and advocates of the long exploded opinion, that monkeys are of the same species with mankind," writes Forster (174). He continues, "I appeal rather to an argument taken from the better half of our species, the fair sex; we all assent to the description which Adam gives of his partner." Citing Milton, Forster finds her to be an exemplary creature:

> *... So lovely fair,*
> *That what seem'd fair in all the world, seem'd now*
> *Mean, or in her summ'd up, in her contain'd*
> *And in her looks; which from that time infus'd*
> *Sweetness into his heart, unfelt before,*
> *And into all things from her air inspir'd.*
> *The spirit of love, and amorous delight.*
> *Grace was in all her steps; heav'n in her eye,*
> *In every gesture dignity and love.*   Milton

Forster continues, "I cannot think that a man looking up to this inimitable masterpiece could be tempted to compare it with an ugly, loathsome ourang-outang! If he still in good earnest be of this opinion, the whole heavenly sisterhood of Eve's fair daughters ought for ever to exclude him from their bright circles: and in case he then persists obstinate, may none but ouran-outangs vouchsafe and admit his embraces" (174). In imagining a human's perversely copulating with a feminized beast, Forster levies punishment on the disbelieving man who fails to recognize Eve's paradisal femininity. Yet Eve is equally of course the object of misogynous satire throughout the eighteenth century. She exemplifies the "fair defect," the monstrosity and deception visited on all women by Eve's fall:

> This Venom spreads thro' all the Female-kind;
> Shew me a Woman, I'll a Monster find.
> They're false by Nature, and by Nature taught,
> The Treachery that *Eve* so dearly bought.[13]

Such contradictory arguments align women, even English women, with the generic deformed who defy gender or specific geographical region, and who are associated with nations and peoples who do not share in being "fair." Like the noble and ignoble savage, the perfect Eve is deeply flawed.

Monogenist and polygenist views of human differences circulated and evolved throughout the eighteenth century, though by the later decades the debates had been complicated by abolition sentiments and the diversity revealed through wider exploration. In the 1770s and 1780s the barbarity of black Africans was often attributed to environmental causes and this led toward a more hierarchical arrangement on the scale of humanity. Stadial theory of course proposed that there had been four stages of socio-historical development after creation in which man progressed from the most primitive state to the most civilized. According to the dominant monogenist view to which Johann Forster subscribed (as well as Adam Ferguson, John Millar, Buffon, and others) the human family constituted one race, and the early books of Genesis furnished the narrative justification.[14] For the monogenists, differences in pigmentation or physical features might then be ascribed to geography, migration, mutation, climate, diet, and cultural customs instead of discrete moments of creation. By midcentury Buffon's *Histoire naturelle* in dialogue with Linnaeus imagined humanity as a continuum and linked through scientific claims distinct degenerate species to "race."[15] Degeneration from the original species occurs especially when women's reproductive capacity is insufficiently regulated or when imperiled peoples relocate to other climes. Women are granted special moral authority in shaping civilization through public and private virtue,[16] and they bear a special responsibility for the preservation and reproduction of the species in its purest form. As superior beings, the fair daughters of Britain are also the designated guardians of their country's distinctive complexion. It is their patriotic duty to preserve a "race" from degeneration and deformity. In the "fairer nations," Forster suggests, women appropriately eschew intermarriage with "negroes, mulattos, or other aboriginal or mixed tribes of hot climates," for interbreeding creates a suspicion "that their character and complexion must generally degenerate, and become more and more debased" (183). Such peoples were believed to lack sufficient education, the ability to propagate, and European advancements.[17] Still, nagging questions persisted about the systematic classification and ranking of variations in an essentially unified humanity. Of course, for monogenists, one single act of creation spawned mankind, and the multiplication of diverse cultures evolved at another time. Unity, however, did not necessarily guarantee equality among all peoples. Perhaps, it was thought, the human species was so various and complicated that more than one scale of progress pertained.

Alternatively, man's history involved falling into barbarism and savagery after having been created in God's perfect image. Renaissance theories linked degeneracy to human taxonomies.[18] Authors such as Henry Home, Lord Kames (*Sketches of the History of Man* 1788), edged toward polygenetic beliefs but held back from a fuller commitment to them because of loyalty to biblical Christian creation myths. In the more secular polygenetic account, inequalities and distinctions were explained by multiple creations having taken place in two or three places on one single historical occasion, and worries about the coloring and degeneracy of the Negro encouraged polygenetic justifications for racism followed by the pseudoscientific racism of the nineteenth century. At the same time, however, Goths, Huns, and Vandals contributed to progressive civilization of the North.

The passion for scientific and ethnographic collection, originating in earlier periods but epidemic in the eighteenth century, sought to clarify social origins and to find a uniform universal order as it derived from particular objects, places, or peoples. Most important to my argument here is the fact that theories popular in earlier centuries about the passing of cultural characteristics from one group to another, from one place to another, held moral implications. Decline was endemic to theories of social change and to systems of cultural diffusion as humanity diverged from its original and purer form. Polygenetic theories were thus open to and even productive of ideas about man's corruption, while monogenesis offered a more neutral foundation for sameness and uniformity. For the polygenist, the direction of cultural evolution rolled unrestrained down the torrent of fate toward greater sin and corruption. This dark shadow troubling the belief in progress of the Scottish Enlightenment *philosophes* pulled humankind into decline. According to Margaret Hodgen's lucid understatement, "Diffusion, contract, mingling, the horizontal transmission of culture from one people to another was branded therefore as something less than desirable."[19] In any of these accounts of the human species – monogenetic or polygenetic, progressive, or degenerative – Eve's problematic potential as a fair defect could be incorporated. Just as defect proves to be foundational to gender difference, degeneration, often believed to evidence itself in physical anomaly, is also integral to ideas of racial difference in theories about human origins that evolve and are transformed by Enlightenment ideas of progress.

Some eighteenth-century travelers recognize that Europeans manage to contaminate idealized societies in spite of protestations that they possessed a superior culture. An anonymous author in the *London Magazine* worries that "we, a more refined race of monsters, contaminated all their bliss by an introduction of our vices."[20] Johann Forster and Captain Cook in their exploration of the South Pacific sometimes share a sense of bewilderment that the happiness of islanders is not increased by emulating European society. These nations find themselves in a decayed state as the result "of a few profligate individuals, very much debased, and mixed with the miseries, which are entailed upon our civilized societies, by luxury and vice" (192). When Forster, Cook, and others come to recognize that European exports such as leprosy, smallpox, and venereal disease may have spoiled the paradisal Oceania and contaminated its purity, they too speculate about the origins of degeneration.

Yet among explorers there is also a disquieting sense that the primitive is not unabashedly ideal, and that the deformed, hideously diseased, licentious, and monstrous insidiously trouble romantic perfection. In ascertaining the causes for the varieties of mankind in the South Pacific islands, the final category Forster discusses is "peculiar defects or excesses . . . of the human body" (180). The depressed forehead of the people of Mallicollo causes those indigenous peoples to resemble monkeys; the Tierra del Fuegians are "a chubbed race," a degenerate type of short and squat people similar to dwarfs, though their large knees are acquired from sitting on their hams; and he remarks on the broad and prominent noses of many South Sea islanders (though as they move toward the West these features are less prominent). Some lack fingers, most have widely pierced ears, and even their circumcision is taken to reflect mutilation. In other groups the

2 William Hogarth, "The Inspection," *Marriage A-la-Mode*, Plate 3 (1745). In this
engraving the anomalous become objects of inquiry, and various irregularities
of nature, human and nonhuman, are compressed into the cluttered space of the
"doctor's" office space.

breasts of the women are "flaccid and pendulous" because of exposure to the
elements which occasions "the greater relaxation of the body in the women
of the lower class" (181). In short, these aberrant peoples display human
variety even as the idyllic status of some South Pacific peoples verifies the
extraordinary exemplarity of Eve as a prototype of the primitive and as an
emblem of Europe's prehistory.

It is in this context that we might also interpret the third plate in William
Hogarth's *Marriage A-la-Mode* (1745), one of a series which in its entirety
is emblematic of a patchwork of notions about the human at an important moment in English domestic and imperial history (illustration 2).
This multifaceted visual satire, like the cartoon of the Duchess of
Queensberry and Soubise fencing, draws into conjunction the categories
upon which I focus throughout this book. Hogarth's full series of six plates

mock aristocratic greed, indolence, and adultery in an English culture obsessed with explaining and excusing its newfound luxury and its attendant indolence. Plate 3 integrates the decayed and victimized feminine into a highly suspect aesthetic taste paired with aristocratic debauchery. The Earl's libertinism in contaminating a young maiden with venereal disease is yoked to monstrosity, colonial curiosity, and a compromised masculinity. A quack doctor (himself infected) and the prepossessing woman (perhaps the maiden's bawd and mother) coupled with him apparently respond to the Earl's anger at his prescribing an ineffectual cure for the younger ruined woman. The pair of debased women – the diseased child and the virago-like bawd – figure doubly and centrally in the picture. A huge phallic-like buttress, a narwhal's tusk, seems to emanate from the head of the large hoop-skirted and pock-marked Amazon, the man-woman who is the focal point of the picture and who brandishes a razor at the apparent attack on the doctor's qualifications.[21] The horn-like object also makes her resemble the apocryphal unicorn, one of the unnatural monsters frequently inhabiting travel books. The sexually rapacious Earl is armed with his own phallic weapon, a walking stick poised to strike at the defective bow-legged and nearly toothless doctor with shrunken shoulders and broad hips. The quack's suspect connoiseurship is figured in a cabinet of curiosities and represented in the instruments and artifacts strewn around the room. His claims to science seem as specious as his medical knowledge. The "civilized" are deeply suspect in their confidence that science can cure civilization's contaminated bodies.

Even the margins of Hogarth's picture are replete with emblems representing the limits of the human. Most interestingly, mounted above the heads of the diseased couple are various collectibles of empire – a stuffed crocodile, the infant propped above the door, huge ostrich eggs, and a monstrous lizard carcass – and on the wall are displayed pictures of a cannibal whose head is beneath his shoulders, a two-headed hermaphrodite, and below them petrified mummy cases. The phrase "anthropophagi, and men whose heads / Do grow beneath their shoulders" (which Shaftesbury had quoted from *Othello*) is given visual realization. From the top center of the picture stares a threatening "goggle-eyed trade model" who is meant to advertize the curative powers of the pill he holds in his mouth. The antediluvian fossil bone behind him is a sign of giganticism.[22] Pictured with animal artifacts, pseudo-scientific claptrap, and the savage man-eater, the young aristocrat and his fallen mistress are more closely aligned with the animal than the civilized. The miscellaneous exotica produce a series of possible narratives: of sexual aberration in the hermaphrodite, of violation of the definition of the human in the cannibal, and of the corrosive power of degenerative sexual disease in the aristocratic world of taste. All are united by the occasion for the encounter – the contagious disease engendered in the seduced maiden that is the sign of a spoiled femininity which has more in common with the savage than the privileged world with which it would seem to be aligned. Savage and civilized would at first appear to be reversed, though neither is firmly tethered to women or men, to a particular class or trade, or to a particular geographical location. The geography of defect and race here intertwine with corrupt femininity and masculinity in England to domesticate and creolize them. The remarkable and regular conjunction of these categories internalizes the monstrous within the domestic and the homeland, and the contradictions among the juxtaposed categories of racial and gendered subjects complicate English perceptions of the defective within and without the country.

III

This book is divided into two sections, one concentrating on anomaly and the other on race, each as it is inflected by gender, but each of the categories easily escapes its moorings to attach itself to another kind of difference. Readers will recognize that this book builds on my previous interests as well as on the rich context of interdisciplinary criticism relevant to eighteenth-century studies.[23] Much of this work focuses significantly on one or another difference but no single book of which I am aware has attempted to make the kinds of multiple connections I am drawing here, especially as they are present in the literature of the period. In the first section I have selected fictions that offer significant reflections on the gendered aspects of extraordinary bodies, many of which are written by women. The second section focuses on representations of racialized bodies but especially through the domesticated performance of the internalized other as witnessed on stage and in London streets. Some readers may wish for a book on each of these topics, for more attention to India or the South Pacific, or to the abolitionist debates, or for a more extended discussion of any one of the topics introduced. These worthy projects await further treatment but are beyond my scope here.

The oppositions I am examining do not long remain secure. I begin with defective women, the best and the worst combined. The first half of the book focuses on a series of women writers central to representing femininity and effeminacy throughout the eighteenth century including Aphra Behn, Eliza Haywood, Sarah Fielding, Elizabeth Montagu and the

Bluestockings, and Frances Burney, but more canonical works by Samuel Johnson and Laurence Sterne are also considered. The first chapter surveys fictions of defect from medical literature and misogynist satires that connect woman's sexual difference to her "fair defect." Yet it is her very blemish, her disfiguring lack of an appendage that also is the mark of her specialness as distinct from the other sex. My reading of Behn's two short tales, *The Dumb Virgin: or, The Force of Imagination* and *The Unfortunate Bride: Or, The Blind Lady a Beauty* (both published in 1700), shows that women who are literally handicapped (in addition to their natural defect as women) may possess unusual capacities for wisdom or understanding. Their special abilities would seem to be dependent upon their freakishness, forming a conjunction that parallels the plight of the eighteenth-century woman writer. Eunuchs, like befouled femininity, are icons for both the worrisome presence and the glorious absence of defect. Similarly Duncan Campbell, the deaf-mute soothsayer immortalized by Eliza Haywood and others, is empowered through his disability and his feminization, and he poignantly personifies the difficulty of finding voice. He resembles women writers in possessing a defect which makes him a commodified object of wonder and spectacle. As a sentient and sexual being, he also defies racialized assumptions about his origins and his supposed bestiality. In this chapter anomalous beings demonstrate alternatives to spoken language as avenues to reasoned exchange and sociability.

Sexual difference figures first in accounts of the loveliest of women, Eve, who repeatedly embodies femininity as unredeemed defect. The section on defect continues with distinctions I draw between *femininity* and *effeminacy* with particular attention to Sarah Fielding's *David Simple* as exemplary of the exchange of gendered characteristics between the manly woman and the parodically feminine man. If British manliness is the opposite of the macaronic fop, and if its absence is a threat to national security, then being effeminate or its opposite – a female who embodies masculinity – is given geographical specificity outside England. Thus, effeminacy lends itself to racial connotations and is yet another of civilization's barometers.

I turn then to the intellectual community of the Bluestockings to suggest the relevance of the correspondence of Elizabeth Montagu, Elizabeth Carter, and Elizabeth Vesey to notions of femininity. When Montagu wrote to Carter, translator of Epictetus, that women's "feminalities" – their weakness and timidity – disgraced the female character, she also worried that learned ladies might appear to be excessively masculine. These learned women were influential in determining the shape of femininity *and* feminism into the nineteenth century. Beginning from a manuscript letter in which Montagu peculiarly labels Samuel Johnson's prose style in the *Preface to Shakespeare* a threat to England because of its effeminacy, this chapter explains her peculiar way of describing Johnsonian language as an exchange of gendered characteristics within the women's social intercourse. Several of the women are themselves accused of intellectual monstrosity, and the allegedly "unnatural" character of their friendships has been the subject of much speculation. Peculiarly aligned with these odd women are the emasculated characters in Laurence Sterne's *Tristram Shandy*. This chapter pairs "the wits and the Blues," as Hester Thrale called them, as they define femininity and effeminacy in the decades of the 1760s and the sexually equivocal 1770s. The comparison supports the argument that defect is fundamental to modern definitions of gender difference, and it stresses the importance of community in turning oddity into innovative sociability.

The section on anomaly and gender concludes with a study of the debilitating effects of smallpox on eighteenth-century women, their beauty, and their prospects. Disease threatens the nation's health and wealth, and its sources are often displaced onto alien peoples whose complexions and bodies are imagined as inferior. Though elaborate remedies were created to avoid residual pitting of the skin and the spread of the disease, fears of contamination of the population persisted into the later eighteenth century. Frances Burney's *Camilla* (1796), like earlier novels and poems in the century (most notably Lady Mary Wortley Montagu's "Satturday: The Small Pox") demonstrates the way that the resultant disfigurement and scarring dislodge later eighteenth-century assumptions. The novel's maimed character Eugenia, rewarded for her pock-marked face by the coins first struck for use in the slave trade, contests expectations of femininity; as its deformed and racialized opposite, she also triumphs as its exemplary representative.

In texts as historically distant as *Oroonoko* and *Camilla*, visible difference, and especially complexion, is an important component in cultural assessments of beauty and of race. The exotic often conveys a sense of the ornamental aspects of racialization, while the attempt to wash the blackamoor white reveals a surface-interior dichotomy heightened by fears that blackness cannot be washed away. The second portion of the book begins by surveying literature in which the authors are vexed by the differences of complexion newly observed in an imperial context and an expanding geographical terrain. In this section I discuss in turn black women, white women, black men (including their impersonation by white men), and juxtapositions of racial representations in drama, poetry, fiction, and lifewriting to conclude with analyses of late eighteenth-century encounters that hint of the struggles to follow regarding miscegenation and degeneration.

For much of the century modern racial classifications were not yet firmly established, but blackness regularly ranks near the bottom of the scale. Yet with the growth of the abolition movement, blackness also inspires the philanthropic and the sentimental. I argue both that racial categories become more solidified as the numbers of freed blacks in England increase, and that abolition coincides with heightened concerns about miscegenation even as a greater expectation of racial realism on the stage develops. As the demand for credibility in travel accounts and fictive representations increases, so does racist thinking, and that abolition paradoxically brings increased fears of intermixture.

Focusing on the transformation of Aphra Behn's Imoinda from the black African wife of the eponymous hero in the novella *Oroonoko* to a white woman in Southerne's play, I also explore the early history of blackface on the eighteenth-century London stage in relation to an invisible difference, white femininity. Chapter 7 offers an explanation for Imoinda's color change. Actresses who first appeared on stage were, of course, often considered to be sexually corrupt, a characteristic which was sometimes portrayed as racialized as well. Unlike the racial mixture embodied in the blackened white actors playing Oroonoko and Othello, femininity resists being reconceptualized as racial mixture in a nation coming to define itself and its women to a significant degree by skin color and quality.

Masculinity as much as femininity is the ground on which racial difference is laid out in the tragedy and comedy of empire. Black men are much more conspicuous than black women within the English culture and within the nation itself in the eighteenth century because of the greater migration of male slaves. The trajectory moves simultaneously toward increased freedom, and equally steadily toward a more focused and intractable racism. To demonstrate this point, I consider the concept of black manliness with special reference to the slave narrative of Olaudah Equiano and the letters of Ignatius Sancho, the two most prominent literate Afro-Britons in the period. Black masculinities, products of white attraction and repulsion, ran the spectrum from classical princeliness to exaggerated sexuality, and they helped to formulate in the later eighteenth century an alternative to the thin range of European masculinities which included the effeminate fop, the hypersexual libertine, and the economic man who was also the sociable gentleman. The highly visible Equiano and Sancho were among those who successfully negotiated this dangerous territory in the European public sphere.

As I show in chapter 8, racialized masculinity in the British theatre of the eighteenth century can be further deciphered from the dramatic repertory acted by Ira Aldridge, the first black actor on the English stage, in parts such as Othello, Zanga in Edward Young's *Revenge*, and the leading roles in *Oroonoko*, and *The Ethiopian, or the Quadroon of the Mango Grove* (*The Slave*). Through an analysis of Aldridge's repertory, I examine a nation's ability to distract itself from the violence perpetrated on the black male body and its investment in the public performance of black masculinity, thus highlighting the black woman's absence from the theatre until the late eighteenth and early nineteenth centuries. Further, I argue that the English stage during the decades of abolitionist activity forged interracial male bonding between black and white men that was predicated on fracturing the feminine and eradicating the black female. As feminism propelled itself into prominence with Mary Wollstonecraft's *Vindication of the Rights of Woman* (1792), these bonds crucially circumscribed white women's emergence into the public sphere.

In short, in this history of early English minstrelsy, the public counterfeit of black face defused the threat of black masculinity and helped regulate racial and sexual relations in much the same way as nineteenth-century American minstrelsy. An embodied black male presence enters the theatre in the same decades when, after ending the slave trade in 1807, slaves were finally emancipated in England in 1833. By figuring blackness in this way on the domestic home stage, the plays, autobiographical accounts, and poems offer a range of dissonant fictions which celebrate black masculinity while easing the path to continued dispossession and exploitation at home and abroad. Finally, I show that the slippage between racial categories decreases at about the same time that a black man appears on the stage, and during the period when the product of miscegenated unions – mulatto children – become increasingly visible in England itself. The cultural function that these figures of shifting complexions had played, moving rather randomly from one geographical location to another, from one tincture to another, evaporates; racial categories and their relationship to geographical identity harden; and the playfulness with which these fictional characters inhabited variously colored bodies becomes a matter of deadly, even legislated, seriousness. Our current difficulties in assigning color to complexion, nationality to a person's name, identity to a geographical region or nation, and a knowing consciousness to unusual anatomies or anomalous beings, appropriately remind us that these categories continue to influence the ways we continue to redefine the boundaries of being human.

PART I
Anomaly and gender

CHAPTER I

Fictions of defect: Aphra Behn and Eliza Haywood

I

Echoing Alexander Pope's sentiment in *Epistle to A Lady*, "Fine by defect, and delicately weak" (1735), an eighteenth-century misogynist tract defines woman as a defective man, less than a man and lacking his perfection, because she possesses less vigor and strength. *Female Rights Vindicated* (1753) continues by asserting that women have been regarded since Aristotle as deformed amphibious things, "neither more or less than *Monsters*."[1] Countering this assumption that sexual difference should be construed as defect, a feminist response to another vindication of women's rights claims, "Each [sex] was perfect in its Way; and it was necessary they should be disposed as we see them, and every Thing that depends upon their respective constitutions, is to be consider'd as Part of their Perfection. It is therefore without Foundation, that some imagine the Women are not so perfect as the Men, and represent that as a Defect, which is an essential Appendage to their Sex, without which they could not answer the Intent of their Creation."[2] The "Appendage to their sex" (called an "essential Portion of their Sex" in an earlier version) refers to women's reproductive organs, and in particular the womb, construed in the earlier Aristotelian and Galenic models to be an interior penis which constitutes the salient biological difference.[3] Unlike a man's appendage, woman's is not palpable or easily visible. The essence of womanhood is her womb, hidden and interior, rather than the exterior organs of femininity. This mysterious female difference is misconstrued, the tract argues, as deformity since men habitually and misogynistically deem women's flaws to be intrinsic to their natural sexual difference. Their defect arises not only from the lack of a penis but from the presence of an alternative, inferior body part. Woman's appendage – the reproductive womb – embodies failed femininity within a striking dynamic of similarity and difference.

This chapter attempts to trace the ways that disability and gender inflect one another in the early eighteenth century, and to show a paradoxical valorization and rejection of anomalous beings. Here I examine the alignment between defect and gender in several early fictions written by women in the context of these vindications and other writings to assess the ways that aberrance and disfigurement helped both to articulate sexual difference and to obscure its binaries. Cultural anxieties about "natural" boundaries between the sexes help constitute the problem they describe and attack. In particular I am discussing fictions that complicate and realign expectations that femininity will prove defective. Aphra Behn and Eliza Haywood, I suggest, celebrate, refine, and counter the prevailing constructions of femininity as deformity. These constructions also extend to the much desired but mutilated man, the eunuch, who veers so radically away from the conquering economic hero crucial to the formation of a British identity; and to a deaf, nonspeaking prophet whose compensatory gift as a soothsayer embodies the paradox of femininity. Thus disabling or disfiguring a woman sometimes corresponds to the equivocal marking of a man as a particularly anomalous being.

A defective man was often taken to be a mere imitation of femininity since defect bears a linguistic and cultural equivalency to womanhood. In this construction, substance signals masculinity while lack signifies femaleness. Another set of oppositions that help to shape the idea of a "normal" body arises between internal and external defect. A woman's value within the sexual economy evolves from her external beauty which is both "*Merchantable*" and the object of contempt, both precious and demeaned, both visible and invisible, as her "defect" is valued as the object of envy, yet the site of monstrosity. *Beauty's Triumph* (1751), a further defence of women, claims that even women's elaborate artifice cannot adequately disguise blemishes. Here the cultural meaning of "blemishes" slips between the metaphorical and the material, between that of character and of a more literal physical disfigurement: "By shewing you to yourselves in a true light, it will, I hope, enable you to improve the real excellencies, and to remove out of sight all the blemishes you may discover in yourselves. And as patches and paint will be useless to hide the defects which this will point you out, it may possibly set you on finding out better expedients to prevent the ill effects of them, than the daubing disguise of affectation."[4] Anatomists of the later eighteenth and early nineteenth centuries sometimes literally erased blemishes to mold representations of the body into more idealized versions.[5] Depicting flaws obviously interfered with portraying womanhood as perfection, but cosmetics were only a temporary and unsatisfactory solution to women's escaping their inherently inadequate state. In short, women's blemishes were often imagined to be the outward manifestation of an internal deficiency, and defects for both sexes could be deemed substantive as well as superficial.

The misogynist male narrator in *Beauty's Triumph* ironically links "blemish" both to women's beauty and to anatomical essentialism. Recalling the assignment of defect to the womb, he offers Salacia as an example of a mother whose interior blemishes result in deformed and monstrous children. For her, blemishes compose the perfection of womanhood, but the ability to give birth, the most potent marker of sexual difference, corresponds with monstrosity and moral perversion. Though women are responsible for reproducing the species, their principal deformity rests in their incapacity to bear healthy "normal" babies: "That WOMEN *are no more to be trusted than their* WOMBS: these being not more liable to miscarry of their fruits, than they of the trust we deposit in them" (124). A particularly defective nature (such as that of a prostitute) suffuses a mother's deformity into her progeny or, alternatively threatens to makes her barren, though even apparently "normal" mothers may give birth to defective children.[6] The womb – in misogynist tracts, the sign of woman's ineradicable defect – either replicates its monstrosity in the children it spews forth or is condemned to forfeit its reproductive function. Woman's monstrous inadequacy, her freakishness, results from having a womb, whether she bears children or is unable to bear them.

Eighteenth-century controversies surrounding the question of the potency of the maternal imagination raised the spectre of extraordinary female power over producing "normal" offspring so that the entire category of the female embodies the difference that deforms.[7] *Orthopaedia: or, the Art of Correcting and Preventing Deformities in Children* connected having intercourse during menstruation to bearing deformed children (illustration 3).[8] Even Mary Wollstonecraft couples what she believes to be a cultural tendency toward effeminacy with a high incidence of mental retardation among the privileged classes, and she asserts that championing women's virtue produces healthy babies for the middling classes. While bearing well-formed children may excuse and justify woman's "defect," her intrinsic femaleness also aligns itself with disfigurement. The defect of womanhood that is concentrated within the womb may migrate to other parts of the body and even to other bodies. Beyond the inherent defect of the sex, *particular* women bear a double defect in also being blind, lame, deaf, ugly, or scarred. Women of both sorts – the general run of femininity and the particular case of anomalous beings – throughout the century focus cultural

Hulett Sculp

3 Frontispiece to Nicholas Andry, *Orthopaedia: Or, the Art of Correcting and Preventing Deformities in Children* (1743). The maternal figure provides the standard measure for the cherubic figures who nestle around her.

anxieties about links between normalcy and gender in fictions of defect as diverse as Henry Fielding's noseless *Amelia*, Sarah Scott's pock-marked ladies, and Frances Burney's lame, scarred, and humpbacked Eugenia.

Deformity, like defect, is a word with eighteenth-century currency. Though deformity was often linked to foreign locales, William Hay, a member of the House of Commons, provided a local instance. Articulating an identity as a disabled person in *Deformity: An Essay* (1754), he employs William Hogarth's admiration of the rounded line in *Analysis of Beauty* to define the curvature of his spine as aesthetically pleasing, and thus to suggest that judgments about attractiveness may be culturally determined. Yet "deformity" most frequently serves as the opposite of beauty in, for example, the treatise *Hebe; or, the Art of Preserving Beauty, and Correcting Deformity* (1786). There a missing eyebrow, large nose, wandering eye, hare lip, wide mouth, chin hair, freckles, and birthmarks signify deformities. Characterized by asymmetrical or misshapen bodies, deformity may be an unnatural and correctable condition, "not as a total privation of beauty, but as a want of congruity in the parts, or rather an inability in them to answer their natural design; as when one arm or leg is longer than the other; when the back is hunched, when the eyes squint, and such similar defects: which, however, are not to be opposed as a contrast to beauty; for the unfortunate object may, in every other part of his body, be exactly well-made, and perfectly agreeable."[9] This problem of anatomical malformation, especially characteristic of women's bodies, may be deemed either accidental, manmade, or attributable to inadequate child care and poor health habits. Yet it may also be permanent and intractable, requiring cosmetic disguise and inspiring pity or derision: "Ugliness always excites our aversion to the object in which it resides; deformity as generally calls up our commiseration."[10] In short, ugliness often reflects an inner evil while irremediable deformity, "an inability to answer nature's design," excites compassion.

Aphra Behn's two tales of defect, *The Dumb Virgin: or, The Force of Imagination* and *The Unfortunate Bride: Or, The Blind Lady a Beauty* (both published in 1700), suggest that all femininity is deformed or monstrous by definition, and that a particular subclass of defective women who populate these fictions is especially disquieting.[11] At one level these doubly defective women stand in for all femininity; at another level they represent women who defy femininity, women writers. In these novellas the unstable relationship of beauty to virtue, of defect to lust, displays the linkages between gender and defect. In *The Dumb Virgin*, a wealthy Venetian senator's wife expresses an unbridled passion to visit an idyllic seat of pleasure, an island in the Adriatic Sea. Renaldo's yielding to his wife's excessive desires rather than taking command results in the birth of defective children. The eldest, Belvideera, a physically deformed daughter "addicted to study" (344) is described as a neutered child without an identifiable gender: "its limbs were distorted, its back bent, and tho the face was the freest from deformity, yet had it no beauty to recompence the dis-symetry of the other parts" (344). Belvideera's femininity is lost because of the unmistakably obvious crippling of her body. The mother's imagination, especially the erotic desire for something exotic and unfamiliar, and her unrealized fears of being taken captive and enslaved, produce defect; but defect also interrupts or complicates desire.

The tragedy resulting from the deformities is compounded when Belvideera's mother dies in giving birth to a second daughter, Maria, who is beautiful but unable to speak, "which defect the learn'd attributed to the silence and melancholy of the Mother, as the deformity of the other was to the extravagance of her frights" (344). In both cases the mother's reproductive power is compromised by immoderate desire, and her womb, the defective appendage, makes manifest her hidden faults to produce a more definitive secondary category of flawed femininity in the second generation. In Maria's case the defect of speechlessness, as in the generality of womanhood, is made invisible through the natural disguise of female beauty; in the witty Belvideera's case, her facility with words distracts auditors from the painfully obvious flaw, and she compensates for her natural impediments by becoming a linguistic prodigy. If Maria's defect results from her mother's timidity, Belvideera's deformity arises from bold desire, thus setting forth a tentative distinction between the causes of defect and deformity.

The beautiful Maria, skilled at sign language but unable to speak, exhibits charm and grace, and her dazzling radiance is so extreme that it cannot be viewed directly. When a portrait painter finds himself incapacitated by her riveting beauty. Maria resorts to completing the picture herself. Silenced in traditional ways and thus excluded from a conventional loquacious femininity, Maria is a creative woman who finds a means to express herself through art. In contrast Belvideera's tongue, in spite of her physical deformity, carries a force that is as compelling as Maria's eyes. As such she typifies the learned, peculiar man-woman whose femininity throughout the eighteenth century is questioned, and she is placed outside the usual sexual traffic.

Both sisters, one beautiful but silent and the other ugly but brilliant, become competitors for Dangerfield, a suitor whose Turkish turban signals his exotic taste.[12] The uncomely Belvideera at first prevents Dangerfield from learning about her sister's mute condition. Maria curses her speech-lessness, a handicap explained as a penance for unnamed sins, that prevents her from voicing her passion. Though Maria pulses with sensual heat, "her breasts with an easy heaving show'd the smoothness of her Soul and of her Skin" (351); it is her searing beauty that inflicts metaphoric wounds on her lover. One sister's contorted limbs are weighed against the other sister's being "dumb" as the women debate whether disfigurement or muteness is the greater public shame; yet both seem united in their sexual desire for Dangerfield and in the fear that their aberrant femininity excludes them from successfully circulating within a marriage economy.

This romantic tragedy inspires women to believe that physical handi-caps, handicaps that exceed the defect of being a woman, need not be an impediment to love but almost certainly preclude marriage. In choosing be-tween the sisters Dangerfield prefers Maria's silent beauty to the deformed Belvideera's wit. Swooning into his arms, Maria scribbles a message that finally reveals her mute state, and he responds, "*Dumb*, (he cryed out) *naturally Dumb? O ye niggard powers, why was such a wondrous piece of Art left imperfect?*" (353–4). Maria figures the very state of being woman in her embodiment of the disturbing contrast between her remarkable ex-ternal beauty and her interior flaw. The plot then takes a startling turn. In Dangerfield's dying moments, his dagger birthmark reveals that he is actually Maria's brother who had supposedly drowned in the Adriatic Sea. This bodily defect signifies the deeply tainted nature of the mother's legacy to her son, and Maria's figurative blindness leads to a greater monstrosity – incest. The recognition that Maria had slept with her brother dawns as "a violent impulse broke the ligament that doubled in her Tongue," and exclaiming "*Oh! Incest, Incest*" (359), she impales herself on her brother's sword. The narrator, herself a playwright, "struck dumb by the horrour of such woful objects," is herself made speechless when the heroine's tongue is loosened.

To suggest that Behn constructs Maria without a subjectivity unwittingly replicates the idea of woman as a defect of nature. One critic has observed that "Maria's entry to subjectivity/speech is then coterminous with her death and with her recognition of her desire as incestuous,"[13] but Maria's subjectivity is not confined to speech. In Behn's tale the disability that defines woman as woman does not completely disempower her, and though Maria struggles to make her wishes known, she is not without will. Maria successfully employs sign language ("her silent conversation," 345) and communicates intimately with her sister in an elegant and original way. The mute Maria conveys a fully developed subjectivity including desire, envy, and surprise through painting, writing, body movements, clothing, and manner: "The language of her Eyes sufficiently paid the loss of her Tongue, and there was something so commanding in her look, that it struck every beholder as dumb as herself" (345). Both subject and object, she in fact turns the tables to disable onlookers with her stunning looks. Similarly, the leveling effect of a masquerade they attend allows Maria to compete for men without having to talk, and it becomes the turning point in creating jealous envy between the sisters: "Poor *Maria* never before envied her Sister the advantage of speech, or never deplor'd the loss of her own with more regret" (348). Though Maria flirtatiously affects an inability to communicate her passion, Dangerfield has no doubt about his conquest over her heart. Finally Maria's recognition of her incestuous desire for her brother prevents the marriage; and Belvideera, assigning her fortune to an uncle, resigns herself to the reclusive virginity typical of a learned lady. Physical deformity, ugliness, and verbal impairment seem to forestall marriage, a marriage that could only reproduce monstrosity. In short, in the novella the more encompassing category of women in general reproduces defect through sexual desire, while the subclass of overreaching ladies defy their defect but die calling out the very name of monstrosity.

Women's empowerment in this period, whether it derives from beauty's empire, linguistic skill, or political and military victory, is deeply bonded to defect and deformity. Beyond the persistent strand of misogynist satire against learned ladies in the eighteenth century, the connection between deformity and female subjectivity easily extends to characterize eighteenth-century women and their literary productions as monstrous, mutilated, and compromised. The connection between women's talent and their double defect is sometimes literal as in the example of the deformed poet Mary Chandler (1687–1745) who established a milliner's shop to support herself; or the blind poet Priscilla Pointon Pickering (*c.* 1740–1801) who celebrated her marriage to a saddler in "Letter to Sister, Giving an Account of the Author's Wedding Day."[14] But more often than not, able-bodied women acting on the Restoration stage or publishing in the literary marketplace are presumed to be defects of nature by definition. Mutilation and deformity are implicated in their perverse desires. We think, for example, of the grotesque image of Eliza Haywood "with cow-like udders, and with ox-like eyes," her works compared to "two babes of love close clinging to her waste" in Pope's *Dunciad* (2: 149–58).[15] This enduring image of the woman writer as the monstrous and repulsive prize bestowed on the winner of a pissing contest should be given equal weight, I think, with the more familiar epithets applied to eighteenth-century women writers such as whore, heteroclite and bluestocking. Perhaps women writers in articulating their deformity are released into an exposition of its history.

In a second tale of defect, *The Unfortunate Bride; or, the Blind Lady A Beauty*, again Behn pairs beauty with disability in the lovely blind Celesia. Again two women compete for the same man, Frankwit, who was "so amiable... that every Virgin that had Eyes, knew too she had a Heart, and knew as surely she should lose it. His *Cupid* could not be reputed blind" (325). Celesia, according to Frankwit, possesses a *"charming Blindness"* (328) and, like Maria in *The Dumb Virgin*, she is able to conquer lovers even with her significant handicap: "You, fair Maid, require no Eyes to conquer" (328). The story is rife with ironic visual metaphors: "her beauteous image danced before him," "he saw his Deity in every Bush" (326), "there were pulses beating in their Eyes" (326), and "he only valued the smiling Babies in *Belvira's* Eyes" (327). After these constant references to eyes, the female voice of the narrator only then coyly acknowledges that she had forgotten to mention that Celesia could not see: "*Celesia* was an heiress, the only Child of a rich *Turkey* Merchant, who when he dyed left her fifty thousand pound in Money, and some Estate in land; but, poor creature, she was blind to all these riches, having been born without the use of sight, though in all other respects charming to a wonder" (327). Being blind is not equated with sexual virtue, but it does happily make Celesia oblivious to the lustre of earthly wealth.

Celesia's blindness, unlike ugliness or physical deformity, does not detract from her charms, and her powers of understanding, in the tradition of the blind prophet, are quite formidable: "Sight is Fancy," according to Celesia. When childhood sweethearts Frankwit and Belvira seek Celesia's advice as to whether they should marry, Celesia confesses her own attraction to Frankwit. Reminding us of the incestuous love in *The Dumb Virgin*, sexual expectation is likened to "A Monster which enjoyment could not satisfy" (329). Thwarted in love, Celesia "thought herself most unhappy that she had not eyes to weep with too; but if she had, such was the greatness of her grief, that sure she would have soon grown blind with weeping" (329). After Frankwit travels to Cambridge where he lodges with a wealthy Blackamoor, Moorea, Celesia miraculously recovers her sight in his absence through the ministrations of an aged matron.

Racialized as a shedevil, Moorea (whose name also implies she is a religious other) intercepts the letters from Belvira to her lover. "The Black *Moorea*, black in her mind, and dark, as well as in her body" (332) is complicit in the evil that befalls the other characters and sends false news of Frankwit's death. When the bewitched Frankwit fails to return, a rival, the rich and manly Wildvil, marries Belvira instead. Reminiscent of the staggering consequences of incest in *The Dumb Virgin*, the narrator reports that her writing powers begin to fail her. Frankwit too is struck speechless by the events that transpire. Killing Wildvil in a fit of jealousy, he accidentally inflicts a mortal wound on his beloved Belvira. The paralyzing effects extend to the narrator who professes to be stymied by the pathetic murder scene.

Regaining her sight allows Celesia to become a legitimate competitor for Frankwit, whom she marries after Belvira's death, exercising an option unavailable to a sightless woman. Yet Moorea's machinations in her behalf release the blind woman into the sexual economy, and when Celesia's blindness is restored, the narrator feels inspired to resume her writing. In each of these novellas, the release from the defect of nature (muteness or blindness) brings misery and chaos. Defects need not render desire untenable; in fact, they may fan women's passions. Desiring women, themselves figured as defective and monstrous, are instead punished by bearing deformed children, breeding incest, and losing their lovers. In these two tales, neither the category of able-bodied "women" or of more literally deformed women can be released from the defective essence of femininity.

II

When at midcentury Samuel Johnson ironically protests in *Idler* 87 that "There is, I think, no class of English women from whom we are in any danger of Amazonian usurpation," he protests too much:

I do not mean to censure the ladies of England as defective in knowledge or in spirit, when I suppose them unlikely to revive the military honours of their sex. The character of the ancient Amazons was rather terrible than lovely; the hand could not be very delicate that was only employed in drawing the bow and brandishing the battle-axe; their power was maintained by cruelty, their courage was deformed by ferocity, and their example only shews that men and women live best together.[16]

Amazons are, of course, widowed warrior women who colonized Asia and built the city of Ephesus. Temporarily defeated by Hercules and Theseus, these barbarous and nomadic natives of Scythia (ancient European and Asiatic Russia) escaped after murdering their guards. They are commanding women who amputate or cauterize their left breasts in order to become better marksmen. Actual ruling women in the contemporary moment of the eighteenth century were imagined to wage war in the Caucasus or to live primarily in Africa where they "kill all the Boys they bring forth, and train up their Girls to military Exploits."[17] Amazons represent an entire "race" of exotic women who are deformed in several senses – physically mutilated, sexually perverse, and possessing a womb, but disinclined to marry and reproduce in the conventional manner. As we have seen, woman's essentially defective nature arises by definition and also when she gives evidence of being insufficiently feminine, and the Amazon personifies this doubly impossible position.

The Amazon, a powerful yet mutilated warrior woman, is a specifically monstrous emblem of women's entry into the public sphere. Her defective male counterpart, the eunuch, figures as man's fear of what may result from exercising that power. Defective women are so closely aligned in the cultural imagination with eunuchs, those "ecchoes of virility," according to the mythology, that it is they who allegedly introduce the practice of castration. In fact, the atrophy of male organs and the loss of masculine attributes characterized a "Scythian" disease named for the Amazon's legendary home, and "Scythian insanity" showed itself in Apollo dressed as a woman among them. Linking Amazons to eunuchs as exotic and sometimes racialized deformed beings, *Eunuchism Display'd* (1718) recounts the commonplace legend that Semiramis, Queen of the Assyrians, having dressed as a man and having led her troops to victory, introduced the practice of castration in order to demonstrate her political power over her lovers, and other legendary manly queens mutilate and maim young boys: "Perhaps this Dress gave Birth to those Reports, that *Semiramis* had made imperfect Men, half-Men, and so on, till at last it was conjectured, that she effectually made People undergo the cruel Ceremony of Castration" (4).[18] Semiramis brought up her son as a girl, took men to her bed, and then executed them.[19] In this cultural parable, male deformity misogynistically results from female authority.

Merely being associated with powerful women may transform men into metaphoric eunuchs, weak and listless men, if not literally castrated beings. David Hume, for example, recounts the legend of Scythian Amazons who conspire against sleeping men to make them defective in another way, to blind them, and to free the women from pleasing men through fashion and display: "It was, therefore, agreed to put out the eyes of the whole male sex, and thereby resign in all future time the vanity which they could draw from their beauty, in order to secure their authority."[20] Hume continues, "There are a few degenerate creatures . . . , they are such only as by conversing with *Womankind*, putting on their foibles, and affecting to be like them, degrade themselves of manhood, commence intellectual eunuchs, and deserve no more to be reputed of the same sex with us".[21] Definitions of defect rely heavily on connections to sexuality, including the question of whether persons are able to become legitimate objects of desire or to reproduce. Women seem doomed to be defined as defective, irritating beings whether or not they possess this reproductive ability since giving birth may simply confirm their monstrosity, while men's ability to penetrate and spend their seed gives them some protection from charges of feminine defect. If they lack one of these, their defect effeminates them. Enfeebled masculinity – enervated, luxurious, and sodomite, and a particular threat to an English nation poised for military victory and continued imperial expansion – finds its most monstrous manifestation in the eunuch.

Women's sovereignty in both feminist and misogynist texts in the eighteenth century rests uneasily upon unmanning men, and yet in possessing a sexual defect they resemble the most reviled of men. The author of *Beauty's Triumph* likens women to impersonations of "that copy of themselves," Sporus, a neutered male wife who is famously "between *that* and *this*":[22] "All the World knows the History of *Sporus*, whom *Nero* caused to be gelt, and whose Folly was so extravagant, that he endeavoured to change his Sex; he made him wear Woman's Cloaths, and afterward married him with the usual Formalities, settled a Dowry upon him, gave him the nuptial Veil, and kept him in his Palace in quality of a Woman, which gave birth to this pleasant Saying, *That the World would have been happy had his Father* Domitian *had such a Wife*. In short, he caused this *Sporus* to be drest like an Empress, had him carried in a Litter, and attended him to all the Assemblies and publick Fairs of *Greece*, and at *Rome* to the *Sigillaria*, and Squares of the City, where he kissed him every Moment."[23] Yet peculiarly in this account, even a manmade eunuch or a natural hermaphrodite is better than a woman: "How well the masterly limner knew them [women], who snatch'd from them the graces he so skilfully bestowed on *Sporus*, that copy of themselves, inspired too by them, as they by *Satan!*" (107):

> *Whether in florid impotence* they speak,
> *And, as the prompter breathes, the puppets squeak;*
> *Or,* Eve's true spawn, and tools of th'ancient *toad,*
> *In puns, or politics, or tales, or lyes,*
> *Or spite, or smut, or rhymes, or blasphemies:*
> Their *wit all see-saw, between* that *and* this;
> *Now high, now low,* now forward, now remiss;
> *And* each herself *one* dull *antithesis.*
> *Amphibious things! That, acting either part,*
> *The trifling head, or the corrupted heart,*
> Bullies at cards, and flirts when *at the board,*
> *Now* jilt *like dames, now* swear *like any lord.*
>
> (107–08)

His gender status seriously at issue, Sporus is a profoundly inadequate copy of women but reminiscent of their intrinsic flaw. He is also a third sex, "neither Male nor Female, but a Prodigy in Nature" (7) whose wit like his sexuality is impossibly compromised. A eunuch could be categorized as a natural or man-made deformity, both a risible object and a prized rarity because of his *castrato* voice. Boys may be born eunuchs, their testicles "lank and flabby," or they may become eunuchs by having their testicles removed, making them, like Sporus, into manmade or artificial monsters.[24] *Beauty's Triumph* argues that whether a eunuch is involuntarily castrated determines the legitimacy and extent of our compassion:

These are imperfect Creatures, in a Word, Monsters, to whom Nature indeed has been sparing of nothing but the Avarice, Luxury, or Malice of Men, have disfigured and deformed. If they have sometimes been raised to the highest Pinnacles of human Glory, ... the People look'd upon them as so many Erroneous Productions of the depraved and corrupted Minds of Princes, who elevated them to those High States of Honour, and when they appeared in Publick, they only encreased and augmented the Hatred and Aversion the People had for them, who laughed at them amongst themselves, calling them old Women, &c. (95–96)

As we have seen, all women share an intrinsic defect, yet some carry the supplementary burden of ugliness, malformation, or disability. Because their defect is "natural," it distinguishes them from the eunuchs whose bodies may be marked by a vicious act intentionally perpetrated upon them. Natural defect and manmade defect do not run strictly parallel. A man in woman's clothing, Sporus dressed as Nero's wife is a precious yet inferior object, a preferable substitute for a woman. In spite of his impotence, his inability to reproduce, the female imposter possesses a cultural value that exceeds that of a natural woman. The affectation of femininity perverts manliness, though the exchange value of both women and eunuchs is high. In an important way, in these texts "woman" is a eunuch.[25]

The author of *Eunuchism Display'd* wonders about the paradox that would grant eunuchs political authority: "I cannot well comprehend how any one who is mutilated, and degraded (if I may so say) from the quality of a Man, should on that Account be *more precious than he was before*."[26] This double attitude of adulation and contempt, of awe and disdain, toward the eunuch replicates the combination of idealization and misogyny for eighteenth-century women and brings to the foreground the artificially social nature of such a defect. These contradictions escape resolution, for to reconcile them would be to recognize the artificiality and contingent status of these categories. It is precisely that constructedness that Amazons, eunuchs, ugly women, or deformed persons of any sort make visible. Yet,

since femininity is also gaining its own substantial subjectivity in the eighteenth century through women writers, the pressure to define womanhood
as *either* deformity or its absence increases while exposing such a resolution
as inadequate, since defect signifies both the inexplicability of difference
and its attraction.

Unlike Aphra Behn's narratives of female defect, Eliza Haywood's
Philidore and Placentia, or L'Amour trop Delicat (1727) is an exotic romance that incorporates deformity through a Christian eunuch. A fantasy
of female power, the first section of the novel set in England mirrors the
second section placed in a seraglio. In the novella, personal merit rests on
one's financial fortune, on moveable property rather than landed wealth.
Though he does not mention the eunuch as an example, Michael McKeon
aptly recognizes that economic exchange in the novel is an endless circuit
in which the movement toward completion and consumption, a perpetual
imagining of an end that must never come, becomes an end in itself.[27] The
eunuch, I suggest, is both a conduit toward the completion of traditional
male–female desire and an emblem of the impediment to achieving that resolution. The eunuch is *himself* a commodity as well as the nonreproductive
circuit, the emissary through which the traffic in women takes place.

The first part of *Philidore and Placentia* focuses on an aggressively sensual
Haywood heroine, Placentia, who is in love with the noble but impoverished
Philidore. As in the Behn novellas, the defective is intertwined with Eastern
exoticism from the beginning. Philidore darkens himself to an "Egyptian
color" and transforms himself into a humble servant who silently worships
his adored object of affection. But his "native whiteness" and nobility soon
show through his disguise to charm Placentia,[28] and she rewards him for
rescuing her from ravaging ruffians by making him groom of her chambers.

At first adopting a manly threat of force to seduce her reluctant slave,
Placentia later shifts tactics to propose marriage to him in spite of the disparity in their fortunes. Steadfastly refusing because of his poverty, he flees
to bury his broken heart. In the story that constitutes the second part of the
novel, Philidore during his adventures in Turkey encounters the Christian
eunuch, a beautiful mysterious man, disguised in blood and dust. The mag-
netic attraction between Philidore and the eunuch is palpable: "Philidore
finds himself attached to him by an impulse which he could not at that
time account for" (188). The homoerotic undertones remain subdued, but
the affection Philidore expresses for the "lovely stranger" continues to resemble that of a lover. To clarify the eunuch's sexual orientation, and to
erase these implications of desire between the two men, Philidore recovers
a picture of a beautiful woman from the stranger's effects, and only then,

by witnessing a medical examination, discovers that "this beautiful person had been deprived of his manhood" (192), not in order to obtain a position in the seraglio, but as a punishment. The exotic stranger finally spills out the history of his emasculation which reminds us of a similar juxtaposition between beauty and defect in Behn's lovely mute heroine Maria whose loosened tongue freed her to speak of monstrosity. The occasion of being made defective or recognizing monstrosity releases the narrative. As Haywood tells it, woman's "deformed" subjectivity, like the subjectivity of the Christian eunuch, is resisted and redefined even as it is constituted by defect.

In Haywood's *Philidore and Placentia* the Christian eunuch, like the female sex he is alleged to personify and parody, is "fine by defect." Of ancient and honorable family, the eunuch, the last surviving male heir and himself an exotic, collects rarities and, as one would expect from an effeminate, attends to fashion. Shipwrecked and captured by Persian pirates, purchased as a favorite by the Bashaw of Lipera, the character soon recognized even before he became a eunuch that he was a feminized commodity at the Bashaw's disposal who possessed use value. The eunuch resembles "a fine garden, a palace, a rich jewel, or any other thing which affords him delight. He [the Bashaw] thinks of those whom ill fortune has reduced to be his slaves but as part of the furniture of his house, something he has bought for his use (198)." To his peril he had fallen in love with the loose and sensual beauty of Arithea, one of the Bashaw's wives, in the seraglio.[29] Disordered by infatuation he refuses to leave when granted his freedom. Both the seraglio and his enslavement are metaphors for the power that love wields in making him forget national loyalties. Entering the forbidden walls of the seraglio disguised as a mute, already taking on the mark of the defective, he risks slavery and exile at his peril. Unsatisfied, Arithea relentlessly upbraids him for his cold European nature and his failure to confront the Bashaw, just as Philidore had failed to be sufficiently aggressive with Placentia in Part 1.

In the conclusion Philidore, still in Turkey, suddenly becomes heir to a great fortune, and the economic impediment to his marriage with Placentia is at last removed. At the very moment of potential climax between the illicit lovers, Turkish slaves capture the European and make him a eunuch, leaving him "nothing but the name of man (206)." Placentia, having followed Philidore to Turkey, resurfaces as the slave of a Persian merchant. Now dispossessed of *her* fortune, she turns tables on Philidore and refuses to marry *him*, but the Christian eunuch is revealed to be the barren Baron Bellamont, her brother who was returning home to claim his inheritance.

The Christian eunuch awards Placentia a third of his newly acquired estate. Firmly situated within the marriage economy, Placentia's capacity to bear heirs is reinstated through the eunuch's good graces. Men who are outside heterosexuality and aligned with women in their defective nature differ in that masculinity is deformed by an inability to reproduce, while woman's status is ambivalent and inclusive of both since her reproductive organ is the very site of her defect.

Ultimately, however, deformity or defect are firmly attached to a male body rather than a female one in Haywood's tale, and the eunuch's defect is the cruel consequence of desiring a woman of the seraglio, a religious and national other, for which the eunuch is condemned to a life outside the reproductive economy. Marriage between two passionate European lovers circulates through the eunuch, a defective imitation of a man, so that money and value are partially transferred to the woman instead. The Christian eunuch's misplaced desire for an Eastern woman, a woman of the seraglio, emasculates him, enriches the European woman, and enables her marriage. There is not a hint in Haywood's novella of a *woman*'s being genuinely defective; rather the sexually charged heroines berate men for their cowardice, and are in fact rewarded with a fortune because a subclass of men is rendered impotent and relegated to a lesser status because of his castration. In Behn's tales, women, both intrinsically and externally defective, were depicted as being on the margins of such a circulation. Haywood's tale suggests that women's empowerment is entangled with their sexual, physical, and moral deformity but not integral to it, and though women's economic fortunes may depend on men's castration, femininity need not be tantamount to monstrosity.

During the eighteenth century, I am arguing, femininity as perfect difference, an inferior perfection, competes with femininity as defect. Amazonian women and eunuchs representing the perversion of desire are the flawed beings who become the collectibles and unnatural exotica of empire along with giants, pygmies, mermaids, hermaphrodites, and mutes. Yet they are also the troubling and fascinating emblems of gendered uncertainty reflecting England's anxieties about its national manliness and its capacity to muster the necessary rapacity for empire-building. Women's defect, their reproductive power, could be manipulated for the transfer of wealth, social status, and political power. In eighteenth-century England women like Behn and Haywood inscribe a subjectivity that queries the concept of a double defect and contests conventional forms of sexual difference which would portray the exceptional woman as defective, deformed, and monstrous, even among the earliest practitioners of women's writing.

III

Eliza Haywood was also fascinated with Duncan Campbell, a deaf-mute secular prophet who flourished from 1710 to 1730. A cluster of publications, some of which have been falsely attributed to Daniel Defoe, centered on Campbell who is the subject of *The History of the Life and Adventures of Mr. Duncan Campbell, A Gentleman, who, tho' Deaf and Dumb, writes down any Stranger's Name at first Sight* (1720); *Mr. Campbell's Packet, for the Entertainment of Gentlemen and Ladies* (1720), Eliza Haywood's *A Spy upon the Conjuror* (19 March 1724) and *The Dumb Projector* (1725); *The Friendly Daemon; or the Generous Apparition* (1726); and *Secret Memoirs of the Late Mr. Duncan Campbell* (1732).[30] Eliza Haywood's two contributions to the Duncan Campbell stories, *A Spy upon the Conjuror* (1724) and *The Dumb Projector* (1725), fit within the context of anomalous beings of both sexes and of women writers in particular. The Scotsman Campbell attracted a parade of the curious and the lovelorn to his door with claims of possessing second sight and foretelling the future (illustration 4). Eliza Haywood was among those who frequented his home as well as Susannah Centlivre, Martha Fowke, Aaron Hill, Richard Savage, and Richard Steele. His story became so popular "that even before the first edition was exhausted, the sanguine publisher Edmund Curll, ordered a second."[31] According to the *Spectator* for 28 June 1714, "the blind *Tiresias* was not more famous in *Greece* than this dumb Artist has been for some Years last past in the cities of London and Westminster."[32] Campbell himself boasts in his memoirs, "But I was once in such a Vogue, that not to have been with me, was to have been out of the Fashion; and it was then as strange a Thing not to have consulted the *Deaf and Dumb Conjurer*, as it is now not to have seen the *Beggars Opera* half a dozen Times, or to admire *Polly Peachum*" (*Secret Memoirs* 13–14). Realizing the benefits of being spectacularly à la mode, he enjoys performing as a man of the moment whose advice is advertised as more valuable than new fashion. For women, soliciting Campbell's advice apparently competed with expenditures on modish clothing for their pocket money. His fame was such that an advertisement in William Bond's *Weekly Medley*, 31 Jan. to 7 Feb. 1719, admonishes female masquerade-goers: "I would therefore advise most Ladies, who are at so much Cost for their Habits, to lay out as they may with much more Prudence and Benefit One Piece of Gold more to see him for so much previous wholesome Advice; or if they are so silly as not to follow my Counsel, they would be at least so wise to themselves" to impersonate Campbell as a mute, and to affect being dumb only when they are solicited by strange masked men.[33]

4 Frontispiece, "The Effigies of Mr Duncan Campbell the Dumb Gentleman," to *The History of the Life and Adventures of Mr. Duncan Campbell* (1720). Later versions attempt to remedy Campbell's concern that he appears too corpulent. Campbell's hands with which he communicated are not visible.

Taking advantage of the popular taste for the odd, Campbell commodi-fies his own person to become the equivalent of a London tourist site, thus avoiding the usual dislocation of the disabled to the marketplace's margins as beggars or ballad-hawkers. Instead Campbell evolved into something of a cultural icon, and he functioned, in the way that we have seen disabled figures so often do, as a corporeal node that tellingly reveals social and historical tensions. The deaf predictor blurs the limits of the human – since speech is so often indicated as a characteristic that distinguishes men from animals – and calls them into question. Articulating these differences also produces the "normal," a word that first appears in 1759, even as the culture seeks to locate the abnormal in place and time, as elsewhere and other.[34]

The Duncan Campbell myth is a kind of secular conversion story that inspires the irrational belief that there may be some connection between uncanny abilities and disability. Eliza Haywood makes use of this intertwining of imaginative power and physical anomaly to connect implicitly Campbell's predicament to that of early eighteenth-century women writers. In spite of being perceived as monsters Campbell, along with able-bodied women who publish, support themselves through intellectual labor.

As Behn's and Haywood's other writings make clear, gender cannot be isolated from other regnant cultural and political values, and Campbell challenged other kinds of assumptions as well. Campbell violated expectations of the deaf as isolated, economically dependent, and lacking in sexual desire, and I am also arguing here that the fashionable Campbell has such peculiar cultural resonance because he represents both the past and the future. As a freak of nature, a human being who employs sign language, and a mute who writes, Campbell sits precariously on the cusp between prehistoric time and the unknown future as a modish rarity within whom past and present intersect. Figured as a remnant of the past, he is also nearly cotemporaneous with Linnaeus' division of man into *homo sapiens* and *homo monstruosus* in *Systema Naturae* (1735; 10th edition 1758; translated into English in 1802), representing a being who evolved from ancient creatures *and* an analog to the noble savage, a marvelous brute.[35] The popular literature of the period including Addison and Steele's *The Spectator* draws associations for example between Campbell as "A Dumb Oracle" and a chattering magpie who is taught to speak. In addition, the fortuneteller made his living as an emblem of the speculative and its promise for the future.

In the eighteenth century defective beings were often associated, not only with a location at the edge of European geographic knowledge but also with an earlier "less civilized" period of history. By defective beings, I mean those with exceptional morphologies such as giants, pygmies, and dwarfs, as well as those with physical and cognitive anomalies including the deaf, the blind, and the retarded. Campbell, then, is an example of monstrosity's temporal location in the prehistoric. Mutant forms are, like race, given geographic specificity; often indicative of a species apart, abnormality is relegated to intemperate climates. The defective, then, are easily intermingled and made synonymous with the racialized since dwarfs, giants, and blacks together compose "deformed races." A "geography of monstrosity" places the freakish at the edges of what is known and beyond, just as the racialization of space took shape in climatic theories that ascribed low intelligence and lax morals to torrid zones populated largely by people of color. Ancient writers such as Pliny and Herodotus, notes V. Y. Mudimbe in *The Invention of Africa*, are among the first to locate a "geography of monstrosity" that distinguishes the savage, black, and strange (the headless, satyrs, cave-dwellers without language) as residing elsewhere than the "civilized."[36] Pollution, deviation, and degeneration of the "race" created social disorder and contamination of the larger social body, and it was popularly accepted that an environmental cause, especially in faraway places could take root in physiology to become hereditary. That is, bodily conditions influenced by the environment may take suffficient somatic hold in the body to be transferred from generation to generation; similarly, skin afflictions may first appear as disease only to become hereditary in a second generation to allow race, like defect, to develop a history.

The concept of the monstrous when taken together with the geography of race complicates what Charles Mills believes to be inherent within the racial contract: that it "norms (and races) space, demarcating civil and wild spaces."[37] In Rousseau's *Discourse on Inequality*, as Mills points out, "the only natural savages cited are *nonwhite* savages, examples of European savages being restricted to reports of feral children raised by wolves and bears, child-rearing practices (we are told) comparable to those of Hottentots and Caribs"; and because the state of nature was deeply racialized, savages were universally defined as nonwhite.[38] This leap from monstrosity to racialization is also compatible with other conceptual frameworks in the Enlightenment. *Spectator* 17 contends that odd creatures are found in "the woody Parts of the *African* Continent, in your Voyage to or from *Grand Cairo*" (1.76). David Hume's racist footnote singles out a Jamaican man of learning as a rare exceptional being who resembles a speaking parrot: the Negro who is aligned with a parrot can be trained to imitate language, and his hybridity is both bestial and incongruous. Similarly Robinson Crusoe taught his parrot to speak well enough to startle him awake by imitating human sentiments: "Poor *Robin Crusoe*, where are you *Robin Crusoe*?" just before locating the puzzling footprint.[39] The parrot is also a familiar means to mock women's alleged talkativeness. Haywood herself adopts the persona of the glib gossiping talking tropical bird in a periodical *The Parrot* (published from 2 August 1746 until 4 October 1746) as a reverse satiric device, and in another earlier historical context, the Renaissance, the parrot also personified a misogyny, as Kim Hall aptly notes, "in which women are said to be incapable of autonomous speech, able only to mimic the language of *man*kind."[40]

Campbell is then a test case employed to determine whether only humans speak even as he refuses the usual condition of the voiceless by writing and gesturing for profit. The deaf and dumb also arouse contemplation of the question of the relationship between animal sounds and the gesticulations and noises that other speechless creatures employ. Such distinctions among modes of communication in various species have a racial resonance. The racial contract, the implicit assumption upon which the social compact rests, means that "a category crystallized over time in European thought to represent entities who are humanoid but not fully *human* ('savages,' 'barbarians') and who are identified as such by being members of the general set of nonwhite races. Influenced by the ancient Roman distinction between the civilized within and the barbarians outside the empire, the distinction [arises] between full and question-mark humans."[41] Among the human traits that distinguish men from brutes is speech, beyond the mere imitation of articulation characteristic of crows and magpies, the ability to talk is crucial to the demarcation of the human race whose origins are located in regions distant from Europe. Jean Coenrad Amman, a late seventeenth-century Swiss physican who tutored a deaf Dutch girl, claimed that whole nations of the speechless who used sign language could be found among indigenuous populations in Africa.[42] This is particularly telling because speech was believed to distinguish man from animal, the civilized from the savage, and the logic was extended also to confound the difference between an oral and a written culture. Lord Monboddo too remarks that "in the woods of Angola, and other parts of Africa . . . races of wild men, without the use of speech, are still to be found."[43] Wondering at the extraordinary effort that Thomas Braidwood (1715–1806) exerts to teach the deaf, Monboddo uses these African examples to argue that articulation is a learned rather than an innate skill. Demonstrating that language is not natural to man, in his account deaf people resemble primitive men in a state of nature who "have inarticulate cries, by which they express their wants and desires" (1. 190), and who resemble Angolan orang outangs who enslave Negro girls for labor and erotic use.

Similarly, gesturing instead of speech was also given exotic flavor in its presumed transmission from Turkey. George Sibscota was among those who reported that the exotic disabled, mutes assigned to the harem, communicated through hand motions: "The Emperour of the Turk maintains many such Mutes in his court; who do express the Conceptions of their minds one to another, and as it were interchange mutual discourse, by gesticulations, and variety of external significations, no otherways than we that have the faculty of signifying our own thoughts, and conceiving those of other Persons by outward Speech. Nay the Turkish Emperour himself, and his Courtiers, take great delight with this kind of Speech shadowed out by gestures, and use to employ themselves very much in the exercise hereof, to make them perfect in it."[44] Sibscota's early linguistics manual shows how the mutes retain their own languages and speak only with gestures when dining together.[45] According to these theories, civilized men possess the capacity to speak while monsters who communicate in unconventional ways exist precisely on the boundary of what is humanoid to define the limits of the human. As Nicholas Mirzoeff has noted, "In this sense, sign language becomes the unstable mark of simian similarity and difference with the hearing/human."[46] The disabled and racialized Other is figured as a means to truth through its becoming the object of scientific experimentation, yet it also figures as a sign of obfuscation in the sense of continuing to pose insoluble mysteries about humanity's essence.

Duncan Campbell becomes the object of Haywood's benevolent scrutiny. Being taken for a prehistoric being who survives in a modern time, yet able to perceive events in the future as if they were in the present, Duncan Campbell also exemplifies this double temporal disjunction. Duncan's father Archibald Campbell, who allegedly derives from the legendary home of second sight, the Shetland islands, married a Laplander woman after having been shipwrecked.[47] In one version of the story, a letter ostensibly from Archibald Campbell to *his* father recounts his experience in Lapland: "When first I enter'd this Country, I thought I was got into quite another World: The Men are all of them Pigmies to our tall, brawny *Highlanders*: They are, generally speaking, not above Three Cubits high; insomuch that tho' the whole Country of *Lapland* is immensely large, and I have heard it reckon'd by the Inhabitants to be above a Hundred *German* Leagues in Length, and Fourscore and Ten in Breadth: Yet I was the tallest Man there, and look'd upon as a Giant" (*The Supernatural Philosopher* 18–19). Laplanders were frequently presumed to be diminutive and degenerate people,[48] and there is evidence that later in the century two Laplander women were exhibited for profit. For Oliver Goldsmith in *An History of the Earth* extreme climates, like those in Lapland, may contribute to the degeneration of an entire population, "as their persons are thus naturally deformed, at least to our imaginations, their minds are equally incapable of strong exertions. The climate seems to relax their mental powers still more than those of the body; they are, therefore, in general, found to be stupid, indolent, and mischievous."[49] Accident, heredity, mutation, and climate all breed the potential for deformity. In addition, Campbell's birth apparently confirmed the Laplanders' superstitions surrounding the maternal imagination as represented in Laplander folklore: "If a Star be seen just before the Moon, we count it a sign of a lusty and well grown Child, without Blemish; if a Star comes just after, we reckon it a token that the Child will have some defect or deformity, or die soon after it is Born" (*The History of the Life* 25). The unknown commentator for *The History of Duncan Campbell*, perhaps William Bond, is the only one who tells this part of the story that relates to Lapland, and other writers – especially Eliza Haywood who resists making his mother's imagination the cause of his deafness – are more especially interested in Campbell's status as a speculator for the lovesick who makes a living from his special gift. As such Campbell escapes being a representative of England's internal colonization, and he enters the laboring economy rather than resting on its margins.

When Campbell first learned the Scots language, according to *The History of the Life*, he learned "to leave off some Savage Motions, which he had taken of his own accord, before to signifie his Mind by, and to impart his thoughts by his Fingers and his Pen" very intelligibly and swiftly (*The History of the Life* 36) (illustration 5). After Campbell had been orphaned at twelve, in reality the precocious deaf and dumb boy became a soothsaying phenomenon who marketed his disability to counter serious debt. The evidence is compelling that Campbell was truly hearing-impaired though he may have possessed some modicum of hearing. But fortunetelling is a questionable avocation, and the validity of the disability (even for modern commentators) is sometimes confused with skepticism about Campbell's second sight, a special talent that Samuel Johnson later defines in *The Journey to the Western Islands of Scotland* as "an impression made either by the mind upon the eye, or by the eye upon the mind, by which things instant or future are perceived, and seen as if they were present... Things distant are seen at the instant when they happen."[50] Haywood's *Spy Upon the Conjuror* begs the question of Campbell's credibility as a fortuneteller while remarking on his amazing capacity to write the names of people he met for the first time, along with those of their former or current spouses.

Campbell defies the usual picture of a bereft and infantilized person with disabilities and is instead idealized as a man who also resembles a woman and takes on the qualities of a third sort of amphibious being. One

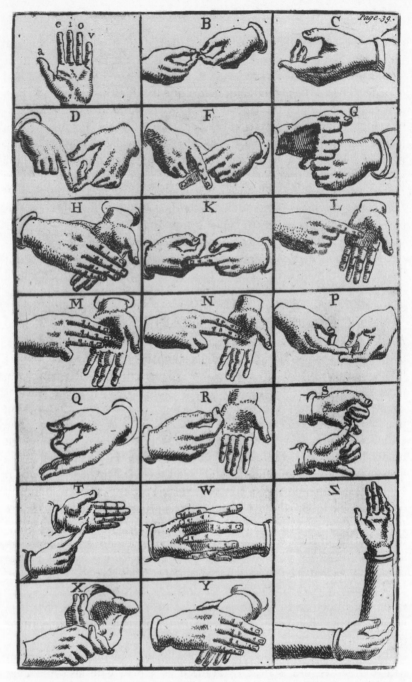

5 Sign-language alphabet, *The History of the Life and Adventures of Mr. Duncan Campbell* (1720). Sign languages for the deaf originated in the seventeenth century, and a literature of "surdo-mutism" flourished among physicians and scientists.

observer of Campbell describes a gathering in which he was the focus of extraordinary adulation:

As soon as I enter'd the Room, I was surpriz'd to find myself encompass'd and surrounded by a Circle of the most beautiful Females that ever my Eyes beheld. In the Centre of this Angelick Tribe was seated a heavenly Youth, with the most winning comeliness of Aspect, that ever pleased the Sight of any Beholder of either Sex; his Face was divinely Fair, and ting'd only with such a sprightly Blush, as a Painter would use to Colour the Picture of Health with, and the Complexion was varnish'd over by a Blooming, like that of flourishing Fruit, which had not yet felt the first Nippings of an unkind and an uncivil Air; with this Beauty was join'd such a smiling draught of all the Features, as is the result of Plesantry and good Humour. His Eyes were large, full of Lustre, Majestick, well set, and the Soul shone so in them, as told the Spectators plainly, how great was the inward Vivacity of his *Genius*: The Hair of his Head was thick and reclin'd far below his Shoulders; it was of a fine Silver Colour, and hung down in Ringlets like the curling Tendrils of a copious Vine. He was by the Women entertain'd, according to the Claim, which so many Perfections joining in a Youth just ripening into Manhood, might lay to the benevolent Dispositions of the tender Sex. One was holding the Bason of Water, another washing a Hand, a Third with a Towel drying his Face, which another Fair had greedily snatch'd the Pleasure of washing before, while a Fourth was disposing into order his Silver Hairs with an Ivory Comb, in an Hand as White, and which a Monarch might have been proud to have had so employ'd in adjusting the Crown upon his Head; a Fifth was setting into Order his Cravat; a Sixth stole a Kiss, and blush'd at the innocent Pleasure, and mistook her own Thoughts as if she kiss'd the Angel and not the Man; and they all rather seem'd to adore than to love him, as if they had taken him not for a Person that enjoy'd the frequent Gift of the Second Sight, but as if he had been some little Prophet peculiarly inspired, and while they all thus admired and wonder'd they all consulted him as an Oracle. (*The History of the Life* 128–29)

In this extraordinarily visual passage, Campbell captures the observer's gaze as well as the attention of the beautiful angelic women who surround him. He is pleasing to both sexes, "divinely fair," a blooming virginal youth ripe for the picking who with his silver shoulder-length hair resembles a prelapsarian Adam, a prophet, or Christ himself. His body parts are associated with natural beauty, his hair tendrils like a vine, his complexion like fruit. The attending women fawn over his toilet, each contributing to bathing and dressing a part of him in turn. He is monarchical and majesterial but also feminized as a sexual object in their loving attention devoted to his body. Campbell, "just ripening into Manhood," inspires a dressing ritual which resembles nothing so much as a royal prince with his English harem, in which the attending women are emboldened to kiss him. His vibrant nature exudes a luscious sexuality. A regal yet approachable androgynous creature, he is a gorgeous if somewhat peculiar specimen who will mellow into something more fully seasoned, and his capacity to prophesy magnetically draws the women to him. In a curious gendering, Campbell seems to exceed being a mere man or woman, yet he participates in both sexes.

Also incarnating the latest fashion, Campbell embodies femininity both as a spectacular object and as an aberration or defect, a connection common to the eighteenth century. Disability is also characteristically linked with effeminacy as in Jean-Nicolas Bouilly's play *Abbé de l'Epée*, when "the character of the signing deaf boy was considered an appropriate role for a woman."[51] Campbell is also feminized because of his epilepsy, a condition that he blames on the extraordinary mental and physical concentration required for fortunetelling: "a Flirt of a Fan has made me sudden drop down in the most terrible Convulsions, and rendered me wholly incapable of answering any Questions that Day . . . I cannot but look on it as a Womanish, or at best, a Pedantick one, but all I can do has hitherto been ineffectual" (*Secret Memoirs* 16).[52] Thus Campbell is a figure who embodies an enfeebled and enervated masculinity while at the same time in other accounts he is regarded as sexually desirable. In either case his potency is unstable and very much at issue. By his own account Campbell is at pains to disassociate effeminacy from his hearing impairment, and he displaces impotency onto blindness. He recounts his meeting with a famous blind man who claimed that he could distinguish colors by touch, and who relished playing card games. After twice losing at cards, Campbell discovers that the blind man's squire secretly marked the cards with pinpricks so that he could distinguish them with his sensitive fingers. The deaf man then teaches the blind man some sign language with great relish: "In fine, no two Persons in Company could be more conversible with each other, than we were within the Time prefixed; on which, said the blind Man, *I* see *by* Feeling, *and you* hear *by your* Eyes." The two engage in a debate over the hierarchy of disabilities, each claiming that his is the more valuable. Campbell insists on the superiority of sight over speech and hearing: "I told the Company, *That I would not lose the Sight of the Sun, and a fine Woman, to be Emperor of the whole globe; and, that I would be deprived of Legs and Arms, nay, endure* Castration *itself, rather than quit so valuable a Blessing as that of Sight*" (*Secret Memoirs* 117). Sight is equated to his sexual organ: to be able to see is to have a penis, to be blind is to be castrated, and Campbell like his commentators tries to make manly what had in the past been associated with "credulous Nurses and old Women" (*Supernatural Philosopher* 6). To be deprived of his eyes would be *worse* than losing sexual prowess, and, curiously, to gaze upon a woman, to see her, in this logic is more significant than bedding her. In Campbell's formulation, as long as he possesses sight he is manly.

Campbell is not emasculated in Haywood's account in spite of his occupying a cultural location that is akin to that of old women and shiftless beggars. Haywood is careful to distinguish Campbell from ignorant fortunetellers who are fear-mongers or who provide love charms, "and a thousand other fantastick, ridiculous Spells, which rather would excite Derision, than raise Belief in the thinking Part of the World" (*Spy* 126). Campbell's misogyny also serves to counter any charges of a masculinity at risk: "He would often smile and write to me," Haywood reports, "*O Woman! Woman! Woman! The Sin of Eve taints thy whole Sex*" (73). Obviously Haywood hoped to cash in on the extraordinary popularity of Campbell's story. Though her biographical narrative reveals little plot, it becomes an occasion for the narrator to expose Campbell's misogyny and even to participate in it. "Heavens! That Women can be mad enough to publish their own Disgrace, and swell the Triumphs of him that has undone 'em! Yet so it is with our inconsiderate Sex! – to vent a present Passion, – for the short-liv'd Ease of railing at the Baseness of an ungrateful Lover, – to gain a little Pity, – we proclaim our Folly, and become the Jest of all who know us" (*Spy* 75–76). Both Haywood and Campbell take women to task for their refusal to heed warnings about men's easily ruining their reputation, and Campbell appears to have possessed unusual prescience in regard to virgins and their future ruination.

For Eliza Haywood, Duncan Campbell, the deaf and dumb seer, is both eroticized and exoticized as an *au courant* forecaster of the future who in spite of being voiceless wields cultural power through translating his imaginative visions into writing. In Eliza Haywood's version, more romantic and scandalous than other accounts, her pose as a voyeur anticipates her later posture as the Female Spectator.[53] Haywood writes in the person of Justicia, the "spy upon the conjuror," who visited Campbell regularly, stole some of his papers that constitute the book in which he is featured, and seems to be slightly in love with him herself, a posture she encourages the reader to share. To be the seer, the spy, is to wield the kind of power usually associated with the masculine appendage, not the female. *The Spy Upon the Conjuror: Or, A Collection of Surprising and Diverting Stories, with Merry and Ingenious Letters* (1725) defends Campbell (also called the "Dumb Predictor" and the "Dumb Oracle") against those who question his second sight and the validity of his deaf and mute situation. Haywood's collection of tales and letters, not quite a biographical narrative, emphasizes Campbell's communicating through writing in the presence of his clients much more than his deafness or communicating through sign language. While Campbell makes of himself a sexual object and acknowledges his own peculiarities as a deaf person, other purported letters Haywood produces engage questions of courtship, rape, sexual harassment, and jealousy. Haywood focuses on his ability to tell stories of love that enrage the auditor yet command sufficient respect to allow him to make a living by fortunetelling. In her version, and in the *Secret Memoirs of the late Mr. Duncan Campbell* (1732), Campbell is accused of appealing mostly to women who are more easily duped because of their sex and who constitute the preponderance of paying customers, but among the other clientele who sought his prophecies were the manly members of the Royal Cabinet.

Haywood emphasizes too the violence and rage directed against Campbell as if to underscore her personal understanding that the culture refused to accept a body it insisted on judging to be defective. From the first she portrays him as the object of scorn: "I believe no Man on Earth has ever met with more ill Treatment, Injustice, and Barbarity" (*Spy* 144). Skeptical customers attack him to prove that he is faking his disabilities: one woman catches his fingers (his means of communication) in a door to trick him into crying out, a man who had never before met him beats him with a cane to get him to protest, and another customer marvels that though he lances Campbell's fistula (a pipe-like sore or ulcer), he does not utter a syllable. Describing a situation analogous to the predicament of various women writers, Haywood tells stories of a culture that tested and tortured Campbell, treating him as less than human, perhaps especially because he had no voice to articulate his pain:

I was one Day at a Lady's, where Mr. *Henry Vaughan*, a Surgeon of very good Repute... told the Company, laughing, that he was going to make the *Dumb* to speak: I ask'd him what he meant; and he reply'd, He was that Afternoon to perform that sad Operation of cutting a *Fistola*, which he assured me was worse to the Patient who endured it, than cutting off Legs or Arms. – *The Person*, said he, *that is to undergo it, is the famous Fortune-Teller*, Duncan Campbell, *who pretends to be Deaf and Dumb; but I'll engage I make him speak before I have done with him.* All the Company was impatient to know the End of this Adventure, and engaged him to come back and give us an Account; which in about an Hour after he did, but in a Humour very different from that in which he left us. He acknowledged his Mistake; and said, he was now convinc'd that Mr. *Campbell* could not speak, since he had endured as much as ever mortal Man went through, and had not utter'd the least Syllable, and in his Agonies vented the Sense he had of them, by a Noise which sufficiently testified he was really denied the Benefit of expressing what he felt any other Way. (*Spy* 147–48)

Campbell's inarticulate but heartfelt noise communicated his agony, shamed those who would disbelieve his disability, and turned potential mockery into sympathetic understanding. Unquestionably, Campbell's status as a hot commercial property motivated Haywood's opportunistic desire to capitalize on the popular rage that made his conjectures marketable. But she may also have found in his condition a cultural parable of women writers' struggles to be heard, their difficulty in speaking, and the paralysis that comes from trying to articulate that condition.[54]

Haywood's attitude is largely one of respect, admiration, and celebration rather than pitymongering. She emphasizes Campbell's second sight more than his disabilities and admiringly notes that much of what he forecasts is not easily predicted. Further, Haywood defends him against charges of being mercenary by pointing out that he refuses to talk to certain offensive women in spite of turning away potential customers in making that decision: "This more amaz'd me, having always thought that Money made every Body welcome" (*Spy* 136). She includes a letter from a gentleman who subscribes to the theory of nature's compensating for his disability "by doubling the Vigour of those Senses you are posses'd of, the Deficiency of those she has denied you. The Want of Hearing and Speaking would to another Person be an inconsolable Affliction; yet you, methinks, appear as gay and unconcerned as those who labour not under either of those Defect. – I guess that you will answer, that that supernatural Gift, called the second Sight, abundantly compensates for what is denied you by the Want of those more common Blessings" (*Spy* 238).

Haywood in her discussion of Campbell also reports some of the ways that visitors questioned, sometimes cruelly, whether Campbell was a sentient being, and such questions take on erotic connotations:

It was of a young Woman who really by her Dress, and Manner of Behaviour, appeared to be not of the lowest Rank of Life; she happened to come when our *Dumb Oracle* was abroad: But being told he would come in soon, she chatted away an Hour or two with Mrs. *Campbell*; and being of a pretty pert Humour, ask'd her how she cou'd be brought to like a Man that could not speak. – *Good God!* said she, *How did he make Love? – Lord! I wonder whether he can feel or not?* – She persecuted her with a thousand such-like idle Questions, telling her she wonder'd how so fine a Woman as she could venture on a Monster. – To all which Mrs. *Campbell* made but short Replys. At last, his coming home cut off any farther Conversation of this kind; but having never seen Mr. *Campbell*, it was not without a great deal of Difficulty she was persuaded it was he, imagining, as she afterwards confess'd, she should have seen something very deform'd, and miserable in his Aspect; ... but by writing her Name, and several Particulars of her Life, he soon made her sensible he was really the Person she came to consult. But the Jest is, that this fine Lady, who was so full of Wonder before, became so diligent in learning the Art of talking on her Fingers, that in a little Time she grew a perfect Mistress of it, and made use of it to invite Mr. *Campbell* to come to see her at her Lodgings by himself... Some Letters afterwards found among those Papers, which I stole out of his Closet, give indeed a too great Demonstration that she liked him but too well. (*Spy* 154)

These skeptics puzzle over his status as a thinking and feeling human being, and as a sexual man, and they afford Haywood an opportunity to titillate the reader with imagining his sexual organ that compensated for his defect.

In Haywood's account, Campbell's divining powers repeatedly assume more significance than his anomalous situation. Haywood's narrator Justicia purports to test Campbell's abilities by interrogating those who consulted him. Here as elsewhere his "supernatural Gift" (*Spy* 238) redresses his inability to hear or speak: "The naturally deficient Organs in so noble a Temperament, indeed, demand Commiseration from all generous Humanity; yet the superabundant Retaliations of Providence in your many unparalell'd [sic] Endowments, almost puts me to a Stand whether I ought not, in some Measure, conclude even those very Defects a Blessing, amidst the universal empty Noise and Depravity of Conversation" (*Spy* 257). This description presents a sympathetic picture of a man who admirably compensates for his disability, and a man against whom Justicia rages as she would against any man when antagonized by his vision of her unhappy future. The narrator acknowledges her disorder, distractedness, and fury making *her* the peculiar one: "How my own Character was made ridiculous, by the Wildness of my ungovernable Rage" (*Spy* 75). Campbell fully participates in print culture by literally inscribing his predictions rather than his resemblance to a stereotypically beastlike being who communicates with hand gestures. Justicia does not discuss signing with the hands until the end of the first volume, and then only incidentally when she characterizes him as civil, sociable, and possessing good sense. Haywood's Campbell, unlike the hero presented in some of the other accounts, is a modern citizen rather than a residual being from an ancient oral past. *The Spy upon the Conjuror* also seems to issue a veiled lament that Campbell may be going out of fashion, and that lesser modes of fortunetelling such as reading tea and coffeegrounds are gaining greater vogue, thus making his skills less marketable. The products that come from imperial trade and speculation may put the more primitive second sight out of business. Yet Campbell's prophesying for profit about an uncertain future, and the cultural imperative to speculate and invest in its promise is made most visible in the nation's South Sea Bubble stock venture (1722) and provides a compelling national fable for the new credit economy.[55]

Haywood, herself the spy upon the conjuror of the title, predictably exploits passion and love more than the other commentator since her version of Campbell makes him seem ordinary except for his very unusual gift of second sight. Misdirected passion creates monstrosity, and in her account Campbell is the very center of reason who risks the venom of his clients, chiefly women, who like Haywood herself perversely transform *themselves* into monsters when faced with the "truth" of Campbell's prophecies: "But I had scarce Time to finish it, before a Woman burst into the Room in a very rude and abrupt manner; and by her Way of Behaviour, shew'd me, as in a Glass, the Transformation I had been under when I was there before, and how monstrously Passion disfigures the *Person*, as well as *Reason*, of those who harbour it. She who, when her Fury was a little abated, I perceiv'd to be a Woman of singular good Sense, and what one might call extreamly handsome, appear'd at her first Entrance, the very Reverse of both. – She had quite forgot all Decorum; lost, for some Moments, all that belongs to a Woman of Discretion, or good Breeding. – Her Eyes shot Fire; her Cheeks bloated with Fury; her Lips trembled; every Feature was distorted; her Voice was big, hoarse, and masculine; and her Expressions such as are ordinarily made use of by Fish-Wives, Market-Women, and others of the same Degree of Gentry" (*Spy* 81). Failing to accept his forecast sends this woman catapulting into the loss of femininity, allure, and class status. The woman who distorts her beauty with rage at Campbell's accurate prophecy regarding her lover's deceit provides a troubling mirror image for Justicia. She becomes a figure for the literal ugliness that misplaced passion evinces when it rails against the inevitable future, and against women's inevitable betrayal by men. Such violent anger also diminishes her social class and makes her indistinguishable from ordinary sellers of goods in the street, unlike Campbell who delivers prophecies from the domestic space of his home. Paradoxically too Campbell is reputed actually to make the crooked straight, defying his own categorization as disabled, as he manages to do when a deformed woman comes to him. Haywood explains his inability to predict his own future as self-neglect rather than a failure of powers (*Spy* 170). Haywood is not much interested in his personal history, his Jacobitism, his Laplander or his Scottish origins; instead Campbell is for her a fashionable yet manly figure who uncannily perceives Englishwomen's present and future and whose misogyny is explained as his recognition of the realities of a sexual double standard.

Though Haywood seems to erase the importance of Campbell's Scottish heritage in order to normalize him, Scotland evokes for English readers an archaic past which Campbell embodies, a theme that Johnson echoes in his description of Thomas Braidwood's school for the deaf in the *Journey to the Western Islands* (1775). Braidwood established a special academy for the deaf and dumb, moving it from London to Edinburgh in 1783 when it became a public institution supported by George III, a man who struggled with mental disability himself. In the *Journey* Samuel Johnson famously compares the Highlanders' culture to the Eskimaux and the Hottentots, and the sign language of the deaf inspires hope after a tour of a nation that Johnson finds to be backward and vacuous: "whatever enlarges hope, will exalt courage; after having seen the deaf taught arithmetick, who would be afraid to cultivate the Hebrides?" (Johnson 164). Scotland, in his formulation a primitive and disabled country, deserves "cultivation" since its elusive oral history defies the written narration that he is attempting. Johnson's metaphor of cultivation also justifies England's usurpation of that role. Johnson found the deaf and dumb to be a sign of Scotland's emergence from the past into a commercial future and a print culture.

Scotland, then, in Johnson's account is "ignorant and savage," a handicapped nation needing special education and happily anticipating "cultivation," a metaphor for colonization by the English who are, in the terms of the *Journey*, the ablebodied and normal (Johnson 51).[56] Clusters of metaphors adhere to Scotland as a nation that first learns to speak, and then to think, parallel to the emergence from the child to the mature adult, the individual to the collective, the barbarous to the civilized. In Col, Johnson remarks, "The uncultivated parts are clothed with heath, among which industry has interspersed spots of grass and corn; but no attempt has yet been made to raise a tree" (124). Braidwood's school instructs the deaf to speak, to write, and to read lips, gestures, and print: like Campbell, "they hear with the eye" (163). Johnson's witnessing their achievement gives him hope: "I have seen so much, that I can believe more." The scholars greet their master "with smiling countenances and sparkling eyes, delighted with the hope of new ideas" and exemplified in the young woman who, "quivering her fingers in a manner which I thought very pretty, but of which I know not whether it was art or play, multiplied the sum regularly in two lines, observing the decimal place; but did not add the two lines together, probably disdaining so easy an operation ... It was pleasing to see one of the most desperate of human calamities capable of so much help ... " (164). Recent critics of the *Journey* have emphasized Johnson's personal identification with Braidwood's pupils as "an image of himself as writer, as well as struggling with the problem of self-inscription and (provisionally) solving it" as well as Johnson's inability to bridge the gap between recovering an ancient national Scottish myth that had not been articulated on the one hand, while documenting it as Scotland's authoritative history on the other hand.[57] Like the deaf and dumb, Johnson is unable to translate what he sees into print for a material and commercial culture: "He portrays himself as writing from a position of silence and solitude (he is 'deaf' and bereft of 'conversation')," as Stuart Sherman remarks,[58] and thus I suggest that he appropriates the women writers' predicament as his own. Johnson remarks on the absence of trees, history, written language, of a naked landscape, emigration, and superstitious culture. But if Scotland arouses fears of vacuity and the mental instability that results from the inability of the mind to fix on an object, it also represents the hope that "cultivation" (a word as important to the *Journey* as "vacuity") inspires. Cultivation is something that Scotland must depend upon England to provide, Johnson implies. It is associated with Englishness concerning everything from turnips that will produce fodder for hungry sheep and cows, to the language: "The great, the learned, the ambitious, and the vain, all cultivate the English phrase, and the English pronunciation, and in splendid companies Scotch is not much heard, except now and then from an old lady" (Johnson 162). The ancient unwritten language is feminized and antiquated. In contrast, Haywood's Duncan Campbell defied the expectation that fortunetellers were doddering old women and could instead be sexy, manly, imaginative, beautiful, powerful and deaf.

In *The History of Sexuality* Michel Foucault posits that the regulation of children in the eighteenth century extends to the publication of popular medical directives that correct the physical impairments in young bodies. As Ann Laura Stoler contextualized Foucault within class relations, "In the making of a bourgeois 'class' body in the eighteenth century, a new field of discourse emerged concerned with 'body hygiene, the art of longevity, ways of having healthy children and of keeping them alive as long as possible.' "[59] Along with this aim to regulate the corporeal, the aberrant are pushed increasingly to the geographical edges in order to "civilize" the social body as a category of the normal evolves. Rosemarie Garland Thomson has demonstrated in relation to American literature that "without the monstrous body to demarcate the border of the generic, without the female body to distinguish the shape of the male, and without the pathological to give form to the normal, the taxonomies of bodily value that underlie political, social, and economic arrangements would collapse."[60] The aberrant are akin to all those who inhabit the margins – "races" other than English, women, those of uncertain gender, the laboring classes – as European nationalisms and the modern body associated with them begin to cohere. Haywood's view of the deaf-mute clairvoyant, when interpreted within this historical shift, is remarkably radical. As an individual evocative of erotic attention and possessed of economic self-sufficiency, Campbell is a Scot who does not need or command pity, prejudice, national chauvinism, or imperial opportunity in the guise of cultivation. We might speculate that in Haywood's imagination, Campbell's predicament shares some similarities to the plight of that other intellectual monstrosity, the woman who writes for money. Though she herself benefits from selling his story, Haywood resists treating the conjuring deaf man Duncan Campbell as a freak of nature who resembles a woman preaching, a dog walking on its hinder legs, a talking parrot, or a learned black man. Haywood instead explores the terms by which an impaired human being who, though voiceless, speaks through writing and gesture and even dares to antagonize the very customers who willingly pay for an inauspicious forecast. Campbell's voiceless struggle to construct a personhood, a subjectivity, in writing the fortunes of others parallels that of other aberrant beings and offers an alternative to normalcy as a means to claim an articulate humanity within modernity. More than a eunuch or an impaired woman, Campbell is able to realize his own sexuality and subjectivity rather than act as a spoiler or a conduit for others.

Blind ladies, dumb virgins, eunuchs, and a deaf prophet have much in common in the cultural imagination of the early eighteenth century. The shared monstrosity between women and the "defective" of both sexes is not easily undone, now or then, though Donna Haraway has argued that the discourses of dismemberment and suffering open up the possibility of a nongeneric, feminist, cyborgian humanity. In Haraway's mythology, that "brokenness" may even paradoxically signify hope since she calls for a language of connection outside Enlightenment thought (and its humanism) that would create bonds between inappropriate/d others. Haraway takes Sojourner Truth's heretical declaration, *"Ain't I a Woman?"* as a prime example because it turns her exclusion and difference from the universal human "into an organon for placing the painful realities and practices of de-construction, dis-identification, and dis-memberment in the service of a newly articulated humanity."[61] But, I suggest, beyond the vexed problem of identifying dismemberment with suffering, defect with divinity, and making Truth into the uncanny or exotic Other, Haraway's utopian vision that would turn suffering into hope and individual dismemberment into collective wholeness, is constrained by its simple reversal of terms. To reject this reversal means that we are enjoined steadily and carefully to articulate the history and genealogy of disability, defect, and deformity in their multiplicity to avoid replicating the seductive but finally pernicious view that the handicapped bear a special mystical responsibility to bring more ordinary folk closer to Truth, or the equally problematic view that those who exceed the social construction of gender – as in the case of Sojourner Truth or of early modern women writers such as Aphra Behn and Eliza Haywood – exemplify defect and deformity.

CHAPTER 2

Effeminacy and femininity: Sarah Fielding, Elizabeth Montagu, and Johnson

There is in general a prejudice against female Authors especially if they invade those regions of litterature which the Men are desirous to reserve to themselves.

Letter of Elizabeth Montagu to Matthew Robinson,
10 September 1769

I

As the various renderings of Duncan Campbell's story demonstrate, among the anomalous beings who help determine the boundaries of the human are those who possess impaired senses or maimed bodies. As I have argued, the earliest fictions of eighteenth-century women writers in depicting the deaf, the mute, and the physically deformed allude to broad-ranging assumptions that align women more generally with sexual ambiguity and imperfection. Aphra Behn and Eliza Haywood contest the idea that exceptional women – and the sexually equivocal men associated with them – are inherently defective, but they also intimate that aberrance can unexpectedly release creativity and imagination. As British nationalism strengthened toward the end of the eighteenth century, relatively fixed masculine and feminine sexual identities become crucial to the installation of the modern nation-state, yet gendered hybridity is everywhere manifest in its cultural representations.[1] While the construction of sexual difference emerges along with modern nationalisms, its significance can be calculated in part by recognizing the extraordinary energy expended in its defence.[2] I want to turn now to examine the relation of anomaly to sexual irregularity in both sexes in mid eighteenth-century England, and to explore the way that feminized and effeminated bodies are perceived as corporeal indicators of national values, interests, and anxieties. They are also perceived to provide keys to the location of a culture's civilization on the scale of progress. Both enraptured and repelled by anomaly within and without its borders, mid eighteenth-century English writers attempt to make something coherent and stable of the curious, the exotic, and the disquietingly unfamiliar.

During the past decade or two, conventional wisdom has held that with the formation of the public sphere, the middle decades of the century usher in the cult of domesticity, companionate marriage, and the retreat of women into the private sphere. According to this familiar narrative, sentimental bourgeois values predominate, and modern, increasingly rigid, notions of gender difference and sexual identity emerge.[3] This description of the early history of contemporary sexual hierarchies is now being complicated by the investigation of women's sometimes subtle strategies for managing professional authorship and public attention, and by the growing attention to masculinity, to explain more exactly the reciprocal nature of gendered relations in the period. Yet Samuel Johnson indicates in *The Adventurer* No. 115 (11 December 1753) that sexual difference was more distinct in *former* times, an era in the long forgotten past, when "ladies contented themselves with private virtues and domestic excellence, and a female writer, like a female warrior, was considered as a kind of excentric being, that deviated, however illustriously, from her due sphere of motion." He continues, "The revolution of years has now produced a generation of Amazons of the pen, who with the spirit of their predecessors have set masculine tyranny at defiance, asserted their claim to the regions of science, and seem resolved to contest the usurpations of virility."[4] The professional writers, "the generation of Amazons" whom Johnson describes clearly resist easy confinement to domesticity or to an image of ideal femininity. Instead such women typify for him an entire generation capable of colonizing the masculine domain. Johnson equivocates in his praise of women's knowledge and judgment: women who excel in their endeavors and exercise their sway against masculine tyranny exceed their appropriate sphere. Alluding to a national disease he characterizes as a "universal eagerness of writing" which has brought a proliferation of publication and an "epidemical conspiracy for the destruction of paper," Johnson especially blames women for the predicament. If Johnson depicts women writers of the mid eighteenth century as feisty women who had happily abandoned the domestic pursuits that formerly satisfied them, why does a narrative about their traditional femininity persist?

In speaking of the works written by contemporary Amazons of the pen, Johnson may have been referring to *chroniques scandaleuses* such as Laetitia Pilkington's *Memoirs* (3 volumes 1748–54); Hannah Snell's *The Female Soldier* (1750); or *An Apology for the Conduct of Mrs. Teresia Constantia Phillips* (3 volumes 1748–49). Or perhaps he was simply voicing his concern about the competitive impulses aroused in men as a result of the explosive increase in women's fiction writing from authors such as Haywood, Sarah Scott, Charlotte Lennox (herself the creator of a woman warrior in *The Female Quixote*, 1752), or Sarah Fielding whose historical novel *Lives of Cleopatra and Octavia* (1757) contrasts the exotic Egyptian queen to the virtuous Roman matron. If Johnson's characterization is representative of a larger cultural perception, the concept of women writers as monstrously perverse would compete vigorously with the idea of proper ladies at the very moment when the contest for the marketplace intensified. We might then ask whether Johnson's view of women writers in the generation before the Bluestockings as being akin to viragos, tommies, mollies, and hermaphrodites, and exemplary of a bold third sex in spite of their alleged retreat into domesticity, was widely shared.

The puzzle as to why femininity of the most private and modest sort becomes dominant in England at midcentury along with frequent accusations of effeminacy is partially resolved in observing the changes occurring at that particular historical juncture in relation to the formation of empire. The middle of the eighteenth century is a critical turning point in the argument I am weaving for several reasons: it marks women's alleged retreat into the private sphere and the ascendance of domesticity; in 1745 the question of the Protestant succession (which had dominated English politics for seventy years) is finally put to rest; the Seven Years' War beginning in 1757 radically changed the outlines of Britain's empire; and the category of "monster" was first introduced by Linnaeus as a scientific classification in 1758. All of these developments relate to the constellation of factors I am considering, and they demonstrate both the superficiality of difference and its immutability.

In this chapter I first explore a novel written on the cusp of the Bluestocking generation, Sarah Fielding's *David Simple* (1744), to show that it refuses a strictly symmetrical understanding of sexual difference or a definition of the woman writer as domesticated. In the novel, I argue, Fielding subtly questions the fantasy of masculine authority in *David Simple* through a strong and witty heroine, and a sentimental hero who is less than forceful, to refract through gender the nation's interests at midcentury. After pausing to consider the complex meanings of effeminacy, applied to both women and men, I turn to the literary relationship between Johnson and Elizabeth Montagu, "Queen of the Bluestockings," as a nuanced exchange concerning attitudes about effeminacy and femininity, and as indicative of Montagu's attempt to jockey with various male writers for public authority, a battle she feels unlikely to win, particularly against Johnson. But there are intricacies involved in the contest since Montagu is defending England's literary centrality, and because Johnson was a living national icon who was heavily invested in displaying his own considerable stature through editing another competing national literary giant, Shakespeare, and in writing authoritative biographies of the country's poets. Bearing some similarities to this contest for supremacy waged over and through the writings of Montagu and Johnson, Sarah Fielding's novel renders a paired mixed gendering through a manly woman and a man of feeling.

II

Eighteenth-century satire has usually been assumed to be a masculine prerogative, especially in the earlier decades, but well-known bawds and prostitutes sometimes appeared in caricature as female satyrs who, when figured in engravings, represent sexual predators rather than sexual prey.[5] Though women writers are still not widely perceived as constituting a satiric tradition sufficient to compete with the Tory satirists, recognition of their role as satirists has recently begun.[6] Aphra Behn, Sarah Fyge, Anne Finch, Delarivier Manley, Laetitia Pilkington, Lady Mary Wortley Montagu, Charlotte Lennox, and Frances Burney are among those prose and verse satirists who employ the very constraints that bind women to transform the stigma against their writing satire.[7] Others engage in self-mocking strategies to deflect reproach or to incorporate witty "masculine" female characters who are themselves the object of satire but who wield considerable power through characters such as Burney's Mrs. Selwyn or Maria Edgeworth's Harriet Freke. Evelina, for example, equivocates in her opinion of Mrs. Selwyn who "may be called *masculine*; but unfortunately, her manners deserve the same epithet, for, in studying to acquire the knowledge of the other sex, she has lost all the softness of her own," and evidences an "unmerciful propensity to satire."[8] Yet Mrs. Selwyn's aggressive intervention in Evelina's behalf secures the heroine's patrimony and her inheritance. Women writers discern that effeminacy is much less a threat to their social wellbeing and economic status than systems of dominance that take root in assumptions of essential characteristics.

Though Burney mocks fops as ineffectual monkeys in *Evelina*, in fact, "effeminacy" in men, when imagined as excessive femininity, is sometimes exciting and immensely stimulating to eighteenth-century women. The softer sculpted male body is reported to have spurred desire in some women observers in the period, while masculine brawniness, considered to be less refined, produced disgust and shock.[9] The great notoriety and sexual appeal of *castrati* such as Nicolini and Farinelli dominated eighteenth-century operatic performances[10] until tenors replaced other *castrati* (including Tenducci, Pacchierotti, Rauzzini, Rubinelli, and Marchesi) who lost popularity in the late 1770s and finally disappeared in the 1790s. These men, neutered before adolescence, evoked astonishing sexual hybridity, enacting an ambiguous and indeterminate gender. The spectacle of the *castrati* authorizes unspeakable desires and arouses same-sex yearnings in men and women, as well as an illicit appreciation for a feminized masculinity: "we had much better lose the Pleasure we receive from that *Species* of *Harmony*, than have the *Eyes, Ears, and Thoughts* of our Ladies, conversant with Figures, they cannot well *see, hear,* nor *think,* of, without a Blush."[11]

In the character of David Simple, Sarah Fielding creates perhaps the first man of feeling, a gentle if ineffectual hero who possesses virtue without licentiousness and is paired with a bold and witty woman, Cynthia.[12] Henry Fielding's puff to the second edition of *David Simple*, at first believed to be written by the author of *Joseph Andrews* (1742), commends Sarah's "penetration" and ability to comprehend the tortuous convolutions of human nature:[13]

For as the Merit of this Work consists in a vast Penetration into human Nature, a deep and profound Discernment of all the Mazes, Windings and Labyrinths, which perplex the Heart of Man to such a degree, that he is himself often incapable of seeing through them; and as this is the greatest, noblest, and rarest of all the Talents which constitute a Genius; so a much larger Share of this Talent is necessary, even to recognize these Discoveries, when they are laid before us, than falls to the share of a common Reader.[14]

How is it possible, we might ask, to attribute a masculine penetration and comprehensiveness of vision to Sarah Fielding who appears to some readers to be in "collusion with the eighteenth-century ideology of femininity"?[15] These virtues that Henry assigns to Sarah are more typically masculine,[16] and the overarching stance he claims for her largely eludes the eighteenth-century woman writer. Mary Wollstonecraft, herself often accused of exceeding gender boundaries, describes women's "individual manner of seeing things, produced by ignorance" as the peculiarly feminine habit, one to which women are educated, that holds women to their inferior social situation.[17] From Wollstonecraft's polemical perspective, women learn to attend to "littlenesses" that degrade them and "have their attention naturally drawn from the interest of the whole community to that of the minute parts," but here in contrast Henry Fielding grants his sister a comprehensive view.

In rejecting the more overtly sexual and political traditions of Aphra Behn or Delarivier Manley earlier in the century, Sarah Fielding adopts an alternative satiric approach that nevertheless shares the tendency to avoid misogynist conventions.[18] Fielding learned, as she describes it, "to practice that [satiric art] with Emulation, which would induce Angels to weep, and set Monkeys a grinning."[19] As a theorist and a practitioner of domestic satire, Fielding attempts to steer a course that shuns the rapier thrust of searing wit. She cites Horace in defence of gentle satire: "*No honest Man shall by my Satire bleed*."[20] How difficult to create mild, effective satire, Cynthia declares, to be "witty without either Blasphemy, Obscenity, or Ill-nature" (106). She wishes that "every Man, who is possessed of a greater Share of *Wit* than is common, instead of insulting and satirizing others, would make use of his Talents for the Advantage and Pleasure of Society." Similarly, in the preface to *The Countess of Dellwyn* (1759), quoting a lost manuscript she allegedly had recovered, she criticizes those readers who abuse people for pleasure because of the impossibility of building community under those circumstances: "But with no such Man would my Soul wish to hold *Acquaintance*: I say not, *Friendship*; because it would be the highest Absurdity to suppose such a one in the least degree capable of being animated with the generous Warmth which that Appellation requires."[21] The best raillery, she continues, is that which falls "only on such Frailties as People of Sense Voluntarily give up to Censure: These are the best Subjects to display Honour, as it turns into a Compliment to the Person raillied." Yoking (masculine) satire and (feminine) sentiment, Fielding in *David Simple* unsexes generic expectations, tempers one with the other, and makes intelligible a gendered hybridity that differs substantially from the distressing mixture that would complicate a national identity.

There is nothing explicitly about British womanhood in *David Simple*, and the novel only obliquely addresses domestic rights for women and political rights for men. Yet it could be argued that Sarah Fielding distinguishes between a domestic English sentimental masculinity bolstered by a benevolent middling community, and the corrupt French aristocratic society that endangers it, and between an internal and an external effeminacy. The external effeminate in the person of the French may be of greater concern to Fielding than any internal threat. The morally degenerate French aristocracy in the tragic subplot contrast to the central English narrative about sibling affection and David's search for a friend. The ill-fated group includes the quick-tempered Marquis de Stainville and Isabelle, his distressed sister, who marries Stainville's penniless schoolfriend Chevalier Dumont. Dumont, like David, possesses a much-desired "mixture of

Softness and Manliness, which were displayed in his Countenance," but in Dumont's case it is "joined to his great Genteelness" (227). This mixture attracts Dorimene, the mad melancholic heiress married to Stainville but whose adulterous desire enacts "the Rage of a Woman, whose Passions have got so much the better of her, as to enable her to break through all the strongest Ties imaginable" (236). Such an excessive self-indulgence, like self-absorbed effeminacy, destroys communal bonds. In both plots a strong woman weathers the miseries of her family and friends, but unlike the heroine Cynthia who steadfastly endures, the disillusioned Isabelle retires to a nunnery. The misguided French aristocracy, ruled by passion, exposes the pollution that can twist friendship into self-love.[22] The subplot delineates the dangerous foreign influences that threaten to neuter England and thus threaten fragile bonds within affective societies.

In contrast, David Simple, ruled by his passions, is less effeminate than feminized: he "had more of what *Shakespear* calls the *Milk of Human Kind*...for his Sensations were too strong, to leave him the free Use of his Reason" (129). Cynthia, the narrator, satirist, and principal female character who befriends David, acts as moral arbiter. She assumes the satiric voice but unlike Burney's Mrs. Selwyn in *Evelina* or Edgeworth's Harriet Freke in *Belinda*, completely escapes becoming the object of satire herself. She instructs the receptive little community by mockingly recounting the story of six English gentlemen (a masculine parallel to the gallery of women in Pope's "Epistle to A Lady") who courted the coquettish Corinna in Paris: an artful man without practical sense, a diffident man of understanding, an unfeeling but good-natured man, as well as three men who are respectively ill-tempered, excessively sentimental, and affectedly witty (256–65). Gently chastening the men without abusive or ill-natured satire, Cynthia applauds Corinna's clever management of them. Corinna ultimately calculates that she will be most empowered by marrying the vain man because "it was too much Love on the Woman's Side, that was generally the Cause of their losing their Husband's Affections." Cynthia satirizes these men as a sex. Though none is judged effeminate, none is able to negotiate a way through life with equanimity and good sense.

Other captivating satiric moments include Cynthia's sharing a stagecoach to London with a Clergyman, an Atheist, and a Butterfly ("his Hair pinned up in blue Papers, a laced Waistcoat, and every thing which is necessary to shew an Attention to adorn the Person," 176) who each accost Cynthia in turn. Flaunting false wit on topics such as gallantry, gaming, and dressing, the Butterfly's self-involvement deeply annoys Cynthia. Together, the other travelers lead her to conclude that men are civil only to the women they seek to subdue. Women too earn Fielding's ridicule, though none of them for being manly. Dorimene, Livia, and Mrs. Orgeuil all give evidence of considerable antagonism toward other women. Cynthia satirizes three feuding sisters who rip apart their father's material legacy, a carpet, rather than accept an unequal inheritance: "They were all vex'd to have it for spoil'd, yet each was better pleas'd, than if either of the Sisters had had it whole" (48). These women destroy both property and family ties because of their graceless greed. Satire of a certain sort, as Sarah Fielding construes it, paradoxically builds community, distributes wealth equitably, serves the best interests of both sexes, and unites the nation. This effect occurs even though men perceive that woman's wit threatens the gendered economy upon which it is based. Cynthia's father grants her no inheritance, and like her sisters he challenges her to survive solely by her superior wit and, by implication, as a whore. One recalls Sarah Fielding's own struggles when the manly Cynthia, discouraged from pursuing learning, is "so teazed and tormented about *Wit*, I really wish there was no such thing in the World. I am very certain, the Woman who is possessed of it, unless she can be so peculiarly happy as to live with People void of Envy, had better be without it" (102). A woman's wit is a marketable commodity which, if fostered within a tight group of like-minded people, may bring her economic independence. Women writers who dare to attack others, even mildly, need protection from public or familial retribution as well as the social support which would allow them to step outside traditional boundaries.

Cynthia's sister connects dissolution and licentious with the word "libertine," a term seldom associated with women. She "*was really afraid what I should come to, as she saw, I fancied it a Sign of* Wit *to be a Libertine*; a Word which she chose to thunder often in my Ears, as she has heard me frequently express a particular Aversion of those of our Sex who deserve it" (103). To be a witty woman, Cynthia laments, is "to be kept back as much as possible, for fear I should *know too much*" (112). Unwilling to prostitute herself, or to be an upper servant to the husband her father has chosen for her, or to be a toady to a tyrannical woman employer who treats her as a slave, Cynthia instead joins David Simple in his search for "a real Friend" (76). In order to survive, a woman satirist requires a community of true friends – David, Camilla, and Valentine – who make it possible for Cynthia to avoid economic dependence as she extracts herself from the patronage of the gentry and frees her tongue from being monitored. Their easy sociability as they survey the world from a London coach contrasts to the harassment that Cynthia experienced with the Clergyman, the Atheist, and the Butterfly. Creating a new "*happy Family*" (327) they substitute a viable economic community for their own unhappy families to cultivate affective bonds instead of relying upon blood ties. This kind of freedom also makes gender fluidity more feasible.

While Cynthia engages in a satire that escapes and defies misogyny, David personifies a sentimentality which is not lachrymose but tender, at once a model of sentiment and a parody of it. Readers have labeled him a "cypher," and "a bloodless, moralizing sentimentalist,"[23] but Fielding creates a man of feeling who escapes the negative connotations assigned to effeminacy. In *David Simple* Sarah Fielding herself defines "effeminacy" as extreme self-interest, a tendency toward economic and emotional self-indulgence that is undesirable in either sex. When the word appears in the novel, it applies to pitying oneself rather than displaying a natural masculine sympathy: "Here Mr. *Orgeuil* stopped, seeing poor *David* could hear no more, not being able to stifle his Sighs and Tears, and the Idea of such a Scene; for he did not think it beneath a Man to cry from Tenderness, tho' he would have thought it much too effeminate to be moved to Tears by any Accident that concerned himself only" (63). Rather than satirizing weeping as effeminacy, or associating it with sodomy, Sarah Fielding criticizes the material effects wrought by luxuriating in such self-interestedness. Simple's ethic of community is set against a counter-ethic of self-interest and arrogance in Orgeuil, a character whose mildly irritating pride in the first two volumes gives way to real malevolence in *Volume the Last*.[24] For Fielding, this kind of effeminacy works against the common welfare.

While David is simple in the sense that he is free of duplicity and guile, like any picaro he is also the object of satire. But most frequently, Fielding's satire inveighs against a world that cannot tolerate a man who prefers true friends to unmitigated self-interest. Often the victim of a harsh world, he searches for the fellowship of individuals, regardless of sex, who partake in an idealized friendship that is free of hierarchies, domination, and servitude. The four friends, models of emotional closeness, share affection and grant mutual economic support to create social configurations that exceed blood bonds or the conventional relations between the sexes. When David offers himself in marriage to Cynthia, she is at first puzzled that David's motives are neither patriarchal nor economic. Her refusal testifies that they are best suited to being platonic companions who will protect each other from becoming the victims of a friendless society. Similarly, women's friendship affords a noncompetitive community of idealized social relations. Camilla and Cynthia exemplify a union of equality in spite of their differing capacities: "so uncommon were [their] Characters..., and so very extraordinary the Friendship, that they had often talked over the Difference of their Capacities and Dispositions with the same Freedom as if they had been mentioning the Difference of their Height or Size" (330). In fact, Cynthia alone enables the survival of the community which, without her canny satiric stance that is lost to the group when she travels to Jamaica in *Volume the Last*, dissolves into hopeless destitution. The community fails when Cynthia is called away to empire and David's irrational tendencies prevail as he is "entangled in the Snare of his Love for others, and his Inclination blinded [by] his Judgment" (352). Deprived of her English community, she loses her characteristic strength.

David Simple, like Henry Fielding's *Joseph Andrews*, flirts with the titillating aspects of incest while firmly insisting that the taboo will be maintained as new forms of friendship develop across sex lines. When Livia, stepmother to Camilla and Valentine, accuses her stepchildren of incest in order to disinherit them,[25] the threat allows for the sexual current buried in *David Simple* to be discharged. In Sarah Fielding's paradigm of community, the specter of incest establishes the limits of male–female friendship in order to avoid the perverse and monstrous. Male–female amity, especially between characters who extend cultural constructions of gender difference, disrupts fraternity and patriarchy; it is cognizant of inequalities based on birth, on "capacities and dispositions," but is not diminished by them. David and Camilla's marriage rises to the status of an ideal companionate marriage, but it is the nonsexual friendship between Cynthia and David, the manly woman and the feeling man, that sustains the novel. The ethic of this mixed-sex community, founded on economic reciprocity without separate property, its passions checked by sensibility, exemplifies the opposite of a luxurious effeminacy for either sex and reimagines the binary of effeminate men and manly women.

These unconventional partnerships between the sexes breed agreeable mutations and pleasing hybridity rather than aberrant monsters. Fielding's novel testifies that there is nothing perverse or morally repugnant in the love between brother and sister, or between manly women and feminized men, or in unsexing satire. Fielding veils the revolutionary implications of her story: that amalgamated sexual identities and nonhierarchical communities based on friendship threaten patrilineage and even endanger a national identity that depends for its security on stricter boundaries between the sexes. Escaping the predictable satires against Amazons and macaronis, the narrator's gentler vision in this domestic prose satire, freed of the misogynist tradition yet spurred by dissatisfaction with the status quo, is a vehicle for imagining a nation strengthened by an interlacing of affective communities.

III

Fielding's *David Simple* also demonstrates the tensions for Englishwomen between being female warriors or the embodiment of perfect femininity, and the novel offers alternatives to these apparent national imperatives in spite of seeming to confine women to the domestic.[26] Midcentury brings the inaugural moment for the celebration of a national female genius that exemplifies public virtue in George Ballard's *Memoirs of Several Ladies of Great Britain, who have been Celebrated for their Writings* (1752), and the biographer brags that "it is pretty certain that England has produced more women famous for literary accomplishments than any other nation in Europe."[27] A number of other biographies attempt to codify a peculiarly *British* womanhood for the first time, including John Duncombe's *Feminead: or, Female Genius* (1754), George Colman and Bonnell Thornton's edition of *Poems by Eminent Ladies* (1755), and Thomas Amory's *Memoirs of Several Ladies of Great Britain* (1755). One prominent alternative to feminine domesticity is the Amazonian exotic addressed by Johnson in the *Adventurer*, a powerful yet mutilated warrior woman, who is an emblem of British women's entry into the public sphere and of sexual difference gone askew.[28] The female representative of the nation, Britannia, sometimes figured with one bared breast, Amazon-style, resonates in her Celtic origins with the ancient tribes. Similar too is Boadicea, revived as the eponymous subject of Richard Glover's 1753, who had historically symbolized the patriotic imperial woman. The virile man-woman contrasts to the male English soldier whose effeminacy, if not remedied, will threaten the future of the second British empire. Though *David Simple* is not an overtly feminist novel, it exposes the inadequacy of domesticity and of the patriarchal institutions of marriage and family as models for women's lives.

Though it may indeed be the case that an especially decorous femininity prevails at midcentury, Johnson's perception that Englishwomen are newly emboldened resonates with other discussions of national identities. The first two volumes of *David Simple* (1744) were published just before the last Jacobite uprising, and its sequel, the tragic *Volume the Last* appeared nearly a decade later in 1753.[29] Fielding's foray into domestic prose satire in the mid 1740s coincides with the deaths of the arguably misogynist Tory satirists, Swift and Pope, as well as with the defeat of the Jacobite Pretender to the throne at the battle of Culloden when the question of the Protestant succession is finally settled. Fielding anticipates John Brown's formulation that the national welfare depends upon eradicating vested commercial interests which can destroy communities of families and friends over issues of property. At the same time effeminacy, surfacing in the public consciousness with the '45, became subject to frequent discussion in the next two decades. In Brown's *Estimate of the Manners and Principles of the Times* (1757), an enormously popular and controversial tract achieving its seventh edition by 1758 which provides a context for Fielding's novel, he launches a diatribe against an English government in danger of losing the Seven Years' War: "How far this dastard Spirit of Effeminacy hath crept upon us, and destroyed the national Spirit of Defence, may appear from the general *Panic* the Nation was thrown into, at the late *Rebellion*" (91). Both Brown and David Garrick, a symbol of masculine theatrical genius who produced the Shakespeare Jubilee and embodied a national idol, considered effeminacy a threat to national prosperity.[30] By 1759 England's military and maritime virility sought to prevail over an effeminate France and a macaronic Italy.

In addition to being a perverse affection of femininity, a "*vain, luxurious, and selfish* EFFEMINACY" came to signify a surplus of self-directed interest, an undisciplined redundancy, and an unwillingness to sacrifice private needs to the public good. Explicitly mapping a gendered construction onto national identity, Brown finds that commerce in its early stages is beneficial to the nation, and in its second stage "national Effeminacy forms the *primary*, and *Avarice* only the *secondary* Character"; but in its third and most excessive phase commerce creates debilitating factions and dilutes the public spirit to "beget a kind of regulated Selfishness, which tends at once to the Increase and Preservation of Property" (14). In Brown's scheme, private corruption yields public effects, though clearly not public benefits. The *Estimate* famously laments the blurring of sexual boundaries: "The Sexes have now little other apparent Distinction, beyond that of Person and Dress. Their peculiar and characteristic Manner are confounded and lost: The one Sex having advanced into *Boldness*, as the other have sunk into *Effeminacy*."[31] Brown deems any sort of surfeit to be effeminate, including lust for gold, gaming, obscenity, "irreligion," the Grand Tour, foreign cuisine, music, and painting. What is less clear – since Brown excludes them from discussion – is whether he is suggesting that bold women, like effeminate men, also compromise the nation with their aristocratic selfishness and commercial greed.[32]

The misogynist male narrator in *Beauty's Triumph* Part II (1751) similarly laments masculine deficiency, blaming it on mothers who engage in "training up our boys, as they do, from their earliest infancy, to folly, foppery, effeminacy, and vice."[33] In contrast, the female narrator in the same treatise contests the rigid opposition between the sexes which language imposes: "When they mean to stigmatise a *Man* with want of courage they call him *effeminate*, and when they would praise a *Woman* for her courage they call her *manly* . . . [W]hen a *Man* is possest of our virtues he should be call'd effeminate by way of the highest praise of his good-nature and justice; and a *Woman* who departs from our sex by espousing the injustice and cruelty of the *Men's* nature should be call'd a *Man*: that is, *one whom no sacred ties can bind*" (56–57). Here the commentator radically attempts to unburden effeminacy of the cultural weight that adheres to it sympathetically to encourage an easy exchange of gendered characteristics beyond notions of essential sexual difference: "effeminacy" like "manliness" takes on a positive valence in its application to either sex. In short, clearly effeminacy was not at all exclusively associated with homosexual behavior, but its excess – the false and exaggerated imitation of femininity, a failure to achieve an appropriate womanliness – was undesirable wherever it was found. Appropriate sexual difference contributes to producing sacred ties among generous and selfless people who seek the larger good. The markers of "effeminacy" in either sex are moving targets which measure divergence from more familiar social categories that shape a sexual economy compatible with a disciplined and civilized nation.

In early eighteenth-century Britain, men's submitting to extreme heterosexual desire effeminates them while in the later eighteenth century (unlike the Restoration period), the term seems to be increasingly focused on the homosexual, the macaronic, and the foreign.[34] Randolph Trumbach believes that all sodomites in the period after the 1720s were stereotyped as "effeminate and misogynist,"[35] but sexual behavior should not be construed as the sole measure of masculinity. Homosexuality could be culturally marked through the display of an exaggerated masculinity, yet by no means were all effeminate men assumed to engage in homosexual practices. The man of feeling might be clearly drawn sexually to women rather than men, saturated with tenderness and compassion and, unlike the fop, innocent of narcissism and affectation. The loss of masculine authority signaled by "effeminacy" parallels the encroachment of women into the marketplace, and men acknowledge and even cultivate strong heterosexual desire without forfeiting their masculinity: in fact, it would seem to be a condition of it. John Barrell identifies an emergent republic of taste negotiated between "virtue and vertù, between manly politeness and luxurious effeminacy," which cultivated the aesthetic by helping to emancipate men from a decadent desire for material goods.[36] A robust heterosexual masculinity characterized by desire for sex if not for economic consumption, and for authenticity rather than politeness, increasingly prevails as an index to a national identity.

By midcentury the term "effeminate" is fairly consistently a derogatory term signifying luxury and sexual excess.[37] A laudable effeminacy, polite and refined without being extreme, is more frequently labeled "feminine." Johnson's *Dictionary* defines "feminine" as "soft; tender; delicate" or more pejoratively "effeminate; emasculated." Another of Johnson's definitions for feminine – "womanlike; soft without reproach" – he believes to be a positive term not in current use. As a word meaning vulgarly or excessively feminine, "effeminacy" could also be a charge directed at women, and thus it floats free of anatomy. In Sarah Fielding's *The History of the Countess of Dellwyn* (1759) the heroine's father believes that her "effeminate Bashfulness" interferes with her prospects for marriage. In this case, "effeminate" does not carry the meaning of luxury, and it alludes instead to an extreme shyness unbecoming in a sociable woman. Woman's "effeminacy" may also hint at an uneducated and unregulated state that allows her to wallow in natural slovenliness and indolence. In *Female Rights Vindicated* (1758) "effeminacy" suggests the physicality of women's identities, as opposed to the more ideal or cerebral subjectivities of the masculine: "Tutors and Lessons are confined to the Men; the greatest Care is taken to instruct them in every thing that may fortify their Sense, and regulate their Judgement; whilst the Effeminacy of Women is left to increase upon them, through Idleness or Ignorance, by the most puerile, or the meanest Vocations."[38] Here there are also intimations that such unpolished women naturally inhabit an earlier less cultivated stage in history. The term "effeminacy" also makes problematic the difference between manly women and effeminate men.

When Peg Woffington acted the breeches role of Sir Harry Wildair in George Farquhar's *The Constant Couple*, she was congratulated for avoiding effeminacy, best understood in this instance perhaps as men's exaggerated rendering of femininity. It was unclear, as Pat Rogers has pointed out, whether Woffington was "to be admired for resembling a man in the role, or admired for not doing so."[39] Most likely, however, it points to her carefully regulated acting which escaped the excess of caricature. As a criticism that could be leveled at a woman in a breeches role, effeminacy at midcentury seems to be less a womanly quality grafted onto a man (womanlike though not a woman) than a primitive child-like state that precedes politeness. In any case, its presence is more a reminder of the unbending nature of acceptable "masculine" and "feminine" behavior, and any connection to sexual practices may be incidental. Virtue and domesticity conjure up the proper feminine, while the overly refined, excessively delicate, and the enervated evoke the surfeit of effeminacy.

Effeminacy at midcentury also involves the mere illusion of masculinity, or impersonating femininity with exaggerated feminine manners, a charge often lodged as a critique of the aristocracy with or without a homosexual content; it may also incorporate a resistance to the predominant types of masculinity, whether aristocratic or bourgeois, though it is most often associated with the luxurious indolence of the ruling class. Real men possess sense and wit, while effeminate men engage in gossip and are ruled by fashion, excess sentiment, and affectation.[40] Whether impersonating a woman or producing the mirage of masculinity, effeminacy, then, is a term with a range of meanings which suggest a complex sexual economy in which neither simple oppositions between the sexes nor an inversion of homosexuality offers a sufficient explanation. Yet effeminate men were accused of polluting women, even manly women, by engaging them in trivial pursuits and selfish frivolity. Effeminacy also threatened rates of propagation and countered the national imperative to encourage marriage and increase fertility. By the decade of the 1770s complaints focused on "the delicate *Maccarony things* we see swarming everywhere, to the disgrace of our *noble patient British race*"[41] who were perceived as sexual mutants. Objectified as an asexual "it" or third sex, these much caricatured macaronis had founded an eating club with a Mediterranean cuisine that rivaled the Beefsteak Clubs reputation for fostering virility because of its bovine dining fare. James Boswell, a Scotsman who longed for a more explicitly English identity when he arrived in London in 1762, was ambivalent about the value of the motto of the Beefsteak Club, *Beef and Liberty*, prominently displayed in golden letters. According to Boswell, being English involved a reputation for being "selfish, beef-eaters, and cruel," given to rituals such as watching cockfights, yet he, a Scotsman, willingly impersonated such a national trait and wrote a biography that defended the masculine credentials of its subject.[42]

In short, effeminacy encompasses among its midcentury meanings the following connotations and more: (1) failing to exercise self-restraint; decadence, luxury; (2) enervation deriving from passionate heterosexual desire, but only sometimes linked to homoerotic desire; (3) in its misogynist connotations, associating oneself with women, imitating, or impersonating femininity;[43] (4) lacking interiority, being superficial and frivolous, producing the illusion of masculinity; (5) resisting identification with normative masculinity; (6) failing to exemplify classical republican virtue and incapable of military heroics; (7) having a Protean nature; instability;

(8) sodomy; and (9) a favorable term meaning soft, kind, or compassionate. Effeminacy is most consistently barbaric, foreign, or anti-British, while manliness in either sex strengthens the nation and is exemplary of it. Effeminacy also encodes attitudes toward public matters including civic humanism, monarchical loyalties, and slavery. Gender-coding relies for its legibility on coherence and predictability, in contrast to the display of effeminacy which sometimes highlights the incongruity between anatomy and other indicators of identity.[44] Accusations of effeminacy thus assume a primary identity from which there is deviation even as they question whether that primary identity even exists. In short, eighteenth-century effeminacy is not confined to the sodomite, the homosexual, the heterosexual, the aristocrat, the foreigner, or even to men.

I V

After our survey of effeminacy it may seem odd to learn that Johnson himself was the object of sexual attack, and that literary women hurled allegations of an insufficient and peculiar masculinity at him, if only in private correspondence. Elizabeth Montagu, Sarah Fielding's benefactor, accused Johnson of being an effeminate beau, and thus an inadequate representative of the British nation in her letters to Elizabeth Carter. Carter had introduced Johnson and Montagu in 1759 in connection with their solicitations on behalf of Johnson's blind friend, Anna Williams, and he visited her Bluestocking assemblies on more than one occasion. After a brief interruption to their friendship, Johnson was after 1775 often a guest at Montagu's home on Hill Street, but their connection was again deeply strained after his publication of *The Lives of the Poets* in 1781.

The troubled relationship between Montagu and Johnson is further complicated by her friendship with Lord Lyttelton. The Bluestockings' protection of Lord Lyttelton's person and reputation occasioned something of a rupture with Johnson for more than one of them. The circumstances of the quarrel deserve some attention. Having met Lyttelton two years before she married Edward Montagu at age twenty, Montagu had contributed anonymously three dialogues to his *Dialogues of the Dead*. Styling her "The Madonna," Lyttelton was later extremely admiring of her *Essay on Shakespeare* (1769).[45] Gossip about the nature of their relationship persisted, especially after he was parted from his second wife. Lyttelton's Whig sympathies did not endear him to Johnson, and he offended Johnson further in having been patron of a satire which mocked his Latinate style in *Lexiphanes, A Dialogue imitated from Lucian* (1767). Later Montagu treated Johnson coldly after having read his *Life of Lyttelton* (part of the *Lives of the Poets*) in manuscript. Horace Walpole recounts the dispute in a widely circulated anecdote dating from 1781: "It has not, I believe, produced any altercation, but at a bluestocking meeting held by Lady Lucan [Elizabeth Vesey], Mrs. Montagu, and Dr. Johnson kept at different ends of the chamber, and set up altar against altar there... There she told me as a mark of her high displeasure that she would never ask him to dinner again." The disagreements between Montagu and Johnson over Lyttelton also occasioned Johnson's famous comment to General Paoli, "You see, Sir, I am no longer the man for Mrs. Montagu." Similarly, when Boswell corners Johnson about his feelings for Mrs. Montagu, he responded, "Mrs. Montagu has dropt me. Now, Sir, there are people whom one should like very well to drop, but would not wish to be dropped by."[46] In addition, according to Hester Thrale, both men were deeply attached to Miss Hill Boothby and were competitors for her attentions. Thrale cavils about Boothby, "Such was the purity of her mind, Johnson said, and such the graces of her manner, that Lord Lyttelton and he used to strive for her preference with an emulation that occasioned hourly disgust, and ended in lasting animosity."[47]

But the most intense feelings about Johnson were perhaps the private ones revealed in Montagu's correspondence with her friends. When Montagu prepares to publish her *Essay on the Writings and Genius of Shakespear compared with Greek and French Dramatick Poets: With Some Remarks Upon Misrepresentations of Mons. De Voltaire* in 1769, the year of David Garrick's Shakespeare Jubilee, she worries that she will appear presumptuous since Johnson's *Preface to Shakespeare* (1765), a work she praises in the main, had already appeared, and it seemed hubristic to take on the same subject. In assessing her predecessors, she suspects she can improve upon them: "When I have put Mr Popes & Johnsons essays together I do not mean to represent them as perfectly similar. Mr Popes is by far I think ye best composition, but he has only gatherd the finest flowers in the Field, Johnson has more nearly glean'd it, but his preface is not so beautifull as the other. His language is laboured, rather too fine for my taste, who love the negligences of genius better than the ornaments of study, but perhaps I judge so for want of refinement. I never love the velvet style, an equal pile [of the cloth] as if cut by an engine, however in these effeminate days perhaps it will be admired for the very thing I dislike."[48] Johnson's refined and ornamental style, Montagu suggests, will appeal to effeminate tastes, tastes reflective of the current love of fashion and excess.

As I have suggested, effeminacy in its eighteenth-century usages is not synonymous with either femininity or the unmanly; and in spite of considerable recent scholarly work concerning sexual difference, there is a regrettable tendency to increase this confusion by using the terms inter-changeably. The advocacy of the English language itself as a manly tongue, elegant and polished, as preferable to the primitive or effeminate languages of other countries, was widespread.[49] In contradiction to this standard, Montagu finds Johnson's prose to be offensively à la mode. Words, she writes, "should [not] astonish by their novelty, nor glitter by quaintness, which to tell you the truth, I think Mr Johnsons are apt to do. The worst fault of language is to be equivocal, the next fault perhaps, is such a sort of novelty from new coin'd words, that the sense is not yet ascertain'd."[50] His language is taken as a sign of his uncertain, irregular sexual difference. Montagu at first complains of being at a loss in seeking a word to describe precisely its flaws, but she settles on a French phrase, "trop recherché." It is Johnson's "ostentation of phrase" which she finds to be affected since, like those who would mimic the feminine, it attracts notice to its extreme and exaggerated style. As for women themselves, Montagu prefers a female character devoid of weakness and timorousness, and a femininity without the "feminalities" or flirtatious affectations that she deems to be excessive, and thus the female equivalent to effeminacy: Johnson "does all he can to cure our sex of feminalities without making them masculine."[51]

Montagu's impulse for writing the *Essay on Shakespeare* arises as much from an impulse to wrest authority from Johnson and to reclaim Shake-speare from the troubling effect of Johnson's effeminate language, as it is an historical moment to define an Englishness which is not superfluous and ornamental. Arguing that human nature achieved its highest expression in Shakespeare, she helped shape a canon of English literature that held the bard at its center: "Our rank in the Belles lettres depends a good deal on that degree of merit which is allow'd to Shakespear, who is more than any other writer read by foreigners."[52] Within the *Essay* all differences are subordinated to a larger notion of humanity which transcends historical particulars as Montagu holds together the tensions of a feudal England and a more permanent idea of nation that transcends its past, as Jonathan Kramnick has argued.[53] Yet her attack on Voltaire evinces a strikingly simi-lar motivation to her critique of Johnson. In his literary criticism, Voltaire's accusations about Shakespeare's barbarity, monstrosity, and ignorance – his apparent recapitulation of the nation's primordial past – are in fact precisely those traits that Montagu finds to be characteristic of Johnson's prose. Re-finement is evidence of advancement toward civilization and its perfection, but it also possesses a double edge since, in its excess, it may be indicative of degeneracy and monstrosity. She portrays Johnson, who is implied to be part of a foreign enemy camp, as ruined by an effeminate indolence which lacks the industry that she possesses: "He wants invention, he wants strength & vigour of genius to go through a long original work."[54] His prose bears a resemblance to the extravagant dress that disrupts appropriate sexual difference: "Too curious adorning of the Person makes a Man appear effeminate, a Woman Coquettish."[55] In her assiduous attention to the ramifications of literary criticism, Montagu implies that *her* style will certainly escape such flamboyant tendencies. In short, the oddity that Johnson displays in his prose is moralized, gendered, and assigned national import.

Such accusations of effeminacy against Johnson's style are especially jarring to those readers who have relied on James Boswell's depiction of him in *The Life of Johnson* as a literary colossus whose manly prose thunders forth in vigorous cadences.[56] In Boswell's rendering Johnson exemplifies both a gladiator from a classical past, and an authoritative national presence as an author who most famously accepts George III's invitation to write the literary biography of the country. Yet Montagu in another letter to Elizabeth Carter charges Johnson with exhibiting a modish extravagance that she believes, if it were to be widely imitated, would actually threaten English liberty and language: "I agree with you in abhorring the ribbaldry with which Mr Johnson has been treated, & have loudly signified my disapprobation of it at the same time he always writes as if he was a parnassian beau, his language is wonderfully dress'd & finical, & I own, I think if he was fashionable enough to be copied, he would ruin the english language for which I have a great respect, as it is noble, strong, & fit for a free people. Let ye trembling slaves of Despotes weigh & measure syllables, & cut their periods by a rule, but let the freeborn britten speak in a manly style!"[57] Johnson's quaint neologisms, Montagu confides in Carter, resemble the contagious affectation of French men who "are become perfect fine Ladies, & pass their summer evenings at a card table," she mentions in another context. Offended by its novelty and glitter she finds the worst fault of language "is to be equivocal, the next perhaps, is such a sort of novelty from new coin'd words, that the sense is not yet ascertain'd."[58] In short, Montagu denounces Johnson's literary style, usually described as ponderous and Latinate, as displaying instead the enfeebled and foreign characteristics which undermine national identity and security.

While the unusual word Montagu employs to describe his language, "finical," was not in common usage now or in the eighteenth century, it features prominently in Frances Burney's *Evelina* (1778). In the town shopping scene when Evelina and her relatives, the female Mirvans, seek stylish clothing to wear at a private ball, the heroine remarks that the male milliners attending them are "so finical, so affected! They seemed to understand every part of a woman's dress better than we do ourselves; and they recommended caps and riband with an air of so much importance, that I wished to ask them how long they had left off wearing them."[59] Evelina is amazed that more male clerks than female ones serve them during their shopping trip, and the implication is clear that these affected men are as foppishly ornamental and redundant as their merchandise. The heroine is speaking here of an effeminacy internal to England and integrally connected to women's fashionable and luxurious display, just as Montagu had suggested.

The offhand comment about the "finical" quality of Johnson's prose also seems a little more understandable when we consider Montagu's fascination with "the science of ornament."[60] She characterizes overwrought ornamentation as an exotic strangeness that is attractive to a mob mentality and uses as an example a Haymarket mob's admiring the sea monsters that adorned the King's coach: "False thoughts & grotesque ornaments may please & surprize but it is only the just, the natural, & the proper, that can engage. The mob indeed are attracted by the exhibition of monsters, & prodigies, & foreign rarities, but the judicious spectator is to be fixed by the regular, beautifull, & orderly productions."[61] In this passage Montagu reveals her belief that a class association exists between the unruly and the unlettered, and that the grotesque, the monstrous, the rare, and the foreign especially allure the mob and inspire lawlessness. In her aesthetic scheme, an implicit connection also obtains between less advanced stages of civilization and the decorative dissipation that is its typical expression. Savages are especially vulnerable to this kind of show since they "still decorate their persons with shells, feathers, skins of beasts, & c."[62] When Montagu assumes the management of her husband's coalmines after his death, she similarly assumes that her "barbarous and uncultivated" coalminers, for example, would be hardpressed to appreciate fully the exquisite taste that she attempts to cultivate and that she determines to be appropriately characteristic of the English nation.[63] Yet Montagu herself developed a reputation for extravagant ornament in dress and interior decor.

Further, we know that Montagu considered Johnson to be rough and unpolished in the polite company of the Bluestocking assemblies. When Johnson visited their sociable gatherings, he often dominated the conversation in language evocative of debauchery and superstition: "the great Dr. Johnson has thundered a declamation in words so harsh of sound and obscure in sense as would have better suited a description of the orgies of Erethro or the dire incantations of Medea."[64] When she became angry at his treating her friend Lyttelton with disdain at one such assembly, she also launched a furious attack on Johnson's physical defects and peculiar attitudes, reverting to an earlier notion of embodied character as if his deformities actually produced his distasteful language and ideas. She writes, "But no more at present on so odious a subject as the Doctor and his malicious falsehoods. I wish his figure was put as a frontispiece to his works, his squinting look and monstrous form would well explain his character. Those disgraces which make a good mind humble and complacent, ever render a bad one envious and ferocious. Lady M: Wortley Montagu says of a deformd [sic] Person who had satirized her, ' 'Twas in the uniformity of fate, that one so hateful should be born to hate.' "[65] Wortley Montagu is obviously referring to Alexander Pope, a poet whose stature was much shortened by his crooked back and whose deformity was legendary. Elizabeth Montagu's biographer attributes this uncharacteristic vituperation to her refinement in the face of Johnson's lack of polish, but as we have seen, the evidence for her animosity toward him is well documented elsewhere in the private correspondence. Fantastic ornamentation is spectacular and bizarre, and it fails to provide the steadier, more cultivated aesthetic offered by the regularity that Montagu seeks in written prose and in social exchange, and that she defines as appropriately English.

In the *Essay on Shakespeare* Montagu portrays the best drama as resembling a perfect human body that is flawlessly beautiful and impervious to defect. Drama possesses "a living body; regularity of features, grace of limbs, smoothness and delicacy of complexion[; I] cannot render it perfect, if it is not properly organized within as well as beautiful in its external structure."[66] Montagu applauded Shakespeare's recognition that Richard III's deformity instigates his cruel ambition when he shows that a humpbacked king's disfigurement does not necessarily prophesy his future behavior; but it instead causes his misery and cruelty because his misshapen body prevented him from appearing to be thoroughly noble. Deformity – part of the irregularity Montagu finds so unappealing and distasteful – also disqualifies Richard III for "the softer engagements of society."[67]

Montagu nevertheless expressed ambivalence about launching even an implicit critique of Johnson's thoughts on Shakespeare. Sarah Scott was among those who had encouraged her sister to charge ahead with writing her *Essay on Shakespeare* and to ignore her misgivings about competing with Johnson's essay: "I have not met with one person who likes Johnsons performance; if they had I do not suppose it wou'd have stood in your way, but certainly the general disatisfaction will make yours be received at first sight with greater pleasure; after reading we may trust for its reception to its own merits."[68] Montagu recognizes the unfriendly nature of the marketplace and her disadvantage as a woman: "I cannot say I am convinced that Mr Johnsons criticisms [of Shakespeare] are just, but I am afraid his talents will make ye scale preponderate, as I cannot put into mine the weight of authority or that prevailing charm of writing which he can throw into his."[69] Montagu plans a slightly different tack in taking a more comprehensive view than Johnson and offering "a more particular consideration of [Shakespeare's] merits & faults, excellencies & defects," though she is not fully confident that her work will be superior to his: "the more I read this preface ye better I like it, & the less I like my own. I have enter'd more into ye subject in a critical way, & I think have better exhibited the perfections of Shakespear, as I have more minutely observed on them, but I shall entertain & please less perhaps, a few general observations will satisfy the generality of readers."[70] Johnson's effeminate prose, then, threatens the security of the nation – a nation plagued with internal defects and external contagion – because its ornamental style aligns itself with the enemies to stability and peace. Johnson's ambigous gender standing compromises the civility of the nation, yet these factors ironically help justify Montagu's Amazonian pen in spite of her misgivings about publishing her own piece of literary criticism.

Montagu's contest with Johnson and her defense of Shakespeare against Voltaire's strictures constitute only a small part of her concern about the moral fiber of the country. She also inveighs against the "Monsters" who manage Parliament whose barbarity seems greater than the country's external opponents, the "Chicksaws and Cherokees" who are at war with England: "I have a great deal of female patriotism, it is not in me an original Affection as it is in you, your Lordship [William Pulteney, Earl of Bath] love England for its own sake. I love it the better for yours, every step we take towards degeneracy makes me jealous that your fame [and] your character should be less understood."[71]

Montagu seeks to incorporate her views at the expense of Johnson's and Voltaire's, within a republic of taste that allows her to make a place for a woman to act as a literary critic. When Montagu first considered writing the essay on Shakespeare, she believed that the superficial taste of the time was too frivolous to regard her serious critical efforts as significant. Montagu anxiously rambles on to her sister, Sarah Scott, that her efforts will perhaps be regarded as inferior to Johnson's, and she openly acknowledges her envy of his achievement with grudging admiration: "his Preface is so ingenious it terrifys me. I want to hear what people say of it, the eyes of jealousy admire a rival tho the tongue does not always confess his merit; however, I assume you have no wicked animosity against ye man, tho I wish he had not written this preface, & I shall do it all possible honors in my way of speaking of it to his friends & his foes; & indeed I am so afraid that where I think I perceive it faulty, that opinion shd arise from the jealousy of another, I shall hardly trust myself to speak of it but with general commendation."[72] In fact, expressing her need for secrecy, she uses exactly the same verb that Johnson had employed in speaking of the generation of Amazons – "invade" – when remarking on the difficulty of intruding into literary criticism: "In the first place, there is in general, a prejudice against female authors especialy [sic] if they invade those regions of litterature which the men are desirous to reserve to themselves."[73] Remarking on the difficulty of gaining public attention through advertising her essay, she exploits metaphors of fencing, an activity uncharacteristic of a proper lady, to suggest that she will continue to contest Voltaire if he provokes her. In defending a feminized and victim-ized Shakespeare, she adopts a masculine stance as a bridegroom rescuing a slightly tainted maiden: "I think poor Shakespear is like an unfortunate maid, whom many lovers have betrothed & none has married. The subject is a little contaminated..."[74] In other words she assumes the persona of a man, something that most of her reading audience at first believed to be the case. Other readers too remark that the author of the *Essay* is a man, "who I suffered to be characterised by *he* and *him*, with a most exemplary acquiescence, while I was inwardly wild to oppose such an injury."[75] In fact, Montagu jokes that she feels a beard coming in response to their as-sumptions, but she is thrilled about her achievement as a female critic, and she feels thoroughly proud of possessing a woman's mind and body. It is not surprising that David Garrick too invokes the image of the Amazon as Shakespeare's defender against Voltaire when he remarks on Montagu's *Essay* upon the occasion of the Shakespeare Jubilee:

> Out rush'd a Female to protect the Bard,
> Snatch'd up her Spear, and for the fight prepar'd:
> Attack'd the Vet'ran, pierced his Sev'n-fold Shield,
> And drove him wounded, fainting from the field.
> With Laurel crown'd away the Goddess flew,
> Pallas contest then open'd to our view,
> Quitting her fav'rite form of Montagu.[76]

Garrick here associates Montagu with a maimed or hermaphroditic being, though to be regarded as an Amazon heightens her pleasure, while being mistaken for a man was ultimately an insult.

It is exactly that sense of a publishing market newly open to those who are not the "superlative geniuses" of the former age of Swift and Pope that

Montagu believes makes possible her writing the essay on Shakespeare. Montagu then worries that effeminate prose enslaves a weak British nation even as Johnson – though often deeply sympathetic to women's publication – suggests that Amazons, unsettling to competing male writers and unlike their more sedate domestic sisters of earlier times, contribute to the nation's Grubstreet mentality. In the light of our reading of Fielding, Montagu and Johnson, the contest between men and women authors would seem to be waged at the fringes of the Amazonian empire, and the battle prize is the possession of the British island. In fact, Montagu actually describes her acreage at Sandleford as "amazonian land" which she expects peasant women to till as much as the men, and she figures herself as their Amazonian queen: "They weed my corn, hoe my turnips, and set my Pottatoes; and by these means promote the prosperity of their families. A landlord, where the *droit du seigneur* prevailed, would not expose the complexions of his female vassals to the sun. I must confess my amazons hardly deserve to be accounted of the fair sex; and they have not the resources of pearl-powder and rouge when the natural lilies and roses have faded."[77] In short, pink cheeks mark a leisured femininity that she proudly distinguishes from those of her brown laboring vassals.

Finally, then, Montagu's decision to attempt to tread in Johnson's territory seems most motivated by her sense that his defense of Shakespeare put him within the devil's party without knowing it. Montagu claims that Shakespeare, not Johnson, represents a brand of Englishness free of the barbarity Voltaire accuses him of possessing, and in defending Shakespeare she also implicitly disparages Johnson. She believes that Johnson's prose was as excessive as Voltaire claimed Shakespeare's plays to be; but in her *Essay on Shakespeare* it is Johnson, not Shakespeare, who becomes monstrous. Voltaire, Montagu finds, calls "our English pride a monstrous spectacle, and takes not the least notice of a speech which may be considered as one of the finest pieces of rhetoric that is extant."[78] Shakespeare comes instead to typify a kind of sublime boldness she defines as characteristically English, and, I would add, as particularly unJohnsonian and remote from the ornate language employed by Johnson. In fact, Montagu maintains that Shakespeare's genius derives most explicitly from his skill in shaping histories from the "heap of rude undigested annals, coarse in their style, and crouded with trivial anecdotes."[79]

In short, Montagu works against the grain in recognizing that strong-minded women straddle the incommensurable cultural expectations between Amazons and matrons, between public display and private virtue, between exemplary behavior and independence, yet she insists on the appropriateness of waging battle against a male writer without compromising her national loyalty.[80] In fact she defines her legitimate critical authority as a gendered claim. In spite of an aesthetic that eschews overly polished prose and spectacular display in favor of Shakespeare's sublimity and boldness, Montagu espouses a regulated femininity exemplifying a taste characteristic of privilege while paradoxically redefining it to incorporate the mangled body, the sunburnt skin, the warring nature, the equivocal sexuality, and the foreignness of the Amazon.

v

In the solemn conclusion to Fielding's *Volume the Last* the manly Cynthia ultimately outlasts gentle David when his rationality gives way to extreme emotionalism, and she triumphs through a tenderness bolstered by reason, perspicacity, and wisdom. Her visionary hope that the sexes may bond together without traditional hierarchies appears to die along with her ineffectual friend. Gently satirical without being vengeful or explicitly personal, Fielding's novels record the miseries that characters suffer when women who resist domestic retreat become wits, and when men disdain displays of virility. As readers accustomed to the "manly" wit of the Augustan verse satirists, we may find such satire irremediably enfeebled. Alternatively, we might consider her domestic prose satire an attempt to negotiate between Johnson's two definitions of the "feminine" – between "soft, tender; delicate" and "effeminate, emasculated." Like other equivocal sexualities such as Amazons and fops, Sarah Fielding's characters are both "male" and "female," yet also neither. In exposing the way that the social constructs gender, and in loosening its connection to genre, Fielding destabilizes the sexual oppositions of boldness and softness, of manliness and effeminacy, on which misogyny and its collusion with English national identity rests. In the process she and other women satirists, penetrating the public with the ostensibly private, avoid binding women's national identity to a cult of domesticity, and their governance to a domestic register. A woman's satiric voice, negotiating fears of effeminacy and forging sentimental bonds tempered by wit, transforms misogynist complaints against masculine women into an alternative way to build and defend the nation. Perhaps Sarah Fielding was, after all, in spite of writing domestic prose, among "the generation of Amazons of the pen" that Samuel Johnson had chided in *The Adventurer* "who with the spirit of their predecessors have set masculine tyranny at defiance, asserted their claim to the regions of science, and seem resolved to contest the usurpations of virility."[81] As such she prepared the way for writers such as Montagu who, by boldly opposing Johnson and Voltaire in public and in print, gained authority as a literary critic and a voice as a public intellectual. Fielding and Montagu accomplished these tasks through assertions that a particular kind of English femininity – strong, witty, anomalous, and even proud of its Amazonian defects – incorporates an equanimity of mind and a regularity of taste achieved without resorting to the extremes of feminalities or to the effeminate excess which both of them disdained.

CHAPTER 3

Odd women, mangled men: the bluestockings and Sterne

I must beg of *you* to decide upon its merits, for it [*Tristram Shandy*] is not a woman's book.

Clara Reeve, *The Progress of Romance*

I

The year 1763 brings a conclusion to the Seven Years' War, Britain's most successful military venture up to that date, which newly incorporates Canada, the West Indies, the Philippines, and India, to give birth to the second empire. While it is true that Pitt's greatest victories began in 1759, the nation was enervated after the years of war and deeply in debt. After Pitt's fall from power, England declared war against Spain in 1762, and the American colonies began to chart a course toward revolution. As we have seen, *within* the English nation struggles to determine normalized sexual differences in conjunction with modern nationalisms are negotiated between effeminate macaronis and a manly John Bull, between the proper lady and Britannia. Paradigms of nationalism especially critical in wartime also become entangled with fictions of the deformed and the otherwise compromised, and they too illuminate notions of the human when we incorporate them into the equation. In these same mid eighteenth-century years Linnaeus provides the scientific classification that establishes norms for *homo sapiens* and revises his categories in 1758 to include "monster" for the first time as natural anomalies, man-made monsters, and imaginary beings test the limits of gender and more broadly, of the human. This peculiar confluence of social changes contributed to an increasing distinction between the sexes after midcentury. This chapter argues that for women such as the Bluestockings, anomaly becomes one important ground upon which to forge an intellectual community, privately and publicly, through the exercise of virtue and reason. In addition fraternal relations frequently emerge among the broken – rather than normalized – bodies of men. In

Tristram Shandy oddity in the male characters signifies not only individuality and isolation but an uncertain masculinity, as the many original characters in Sterne's novel enact their impotence by forwarding eccentric hypotheses as intellectual and sexual hobbyhorses. Their communications, laced with sentiment, succeed best with wordless gestures while the Bluestocking women on the contrary place their highest hopes in the efficacy of language and reasoned exchange.

In the midst of these changes, the Bluestocking women in the second half of the eighteenth century begin to form a republic of letters and invent a new mode of elite rational sociability. A term that persists until the present time, "Bluestockings" first referred almost exclusively to the male philosophers in attendance at their public gatherings every second Tuesday. Frances Burney recounts an engaging if not altogether reliable story about its origins: Elizabeth Vesey "told Benjamin Stillingfleet that he need not worry about coming to a party in his blue stockings."[1] " 'Pho, pho,' cried she, with her well-known, yet always original simplicity, while she looked, inquisitively, at him and his accoutrements; 'don't mind dress! Come in your blue stockings!' "[2] Counting himself among the Bluestockings, one observer described the women's meetings in Hill Street and later in Portman Square in military terms as "a very numerous, powerful, compact Phalanx, in the midst of London."[3] Though not known for his polite or sociable manners, Samuel Johnson figured importantly within the group, as did the Burneys (father and daughter), Sir Joshua Reynolds, Edmund Burke, Thomas Erskine, and many others.

Though Elizabeth Vesey is probably the first to attach the term "Bluestockings" to these gatherings, it soon became an unflattering term that resonated with the eccentric nature of the women's Bas Bleu societies. As is well known, the point of the "blue parties" was to dispense with the usual social activities of cardplaying, gossip, gambling, and dancing in favor of more intellectually satisfying activities. Burney provides the liveliest description: "And such meetings, when the parties were well assorted, and in good-humour, formed, at that time, a coalition of talents, and a brilliancy of exertion, that produced the most informing dissertations, or the happiest sallies of wit and pleasantry, that could emanate from social intercourse."[4] They constituted, she writes, "splendid, and trully uncommon assemblages."[5] The frequent meetings, characterized by "bluism," took place most famously at the homes of Elizabeth Montagu and Vesey, but Hester Thrale, Mary Monckton, Frances Boscawen, and Sir William Weller Pepys, Master in Chancery, also acted as hosts. Though Bluestocking rivalries with individual men (such as the one between Montagu and Johnson discussed in the previous chapter) arose, their loosely affiliated societies were constituted of both sexes. These assemblies stand in singular contrast to the thousands of exclusively male clubs and societies that provided social connection and camaraderie for men.

The occasional lament voiced by critics that the early British novel concerns itself largely with the private and the individual, that it resides in the domestic rather than the public, is often coupled with a sense of the genre's wimpishness, its apparent effeminacy, and its failed masculinity. In contrast to the isolated self explored in the novel, Robert Allen, John Brewer, and most recently Peter Clark have instead emphasized the communal aspect of eighteenth-century culture, the vitality and growth of British clubs and societies during the later eighteenth century. These historians have showed how these associations helped a British identity to cohere within an emergent consumer society that accompanied the movement to the metropolis from rural areas and the elaboration of a public sphere. It has seldom been remarked, however, that because the composition of these clubs was almost exclusively male, an analysis of the gender issues involved might also contribute significantly to our understanding of their formation. Clark notes that even as late as 1803–04, only five percent of English benefit societies were regarded as female clubs, and women's opportunity for meeting together was largely limited to philanthropic activities, to music or to the arts.[6] Though women occasionally formed debating societies, the opportunity was sufficiently rare to occasion frequent comments upon its oddity. It is all the more remarkable, then, that in the Bluestocking societies men and women intermingled to engage in serious intellectual activity during this time.

Samuel Johnson's literary club, founded in 1764, was perhaps the most famous of the congregations of men gathered for intellectual exchange in the eighteenth century, a club that notably excluded women, yet he repeatedly testifies that the company of women elevates the level of civility.[7] In spite of Johnson's rather chequered attitude towards women's public performance, in his view intelligent women serve to revitalize masculine virtue and promote the common good.[8] According to Johnson, Englishmen dare not excuse their own intellectual and social failings because of a female presence: "They talk in France of the felicity of men and women living together: the truth is, that there the men are not higher than the women, they know no more than the women do, and they are not held down in their conversation by the presence of women."[9] The stellar group assembled when Johnson speaks these words – James Boswell, Allan Ramsay, Sir Joshua Reynolds, the Bishop of St. Asaph, and Bennet Langton – could not, he insists, be duplicated in Paris. Johnson xenophobically maintains not only that English conversation towers over Parisian, but also that English women's knowledge and wit are superior to those of Frenchwomen.

While discussions in coffeehouses of town gossip and recent events in the late eighteenth century would have largely excluded women, what might such broad interest in collective activity in regard to almost every aspect of masculine endeavor signify? Clark remarks that because the club members often indulged in ritual drinking and vulgarities, they "served as bastions of traditional male perceptions of sociable behaviour, against new, more refined notions of manners favoured by women and increasingly coloured by the culture of sensibility."[10] These clubs, then, would seem to be formed in relation to and even in reaction against, women's movement into public social spaces. Almost exclusively sex-segregated, such clubs fostered men's affective bonds, especially for a newly urban population uprooted from its origins, and against women's ascendancy. Many of these societies promoted the patriotism and national sentiment that joined Britons together in spite of emphasis on the individual, and against internal *and* external threats to a stalwart nation, against effeminacy within and without, and against the foreign. These clubs reflect a cultural longing to establish multiple kinds of social connections based on commerce, trade, and leisure for men as family, rank, and real property shifted in the significance they were accorded.

Elizabeth Montagu, "Queen of the Bluestockings," along with Elizabeth Carter, Hester Chapone, Sarah Fielding, Clara Reeve, Anna Seward, Catherine Talbot, Elizabeth Vesey, and later Hester Thrale offered unprecedented intellectual companionship for a burgeoning group of women writers and thinkers. "Bluestocking philosophy" referred to intellectual companionship between the sexes, but in the late 1770s, it almost exclusively referred to women, and it carried with it the aspect of ridicule. After that time the term "Bluestockings" was applied to women writers who spanned the generations from Charlotte Lennox at midcentury to Hannah More in the later years. Divided roughly into three periods beginning from 1740–58 and continuing during 1758–75, in the last quarter of the century they flourished as a highly visible social phenomenon, eventually fading from view at the turn into the nineteenth century.[11]

How then, one might ask, did the idea of the Bluestocking society come to designate women intellectuals when it originated as a description of unstylish men? Frances Burney too stresses the eccentricity of the cultural phenomenon when she describes a typical evening: "And however ridicule, in public, from those who had no taste for this bluism; or envy, in secret, from those who had no admission to it, might seek to depreciate its merit, it afforded to all lovers of intellectual entertainment a variety of amusement, an exemption from form, and a *carte blanche* certainty of good humour from the amiable and artless hostess, that rendered it as agreeable as it was singular."[12] This change from an epithet for a man in bluestockings to the ridicule of a learned woman may have occurred, I suggest, because denigrating these women effaced the powerful ameliorating function they performed in refining men through social and intellectual interaction, as Johnson himself had acknowledged. If sincerity replaces politeness as a masculine ideal in the final decades of the eighteenth century (as Michèle Cohen and others have argued), and if the high politeness inspired by mixed gatherings became linked with an objectionable effeminacy, then English men might wish to dissociate themselves from the social spaces that involved intellectual exchange between the sexes in favor of same-sex clubs.[13] As the term became more generally applicable to designate all learned women as affected and opinionated, the traits of the Bluestocking society, of their writings and persons become more firmly fixed in the popular imagination as belonging exclusively to odd, anomalous women, an "odious thing" as Elizabeth Montagu with some irony characterizes herself.[14] The strangeness of these remarkable gatherings at once provided their charm and made them vulnerable to derision.

The women who participated in the Bluestocking assemblies throughout these decades were among the first to be celebrated as individual representatives of a national female genius. Often grouped together as luminaries in the popular imagination, they featured most prominently in Richard Samuel's painting, "The Nine Living Muses of Great Britain," reproduced frequently and sold in publications and painted miniatures. Enlisted on behalf of national pride as muses of the country, such groups of women also aroused serious concerns about the ill effects that public displays of female learning might wield. "Extraordinary Talents may make a Woman Admired, but they will never make her happy. Talents put a Man above the World, and in a condition to be fear'd and worship'd, a woman that possesses them must be always courting the World, and asking pardon, as it were, for uncommon excellence," writes Montagu.[15] Learned women were idealized representatives of the nation, yet they were also considered aberrant in terms of their singular brand of femininity. Called Amazons and muses, the Blues wrestled in their epistolary exchanges with concerns about the ways that definitions of womanhood would need to be reimagined in order to include them in relatively public forums. These women in all their oddness took some pleasure in a sense of unified purpose, a common commitment to the considerable virtue and intelligence among them while recognizing that others often regarded them as a group that was differently gendered. Horace Walpole vilified Montagu and her friends, labeling them Maenads or mad women, and thus linking the deformation of womanhood brought about by learning to sexual passion as well.[16] When Montagu confided to Elizabeth Carter that "feminalities" – traits associated with women's characteristic weakness and timidity – were a disgrace to true femininity and a parody of them, she also worried that learned ladies might appear to be excessively masculine. Yet Montagu proudly cites a review of her *Essay on Shakespeare* in a letter to her sister Sarah Scott (21 October 1774) that calls her "the literary Amazon" against whom Johnson "gains no ground," and as we have seen, she accepts the nomenclature with amused pleasure. She adds sardonically, "Very civil of Messieurs the Reviewers to stand by the Amazon" (vol. 1, p. 289). Elsewhere, however, she figures her writing as inadequate to the more daunting Elizabeth Carter and Hester Chapone whom she admires: "I shall desire not to measure my sword with the Amazons; there are some Infantry at Cambridge and near the Inns of Court, with whom I can better contend" (vol. 1, p. 37). At times Montagu consciously mocked the satirical conventions attached to Bluestocking women, including an unkempt appearance. Grooming herself, she self-mockingly claims to be "meek in my Manners and humble in my apparel but rather more clean than is usual for a female Philosopher" (vol. 1, p. 100), having combed loose powder from her hair.

In the remainder of this chapter I describe how the public and private congress in Bluestocking letters is highly valued but also regarded as freakish in ways which complicate ideas of sexual difference in the second half of the century. In a somewhat unlikely pairing I relate the more troubled and aborted sociability of the predominantly male community in Laurence Sterne's anti-didactic novel of masculine domesticity, *The Life and Opinions of Tristram Shandy, Gentleman* (1759–67), to the reactions of these unprecedented women. In the writings of the Bluestockings and Sterne, I argue, sexual, social, and intellectual congress become dissimilarly configured for men and for women even as they are conflated. It is this blending, its interruption, and its failure, especially during the decades of the 1760s and 1770s, which this chapter explores in the "uncommon assemblages" of real-life Bluestockings and in the fictional characters in Sterne's novel, where purity of sexual identification is deeply suspect.

II

The Bluestocking women were influential in determining the shape of feminism *and* femininity well into the nineteenth century. The women largely identified with a traditional domesticity, sociability, and moral respectability that moderated and refined the passions. Spurred by the pious polemic of moral essays and conduct books such as Dr. James Fordyce's *Sermons to Young Women* (1765), Hester Chapone's *Letters on the Improvement of the Mind* (1773), and Dr. John Gregory's *A Father's Legacy to his Daughters* (1774), eighteenth-century women were well schooled and disciplined in cultural expectations that private will should be subordinated to parental, spousal, religious, and social judgments. These and other similar texts value the conventionally feminine over civic virtue and heroism, but at the same time expose myriad contradictions. They enabled a peculiar kind of moral agency and power while shaping a critical realm in which reasoned opinion can be shaped in the public and private spheres to provide a principled undergirding of the country through women's virtue. Popular conduct books, encouraging restrained social behavior, also promulgated the view that enlightened conversation relies on serious and purposeful introspection or "self-discourse."[17] Conversation is one means of accomplishing this in offering up through sociability a continuing education to professional and philosophical young men: "There is, perhaps no method of improving the mind more efficacious," according to Vicesimus Knox, "and certainly none more agreeable than a mutual interchange of sentiments in an elegant and animated conversation with the serious, the judicious, the learned, and the communicative."[18] Such conversation should, of course, appear to be effortless in achieving a grace beyond the reach of art. As Catherine Talbot remarks, "The true art of conversation, if any body can hit it, seems to be this, an appearing freedom and openness, with a remote reservedness as little appearing as possible." The art of speaking well involves offering "instructions in a pleasing way, to introduce useful subjects by unaffected transitions, and to adorn truth with a mixture of pleasing fictions."[19] Deborah Heller has shown that Shaftesbury's views on conversation assume, not surprisingly, that a particular kind of rational discourse was largely restricted to aristocratic men,[20] and that men's and women's words carry different social valences. Samuel Johnson's apparent domination of conversation in London gatherings of the mid and late eighteenth century would suggest, however, that such principles extended beyond aristocratic men to the male literati of the middling classes, and that Johnson encouraged heated debate as rather more manly than gentlemanly. Representative of a more bourgeois masculinity, Johnson was renowned, of course, for talking "for victory," though as frequently he used conversation as a pedagogical tool. In any case, conversation became, as Boswell puts it, "a trial of intellectual vigour and skill," and as such its efficacy becomes, at least as Johnson's biography portrays it, a measure of Englishness manliness.[21]

In their copious letters among themselves and to others the Bluestocking women discuss poetry, criticism, politics, religion, and taste – all matters that bear on public issues to extend well beyond gossip and platitudes. As recent critics have shown, in addition to the formation of distinct public and the private spheres in the eighteenth century, Jürgen Habermas describes "an intermediary zone between the family and the official sphere of the state"²² in which women acted as agents of politeness in a salon culture. If "the presence of both sexes was required to nurture a conversation that was both substantive and sociable," as Lawrence Klein has argued, anticipation and preparation for civil conversation, and for honing the virtue necessary to it, I suggest, often took place among Bluestocking women in the more private epistolary circulation. Thus, the private sphere served not only as a site of domestication but also as an apprenticeship and a substitute activity for conversing and acting in public. As the domestic merges into the public, the private space of writing thus prepares women for a more public sociable and rational exchange.

The Bluestockings most consistently found support for their learning and originality in the realm of the letter, a sphere even more private than the salon if the letters were not intended for publication. The women of the Bluestockings were, of course, less socially and geographically mobile than the men. Many of the Bluestockings retreated from public life for long periods of time including Sarah Scott, Elizabeth Carter, and Elizabeth Vesey. Letters afforded a community, especially a community of women, unavailable to them in other ways. The women's exchange in letters partly substituted for the urbane social intercourse more easily available to men. In the words of the expatriate Scot, Alexander Hamilton, "We meet, converse, laugh, talk, smoke, drink, differ, agree, argue, philosophize, harangue, pun, sing, dance, and fiddle together"²³ was a frequent refrain for the men, but – with the exception of smoking, dancing, and fiddling – these descriptors could as easily be applied to the Bluestocking correspondence. Montagu's letters to Elizabeth Carter reveal a passionate intensity forged by sharing intimate confidences over many years. Similarly, Montagu writing to Vesey insists that her letter should remain shielded from other readers, including especially Vesey's mate: "I wd not trust my letter in any hands but yours, & I beg of you not to copy ye words, only to give ye substance to Mr Vesey. It wd make me very uneasy to have ye words copy'd so I confide in your honour. Pray take care not to lose my letter."²⁴ Female friendship, one which often rivaled their affections for their husbands, built the strongest and most intimate of ties among the correspondents.

The conversational aspects of the written exchanges between the women (who of course write to many notable and cherished male correspondents as well) are somewhat muted in modern published biographical accounts and selected letters because the quotidian details of their private lives are often excised in favor of historical or political events. The manuscript correspondence provides a much fuller accounting. In a letter to Vesey, for example, Elizabeth Montagu grumbles about the "jingle jangle of society" and prefers the virtual presence of her friend to the press of a social gathering: "Your letter this afternoon revived me. I have lived a kind of *as it were* since you left me, I look for you, I sigh for you, I dont find you & where alas! Can I find any thing like you. I am now sitting in expectation of a strange olio of people. Coquettes, Prudes, Bishops & beaux esprits. Quels egaremens de caus a desprit & how preferable is the unison of friendship to all this jingle jangle of society!"[25] Describing only their exchange of letters rather than their being in each other's actual presence, the more fragile Elizabeth Vesey seeks soothing consolation from her friend, "Accept, my dear Mrs. Carter, my last thanks for the benefit and delight of your friendship and conversation."[26] Because letter-writing involves "conversing with a friend," it also relieves low spirits,[27] but conversation need not require the material presence of her friends whom Carter can as easily picture sitting with her "in a crowded circle" and whose spoken words she enjoys imagining.[28] Even Carter's published letters emphasize the ways in which conversation, intended to exercise and improve the mind, is cumulative in building enduring friendship. Insisting on engaging her reticent correspondent, she repeatedly complains about Vesey's emotional distance which belies their longstanding epistolary familiarity: "One would imagine you were addressing yourself to a mere visitor, whom you had met for twenty years together twice in a winter in a formal circle; instead of the person who for several months had the happiness of conversing with you almost every day."[29] In short, letters do not merely simulate conversation or act as a substitute for it: they are often the thing itself. "A weak head and fluttering nerves have obliged me to quit a large jovial company and a heated room," writes Carter, "and I am retired to muse, and sip my solitary tea in the cool silence of my own apartment, where there is nothing to interrupt my conversation with you, for which I willingly leave all the philosophers, historians and poets on my shelf."[30]

While letter writing is most certainly a way to practice what it means to be a sociable being, it is for these women correspondents, then, not merely preparatory but an actual form of sociability that is the welcome equivalent to intimate conversation. Montagu, who claims to write five or six letters a day, vigorously makes the point with great intensity: "I dont [sic] see how a sociable Being can live without writing."[31] Elsewhere she remarks, "This faint & distant conversation by letter keeps up an intercourse, & I fancy I am not quite separated from my Dear friend while I am thus corresponding with her," a virtual exchange which she much prefers to "the din & chatter of London conversation."[32] Vesey tells Montagu that she admires the "inestimable treasure of your own Letters, wishing much you would give them for the improvement of future minds."[33] In fact Vesey's claim that she requires continuing correspondence in order to maintain her health is actually a credible one, especially considering the vulnerable state of her uneasy mind. Letters seem to keep her alive. In Carter's didactic letters to Vesey, she presents herself as the stronger, more substantial being who, grounded in the everyday and the real, can quiet the anxieties plaguing Vesey's ethereal self. Taking long walks that stretch her physical abilities to the utmost, she teases her friend about the contrast between them: "That is, perhaps, a limitation which you do not understand, for you Sylphs who range 'the chrystal wilds of air' can have but very little notion of the difficulties which impede poor wayfaring mortal gentlewomen, condemned to trudge up and down the surface of the earth in leaden shoes."[34] Their close community is forged through infirmity and in spite of it. Letters exchanged between them share sympathy for bodily aches; the act of writing sometimes begets a mutual remedy for illness or for alleviating depression.

In short, the balm of companionate Bluestocking wisdom expressed through letters works gently yet forcefully to assuage malaise or cure disease. When an expected letter from her negligent correspondent Vesey fails to arrive, Carter misses their "conversation" which would have soothed her fierce headache, and she imagines that Paradise is a place where no one suffers any longer from an aching head. Montagu laments to Carter, "[Vesey] complains of [crossed-out word] stomach, & says she is languid, but I hope the late hot weather may have occasiond her languor more than any thing else. Philosophical blue stocking doctrine apply'd to her ear is the best cure for all her complaints. Sensible & ingenious minds cannot subsist without variety of rational entertainment; & then the languor of mind is charged on that most innocent Hulk ye body. If a person is robust enough to bear a course of hard study they may live in any place with dull society sometimes, or in retirement without any society at all; but in a delicate state of health it wont do... Poor Vesey complains of want of rational conversation."[35] Through correspondence the Bluestocking women bridged their isolation, shared confidences and information, gossiped, bore witness to affection, engaged in self-mockery, and generally, according to Elizabeth Carter's characterization of their letters, conveyed anything worth the threepence postage. In addition, the women's letters served as an ongoing apprenticeship for their published writings and allowed them to offer criticism of a correspondent's work or the latest publication of the day. Setting identities in ink, their private correspondence built a community less susceptible to intervention or contest and gathered strength from its collectivity. In fact, one might argue that, taken together, the Bluestocking correspondence quietly rivaled the *Spectator, Guardian, Rambler, Connoisseur,* and other widely read periodical publications in topic and scope, thus creating a consensual community in the shelter of privacy before risking unleashing those ideas on the world. For these inveterate writers, the private conversation of correspondence, collateral surreptitiously invested in advance of the public conversations of the assemblies and preparatory to them, helped shape the nation's reasoned exchange.

We should not, however, underestimate the importance of the actual gatherings of Bluestocking women who also enjoyed the pleasures of the gentle combat of conversation ("argumentative skirmishing"[36]) that aimed to polish or refine their understanding, but there was good reason for the women to be uneasy when in attendance. In the case of Montagu's social gatherings, she gained authority and aimed for a sense of equality among the participants in literally placing the chairs in a formal circle, but others felt that the circle formation left the participants feeling alone and vulnerable when conversing on an assigned topic.[37] Crucially N. William Wraxall among others chided Montagu for her rough voice and manly attitude as instigator of conversation:

There was nothing feminine about her; and though her opinions were usually just, as well as delivered in language suited to give them force, yet the organ which conveyed them, was not musical. Destitute of taste in disposing the ornaments of her dress, she nevertheless studied or affected those aids, more than would seem to have become a woman professing a philosophic mind, intent on higher pursuits than the Toilet. Even when approaching to fourscore, this female weakness still accompanied her; nor could she relinquish her Diamond Necklace and Bows, which . . . formed, of Evenings, the perpetual ornament of her emaciated person. I used to think that these glittering appendages of opulence, sometimes helped to dazzle the disputants, whom her arguments might not always convince, or her literary reputation intimidate. Notwithstanding the defects and weaknesses that I have enumerated, she possessed a masculine understanding, enlightened, cultivated, and expanded by the acquaintance of Men, as well as of Books.[38]

A proper femininity escapes Montagu, her voice betraying her lack of studied graciousness, her ornamentation perversely adorning her "emaciated person" instead of highlighting her beauty. Her "defects and weakness" included her tendency to domineer, her want of sociability, and her highly decorative dress incongruously joined to a philosophic mind and a masculine understanding.

The peculiar hermaphroditic combination of gender codings in the Bluestockings inspires both admiration and contempt in their observers, and Montagu's wealth, emblematic of an inappropriately conspicuous feminine luxury, here seem to be judged to undermine rather than heighten her intellectual brilliance. As we have note, to Montagu it was "pinching poverty" rather than ugliness which "deform'd the human face & form,"[39] and she was sometimes accused of ostentatiously displaying her wealth in the lavish foodstuffs provided, as if to set a standard through that repast for the refined taste she expected of her guests. Contemporary commentators remarked with ill-disguised envy upon her flaunting of economic as well as intellectual resources, to suggest the vulgarity of both. Montagu's house, Burney carps, "appeared to be rather appropriate for princes, nobles, and courtiers, than for poets, philosophers, and blue stocking votaries."[40] Montagu seemed to hope that her decorative fashions and surroundings would compensate for failed femininity and distract from the ugliness inevitably associated with intelligent display.

Montagu's Irish friend and fellow salonière, Elizabeth Vesey, daughter of the Bishop of Ossory and wife of a member of Johnson's literary club, Agmondesham Vesey, also organized mixed gatherings for men and women. Vesey first met Elizabeth Montagu in Tunbridge Wells in 1755, and their memorable parties date from the late 1760s until the mid-1780s. Flighty and forgetful, Vesey bore the nickname the "Sylph" because of the airy spirit which seemed to lift her body. Montagu happily describes her friend as a fairy-like rarified Irish creature who dipped her pen in morning dew, and other correspondents also maintained the appealing fiction:

I am convinced that our sylph Vesey is now quite disembodied; she rode on a moon beam to the place she describes & truly it is a fit haunt for a ghost of taste. The Hermit she describes on his knees, was some lover of hers in disguise, who knew he should win her heart by appearing in such picturesque figure & attitude[.] I rejoyce that the Vesey is past the high day of the blood, for if her frozen virtue had ever melted before the fire of some amorous swain, it must have been one who at the foot of a Rock, shaded by a trembling willow, had languish'd in the moon beams at the ball & masquerade ... And still I say, may the chaste dryads of Lucan guard her from Oberon; his midnight ball illuminated by glowworms when he tends the dance on the green ringlet, & refreshes his fair partner with may dew out of an acorn goblet might lead her astray, from the dull creatures of earths mould I think she is safe.[41]

"The Vesey" embodied gleeful playfulness and absurdity as the head of social evenings from the 1760s, and her mere presence, Elizabeth Carter suggested, "would have thrown a most delightful irregularity into the form" of the conversational circle.[42] Sometimes serving lemonade, biscuits, and tea, Vesey held Tuesday parties which Horace Walpole called "babels." Vesey's very quirkiness provided an exceptional model, and she was capable of being quite raucous: "Mrs Vesey has been here making a riot in my dressing room;" writes Montagu. "She is a boisterous creature, seizes over letters & uses one in a strange manner."[43] Even in her earliest days, her letters to Montagu are wispy fragments reflecting her undisciplined association of ideas. Yet in the midst of their apparent lack of focus, the letters give evidence of her bold creativity. Vesey emotes to Montagu on 10 October 1766, "What ever I may retain of those discouraging feelings I have one much stronger which I leave you to gues & which will impel me to extort a letter from you as often as I can in spight of all the impediments of dulness langour & the dreary dripping Scene which is gathering about our old walls where Mrs. Handcock & I are the only inhabitants *save where from yonder ivy mantled Tower the morning owl does in the moon complain.*"[44] Beyond the more familiar shape of reflective subjectivity we are inclined to see within these Bluestocking letters, the correspondence also delineates a full, rich, and private sociability equally as energetic as the public gatherings, and perhaps even exceeding the salon congress. Correspondence offers these women spirited preparation for public conversation and, most especially, a satisfying private, personal exchange. Though the Bluestockings' public gatherings attracted more notice, then and now, than their letters, their correspondence was at least as important in forging bonds among the women, and in girding them to engage in a public life with a difference.

Hannah More's clever tribute to these women, "The Bas Bleu: or, Conversation" published in 1786, is addressed to Elizabeth Vesey, "of Verse the judge and friend."[45] The mock-epic poem, suggesting Greek and Roman precedents for the Bluestocking regal gatherings, begins *in medias res*. Happily criticizing the card games quadrille and whist that had long interfered with enlightened conversation, and expressing weariness for "twisted Wit" and "labour'd ingenuity," More awards "the vanquish'd triple crown" to the organizing forces of Boscawen, Montagu, and Vesey. She remarks in particular on Vesey's employing her creative genius to change the conversational salon circle into irregular formations:

> Nay, shapes and forms, which would defy
> All science of Geometry,
> Isoceles, and Parallel,

> Names, hard to speak, and hard to spell!
> Th'enchantress wav'd her wand, and spoke!
> Her potent wand the Circle broke:　　(297)

Conversation in the Bluestocking assemblies, "Thou bliss of life, and balm of care," offers healing power to the society just as the letters mollify the pairs who correspond privately. Weaving a commercial metaphor into the verse, More suggests that conversation mints the educational gold:

> But 'tis thy commerce, Conversation,
> Must give it [education] use by circulation;
> That noblest commerce of mankind,
> Whose precious merchandize is MIND!
>
> (301)

In this poem conversation offers imagined travel through varied ruins and far-flung sights in order to encourage forming new understandings, especially pragmatic and functional knowledge, through "strong collision" (302). Conversation energizes and exercises the mind and polishes raw information. Further, it provides the social glue that binds souls to souls. A "trade" (303) with affinities to commercial exchange, it can be employed to breed connection and offer a ladder for social elevation. Yet More thinks of conversation as a specialized language, filled with allusion and dependent on memory: "Virtue sunk what Wit inspir'd" (304). More's poem, while acknowledging the sometimes idiosyncratic nature of Bluestocking assembly, emphasizes instead the usefulness of regular and orderly conversation as a sign of the polished and refined, and thus echoes Montagu's aesthetic as we have defined it here.

Unlike Montagu who usually kept a formal circle through the entire evening of her assemblies, "the Vesey," true to her idiosyncratic bent, breaks the circle of conversants into unusual and peculiar shapes. Lord Harcourt in particular remarks on her tendency to construct conversational triangles, "for her eagerness to break a circle is such that she insists upon everybody sitting with their backs one to another; that is, the chairs are drawn into little parties of three together in a confused manner, all over the room."[46] Perhaps these triangles (like Clara Reeve's dialoguing speakers in *The Progress of Romance*), contravening the more conventional pattern of sexual traffic, included two women and one man. Or perhaps these triangles were Vesey's innovative solution to actually hearing what her guests had to say in spite of her much-remarked upon deafness.

Vesey's significant hearing impairment apparently challenged her friends to speak loudly into her several ear trumpets. Her deafness licensed the gentle but persistent mockery of her friends. Not surprisingly Burney finds this aspect of the "grotesque" Vesey to be a subject worthy of her sharpest satiric skills. The pointed raillery of Burney's caricature is the first and longest description of a Bluestocking in her memoirs, as if to suggest that her disability makes her prototypical of them, "for Mrs. Vesey was as mirth-provoking from her oddities and mistakes, as Falstaff was wit-inspiring from his vaunting cowardice and sportive epicurism." The burlesque description merits quotation in full:

> With really lively parts, a fertile imagination, and a pleasant quickness of remark, she had the unguardedness of childhood, joined to an Hibernian bewilderment of ideas that cast her incessantly into some burlesque situation; and incited even the most partial, and even the most sensitive of her own countrymen, to relate stories, speeches, and anecdotes of her astonishing self-perplexities, her confusion about times and circumstances and her inconceivable jumble of recollections between what had happened, or what might have happened; and what had befallen others that she imagined had befallen herself; that made her name, though it could never be pronounced without personal regard, be constantly coupled with something grotesque.
>
> But what most contributed to render the scenes of her social circle nearly dra-matic in comic effect, was her deafness; for all the pity due to that socialless infirmity; and all the pity doubly due to one who still sought conversation as the first of human delights, it was impossible, with a grave face, to behold her manner of constantly marring the pleasure of which she was in pursuit.
>
> She had commonly two or three, or more, ear-trumpets hanging to her wrists, or slung about her neck; or tost upon the chimney-piece or table; with intention to try them, severally and alternately, upon different speakers, as occasion might arise: and the instant that any earnestness of countenance, or animation of gesture, struck her eye, she darted forward, trumpet in hand, to inquire what was going on; but almost always arrived at the speaker at the moment that he was become, in his turn, the hearer; and eagerly held her brazen instrument to his mouth to catch sounds that were already past and gone. And, after quietly listening some minutes, she would gently utter her disappointment, by crying: "Well! I really thought you were talking of something?"[47]

In this passage Vesey shares a childish confusion and Hibernian vagueness with the other deaf person of equivocal gender I have discussed, Duncan Campbell, for both inhabit a familiar geographical and historical map-ping of disability. Her attempt to cope with deafness and her desperate Johnny-come-lately attempts to engage in conversation afford amusement to onlookers. Most amusing of all to Burney is Vesey's futile juggling of multiple ear trumpets, and her near-hopeless faltering when attempting to participate as an intelligently sociable being. In Burney's cruel phrase, Vesey's her "socialless infirmity" exacerbates her otherworldliness. For her, like Campbell, the hope of escaping isolation to participate in "the first of human delights" is laughable. The passage shows with startling clarity that letterwriting, along with smaller discussant groups in triangles, might have been especially welcome because it leveled the conversational playing field for Vesey.

Montagu's sister Sarah Scott, who included the deaf among the fictional female community attached to Millenium Hall (the novel of the same name published in 1762), was especially conscious of the extraordinary physical and mental efforts that those with impaired hearing must make in attempting to be sociable. But in describing another conversational scene with those who could not hear in a letter to Montagu, Scott found the labor expended in achieving a semblance of normal exchange less risible, less ludicrous, and more troubling than Burney:

It is really dreadful to see two people who can hear so little; no conversation can pass between them which will not sooner be heard by the whole house than by themselves, and . . . their acquaintance have a hard task; their minds can not supply the chasm of even one sillable in a sentence, therefore many repetitions are necessary before they catch one sentence entirely unmutilated. They give one some bodily exercise too, for one has to walk from the ear of one to that of the other in order to keep up a tolerable appearance of conversation . . . A visit of several hours from persons in that condition was tolerably fatiguing, and more vexations for the censure one can not refuse passing on oneself for being so tired . . . what to them is really so grievous a misfortune . . . it is great want of charity not to scream oneself hoarse with pleasure, but I find I have not enough to hold out above an hour or two under so laborious a trial.[48]

Scott here intuited the crude alignment between a nonhearing minority and women in general that we have been tracing, and she expresses a more sentimental, less antagonistic attitude toward "defect." If Montagu, Vesey, Carter, Talbot, and others regarded themselves as anomalous, as new kinds of women who upheld valued feminine characteristics that led in unorthodox directions, others such as Burney and Wraxall mocked women's compromised natures.

III

As Hannah More argues in "The Bas Bleu," good conversation affords the best kind of commerce. But "conversation," and especially "criminal conversation," were also synonyms for illicit sexual congress between men and women in the latter eighteenth century. For the Bluestocking women the element of sexual connection, conversation of a different sort, is largely absent from their written exchanges, though occasionally hints emerge of the highly charged feelings for each other which regular, intense correspondence can only heighten. In addition, some of the women were subject to more explicit speculation about their erotic lives. As we have seen, Montagu and Lyttleton were suspected of criminal conversation, and rumors of an illicit liaison between Elizabeth Vesey and Laurence Sterne abounded after a series of apocryphal obscene amorous letters from Sterne to Vesey surfaced. Though the two apparently did not engage in an affair, meeting only briefly at Scarborough, to assume a connection between them – both born in Ireland, both linguistically playful, both taking pleasure in disorder and sharing eccentric tendencies – seems quite natural when one peruses Vesey's legitimate correspondence. In seeming imitation of Sterne's whimsical style, Vesey's letters, less veiled than those of the other Blues, exude breathless romanticism, conceits, and exuberance, though they lack Sterne's ribaldry. In addition they reveal that Vesey's later years were plagued with deepening depression and mental distraction, especially after her philandering husband died leaving her with no means of sustenance.

Sterne, like Johnson, was not notable for his enlightened attitudes toward women. In Clara Reeve's *The Progress of Romance*, a Bluestocking dialogue among Hortensius, Euphrasia, and Sophronia, defines morally edifying reading material, especially for mothers charged with educating their children. Hortensius remarks that in assessing recent novels, his female friends have neglected Sterne's *Tristram Shandy*. Euphrasia retorts, "I must beg of *you* to decide upon its merits, for it is not a woman's book."[49] When Hortensius presses her to elaborate, Euphrasia, claiming to having read only half the book, disdainfully remarks "but what can I say of it with safety? – that it is a Farrago of wit and humour, sense and nonsense, incoherency and extravagance" (235). Though *Tristram Shandy* is a domestic novel of sorts, it is clearly *not* a woman's book for a variety of reasons: women are implicated as readers who understand more of the racy Rabelaisian material than they might wish to acknowledge; the male characters in the novel bond over bawdy jokes at women's expense; the novel excludes female characters from participating in men's conversation, and evacuates their identity while holding them responsible for mangling men. In short, women ironically seem irrelevant to a story that begins with sexual congress and childbirth.

Reeve's *Progress of Romance* recommends instead the best contemporary women's novels, noting without prejudice how they interconnect with romance. In the *Progress*, as I have remarked earlier, the triangle of debate among the three interlocutors inverts the usual male–female–male arrangement of romance to imitate an actual Bluestocking conversation during which a man gradually concedes authority to the two women united in expressing their opinions against his. The verbal contest begins heatedly, if politely, as a duel of wits between a man and two women – "Artillery and fire-arms against the small sword, the tongue" (170) – to afford an harmonious surface in spite of the colliding ideas. Hortensius first throws down the gauntlet in demanding a full explanation of Euphrasia's degradation of epic poetry to a status no better than ancient romances. Holding her ground without taking shelter in tears or intellectual cowardice, she pursues a restrained attack and achieves a modest victory. The authoritative Euphrasia takes command of the conversation to present a reasoned history of the romance and to defend reading novels. (Sophronia largely reiterates Euphrasia's ideas and defers to her superior understanding.) At the end of the second evening, Hortensius appears to be rather cowed by the women's reasoned opinions: "I find I must take care of what I say before you" (179), and Euphrasia quickly assures him that the conversations will remain private. Hortensius concedes that Euphrasia has convinced him and the dialogue concludes in cordial consensus among them: "Then we are agreed at last" (261). The two women, having offered their interpretation of the writing and reading of romance, consequently succeed in improving and cultivating Hortensius' taste. *The Progress*, then, exemplifies an idealized exchange between the sexes which displays women's learning and heightens their intellectual confidence.

In the *Progress of Romance* Reeve assumes that intellectual and sexual differences are sufficiently distinct so that men and women may resolve their disagreements civilly. In contrast, Sterne's *Tristram Shandy* conversation most often resembles the frustration of *coitus interruptus*. *Shandy* engages long-suffering readers in the playful combat of unfinished conversation, constantly interrupted for apparently frivolous reasons, and it fails to culminate in a union of either bodies or minds. Of course, the wickedly funny novel relies principally on phallic humor, a fact which helps explain why contemporary responses to it (such as Euphrasia's in *Progress of Romance*) largely divided men from women, most often on the grounds that it exceeds the bounds of decency. Lady Dorothy Bradshaigh remarks, for example, "Upon the whole, I think the performance, mean, *dirty Wit*."[50] Mary Granville Delany writes to her sister Anne Granville Dewes, that *Tristram Shandy* "*has not* and *will not* enter this house."[51] Grudgingly admitting to having read the book, Elizabeth Montagu (incidentally the cousin of Sterne's wife), criticizes the novel while admiring the man. She remarks, "Nothing gives me such a contempt for my cotemporaries as to see them admire ribbald facts and ribbald witts, it speaks a bold licentiousness that if it was not softened by fribblism might break out very dangerously. I like Tristram better than his book... A man of witts, and such he certainly is with all his oddities, that never makes use of the sharp weapon ever at his side to alarm or to wound his neighbour, deserves much indulgence."[52] Though Montagu was "ashamed to hold long converse... with the author of a tawdry book," she recommends that her sister Sarah Scott visit with Sterne in April 1765: "He is full of the milk of human kindness, harmless as a child, but often a naughty boy, and a little apt to dirty his *frock*."[53] Elizabeth Carter and other first generation Bluestockings seem to emphasize that his sensibility is perverse and unproductive, even sterile, because it is merely a form of physical affection expressed through gesture and speech rather than heartfelt benevolence.

Conversation in the novel often serves as a metaphor for sexual congress, of course, and it acts also as a symptom of the broader cultural barriers standing in the way of men's and women's sociable interactions. Tristram, his father Walter, his uncle Toby, and Toby's man Trim substitute building military fortifications, riding hobbyhorses, delivering lectures, and writing novels for effective communication or sexual consummation. The narrator in *Tristram Shandy* affects to converse with a woman reader, but the book also implicitly refuses to allow that conversation to reform men's obscenity. Sterne's narrator flies in the face of such platitudes and refuses to be civilized by such a reader. If the *Progress of Romance* recognizes women's contribution to the novel and offers a tribute to the pedagogical effects of their reasoned debate, *Tristram Shandy* is its opposite – a testament to an impotent masculinity threatened by generic expectations.

Unlike Bluestockings conversations, those in *Tristram Shandy* often proceed in fits and starts to end in utter silence, loss of temper, or comic misunderstanding. Orations and harangues characterize the character's communication, or lack of it, rather than polite sociability. Tristram's ubiquitous dash operates to demonstrate the interruptions in thought that convey nuances within the narrative silences, blank pages, and typographical eccentricities. Most hilarious among the miscommunications is the abbess of Andoüillets' frustrated shouting and the novice Margarita's attempt to move a mule, an obvious symbol of sterility and miscegenation, by dividing the offending words in order to avoid blasphemy and pollution: "Bou–ger, fou–ter."[54] Able to commune with an ass, unlike any other human or animal, Tristram imagines the animal's part in the conversation. As the mule (Tristram's very own ass or rear end) accompanies him on his grand tour, Tristram remarks on the fine company it provides, "as my mule loved society as much as myself, and had some proposals always on his part to offer to every beast he met" (VII.43, p. 430). Here as in other places in the novel, speaking (from either end) resembles a sexual act. The lonesome friction between a man and his hobbyhorse, Tristram asserts, offers the best communication available.

Tristram pens the entire book worrying over his failed effort to make the reader comprehend his salacious jokes as readers ponder the multiple meanings of whiskers, buttonholes, things, chamber-maids, noses, and bridges. The decorous and proper Madam Reader, to whom much must be explained because of her alleged innocence, is prodded and embarrassed into comprehending his low humor in spite of "that female nicety, Madam, and inward cleanliness of mind and fancy, in your sex, which makes you so much the awe of ours" (1.21, p. 54). Uncle Toby's modesty allegedly rivals a woman's, and finding himself reduced to silence, he whistles Lillabullero while building his replica of the Siege of Namur. Gestures expressing simple and immediate sibling attachment substitute for words between Walter and Toby in Sterne's paean to sentimentalism. "The brothers never reach an understanding on intellectual terms," observes Alan D. McKillop: "Walter derides Toby's hobbyhorse with great eloquence and a battery of technicalities; at the same time he is always trying to impose his own ideas; on this level the brothers can never get together, whether Walter is using Latin or English."[55] The male characters in the novel violate cultural expectations of what is required of a "man" in the later decades of the eighteenth century.

The understandable emphasis on Tristram's psychology has sometimes distracted critics from attending more closely to the way that the novel itself is firmly tethered to the social history of the period. When clubs, coffeehouses, and print, the centers of male culture, help to shape a public sphere of civil discourse, what ideas of a more private masculinity balance the cult of domesticity in the age of male foppery? The novel first and most obviously depicts an imperilled English masculinity in Toby's and Trim's obsession with virility through their military past. Especially after 1763, flagrantly dressed macaronis rival the manly Beefsteak Club, even though John Bull persists as a national symbol. These cross-bred hybrids, Elizabeth Carter remarked, were "a species of animal . . . not an English character. Such a composition of monkey and demon, as at one half of the day appears to be studying all the tricks of the most trifling and contemptible foppery, and in the other is raving and blaspheming at a gaming-table, must be an aggregate of all the follies and all the crimes that a worthless head and a profligate heart can collect from all parts of the globe."[56] Seeming to be another species, these macaronic men define the limits of the human for Carter, and they represent the least desirable aspects of foreign peoples. *Tristram*

Shandy undercuts masculinity as public reputation to display the tension between man and beast, between male domesticity and (homo)sociality in the eighteenth century, and of their expression within the private and the public spheres.[57]

Many historians have come to believe that the latter half of the eighteenth century is also characterized by increased tendencies to engage in reproductive sex and to marry, and that both occur for men at a younger age than in the earlier decades of century.[58] The understanding of eighteenth-century masculinity is less and less clearly defined as an emergent "molly" subculture of homosexuality competing with a masculine heterosexuality amassed through penetrative, reproductive sexuality. Lawrence Stone has argued, in what is by now a familiar though contested thesis, that greater intimacy and companionate marriage were typical of heterosexual relations.[59] But *Tristram Shandy* (in spite of Tristram's erotic desire for Maria) would seem to thwart this supposed tendency with its virtual elimination of women from social and even familial scenes, and its unmanly inability to enjoy conventional sexual relations. The book expends its energy in relegating women's complaints out of print and making them illegible, from Widow Wadman's concerns about Toby's wound to Mrs. Shandy's issues about childbed delivery. Tristram's verbal assaults on Madame Reader are saturated with double entendres dually designed to embarrass and titillate. The novel's impotence extends to the difficulty of communicating with a reader, the impossibility of sustaining a story line, and the artificiality of realist fiction; but the novel also takes its impetus within an historical moment critical to shaping new modes of masculinity to testify to the tortures of shaping a refined, public, and clubbable masculinity from a scarred and singular interiority.

As the men of *Tristram Shandy* come to embody the defective nature more usually represented as female, the women characters fall silent or become invisible. While Carol Kay has interpreted the novel as displaying an anachronistic misogyny, its relevance to the fraught gender politics that I have been tracing here suggests instead that its misogyny takes on special functions which are in fact characteristic of the 1760s and 1770s.[60] Women figure much less prominently than men, though their ostensible absence except as auditors bears significantly on the novel's meaning. Mrs. Shandy labors upstairs out of the reader's sight in childbirth through much of the novel, Widow Wadman pursues Toby while being characterized as a blank page, Susanna allows the window sash to drop on Tristram's generative organ, and the Negro girl, an object of sentimentalism, inspires Tristram's pity. Instead of cultivating manners and civilising men's social behaviour, women in *Tristram Shandy* wreak havoc on men's bodies and their sexual desires. Mrs. Shandy interrupts Walter mid-orgasm to ask whether the clock is wound, and she inconveniently demands a trip to London for birthing, a normal delivery, and a midwife attendant at the birth. She also destroyed the family's hopes in giving birth to Tristram's older brother, Bobby who, before his untimely death, was apparently mildly retarded. Bobby's having entered this world head-first results in his being "a lad of wonderful slow parts" (II.19, p. 121). In fact, Walter, "odd and whimsical" (II.19, p. 115) and possessing an "infinitude of oddities in him" (V.24, p. 306), characteristically weaves an hypothesis that "accounted for the eldest son being the greatest blockhead in the family" to unriddle "the observation of drivellers and monstrous heads" (II.19, p. 120). The allure of the irregular and discomfiting characters in the book is not unlike the perverse fascination aroused in peering at cabinets of curiosities and other exhibits of human defect enjoyed by an English public during this time.

While mangling men into eunuchs, as I have argued in an earlier chapter, paradoxically increased their value, Tristram, comically wrestling with the circumstances of his birth and childhood, wonders what possible value (other than producing a novel) might result from recording the history of his defective and ineffectual family. The raging hobbyhorses of Walter and Toby and Tristram alienate them from family and friends as they pursue their "disabilities of temperament," their serpentine paths in philosophy, fortifications, and personal history. As Martin Price puts it, "Sterne plays off the crippled body or temperament, seen from the outside as the ludicrous victim of circumstance, with the expansive mind."[61] The book, we know, celebrates as well as bemoans strangeness, a fact which enchanted some readers and disgusted others. As Samuel Johnson put it, "Nothing odd will do long."[62]

But of course it is precisely the oddness that has lasted. In *Tristram Shandy* we find the twisted, maimed, and mutilated men among the first fictional characters whose defective bodies figure significantly as part of their characterization. Deformity is also reassuringly diverting throughout the novel to embody Hobbes' contention that "laughter is a 'sudden glory' which is likely to be raised by the apprehension of some deformed thing in another, by comparison where of they suddenly applaud themselves."[63] Each of these tales is propelled on its meandering and seemingly random course by male impotence to mark the effects of malformation or disabling injury, "For all the SHANDY FAMILY were of an original character throughout; – I mean the males, – the females had no character at all, – except, indeed my great aunt DINAH" (1.21, p. 53). Toby himself acknowledges that in regard to women, "I know nothing at all about them" (11.7, p. 82). In the case of the Shandys, the family abysmally fails in attempting to re-produce itself. Tristram and Toby are aligned with women through their inadequacies; their alleged defects, like women's, lodge in their injured reproductive organs. In *Shandy*, the absence of defect signifies an absence of character. In fact the odd, singular, and defective originals in the novels of Sterne (along with Henry Fielding's *Amelia* and those of Tobias Smollett) might arguably be termed the first major characters in the novel to display disability *as* character.

The Shandy family, of course, is prone to mishap and mayhem to such an extreme that Tristram is his father's final hope: Walter "had lost my brother *Bobby* entirely, – he had lost by his own computation, full three fourths of me – that is, he had been unfortunate in his three first great casts for me – my geniture, nose, and name, – there was but this one left" (v.16, p. 298). Yet Tristram complains that his father was so much preoccupied with writing the family's history, the *Tristrapaedia*, that as a child he had unfortunately been abandoned to his mother for three years straight until he was taken "out of these women's hands" (vi.5, p. 332) to be properly educated. In this case, Walter's obsession with writing literally creates deformity and for Tristram, defect releases him into writing. The heir apparent to the Shandy fortune is mangled at the hands of Susannah, a fact that forecasts its future. Not surprisingly the congregation of men at Phutatorius' dinner, obliterating the essential function of women with one swipe, conclude that a mother is not kin to her child (because the child is of the blood of the parent, but the parent possesses none of the child's blood). Bonding together in masculine pain and potential genital injury to eradicate the female through the intellect as well, the men clarify that by this standard Mrs. Shandy, Tristram's mother, is unrelated to him. In *Tristram Shandy* masculine impotence has both a family history and a history intertwined with that of England and Ireland.

The defects extend to other characters as well. Upon the death of his retarded brother, Tristram inserts a tale about Walter's pairing of a favorite mare and an Arabian horse resulting oddly in a mule, as if to reinforce its comparison to Bobby as an imperfect and perhaps sterile offspring: "By some neglect or other in *Obadiah* [the servant who had brought the news of Bobby's death], it so fell out, that my father's expectations were an-swered with nothing better than a mule, and as ugly a beast of the kind as ever was produced" (v.3, p. 283). Tristram narrowly escapes castration because of Susannah's unthinking removal of the sash window weights, and in a vaguely racialized deformity, his nose is flattened to his face. Dr. Slop suggests that Trim's left leg is so lame as to be able to take only a small portion of his weight. Yorick, in a reference to the mercury treatments Sterne is known to have taken for his venereal disease, is "as mercurial and sublimated a composition, – as heteroclite a creature in all his declensions," as can be found (I.II, p. 22); even the ineffectual Dr. Slop, reminiscent of Alexander Pope's much caricatured physique, is an anomalous being, "a little, squat, uncourtly figure...of about four feet and a half perpendicular height, with a breadth of back, and a sesquipedality of belly" (II.9, p. 84).

In *Tristram Shandy* these mangled men seem naturally to belong to an inarticulate club from which women are justifiably excluded. In contrast to the gatherings of Bluestockings where intellectual exchange is explicitly cultivated within sociability, the best communication, Sterne's novel relies upon appeals to the heart, to feelings men possess, rather than the mind. It is as if all men have developed the difficulty in speaking that Duncan Campbell had inherited. Yorick embodies the superiority of sentiment over wit. Corporal Trim drops a hat upon hearing about Bobby's death, the meditation upon which brings forth Susannah's tears. In the dinner conversation among the men Didius, Gastripheres, Kysaricius, Homenas, Triptolemus, Toby, Walter, and Yorick, the bits of the parson's sermon, produced by his head rather than his heart, are used to light Walter's pipe amidst discussions of the canonical intricacies of Tristram's christening in order to determine whether his misnaming can be reversed. Perhaps the most famous of manly interruptions occurs as Toby rises to remark on projectiles. Phutatorius, author of a treatise on keeping concubines, cries "ZOUNDS! ———" (IV.27, p. 254) when he finds himself wounded by a hot chestnut landing in the aperture leading to his groin, enacting yet again ludic impotence. Phutatorius' yelp testifies to the clarity of his unfiltered expression of masculine pain. And finally Parson Yorick, Sterne's version of Shakespeare's character, labels the history of Tristram's broken nose and injured testicles "A Cock and a Bull" fable to mock the family's propensity for genital accidents, and he remarks that the parish bull may also mirror the Shandys' impotence and failure to reproduce. The entire cock and bull story of a cow's failure to calf and a bull's inability to perform, as we are reminded in the last chapter, threatens to be as infertile and maimed as the Shandy men. Tristram's personal family history of decline threatens to parallel that of Great Britain itself.

Elizabeth Montagu, scolding Sterne for providing an indecent example in his writings, believed that his reliance on fashionable oddness, his wit à-la-mode, constituted a dangerous menace to the stability of the country: "The great who encourage such writings are most to blame, for they seduce the frail witt to be guilty of these offences, but we are now a Nation of Sybarites who promise rewards only to such as invent some new pleasure."[64] *Tristram Shandy* aroused charges of novelty for novelty's sake. The focus in the novel shifts unpredictably from effeminacy, luxury, and refinement made familiar in earlier fictions to impotence and wounded masculinity. It is not luxury or excess or rarification which troubles these male characters so much as the incidental defects of sexual and intellectual impotence that inevitably reflect the human condition. These male characters *acquire* their defects through accident or heredity, while for women their reproductive organ, the site of their inherent defect, is a fundamental aspect of their sexual definition. In the very eccentricity of Sterne's domestic novel, we find a turn toward a sexual difference that anticipates modern concepts of masculinity because the Shandy men define themselves through their concerns about potency, and through the correspondent silencing of women. As we have seen in the novellas of Aphra Behn and Eliza Haywood, defects are closely linked to aberrant sexuality and its performance. Associated in Elizabeth Montagu's mind with an effeminate luxury that contaminates the nation, and in Clara Reeve's with an uncompromising masculinity, *Tristram Shandy* displays men's corporeal and mental oddities in the interests of singularity, scabrous humor, and homosocial bonding, while the Bluestockings enlist women's "defects" to build a community of women – and men – founded in virtue. In the later eighteenth century defect and its absence, the socialless *and* sociable infirmities of extraordinary beings, continue to be at the root of modern gender difference as it takes shape within the limits of the human.

CHAPTER 4

Scarred women: Frances Burney and smallpox

"Scar that vhiter skin of hers than snow."
                    Othello in Frances Burney, *Camilla*

I

During the decade of the 1790s both Mary Wollstonecraft's *A Vindication of the Rights of Woman* (1792) and Frances Burney's *Camilla* (1796) made critical use of the concept of woman as a defective being. In a broad metaphoric sweep Wollstonecraft associates femininity at its most egregious with women of the seraglio, with Eastern princes, with "poor African slaves," and with effeminate behavior. Though the female condition is for Wollstonecraft a consequence of insufficient education, women everywhere resemble "beautiful flaws in nature," like Pope's characterless women who are "fine by defect" and Milton's Eve who embodies "fair defect."[1] Wollstonecraft connects deformity with vice (12), idiocy with royal in-breeding (16), and monstrosity with sybaritic pleasures (18). Effeminate young men who conceal themselves "under gay ornamental drapery" (17) also share these defects with "weak enervated women" who, in being excessively desirous of these rich depraved libertines, will conceive "only an half-formed being that inherits both its father's and mother's weakness" (139) to reproduce an increasingly degenerate social body that is corrupted both by its sensuality and its luxurious consumption. Seeking to free the female sex from being perceived as possessing inherently crippling traits, Wollstonecraft claims that maimed or deficient human beings are completely different from the rational and enlightened women of unblemished character she envisions. In fact, the *Vindication* cordons off those with crippling anomalies rather than aligning women's cause with the disabled and afflicted. In Wollstonecraft this rhetoric of degeneracy emerges through references to gross sexuality, venereal disease and its attendant dangers to progeny, and hints at the polluting effects of miscegenation. "I believe," she charges, "that the human form must have been far more beautiful [in the past] than it is at present, because extreme indolence, barbarous ligatures, and many causes, which forcibly act on it, in our luxurious state of society, did not retard its expansion, or render it deformed" (171). Similarly, the *Rambler's Magazine* alerts the country to worrisome signs: "It is therefore incumbent on us to restore that manly firmness and vigour, which, from the depravity of human nature, by means of luxury and dissipation, has for more than a century been lost: this has brought on disease which has innervated [sic] and debilitated the human race... [T]he inhabitants of this island have decreased amazingly, and every succeeding generation becomes more and more weakly... [T]he degeneracy and imbecility of body and mind, so prevalent in this country, not only destroys the state, but likewise the peace and happiness of individuals."[2] If these entreaties for turning away from sexual dissipation are sufficiently heeded, this writer speculates, "There would soon be such an offspring, sufficient to man our fleets and increase our armies, as would bid defiance to our most inveterate foes" (6). Again and again, eighteenth-century texts warn that luxurious living contributes to poor health, a weak nation, and a shrunken population. In addition, degeneration and decay accompany migration, displacements, and increased contact between peoples even within monogenetic theory.[3] The linguistic diffusion resulting from the Tower Babel when the single language of the world was riven into multiple languages brought about a diversity associated with sin and leading to corruption. In these texts degeneracy and disability corrode the nation, especially its polite classes, and its characteristic sexual difference.

Near the end of the eighteenth century the scarred or disabled body becomes a locus of these intense national fears about encroaching degeneracy in the population, the impending contagion of race, and urban pestilence. Anxieties about the nation's health in the face of contamination and disease – and in particular the fear of smallpox – are projected onto imperfect bodies, including the excessively feminine and the exotic other, and the irregular and atypical help form a "normate" identity as they provide the negative measure of the nation's physical and moral health. Theories of degeneracy also figure importantly in the shift from an emphasis on inherited privilege and rank to the formation of a self-conscious middling class as the hallmark of a thriving nation. As was the case in the pamphlet wars on effeminacy at midcentury, modern luxury is charged with wreaking deleterious effects on English bodies. By the end of the eighteenth century fashion and its attendant sybarite pleasures – those which Elizabeth Montagu had also believed would spoil the nation – are increasingly entwined with threats posed by sickness and degeneration. Both the lower and the upper classes are potential sources of infection, as are foreign bodies. Imbecilic, misshapen, or exotic racialized bodies allegedly derive from the licentious aristocracy, or perhaps from the unhealthy working classes, but only rarely from the middling sorts. Physically anomalous individuals such as conjoined twins, dwarfs, and macrocephalics who had often been the object of spectacle in fairs and marketplaces gave visual reality to a nation's fears about the persistent dissipation of the British race. The periodical literature is filled with injunctions to marry and reproduce an ablebodied population in order to replenish a nation weakened by wars and exploration. These are supported by warnings about the potential deterioration of the remaining populace since signs of dissipation produce visible effects. Health (and in particular countering the ravages of veneral disease) *is* the national wealth. A middle class feels itself vulnerable to the potential contagion of both aristocratic profligacy and laboring-class stupidity as fertility and mortality dominate social concerns about an increasingly mobile English population focused on health as a measure of its humanity.[4]

On 12 July 1796, *Camilla*, Burney's commercially successful novel in which smallpox and deformity figure centrally, was published in five volumes. Just two months earlier on 14 May 1796, the first cowpox vaccination had been performed on James Phipps, aged eight, by Edward Jenner. Contagion and disease restricted trade and interfered with commercial ventures, but the invention of Jenner's cowpox vaccine (as distinguished from the earlier practice of inoculation with active smallpox virus) in 1796 brought the beginning of the end to such epidemics. Though debates about the value of inoculation are largely concentrated in the earlier decade of the 1720s, the controversy persists throughout the eighteenth century and into the next. In 1790 Sir Robert Walker, Fellow of the Royal College of Surgeons, indicates that "the mortality by small-pox has not been reduced by inoculation; but rather since the æra of that practice, or soon after, there appears to have been a considerable annual increase of deaths."[5] Children were especially vulnerable to its most tragic effects. Women and those from foreign lands were largely condemned for their efforts to quell the epidemic through inoculation, but they were also associated with disfigurement itself. This deeply feared corporeal consequence of smallpox was in the eighteenth century closely identified with abandoned women who wept over lost beauty and fortune, as well as with the purported ugliness of peoples other than European whose bodies did not so closely resemble ideal classical form. England seems to project its fear of smallpox outbreaks onto women and non-Europeans of both sexes. Smallpox, an eighteenth-century

disease which is now no longer a threat except through the release of viruses
sealed in scientific laboratories, claimed the highest rate among infectious
diseases except for "consumption and 'fevers,' which included typhus, ty-
phoid, and scarlet fever."[6] Smallpox changed the course of wars, lives, royal
families, and empire, and the frequent epidemics impeded the activities
of the marketplace; epidemics erupted during migrations from country to
city and through new circuits of global interchange.

Though smallpox appeared as early as 1200 BC in China and Africa and
entered England in 1240, it was not until the 1630s that an especially virulent
mutant strain caused widespread mortality and scarring: smallpox deaths
in Europe are believed to have averaged between 200,000 and 600,000
during each year of the eighteenth century.[7] Estimates of the number of
deaths indicate that up to a fifth of all those who contracted smallpox died,
and up to an eighth of all deaths throughout Europe came from smallpox.
The rules of prevention, indicating the emerging knowledge regarding the
means of contagion, were explicitly spelled out even as late as 1790:

1. Suffer no person who has not had the small-pox, to come into the infectious
house... II. No patient after the pocks have appeared, must be suffered to go
into the street, or other frequented place. III. The utmost attention to *cleanliness*
is absolutely necessary... IV. The patient must not be allowed to approach any
person liable to the distemper, till every scab is dropt off, till all the clothes,
furniture, food, and all other things touched by the patient... have been carefully
washed.[8]

Fatalities were swift and cruel, often occurring during the second week
of infection though sometimes occurring up to a month after the onset
of illness.[9] The lethal disease flourished, as epidemics occurred at regular
intervals over the next two centuries until the salutary effects of inoculation,
and eventually vaccination, began to prevail.

Smallpox develops into an acute infection when the victim inhales the
virus through the upper respiratory tract. After about two weeks' incuba-
tion, extreme influenza-like symptoms ravage the body with fever and
aching. Pustules begin to show themselves on the face and travel the length
of the body, though the upper half of the body usually sustains a greater
number. These noxious smelly pits eventually crust over, and the individual
remains contagious until all the scabs have fallen off. Fear of death was
always paramount, but smallpox also caused inflammation of the eyes,
blindness, and hideous scarring, often about the face and neck. To alleviate
suffering and to attempt to minimize permanent pitting of the skin, physicians treated the sores by applying cool air, rubbing fresh butter and beet

leaves into them, or spreading lineament on a fine cambric mask placed gently on the face.[10] "I think the chief Endeavour must be," one physician counseled his fellow practitioners, "to mollify and supple that outward Pellicle which involves the Humour of each Pustle, so that it may be disposed to give Way and stretch the more easily. By this Means the Purulent Matter, meeting with the less Resistance, will be forced into the Pustles out of the Parts beneath, which want to be filled up; and thus the *Pitting* will be avoided."[11] The most effective means of preventing scarring was to keep the skin soft during the active phase of the disease. Other somewhat arbitrary remedies included oil of tartar, myrrh, gum arabic, a mastic resin patch, saffron, and turpentine. In addition, dangerous skin peelers such as the poisonous sublimate of mercury or ceruse (a white lead ointment) were sometimes applied to the skin to remove women's smallpox scars.[12]

Inoculation was practiced in China and other Eastern countries as early as the eleventh century, where it consisted of placing bits of the virus into the nostrils. In early eighteenth-century England, inoculation was seen as a dangerous importation from Turkey, other Islamic cultures, and foreign peasant women.[13] These assumptions about inoculation's origins deflected attention from the fact that smallpox was on more than one occasion a contagion that Europe spread to the empire. Johnson's *Journey to the Western Islands of Scotland* remarks upon devastation the disease brings when introduced into the Hebrides. Smallpox also killed hundreds of Aborigines in Port Jackson and beyond, spreading with "irresistible fury," perhaps contracted from matter that was purposely introduced by the First Fleet surgeons.[14] The physician Robert Walker in his "Medical and Political" treatise on smallpox of 1790, recounts a history of Europeans' near genocidal infecting of the ports they visited: "In the year 1718, the tribe of Hottentots on the Cape of Good Hope, were almost extirpated, by means of some linen sent on shore to be washed from a Dutch East India ship, where a few boys had the small-pox on the passage, but were then perfectly recovered."[15] Further, visitors mingling with the English such as Prince le Boo from the Pelew Islands and Sartje (the "Hottentot Venus") died of smallpox after having been exposed to an unfamiliar germ pool. Contaminated blankets may well have transmitted the disease to Aztecs and North American Indians.[16] Yet in Walker's account he insists that Arabia is responsible for spreading the smallpox: "We are indebted to the Arabians for the first accounts of small-pox, among whom the disease appears to have been common, and who were the means of spreading its infection through the different kingdoms of Europe," including especially Persia and Avicenna.[17] By the early nineteenth century, inoculation's Middle Eastern origins are obscured, and the disease itself is condemned as infidel, a condemnation that in turn justifies inoculation.

Lady Mary Wortley Montagu refutes these terms of analysis in the early eighteenth century, valuing the knowledge of women folk healers over male professionals and becoming herself an embodiment of the infidel who refused to accept her nation's ignorance. In 1717 Lady Mary, whose brother Lord Kingston had died of the disease at age twenty, allowed her son to be "variolated" in Turkey, and later, in 1721, replicated the procedure in England for her daughter. This technique involved placing a small amount of the variola virus under the skin to induce a very mild case of smallpox. In her son's case the inoculation site became inflamed, and he sustained about one hundred pocks without any subsequent scarring.[18] The fact that an old Greek woman ingrafted the young boy, and that women possessed this medical information and skill, may have slowed the acceptance of inoculation in Europe despite Lady Mary's efforts and example. William Wagstaffe's famed anti-inoculation stand is typical: "Posterity perhaps will scarcely be brought to believe, that an Experiment practiced only by a few *Ignorant Women*, amongst an illiterate and unthinking People shou'd on a sudden, and upon a slender Experience, so far obtain in one of the Politest Nations in the World, as to be receiv'd into the *Royal Palace*."[19] Montagu defends in detail the nurse's ingrafting of a tiny amount of pox in her impassioned "A Plain Account of the Inoculating of the Small Pox by a Turkey Merchant,"[20] and she accuses the "learned" members of the Royal College of Physicians of committing murder and causing mayhem: "The miserable gashes, that they give people in the Arms, may endanger the loss of them, and the vast Quantity they throw in of that Infectious Matter, may possibly give them the worst kind of Small Pox, and the cordials that they pour down their Throats may encrease the Fever to such a degree, as may put an end to their Lives."[21] In turn Caroline, Princess of Wales, wife of the future George II, encouraged royal involvement in the practice of inoculation. Eighteenth-century women were in fact courageous pioneers in advancing medical knowledge and the public health.

As England emerges into a colonialist modernity, its wish to amputate from national memory a past associated with the ancient and the Arabic reaches crisis force and is strongly evident in discussions of smallpox and inoculation. "Disease and death are, throughout scripture," warns James Plumptre in his 1805 polemic on smallpox, "considered as the effects and punishments of sin; and sin itself in a figurative sense, is expressed by the emblems of disease."[22] Plumptre cites numerous authorities who share this view in his sermons, which support inoculation against "the Arabian Pestilence": "This disease, we are informed by writers upon the subject, had its rise in Arabia, at the very time of the Imposter Mahomet, and was spread abroad by the Saracen invaders whithersoever they carried their arms and doctrines."[23] Plumptre further draws upon John Haygarth, Richard Mead, and William Woodville to document the claim that smallpox first appeared at the time of Mahomet's birth. To borrow inoculation from infidels was fraught, its importation justified as a tradeworthy commodity, and its distribution to the poor encouraged as a benevolent act: "Many good and most zealous Persons exclaim against Inoculation, because it is transplanted out of a *Mahometan* Country into *Great Britain*, which is Christian."[24] Plumptre fears perhaps more the potential religious contagion from a Muslim to a Christian country, and he collapses the distinction between medical and religious practices. In the early part of the eighteenth century, too, physician Philip Rose argues that "the *Turks* are to us Infidels, and . . . the borrowing of Inoculation from *Mahometans*, seems a kind of Scandal to Christianity."[25] Even Rose pleads, however, that Turkish ideas need not be rejected out of hand simply because they are foreign, and he proposes that inoculation be considered as a tradeworthy commodity that England exchanges in a neutral rather than a philosophical or spiritual importation, similar to a captain's sailing a ship to a foreign land. By the late eighteenth century the expertise concerning inoculation was exported as if it had been an English invention. Thomas Dimsdale, a well-respected physician of the eighteenth century, traveled to Russia to inoculate Catherine the Great and her son, the Grand Duke Paul.

In Europe the young, the impoverished, and tradespeople without benefit of inoculation suffered most severely. Not surprisingly, inoculation began with the upper classes and the urban population who were most able to avail themselves of the current medical wisdom. Dimsdale worried that inoculation had been "upon the whole rather hurtful than advantageous to the city of London" since, in spite of the wealthy's having been inoculated, smallpox incidence had increased: "the loss has fallen principally among those who are not the least useful members of the community, viz. on young persons, the offspring of inferior trades-people, and the labouring poor." Among calls to encourage the lower classes to abandon their suspicions of the procedure, Haygarth proposed that the wealthy should be encouraged, in the national interest, to support the cost of inoculating the less fortunate: "Indeed, a reward, in one case, may be properly offered for the inoculation of a poor family; because it would be a publick as well as a private benefit."[26] He and others fretted that the lower classes, especially susceptible to the disease because of poor hygiene and sanitation, needed to be disabused of their fear of inoculation in order to eradicate the disease; these concerns are supported by accounts of the poor becoming beggars because of the affliction. Hospitals specifically dedicated to inoculation rather than treatment were established beginning in 1746 so that in the very process the inoculated who were temporarily infectious did not spread the disease.[27] The midcentury smallpox epidemic raged at the same time as increased attention was devoted to drainage, lavation, and ventilation which in turn led to disinfecting the sites where the virus was transmitted including hospitals, and eradicating the places where filth gathers. Institutions and public places became the objects of these remedies of improved methods of sanitation and hygiene. Trying to convert inoculation into a specifically English remedy for a foreign disease, clergymen, doctors, and essayists interpreted its nagging persistence to be further evidence of the nation's degeneration. Believed to impede national security, the malady extended beyond the individual organism to the social body; and because the value of the country was measured by the health of its population, its disabling effects became an economic as well as a social phenomenon.

II

Surprisingly, most medical tracts on smallpox assign little attention to the prevention of scarring or to the social effects of the disease, but in literature disfigurement figures importantly. Smallpox often produces abrupt turns in the plots of eighteenth-century novels and its effects drive the stories. John Cleland's Fanny Hill commences telling her whore's story because her parents' death from smallpox leaves her destitute in *Memoirs of a Woman of Pleasure* (1749). In Eliza Haywood's *Betsy Thoughtless* (1751) the heroine is finally free to marry her ideal, Mr. Trueworth, after smallpox claims his first wife. In Elizabeth Griffith's *The Delicate Distress* (1769) Lady Straffon determines to inoculate her children during her husband's absence to spare him anxiety, and her sister exposes herself to the disease in order to protect her fiancé from the possible misfortune of a wife irremediably altered. Smallpox scars were legitimate legal grounds for dissolving a marriage contract.[28] For Sarah Scott in *Agreeable Ugliness* (1754) and *Millenium Hall* (1762), ugly women welcome their poxed fate because it ratifies and makes visible their virtue. Their unsightliness becomes a legible rendering of a highly valued interior state and a virtuous femininity. Even late into the eighteenth century women are popularly perceived to be inherently defective, yet some – like their sister characters in Behn, Haywood, and Scott – carry the additional stigma of physiological and anatomical anomalies.

Disease and defect, as we have seen, come to define sexual difference and to stabilize a non-normal personhood, though at the same time some fictions of defect such as Burney's *Camilla* hint at alternatives to conventional femininity and masculinity. Certainly men as well as women who suffered the worst effects of the disease must have found their lives permanently altered. Surely these men grieved, though perhaps secretly, because of the social or sexual disappointments that resulted from their lost attractiveness. But the *literary* representations of living with smallpox's miseries are largely confined to women, and the fearsome effects of the disease are most often visited on lovely young virgins. The price of a pit-marked face is most poignantly portrayed in Henry Jones Bath's *Inoculation; or Beauty's Triumph: A Poem, in Two Cantos*, an ode to women's beauty written just after the 1750 epidemic. It praises Sir Robert Sutton's improved method of inoculation involving slight prickings of the skin instead of deeper cuts.[29] Claiming that the English have conquered smallpox as they have conquered portions of the world, this poem describes Sutton's "nobler and unmatch'd Discovery" as superior to Columbus' discovery of America because saving a human life is of greater value than capturing diamond quarries or gold mines. Recovery without facial blemishes results in the possession of real and valuable property, not coin or credit.

Inoculation credits an English surgeon rather than suspicious Levantine medical practices, and then the poem shrinks the colonial issues to domestic romance. After seeking his fortune in the Indies, Strephon returns home to seek his beloved Flavia. Eager to behold her beautiful face, he is instead struck dumb at "the Tomb of her departed Beauty" after her bout with smallpox:

> He stops, he gazes, and he starts aside,
> With dumb Astonishment he gazes still;
> His Hair erect with Horror stood, his Knees
> Together struck, and freezing Drops bedew'd
> His trembling Limbs; he wist not what to do,
> But like a wretch quite Thunder-struck he stood,
> Whilst Flavia rush'd upon his troubl'd Breast,
> With mad Impatience, and exclaim'd aloud!
> And was it then my Face alone you lov'd!   (18)

Paralyzed by her scarred face, the fickle Strephon shuns his beloved. Later Flavia's stunning beauty is miraculously restored: "When Phoenix-like her new Complexion rose, / With tenfold Splendor, and amaz'd the World" (23). But in the interim Strephon's impregnating Flavia's beautiful sister elicits the recurrent theme of discord between a beautiful and ugly pair that Aphra Behn had exploited earlier in the century. The distraught Flavia finally retires to a convent.

Inoculation reiterates the now familiar theme that the disfiguring tragedy of smallpox is somehow intrinsic to being female: "With marking, deep

degrading Spots, those Banners / Of frail Defect, those Legacies of EVE"
(7). The scars of smallpox are the visible marks of feminine defectiveness,
inadequacy, and inferiority. The poem is instructive about the devastating
effects that smallpox causes in women's lives – Flavia loses both her lover
and the global wealth he represents – but the explicit moral of the didactic
poem is that this tragic tale could have been averted if Flavia had simply been inoculated. For both real and imagined women, being maimed or
deformed by the disease transforms their subjectivity and threatens to alienate them from themselves.[30] The problem extends beyond the mere loss of
beauty to deeper questions of identity. A woman's prospects depended upon
possessing an unblemished beauty, and the traits that most tightly adhere
to identity are those most consistently associated with a fair and flawless
complexion of the face: "I have nothing of my self left which I like," opines
Parthenissa in *Spectator* No. 306 (20 February 1712), and Monimia remarks
that, because her pock-marked face makes her "quite another Creature,"
she will retire from the public arena to tend to needlework.[31] Both disasters
become the excuse for the Spectator to lecture against beauty as the basis for
love: he congratulates Monimia on contracting her pox since it will spur her
to pursue avidly moral improvement. In all of these cases smallpox is taken
as a test case as to whether beauty and virtue naturally co-exist, and whether
ugliness spawns renewed virtue or is a condition for which there is no happy
remedy.

Inevitably changed by the disease, did a woman dare to claim the same
personhood she possessed before its onset? The question was central to
femininity. "Many have experienced such an alteration in the countenance
of their friends and children, from the effects of this disease," writes Robert
Walker, "that they could scarcely know them again."[32] Newly scarred by
smallpox, Parthenissa laments that she does not know how "to Act in
a new Being" or to behave in a way that would be consistent with her
ugliness.[33] The change in identity wrought by smallpox could destabilize
a woman's social position, sexuality, and even racial identification, since
having a deeply pitted complexion also becomes a kind of ready disguise.
Elizabeth Robinson Montagu and her sister Sarah Scott were regarded
as two peas in a pod in their childhood, but after Sarah contracted the
disease, she was no longer known by the nickname "Pea."[34] Acquiescing
to a culture's idealization of white and smooth skin, Montagu desperately
feared the disease all of her life and assiduously tracked its course among her
friends. Yet Sarah Scott, like the *Spectator*, suggests the reverse effect: that
in contracting smallpox, the woman who loses her beauty finds her soul.
In Scott's *Millenium Hall* Harriot Trentham becomes "perfectly contented

with the alteration this cruel distemper had made in her," eccentrically imagines it to be "a reward for the good she had done Mrs. Tonston," and welcomes as a test of character the loss of her lover to another woman.[35]

Physical beauty – or at the very least a lack of deformity – grants the possessor authority to conquer and enslave, elements that enliven the dead metaphor of beauty's empire and extend it from the individual to the social body. In Johnson's *Rambler* No. 130 Victoria, resembling an "old knight-errant at his first sally" to "prosecute my victories," acquires a fortune but is attacked by "that dreadful malady which has so often put a sudden end to the tyranny of beauty."[36] Thus Victoria's pleasure and sway, those two characteristics alleged to define the sex, come to an abrupt end, and her name lingers as an ironic remnant of her lost ability to rule over her lovers. Victoria, whose mother would prefer that she died rather than be disfigured, embodies a morality lesson on the ephemeral nature of beauty. These conduct lessons, like Plumptre's sermons, deliver forceful messages to women that put the disease within a moral *and* sexual economy. No matter how morally uplifting, the ravages of smallpox wrought real economic consequences for women since the disease often destroyed their marketability for marriage. As Swift, Pope, and other satirists regularly reminded women, all are subject to aging. Unlike the lengthy process which ages them, smallpox is a catastrophic occurrence that abruptly changes their appearance.

Lady Mary, herself a victim of the disease that left her permanently without eyelashes, cleverly documents the way that smallpox exposes the commodification of beauty in an ecologue "Satturday: The Small Pox."[37] In addition to shunning the mirror that would remind her of lost beauty, Flavia angrily laments the loss of material benefits that scarring has occasioned:

> There was a Time (Oh that I could forget!)
> When Opera Tickets pour'd before my Feet,
> And at the Ring where brightest Beauties shine,
> The earliest Cherrys of the Park were mine.
> Wittness oh Lilly! And thou Motteux tell!
> How much Japan these Eyes have made you sell,
> With what contempt you saw me oft despise
> The humble Offer of the raffled Prize:
> For at each raffle still the Prize I bore,
> With Scorn rejected, or with Triumph wore:
> Now Beautie's Fled, and Presents are no more.
>
> (201–02).

Unspoiled by smallpox pits, beauty inspires a suitor's gifts associated with luxury and empire, ranging from opera tickets to coveted delicacies, rare perfumes, and Oriental fans, silks, and porcelain. Since empire requires women to be the intended market for its wares, lovers, fashion, power, and fortune disappear along with Flavia's former self. Her "fortune" signifies her fateful loss of wealth of every kind as smallpox robs women of identity and riches.

Montagu was not alone in her plight nor in the ability to wrest art from physical misfortune. More generous to women is John Whaley's poem which consoles a fair nymph who has been disfigured.[38] But it remained for Esther Lewis (later Clark), a poet who had herself contracted smallpox, to align the disease's lasting blemishes with the flaws intrinsic to women's published writings in "A Mirror for Detractors" (1754):

> That when a woman dares indite,
> And seek in print the public sight,
> All tongues are presently in motion
> About her person, mind, and portion;
> And every blemish, every fault,
> Unseen before, to light is brought.
> Nay, generously they take the trouble
> Those blemishes and faults to double.[39]

Again twice-flawed women stand in for all femininity and, at another level, their visible blemishes and invisible but endemic defects make them exemplary of all women writers. Smallpox and other disfiguring effects ruined women's prospects while offering escape from traditional femininities and enabling compensatory expression in their lives and work. As Cora Kaplan astutely notes about Dinah Craik's *Olive* (1850), defective parts or atypical bodies may operate as "fortuitous moral testing ground for the development of ethical and autonomous selfhood."[40] Disease and its unhappy consequences function as a moral standard for women writers and their female characters. As I have been suggesting, smallpox tests the individual's physical and moral health and extends it beyond a woman's personal domain to weigh the nation's stature as measured by the healthy appearance of its women. Their beauty or ugliness is at least as important as effeminacy or manliness in determining the island's well-being at home and in the colonial trade.

III

Perhaps Frances Burney was not speaking simply metaphorically when she compared the effects of bad reviews to disfigurement; upon the publication of *Camilla*, she anticipated that would "be horribly mauled" by the reviewers who would "mar" her.[41] Burney herself read medical texts which documented the disfiguring effects of smallpox, and her son Alex was inoculated a year after the publication of *Camilla* in 1797.[42] Burney's *Camilla* begins dramatically with Eugenia's degeneration from the lovely daughter of a country parson into a pock-marked humpback when her wealthy foolish uncle, the baronet Sir Hugh, indulges her desire for trinkets at the country fair and allows her free rein in that public forum.[43] As a result she contracts a serious and disfiguring case of smallpox. Though her beauty had originally exceeded that of her sisters Camilla and Lavinia (and their cousin Indiana, "an exquisite beauty"), Eugenia is the only one who is afflicted by smallpox and permanently scarred. Incredibly, Sir Hugh engages in further negligence and presides over her dislocating her shoulder and knee in a fall from a seesaw. Like the women of the poems and periodical literature I have discussed, Eugenia's original identity and her prospects are abruptly transformed by her crooked body which becomes an obvious affront to the prevailing standards of beauty and symmetry.[44] Polluted by the public nature of her fall and by the casual inattention of the aristocracy to the hazards of disease and deformity, she embodies the extremes of masculine carelessness perpetrated on a woman, of the deformity produced by contemporary society, and of the pervasive threat of contagion.[45]

If, as I have suggested earlier, the defect of female difference is the sign of the feminine, how does the multiply defective, "diminutive and deformed" Eugenia (1.3.33), figure in the novel? Is she emblematic of defect, or released from its stigma because of her newfound moral standing? As our readings of Behn, Haywood, and Scott have demonstrated, beyond the inherent defect of the sex, particular women bear a double defect in being blind, lame, deaf, ugly, or scarred. Eugenia's character as a woman is reduced to a very few significant traits: she is a blemished, crippled learned lady once she contracts smallpox and falls from the teeter-totter. This now-standard playground equipment was in the eighteenth century an exercise machine sometimes curiously prescribed as treatment for patients to correct the very deformity of the back that her accident caused.[46] (See illustration 6.) Similarly, swinging from heights was often associated with imperial locations, and travel narratives often display such recreations as exotic. An Indian ceremony reported in 1793 (staged as penance to the goddess of smallpox, Mariatale) involved hooking a man, allegedly through the skin of the back, and suspending him high in the air on a levered pole, not unlike a teeter-totter. In addition to worrying over the degree of pain experienced by the suspended man, the text accompanying the picture of the "barbarous ceremony" speculated that even the Brahmins of India might

6 "The teeter-totter," Plate 57 from Jacques M. Delpech, *De l'Orthomorphie par rapport à l'espèce humaine* (1828). Exercising in this manner was prescribed for maintaining women's health.

be convinced to accept a vaccine derived from their god of virtue, the cow (see illustration 7).[47] Again, British anxieties concerning the disease and its prevention are blamed on the East, and they provide a strange connection between the deadly disease, Eugenia's accident, and the healthy activities that bring about her fall.

7 "Barbarous Ceremony" from Charles Gold, *Oriental Drawings: Sketched between the years 1791 and 1798* (1806). The text notes, "From the *Cow*, their God of Virtue, even the Brahmins might consent to be inoculated without danger of pollution."

In the earlier examples from didactic poetry and periodicals, disease produced economic disadvantages for women, though in *Camilla* the reverse obtains. Reliant on the modest living of their father (a younger son), none of the girls has prospects of marriage without receiving an inheritance from Sir Hugh, an estate which he at first determines to settle upon Camilla but, after the dual deformities, transfers to Eugenia who brings into focus the values embedded in economic and patriarchal structures. Because of the contrast with Eugenia's disfigurement, however, the attractive, well-meaning Camilla can appear to be an "unmarked, unblemished, normate"[48] in spite of her naive social errors and her terrible descent into madness. In the narrative Camilla escapes being maimed in a carriage accident, though the phaeton breaks into pieces, the horse is disabled, and Sir Sedley goes temporarily lame. The disastrous potential for disabling not one but two of the sisters is displaced onto the horse, and onto the effeminate man who is revived into manliness by tending to Camilla when the horses go wild. Camilla is also systematically distinguished from Eugenia in her interaction with Edgar Mandelbert, her suitor who is heir to an estate. Coached by the misogynist Lord Marchmont, Edgar repeatedly tests Camilla to be sure that she, unlike her sister Eugenia, is free of defects, a trial that leads to a convoluted history of misunderstandings during their protracted courtship. On the other hand, Camilla's affinity with Eugenia's disability is exemplified in her inability to remain economically viable. Demonstrating her own flaws in judgment, Camilla makes serious financial mistakes as her attempt to keep up with her wealthy and modish friends creates an unending source of public embarrassment.

Advantages continue to accrue to the "mangled, deformed, – unfortunate Eugenia!" (723) because of her misshapen and scarred body that renders her an anomaly who exists in a vexed relationship to the consumer culture. "They tell me, ma'm, that ugly little body's a great fortune," Mr. Dubster crudely remarks as he compares her to a dwarf in a freak show at Exeter Change (2.2.77). While for most women beauty is commercially viable merchandise, Eugenia's *defects* grant her unearned wealth. Eugenia elopes to Gretna Green with the impoverished and disguised Alphonso Bellamy who finds that her inheritance allows him to forget her ugliness. When the fortunehunting suitor accidentally dies by his own hand, she is released from the marriage. Though she finally falls in love with Frederic Melmond, his initial preference for her cousin makes Eugenia generously offer to share her estate with them if the couple marry. Her deformities produce an unmerited and unequaled "accumulation" (4.5.303) of value which serves as a grotesque substitute for the kind of credit she would have earned as a beauty. The very antithesis of a goddess of credit, she becomes instead the cultural symbol of a kind of moral credit that is perversely invested in ugliness and disease. Infectious disease in *Camilla* then both mars a woman and, strangely, makes her valuable. In short, Eugenia's predicament as she regards herself in the mirror and shudders at her recognition of beauty's power is the reverse of Flavia's in *Inoculation* or "Satturday." Flavia finds that beauty's rewards evaporate because of smallpox, while in *Camilla* Sir Hugh arbitrarily bequeaths his fortune solely to Eugenia as compensation for his appalling neglect, promising "a guinea for every pit in that poor face" (1.3.30). He links her scars and her pitted face to the gold coins that are historically linked with the slave trade. Eugenia's smallpox scars are rewarded with slavery's profits, racial violence thus compensating for the white Englishwoman's lost beauty.

We might make something more of the origins of the coin Sir Hugh offers in exchange for Eugenia's smallpox pits. When the Royal Mint first struck the gold guinea coin in 1663, it was worth 20 shillings, later becoming

21 shillings "in the name of and for the use of the Royal Company of Royal Adventurers of England trading with Africa."[49] Though Guinea's territory extended from Sierra Leone to Benin on the West African Coast, the area rapidly became synonymous with the slave ships that carry human cargo to the New World. These gold coin pieces, distinguished by an engraved figure of a little elephant, encouraged the popular use of the name *guinea* employed in the Guinea trade and produced from Guinea gold. The year 1663 also marks the historical moment when the Royal Adventurers sought a charter to purchase slaves to be transported to the plantations of America.[50] Thus the guinea, the gold standard of England's wealth, was from its inception extracted from its slave trade. Sir Hugh's remuneration for smallpox in willingly trading a guinea – the monetary symbol of the slave trade – for every scar revives the original connection in the potential equivalency between race and defect.

Eugenia, ugly and misshapen by accident, resigns herself to becoming a woman who defies the usual definitions of femininity, one who positions herself both inside and outside the category of woman and its sexual economy. Eugenia, I am also arguing, like others who possess extraordinary non-normate bodies, represents a "cultural third term," both "the opposite of the masculine figure" and "the antithesis of the normal woman."[51] As a triangulated gender anomaly, her character transforms disability to empower her to escape the usual trivial feminalities.

For example, when Sir Hugh bumbles through a comic speech in trying unsuccessfully to entice his nephew Clermont Lynmere into marrying Eugenia whom he had "brought up in the style of a boy, for the sake of [his] marrying her," Lynmere not surprisingly responds, "What have I to do with marrying a girl like a boy? ... Besides, what has a wife to do with the classics? will they shew her how to order her table?" (7.12.592). Eugenia's hermaphroditic status unsettles the sexual identity of her intended husband as well, implying that he is attracted to her boyishness. Lynmere like Sir Sedley is effeminate, an "unmanly" foppish narcissist who regularly admires himself in the mirror. He despicably expresses "ridicule ... suppressed by contempt" (7.8.565) toward Eugenia, who as a result experiences "for the first time, a sensation of shame for her lameness, which, hitherto, she had regularly borne with fortitude, when she had not forgotten from indifference" (7.8.566). In his presence Eugenia actually feels as if her disease is returning and that her deformity interferes with her being perceived as feminine: "Young Lynmere, under an appearance of mingled assurance and apathy, the effect of acquired conceit, playing upon natural insipidity, was secretly tormented with the rueful necessity of sacrificing either a noble fortune, or his own fine person;...Eugenia had never yet thought herself so plain and insignificant, and felt as if, even since the morning, the small-pox had renewed its ravages, and she had sunk into being shorter" (7.10.577). Inverting the gender relations depicted in the poems *Inoculation* and "Satturday," Burney's novel *Camilla* questions more explicitly the relationship between deformity and social value; the critical issue for Eugenia is whether or not Lynmere will be able to take possession of her substantial inheritance earned through stigma, "a guinea for every pit," that substitutes for luxurious commodities that naturally attach themselves to beauty.

Thus the context of deformity in the novel curiously offers opportunities to renegotiate sexual difference. Kristina Straub aptly points to the male incapacity of Burney's masculine characters, including Sir Hugh's symbolic castration and the fact that the brothers of Camilla and Indiana are respectively a wastrel and a fop. When the child Camilla dresses Sir Hugh as a female with black cork whiskers, handing him a doll to nurse, she creates a female grotesque, a "she-male," by subjecting the male body to the specular indignities that women regularly suffer.[52] At the same time, exulting in her ability to "govern and direct" her uncle, she boldly dons his wig (1.2.18). And similarly, in a carnivalesque moment Lionel, dressing in maid's clothes in a dramatic moment of class counterfeit, briefly turns into a transvestite (3.13.264), while Miss Dennel wears Ensign Macdersey's cocked hat, and Macdersey himself ends up with the coachman's bobwig (3.13.265).[53] These reconfigurations of gender set the stage for deformity's capacity to reshape definitions of femininity and masculinity in the person of Eugenia.

Strengthening her intellect to make up for her maimed body, Eugenia accepts the Reverend Mr. Tyrold's arguments that classical learning will sustain her new identity rather than make her freakish, and, after a brief embarrassed retreat to hide her body, she accedes to his wish to re-emerge into the public world with a new identity in which virtue substitutes for beauty.[54] Tyrold attempts to circumscribe Eugenia's future within the conventional strictures on deformity to prevent the deformed, sexually ambiguous Eugenia from rivaling masculine power. In paired chapters on "Strictures on Beauty" and "Strictures on Deformity," Tyrold counsels Eugenia to compensate for her loss through moral and spiritual calisthenics rather than remain distraught over her injuries. He cautions her to squelch any niggling desires for what she has missed, taking as his text the *Spectator* rather than the Bible: "A too acute sensibility of personal defects, is one of the greatest weaknesses of self-love" (4.5.302). On the contrary, though her family and acquaintances seem to make the transition nearly instantly from the hope of marriage and family to lost prospects, Eugenia at first seems *insensible* to her defects and, complaining that she has been brought up in "worldly darkness" (IV.5.301), the fifteen-year-old holds her family and friends responsible for what she perceives to be their deception in protecting her from self-knowledge. Eugenia abruptly and painfully recognizes that, in spite of her resignation to her unusual body, she is severely deformed and ugly in the eyes of the world. It is her peculiarity as a disabled person that she had underestimated, and it was the "*abuse*" of others that "shewed me to myself!" Belatedly finding that she had erred in believing "the world to be full of people who had been sufferers as well as myself, by disease or accident" (4.5.303), Eugenia learns instead to identify herself as an aberrant female, more defective than the generality of the sex, because the stigmas assigned to disabled people attach to her in spite of her own self-definition.

When women in the country returning from the market insult her shrunken body, it is a class equalizer. Being ugly and deformed means that the local laborers' children mock her as "the little hump-back gentlewoman!" though they quickly succumb to a bribe when she throws them money (4.6.305). Their kindness can be purchased, and the class privilege that her deformity had threatened is re-established when their taunts yield to her "gentlewoman" status, the class position she attained because of the wealth that her deformity earns her. Eugenia retrieves her foundering gender to reassert her philanthropic role, a role perfectly compatible with her newfound wealth if not her physical anomalies. Eugenia reverses the common association between being "crippled" and being economically dependent as well as the supposed relationship between begging and disability.[55]

But it is the "Strictures on Beauty" that finally prevent Eugenia from imagining any collective bond with others who share the marks of difference. The Reverend Mr. Tyrold creates an artificial occasion for pedagogical purposes when he arranges for Eugenia to meet an attractive "ideot" by chance. Upon encountering the grotesque spectacle of the beautiful but disoriented retarded girl (forecasting the temporary derangement of Camilla, the heroine), Eugenia remains unconvinced and unconsoled about any advantage wrested from ugliness: "I would purchase a better appearance at any price, any expence, any payment, the world could impose!" (4.6.308). The irony, of course, is that in spite of Sir Hugh's economic generosity to her, the price of purchasing beauty exceeds her income. Her *value* is lost, and it must be repurchased, both by her own benevolence in the village and by the commodification of her disability in Sir Hugh's exchange of her scars for guineas.

When the mentally impaired beauty who sparks these meditations acts
in a bizarre fashion, displaying her madness with loud laughter and strange
courtesy, she becomes contorted and racialized; and like the conversion of
Eugenia's smallpox pits into guineas, defect turns into a commodity to be
exchanged for coins: " 'Give me a shilling!' was her reply, while the slaver
drivelled unrestrained from her mouth, rendering utterly disgusting a chin
that a statuary might have wished to model...almost black in the face
before she would allow herself to take another breath" (4.6.309).

This association between mental deficiency and female facial scarring
evokes connections with blackness not only in Burney's novel but in
eighteenth-century culture more broadly. *An Enquiry Concerning the Principles of Taste, and of the Origin of our Ideas of Beauty* is typical in connecting
blackness with mental deficiencies and to an earlier, more barbaric, stage of
civilization: "The negro-race seems to be the farthest removed from the line
of true cultivation of any of the human species; their defect of form and
complexion being, I imagine, as strong an obstacle to their acquiring true
taste (the produce of mental cultivation) as any natural defect they may
have in their intellectual faculties."[56] The beautiful idiot meant to serve as
Eugenia's object lesson turns quite savage and bestial. The epitome of fair
degradation, she is oblivious to a cat scratching her beautiful face: "she tore
her handkerchief off her neck, put it over her face, strained it as tight as
she was able, and tied it under her chin; and then struck her head with
both her hands, making a noise that resembled nothing human" (4.6.310).
A kind of racialized precursor to the mad Bertha in Brontë's *Jane Eyre*, this
woman then warns of beauty's ungovernable power. Eugenia's encounter
with the madwoman transforms her self-pity into a contented acceptance
of her father's declaration that "beauty, without mind, is more dreadful
than any deformity" (4.6.311). Through her father's contrived and violent
lesson Eugenia accepts her new role in inhabiting an anomalous body.

The connections between deformity and race extend further. Immediately following these instructive scenes, the entire party of young cousins
and friends watches a wretched performance of *Othello* presented by
strolling players, a motley group of actors so poorly outfitted that the
Othello character dresses as Richard III with a woolly black wig and a face
"begrimed with a smoked cork" (4.8.318).[57] The central character in the
strollers' production is deformed, racialized, and turned topsy-turvy as a
blackened Richard III and a crooked Othello. The dual tragedies turn farcical as race and deformity incongruously are collapsed into one person.
Other outrageous costuming also destabilizes race and sexuality: Iago is of
necessity dressed effeminately as Lord Foppington, Cassio as a Turk, and

Roderigo as the Jew Shylock. None of the actors is able to disguise their class or their various Norfolk, London, Somersetshire, and Worcestershire dialects. Camilla and Lavinia (Eugenia has not accompanied them) laugh uproariously at the discovery scene between Othello and Desdemona in the last act, the precise moment in the play when scarring, whiteness, beauty, and Othello's blackness are most powerfully visible. When the bewigged Othello, caricatured as a noble humpback in blackface in this production, protests that he does not desire to "Scar that vhiter skin of hers than snow" (4.8.322), he rails against a literal scarring as well as the supposed blight that would result from miscegenation. In this strikingly theatrical scene, the visibility of a defective body, of alternative renderings of the human form, of sexuality, race, and their arbitrariness, thematically highlight the issues that underlie the public display of Eugenia's deformity throughout the text.

On the Renaissance stage the black Othello and the white Desdemona were of course both actually played by white men, one blackened by burnt cork and dark pigment, the other crossdressed as a woman, while in the eighteenth century Desdemona was for the first time played by a female actor instead of a boy. In *Camilla*'s farcical production Desdemona escapes death because Othello's black woolly wig, the signal of his race, catches fire, and she reveals herself to be ready to walk home after the theatre dressed in a dirty red and white linen gown, the rosy and fair sign of perfect English womanhood, here besmirched. Othello, attempting to snuff out her light, drags her violently back to bed to finish the scene: "I know not where is that Promethean heat / That can thy light relume. When I had plucked thy rose / I cannot give it wital [sic] growth again. It needs must vither [sic]." The audience, convulsed with laughter at the moment of murder, speaks through Sir Sedley, "Poor Blacky! Thou hast been most indissolubly comic" (4.8.323). Camilla, who had been attempting to conceal her attendance un-chaperoned as the play is, before it concludes, loudly paged and told of her uncle's alleged impending death. Thus the play works to "out" Camilla as it makes light of monstrosity, here displaced onto exotic deformity and merged with Othello's blackness. Camilla's suitor, Edgar, resembles Othello with his misplaced rage and jealousy in misjudging the heroine throughout the main plot.[58] But Othello, a sign of contamination and degeneration made comic and masculine and divested of his evil potential, also acts as surrogate for the absent Eugenia. The farce of *Othello* provides a dramatic opening for the representation of the monstrous, "a sense of bringing forth to 'show' some 'monster' too 'hideous' to be 'shown.' "[59] At the same time *Camilla* here displays British fears of the entanglements of race, disease, and degeneracy in the threat of interracial romance. Othello's scarring of Desdemona's white face would disfigure her; the mark of Othello on Desdemona signifies the potential violence in the black man's miscegenetic and disfiguring marking of the white woman's body. But Burney's crooked and ill-dressed Othello makes something ludic of the threat. Burney's parodic version of the drama suggests that Eugenia, as an emblem of every woman and none, of the defect of womanhood and of the denial of gender, appearing in public and exposing her deformity to the light, is both insignificant and momentous. The contrast of her newly stable identity to the silly, apparently inconsequential, performance is highlighted by her absence from it.

Desdemona's paleness and alabaster skin contrast her to her lover's in any production, of course, but Karen Newman argues that femininity is also *aligned* with the blackness and monstrosity embodied in Shakespeare's original raging Moor.[60] Burney's comic inversion of *Othello*, as it reflects upon the novel, rearranges the relationships among femininity, race, and monstrosity. Femininity's identification with the monstrous, with blackness and, I would add, with the laboring classes and an enfeebled aristocracy, is located briefly in the heroine Camilla, but more centrally in Eugenia. The consolidation of an idealized and virtuous femininity – heterosexual, passive, domestic, white, and of a certain status – involves occupying at least three contradictory states at once: being the same as the monstrous, the black, and the laborer; sympathetic and benevolent to them; and yet quite distinct from them all. Eugenia manages to position herself as the epitome of a proper femininity in this way in spite of her unfeminine body, thus interrogating the very categories she occupies. The infectious deformity threatening England is embodied in smallpox and its marring of beautiful femininity. But an alternative feminine ideal, represented in her character, mobilizes the images of race, disfigurement, and contagion so as to offer, peculiarly enough, an avenue for rethinking the formation of particular categories of the human.

Eugenia's triumph in being loved in spite of her scars, of finding a husband who sees beyond the surface, is the triumph of a class besieged by aristocratic imprudence and susceptible to the guilt fostered by working-class bribery. Coinage and property, guineas and status, are the levellers assigned to Eugenia *because* of the defects that make it possible for her to compete on the field of femininity. An ugly woman can apparently achieve a sufficient femininity in this novel, though Burney, like Scott before her, seems in the last instance to claim that Eugenia's affliction happily spurs her toward a more traditional virtue: "Eugenia once loved, was loved for ever. Where her countenance was looked at, her complexion was forgotten; while her voice was heard, her figure was unobserved; where her virtues were known, they seemed but to be enhanced by her personal misfortunes" (10.14.912). Eugenia stands as a doubly defective woman who memorializes her subjectivity *because* of the visible defect that is its cause. While Edgar chides the lovely Camilla for her instability of character, an ugly woman's character is presented as determinate and unified. While it is true that Eugenia evidences a kind of stable subjectivity that Camilla lacks,[61] she – rather than the other women who might have inherited Sir Hugh's money (Camilla, Indiana, or Lavinia) – is most intensely engaged in composing her mangled subjectivity into journal form. Her memoirs include meditations on what is required to maintain equanimity in spite of a crooked body and a blemished face as well as a picture of her. In constructing a legible subjectivity, Eugenia recognizes both the limitation and the moral potential that dwell within deformity. As in the case of Behn's defective women, Eugenia's deformity releases her into narrative and assists her in establishing agency, though they are regulated by societal expectations. Her claim to selfhood marked by accident, disease, and disability, is founded on a broken femininity, and it offers a paradigm for sexual difference that relies on defect for its formation. Burney has written a novel in which the legitimacy of the familiar dichotomies – male and female, perverse and ordinary – are called into question. Unusual women, ugly, smallpoxed, deformed, physically impaired, or mentally deficient, are indices both to the gendering of virtue and to a nation that wishes to eradicate from within signs of the effeminate and of miscegenated decay. Rather than rejecting outright women's social malformation as Wollstonecraft's *Vindication* does, Burney's *Camilla* embraces it to offer an original and fanciful interpretation of a mangled femininity, a romance of defect embodied in its secondary heroine who thinks, writes, marries, and remains contentedly, appallingly, and unmistakably mutilated. In short, in the fictions of Aphra Behn and Eliza Haywood, the poetry of Lady Mary Wortley Montagu, the letters of Elizabeth Montagu and other Bluestocking, and the novels of Sarah Fielding, Laurence Sterne, and Frances Burney, "defects" in their natural or unanticipated occurrences help us to draw a new kind of map of eighteenth-century gender as women and men employ broken, twisted, deformed, compromised, and other anomalous bodies in the service of alternative femininities and masculinities. Sometimes those who inhabit these bodies engage them to break the boundaries of sexual difference, taking full advantage of a society that would limit them to the more conventional. Some, as in the case of Elizabeth Montagu, take comfort in restoring regularity as a standard of taste, even as she violates those measures herself. Others such as the characters of Behn and Haywood indulge the misery of impotence or injustice before turning it to unexpected effect. As we have seen, authors – especially women – frequently find within defect a metaphor or a material fact that releases them into writing, and into a subjectivity that can manipulate a print culture's assumptions about their capabilities.

As I have argued in this chapter, Eugenia's scarred face and unsightly back at once signify a reassuringly virtuous femininity, and the threat that a racial and sexual other poses to the country. Turning now to focus more specifically on race and gender we will find that complexion is a standard of beauty and value in relation to the emerging empire and a crux of racial and sexual negotiations. Englishwomen in particular are the guardians of skin as it is characteristic of the health of the nation, and their unblemished white and red complexions, their "white cheeks of Europe" are fragile shields indeed against the fatal contamination introduced by colonial exploration and imperial designs.

PART II

Race and gender

CHAPTER 5

Racial femininity: "our British fair"

Our heroines, tho' seeking regions new,
To English honor both hold firm and true;
Love-struck, indeed, but yet a charming pair,
Virtuous and mild, like all our British fair!
George Colman, "Prologue" to Mariana
Starke's *The Sword of Peace*

I

The racial history of eighteenth-century England is marked at its beginning by the Royal African Company's relinquishing its monopoly over slavery, and at its conclusion by the growth of the abolition movement. In 1729 the joint opinion known as "Yorke and Talbot" established that a slave was not guaranteed freedom by baptism nor by setting foot in the mother country, and his owner might legally insist that the slave return to the islands or the colonies. Any Englishman possessed the right to trade in black flesh. At the same time that 15,000 Negroes lived in London and many thousands of slaves were transported to the West Indies and to the American colonies, Lord Mansfield, a Chief Justice of England, finally extended the protection of habeas corpus to the slave James Somerset in 1772, and thus to all black people in England, though he did not grant them wages or poor law relief. Because chattel slavery persisted until the official abolition of colonial slavery in 1834, the actual legal status of slaves in Britain remained ambiguous. As Folarin Shyllon observes, "Although the opinion was overruled in the Somerset case by the Mansfield decree, the 1729 opinion issued at Lincoln's Inn Hall remained the slave owners' Bill of Rights and the slave hunters' charter, and made every black man, woman, or child unsafe and under imminent threat of removal by force into slavery, until Emancipation in 1834."[1]

Though "race" has been described as "one of the central conceptual inventions of modernity," it is also troubled by a "liberal paradox." That paradox arises from the conflict between modernity's principles of liberty, equality, and fraternity; and the subsequent "multiplication of racial identities and...exclusions that prompt and rationalize, enable and sustain" inequalities.[2] Debate persists as to whether the early versions of racism which foster these exclusions were significantly different from the biological racism of later periods. "Some argue that racism was systematically embraced by the seventeenth century, others hold that it had not yet emerged in its consolidated, pure somatic form," writes Ann Laura Stoler. Since early racial thinking evolved into "the organizing grammar of an imperial order in which modernity, the civilizing mission and the 'measure of man' were framed,"[3] did these discourses already dominate eighteenth-century conceptual frameworks? George L. Mosse, for example, believes that in the eighteenth century "the structure of racial thought was consolidated and determined for the next one and three-quarter centuries."[4] But race is, of course, neither simply a biological essence nor a discursive practice nor is its meaning located outside of history. It is instead, as Michael Omi and Howard Winant have argued, *"an unstable and 'decentered' complex of social meanings constantly being transformed by political struggle."*[5] The chapters which follow show that both an essentialist racism ("race" as a series of exclusions based upon biological and behavioral traits) and the language of cultural nominalism (the recognition that classifications are simply convenient labels) pertain to the period.[6] I argue that, rather than congealing into modern racism, incongruent manifestations of "race" in language and culture coexist in the eighteenth century, and that strategic confusions persist regarding the meanings assigned to skin colorings, physiognomies, and nations. Examining these contradictions at their historical formation helps us to loosen pigmentation from its current local and provincial meanings. These unfamiliar hybrids of racial attitudes suggest that the twenty-first century's pleading against race or to move beyond its boundaries may perhaps find more in common with earlier racial confusions and contingencies than with the nineteenth-century's scientific racism.[7]

Debates about race extended to defining boundaries between humans and animals, centering partially on linguistic abilities since, as we have seen in the case of Duncan Campbell, mute beings limited to imitation, sign language, or brutish social exchange were excluded from rational humanity. David Hume, drawing a comparison between a Negro and a parrot in a notorious footnote in the 1753–54 edition of his essay, "Of National Characters," singles out a Jamaican man of learning as an exceptional being akin to a speaking parrot; he claims that the educated Negro (almost certainly Francis Williams), a freakish example of his species, resembles a parrot in his ability to imitate a few words.[8] Similarly, in an earlier reference to parrots in Richard Steele's *Tatler* No. 245, a Black-moor servant boy asserts his spiritual worth but acknowledges that his value to his owner is simply commercial: "I am as good as my Lady her self as I am a Christian, and many other Things: but for all this, the Parrot who came over with me from our Country is as much esteemed by her as I am. Besides this, the Shock-Dog has a Collar that cost almost as much as mine."[9] In these examples from Hume's footnote and Steele's *Tatler*, the parrot and the lapdog possess an equivalency to an African and the lines among man, commodity, and beast are blurred. The principles of discrimination are calibrated along a color line (the lighter shades are superior to black) and along a hierarchy of creatures (human is superior to animal); and the lower ranges of each are assumed to be parallel. The status of the Negro as man, property, or exotic bird seems perilously uncertain, especially when we try to reconcile Hume's assertions that learned Negroes are analogous to talking parrots with the antislavery stand that he adopted elsewhere.

Novelist and essayist Eliza Haywood also alludes to the relationship between skin color and cognitive ability in *The Parrot* (1746),[10] a gossipy but politically astute periodical. The parrot, a well-travelled East Indian linguist, chats about "whatever either the public Prints, or such private Conversation as I am let into, can furnish" (No. 1). In Haywood's rendering, however, the parrot becomes a subversive (though somewhat camouflaged) agent of both antiracism and antislavery in an account that satirizes facile connections drawn between color and ability:

The Color [green] I brought into the World with me, and shall never change, it seems, is an Exception against me; – some People will have it that a *Negro* might as well set up for a *Beauty*, as a *green Parrot* for a *good Speaker*; – Preposterous Assertion! As if the *Complection* of the *Body* had any Influence over the *Faculties* of the *Mind*; yet meerly on this score they resolve, right or wrong, to condemn all I say before hand.

But pray how comes it that *green* is a Color so much disrelished in *England* at present? – Time was when it was otherwise. – Can any Arguments, drawn from Reason, be given why *red, yellow*, or even *blue*, much less a *motley* Mixture of various Tinctures, should have the Preference? . . . I should have been wholly silent on the Occasion, if it had not reminded me how predominant this Humour is in Mankind, in relation to Things of more Consequence than the *Parrot*.

There is a Nation in the World, I won't say the English, because I have always heard it was unmannerly to expose People's Faults before their Faces; – but there is a certain Nation, who notwithstanding their Reputation and good Sense in some Things, have rendered themselves pretty remarkable for their *liking* and *disliking* to an Excess. (2 August 1746, B 3–B 4)

Haywood impersonates a parrot, a foreigner, who critiques England for its prejudice against parrots of color. While in Hume's essay skin color as a racial indicator hardens into black versus white, Haywood's periodical paper transforms the parrot into an antiracialist figure whose rational capacity cannot be determined by his color. On the other hand, the passage satirically indicates, it would be as preposterous to contend that a Negro with his dark complexion is beautiful as to assume that a parrot may be eloquent. In comically delineating the problems with greenishness, a color against which there was some political prejudice, Haywood refuses to consent to the privileges of "whiteness," or to assume that a white complexion signals rational capacities; yet at the same time *The Parrot* also elides the categories that carry real social meaning in regard to race. It's not easy being green, but even in the eighteenth century, the only beings held captive because their complexion tended toward a verdant hue were parrots.

Writing at mid century before antislavery debates began to come together into a more coherent abolitionist discourse, both Eliza Haywood and David Hume are situated in the wake of Linnaeus' first edition of *Systema Naturae* (1735) in which man is treated as being a species continuous with animals. In the much-revised tenth edition (1758), the elusive nature of complexion hovers over the text in which primate mammals are divided into six categories of *homo sapiens*:

(1) HOMO
  Sapiens. Diurnal; varying by education and situation
(2) Four-footed, mute, hairy. *Wild Man.*
(3) Copper-coloured, choleric, erect. *American.*
  Hair black, straight, thick; *nostrils* wide,
  face harsh; *beard* scanty; *obstinate*, content, free.
  Paints himself with fine red lines. *Regulated* by customs.
(4) Fair, sanguine, brawny. *European.*
  Hair yellow; brown, flowing; *eyes* blue; *gentle*, acute, inventive.
  Covered with close vestments. *Governed* by laws.
(5) Sooty, melancholy, rigid. *Asiatic.*
  Hair black; *eyes* dark; *severe* haughty, covetous. *Covered* with
  loose garments. *Governed* by opinions.
(6) Black, phlegmatic, relaxed. *African.*
  Hair black, frizzled; *skin* silky;
  Nose flat; *lips* tumid; *crafty*, indolent, negligent. *Anoints* himself
  with grease. *Governed* by caprice.[11]

This version translated from the Latin in 1802 elaborates on earlier categorizations to extend the number of possible categories for discrimination beyond geographic region and skin color to facial features, hair texture, and social organization.

In Linnaeus' categorical distinctions the concept of "complexion" in the mid eighteenth century combines both visible and invisible characteristics that reflect aspects of character. Residual elements of medieval and Renaissance concepts of complexion surface in Linnaeus' scheme. This framework had incorporated the entire body rather than simply the face and divided temperament into sanguine, phlegmatic, choleric, and melancholic examples.[12] Something shared by all humans, complexion, like character and "blood," is an unstable racial identifier that may be interpreted as reflecting an intrinsic moral caliber, as restricting the range of human abilities, or paradoxically, as a chance variation of nature with only incidental meaning.

Linnaeus' categories in *Systema Naturae* are widely cited, but their significance as indicative of early racial thinking is much debated. Mary Pratt, for example, finds that this "explicitly comparative" scheme serves to " 'naturalize' the myth of European superiority," while Winthrop Jordan believes that only "hints of ranking" arise, and that the categories are less hierarchical than the more discriminating groupings in the Chain of Being.[13] What seems most salient about these divisions is that the culturally weighted groupings by which race is made visible are explicitly named: skin color, humor, and physique are primary indicators of each distinct geographic region as well as eye color, hair texture, lip size, the absence or presence of a beard or bodily ornamentation. It falls to interpreters to assign variously the extent to which visible features of the body and face, of biology and physiognomy, disclose faculties of the mind; but the systematic citation of these corporeal indicators is critical. Concepts of race and its signifiers were sufficiently incoherent and inconsistent to make launching of a stable identity for English people versus the non-English fraught and complicated, though not impossible. In sum, inconsistencies and confusions are *characteristic* of racial discourse and related cultural practices in mid eighteenth-century England rather than the exception.

II

In the late seventeenth century and the early eighteenth century in England, fantastic ideas of racial identity circulated as speculation about the world at large encouraged artists to ornament maps with cartouches of imagined and monstrous beings. In the later decades of the eighteenth century, as geography, natural history, and protoanthropology become more realistic in description and precise in classification,[14] the physiognomic features of people around the globe are arranged in hierarchies to code racially the regions of the globe. Racial identity during the period was often represented as temporary and contingent – as dress-up costuming or as a color that could be washed off or revealed to be only skin-deep to expose the monogenetic whiteness underneath – rather than as a fundamental aspect of character. I show in this chapter and those that follow that, in part because such identities included a significant constructed component, sexual intermixture *in England itself* was most often understood to be an erotically charged object of curiosity rather than repulsive or offensive until the abolitionist movement was in full force during the last two decades of the eighteenth century. Racism was much in evidence in material practices and representations, but its exact parameters remained elusive.

Feathers, tattoos, and animal skins may also be other indicators of a slippage between beast and human as demonstrated, for example, in the many references to "feathered people" or "the feathered race" as epithets for American Indians or other indigenous peoples.[15] These artifacts of exoticism and emblems of excess lend credence to racial charade as the items are converted from ornament into something consumable through exchange and collection. At masquerades and on stage animal furs, plumage, and the painted colors of complexion are highly popular indicators of the exotic and the savage in costumes donned by actors in the theatre of empire. In many plays of the period we can see from prints and engravings that these costuming properties figured importantly in creating a simulated map of the world. Feathers, for example, migrate easily from East Indian to West Indian, from Native Americans to Tahitians, as generalized and metonymic representations of the ineluctably foreign on maps, in prints and portraits, and on the stage. At this juncture in history, collectible artifacts remain discrete objects without keying into an immediately recognizable master narrative. As Nicholas Thomas has noted, they "are not self-evidently part of an imperial, totalized knowledge 'of the other'; rather, they are somewhat opaque images that attest more to insecurity than to mastery, and to a disputed knowledge of the exotic."[16] Material objects thus substitute for a more refined geographical knowledge. Their lack of specificity in relation to geographic regions is another indicator of the mobility of objects in representing one or another area of the world before scientific racism was more coherently and rigidly organized.

In the home territory of England, racial difference on stage and in public gathering places was something to gawk at, to perform, and to impersonate. Bluestocking Elizabeth Montagu gossips snidely to her friend Elizabeth

Carter in 1764 about women's studied attempts to be *au courant* by impersonating savages at masquerades. She confides, "I never saw such a set of people as appear in the publick rooms[.] [T]heir dress is most elaborately ugly. A friseur [to curl the hair] is employ'd three hours in a morning to make a young Lady look like a virgin Hottentot or Squaw, all art ends in giving them the ferocious air of uncomb'd savages."[17] Montagu has disdain for the way in which such attempts to imitate the "natural" look of "real" savages deform women's appearance. Artful deception makes the counterfeit possible, as women of rank feign inhabiting the bodies of those of other races, noble and otherwise. There is to be sure a sense in which this transracial bonding with the savage through impersonation could be interpreted as European homage to primitive innocence.[18] Yet the practice is also a mockery of that innocence which reveals the real difference between actually being a savage and merely simulating a Hottentot or a squaw.

The European appropriation of indigenous materials such as parrot feathers and animal skins – signs of luxury and abundance – began during the earliest stages of colonialism. "We trade for feathers," writes Aphra Behn in *Oroonoko*, and turn them "into all shapes, make themselves little short habits of them, and glorious Wreaths for their Heads, Necks, Arms and Legs, whose Tinctures are inconceivable. I had a set of these presented to me, and I gave them to the King's Theatre; it was the dress of the *Indian Queen*, infinitely admir'd by persons of quality."[19] Once transferred to the merchant or colonizer through trade, the feathers are the coveted artifacts of empire sought by people of quality in their playful attempt to imitate "uncomb'd savages." These signs of abundance are transformed from being attached to the parrot or other tropical bird into the dress of the noble native, to adorn the European person of rank who impersonates that native. In changing from one habitat to another, the natural is transformed from its original state into a decorative and exchangeable object. Feathers, skins, and other material objects are recontextualized to be given different meanings as they pass through various cultures and social formations.[20] Like the painted skins of white actors that I will explore in detail later, the feathers enable geographical, racial, and even species mobility.

Yet another function of feathers was as highly valued properties that were exchanged for women. Made equivalent to exotic birds, native women, commodities to be traded and exchanged for feathers and skins, are fetishistic objects to be collected. When in George Colman, Jr.'s play *Inkle and Yarico* (1787), a comic opera to which I shall return later in this book, the protagonist's cockney sidekick Trudge cautions his black girlfriend Wowski, "Take care of your furs, and your feathers, my girl . . . Somebody might steal 'em," he indicates his temptation to abscond with the decorations lining her cave, and he suggests that the traffic in furs and feathers, in which he readily participates, resembles the traffic in women. Among other examples is Wainee-òu in the South Sea Islands whom Johann Forster reports was prostituted "as a ready victim" in exchange for parrot feathers that Cook's sailors had gathered (though the islanders may well have held a different view of her status).[21] In the trade between islands red feathers were objects of considerable scarcity and value, and circulated around the islands, but clearly Europeans disturbed the system of exchange. Like chastity, feathers and skins also might be stolen. They sometimes become a metonymic sign of the women themselves since these women can literally be bought and sold as slaves in the case of Wowski and Yarico (the native woman Inkle wooed, and whose story will be recounted in more detail) or taken to be prostitutes in the case of the South Pacific maiden. Thus feathers and animal skins, like native *women* especially, are commodities that can be stolen, bought, sold, and traded to denigrate the native to a beastly status. At the same time, covetous of these precious objects without heeding their affinity to the bestial, European men and women seek to convert them into the highly valued ornamental properties of racial and species difference. The difference between imitating a savage or being one, of having dark skin or painting on blackness for a night of masquerade, is heightened in a number of writers who emphasize that a complexion, even if it seems indelible, may be an inadequate index of character and to being human. In the examples which follow I argue that complexion in its many hues is often represented, sentimentally to be sure, as being as arbitrary as costume and stage properties, feathers and animal skins, tattoos and lacquered fans, in novels and plays of the period. At the same time its stubborn indelibility and the casual attachment of blackness to varieties of peoples gives the lie to claims of color blindness.

III

British women serve both as subjects of a racialized femininity, and as the perpetrators of it. Writers in the later eighteenth century such as Hannah More, Charlotte Smith, Mary Wollstonecraft, and Ann Yearsley recognized powerful similarities between a tyranny based on color and one based on sex. Yet slavery and gendered oppression were also uneasily and inappropriately equated, erasing crucial differences between them.[22]

A pivotal text – Sarah Scott's *Sir George Ellison* (1766), later revised and condensed as *The Man of Sensibility* (1774) – demonstrates the way that external indicators of "race" – skin tone, physical traits, and ornamentation – relate to ideas of interior worth just after the Seven Years' War and before abolitionist discourse coheres. That popular novel reflects the contradiction that complexion is ephemeral and arbitrary, on the one hand, or on the other, that complexion explicitly reveals inherent properties as the nation continues to define the parameters of the racial and gendered complexion of British identity vis-à-vis its colonial others. The novel recounts the eponymous sentimental hero's gaining a fortune through his marriage to a Jamaican plantation owner, his strategies for improving the institution of slavery, and his return as a widower to England where he remarries and develops elaborate reformative programs for abused women, the poor, prisoners, and the disabled.

Sarah Robinson Scott, sister of Elizabeth Robinson Montagu, was born in 1720 into wealth, privilege, and education. Scott engaged in philanthropic endeavors with her dear friend Lady Barbara Montagu ("Babs") to assuage the conditions of the less fortunate. On a visit to Bath in 1765 Scott met Laurence Sterne who would have shared and supported her sympathies for slaves.[23] In fact, when writing to her sister, Scott equivocates: "I am not Politician enough to fancy I can form any proper judgement on the subject of their [West Indians'] grievances, so I hear all sides in silence & am not at all the wiser for what either say, tho' I have friends who are very warm on each, but their warmth is not likely to make them the more instructive."[24] The novel encourages the kind treatment and education of slaves, but one can claim that the novel is abolitionist only by understating the hero's economic collusion and ignoring the way that his charitable impulses rely upon the spoils of slavery for funding.[25]

Scott's manuscript letters to her sister show that the character of Sir George Ellison, a sympathetically portrayed merchant of "sugars and spices" who also appears in her earlier feminotopic novel, *A Description of Millenium Hall* (1762), resonated in her mind with her philanthropic sister Elizabeth Montagu. In a passage previously unnoticed, Scott draws parallels between the West Indian slaves that the fictional Ellison owned, and the restless coalminers ("black subjects") who worked in the pits controlled by the Montagus. "Having on some occasions a sort of enthusiastic warmth in my nature," Scott writes, "I can fancy that I see you among the Colliers what I made Sir George Ellison among his Blacks; your Subjects are little inferior either in untowardness or gloominess of complexion."[26] Scott continued, "However, I am persuaded you will find less ingratitude among colliers than among their superiors, it is the refinements of life that give the pride and petulance which are the great sources of ingratitude, we see little of it in untaught nature; savages are won by the smallest benefits, they give their very souls in return; unaccustomed to refine away obliga- tions, and too humble to be pained by the weight of a favor, they love their benefactor in proportion as they feel the benefit; the sensations of pleasure and affection rise together."[27] Scott asserts that colliers resemble slaves in feeling natural gratitude toward their superiors, and that the blacks' dif- ference of complexion, the mark of their savage state, is analogous to the colliers' "untaught nature."

In her response to Scott, Elizabeth Montagu judges colliers, "barbarous & savage people,"[28] to be as unruly and difficult to manage as slaves, yet she attempts to tame them through studied beneficence. She agrees that the coalworkers' lack of insolence makes their feelings akin to the naive affection of noble savages. Racial discourse is evacuated of its assumptions of inferiority when its objects are regarded as sweetly simple rather than bestial. Still, in controlling the coalmines she inherits, Montagu finds the pitmen of Northumberland impossible to "civilize" and quells their mutiny when she suspects them of fraud. Even as she is empowered to a position of authority rarely achieved by an eighteenth-century woman, she believes that her economic privilege provides that authority; but she, like Ellison, also believes that managing a coalmine enslaves *her* into becoming a "negro slave."[29] Though Montagu elsewhere expresses her wish to abolish the slave trade, she also exemplifies the way that eighteenth-century racial dis- course serves, as Michel Foucault has demonstrated in another context, as a " 'defense' of the nobility against encroachments on its privilege and sources of wealth."[30] In the economy of philanthropy operating here, the smallest amount of payment is proffered for the most substantial return in labor. Scott too justifies Montagu's less than admirable views. For Scott, her sister and Ellison are interchangeable privileged philanthropists who apparently deserve to determine the fate of those who labor in their behalf.

Interested in the family's investment in Northumberland coalmines as early as the 1760s, Montagu became the principal manager after her hus- band's death in May 1775. On occasion she gave the colliers, her "black friends" as she labels them, a feast as a perquisite of their employment in the mines:

I used to give my colliery people a feast when I came hither, but as the good souls (men and women) are very apt to get drunk, and, when drunk, very joyful, and sing, and dance, and hollow, and whoop, I dare not, *on this occasion*, trust their discretion to behave with proper gravity; so I content myself with killing a fat beast once a week, and sending to each family, once, a piece of meat. It will take time to get round to all my black friends. I had fifty-nine boys and girls to sup in the courtyard last night on rice pudding and boil'd beef; to-morrow night I shall have as many. It is very pleasant to see how the poor things cram themselves, and the expense is not great. We buy rice cheap, and skimmed milk and coarse beef serve the occasion. Some have more children than their labor will cloathe, and on such I shall bestow some apparel. Some benefits of this sort, and a general kind behaviour gives to the coal-owner, as well as to them, a good deal of advantage. Our pit-men are afraid of being turned off, and that fear keeps an order and regularity amongst them that is very uncommon.[31]

The parallel to Ellison's treatment of his slaves is remarkable, and "blackness" is figured here as a sign of labor and social rank independent of actual skin color.

In the midst of news of the horror wrought by the French Revolution, Elizabeth Montagu celebrates in May 1792 what her sister Sarah Scott calls a "sable Gala," an occasion when Montagu invited the London chimney sweeps to dine in her garden each May Day. The mode for discussing their "blackness" is clearly that of a benevolent superior providing entertainment for lesser beings, though the exact nature of that inferiority is not exactly conveyed: "In the hearts of your black Guests too [the gala night] wou'd reign unmixed with ennui, or envy, or any of the malevolent & baleful passions, a happiness perhaps seldom to be found in so large a company of superior orders. One shares too in that festival the pleasure the young ones of sable receive from the sight the more for thinking it a lesson of benevolence for their hearts which may have lasting good effects, after the sport is over."[32] As patron of the sweeps who share the colliers' savage nature, Montagu annually diverted them from the tedium of their task in this "fête chrétienne." Montagu's racialized language in which the sweeps are untaught savages, their coal-dusted skin earning them the appellation "blacks," is applied to the laboring classes in order to justify profit-taking, and it also elides the difference between chattel slavery and paid labor. Both Ellison and Montagu use them to display their virtue. Social rank becomes the obfuscating mask to maintain difference and to assume an inferiority specified as "blackness" and "savagery," but within humanity. The "blackness" of slaves, chimney sweeps, and coalminers makes them identical, and class serves to supplement race.

"Race" and "complexion," like race and slavery, of course were not synonymous. According to the first edition of Johnson's *Dictionary* (1755), race simply connotes lineage: "a family ascending," "a family descending," "a generation," or "a particular breed."[33] After Ellison marries a wealthy widow in Jamaica who possesses "a considerable plantation, cultivated by a numerous race of slaves,"[34] the sentimental manliness of Scott's hero contrasts to the first Mrs. Ellison, whose racist attitudes are linked to a skewed femininity. Sir George strongly contests her views even as he displays various traditionally defined feminine characteristics. By depicting this unhappy first marriage Scott strongly resists the idea that women are inherently more sentimental than men or kinder to slaves; in fact, the opposite would seem to pertain when applied to an Englishman abroad and a Jamaican-born woman. Mrs. Ellison exemplifies the special inhumanity of a plantation owner's wife who is capable of perhaps greater cruelty than her husband. Thus Ellison's economic motives seem less vicious, and Englishwomen at home, such as the second Mrs. Ellison, appear in their domestic context to be appropriately sentimental without the gross sensuality of nativeborn women or the cruelty of Englishwomen abroad whose moral principles, like their complexions, have baked in the tropical sun.[35]

George's masculinity also is at issue because he dares to engage in amelioration, though his brand of sentimentality seems thoroughly admirable in Scott's eyes. Sir George and the first Mrs. Ellison debate as to whether slaves are fellow creatures and worthy of the same excessive sentiment that the wife lavishes on her lapdog. The controversy occasions Mrs. Ellison's insulting her husband for possessing "less spirit than a sucking babe" and for "tamely forgiving" the slaves. In a sense too, Sir George's first marriage demonstrates the dangers of intermarriage. It is not too much of a stretch to say that in marrying a (white) Jamaican woman rather than a native Englishwoman, Ellison treats his stint in Jamaica as the rite of passage that truly meritorious Englishmen must endure before they can earn their racial and class privilege. Eighteenth-century Jamaica represents a site of persistent violence and turbulence, curiously embodied here in a woman who exemplifies the worst aspects of the islands. Mrs. Ellison is the antithesis of the proper English lady: manly, emotionally controlling, weepy, a bad mother, and a racist. In contrast to her, Sir George opines that the subordination of slaves "makes me hate the country" (15), and he determines to educate the progeny of their marriage in England against his wife's wishes: "as she has conceived a dislike to England, which even her son's being there could not conquer" (29). Their nasty Jamaican-born child is a parody of imperial arrogance in acting as lord over the world, "a little fury, bursting with pride, passion, insolence, and obstinacy" (29). When Ellison wants to transport his son to England to improve his temperament, Mrs. Ellison abruptly and conveniently dies of a tropical fever just as the novel shifts its venue from periphery to metropole.

Upon his return to British soil, Ellison at first sublimates his desire for the idealized and delicate Miss Allin whose complexion is "extremely fine, clear as alabaster, and heightened with a gentle blooming red in her cheeks" (54), which contrasts with the brash yet saccharine temperament of the first Mrs. Ellison whose English complexion was irreparably spoiled by the Jamaican sun.[36] Once his son's naturally violent temper is tempered by an English education, Ellison grants him "a proper sum of ready money to purchase new slaves" (138) without acknowledging any contradiction between his attitudes toward complexion and slavery.

George Ellison's sympathetic disposition toward the slaves, like Montagu's toward the colliers, stresses that "blackness" should not be the basis for cruelty, though Ellison unselfconsciously defends his profit motive as a slavemaster. Ellison's sentimental attempts to alleviate his slaves' misery reverberate with the language of antislavery arguments. Yet the "difference of complexion" seems crucial to sorting out the conflicting attitudes that Ellison reveals, and in three specific passages worthy of close attention "complexion" figures centrally:

The thing which had chiefly hurt him during his abode in Jamaica, was the cruelty exercised on one part of mankind; as if the difference of complexion excluded them from the human race, or indeed as if their not being human could be an excuse for making them wretched. (10)

Mr. Ellison's house contained also many children of inferior rank; his servants had intermarried, the blacks with blacks, the white servants with those of their own color; for though he promoted their marrying, he did not wish an union between those of different complexions, the connection appearing indelicate and almost unnatural. (139)

"Indeed, my dear ... I must call them so [fellow creatures], till you can prove to me, that the distinguishing marks of humanity lie in the complexion or turn of features. When you and I are laid in the grave, our lowest black slave will be as great as we are; in the next world perhaps much greater; the present difference is merely adventitious, not natural. But we will not at present pursue this subject." (13)

The nuances in these passages reveal connections between gender and race in the first instance, and between the animal world and race in the others. These three examples incorporate the incongruity between – to use modern terminology – a conceptual grammar of antiracism and a racist essentialism. There is something of a gap, for example, between Ellison's stand against sexual intermixture as unnatural and his argument that "the present difference [of complexion] is merely adventitious, not natural." In particular in the first passage Ellison objects to a difference in complexion as the justification for cruelty, and yet complexion is the racial marker that determines the right to inclusion or exclusion from the human race. Ellison entertains both the possibility that a dark complexion indicates the limits of the human, and that it does not. In the first quotation affinities are to be honored among different complexions because of a common humanity, while in the second passage differences supersede affinities when intermarriage within England is threatened as indecorous and "unnatural." Finally, in the third passage the question of the significance of blood affinities and variations in pigmentation are deferred until the afterlife when moral barometers determine that black is sometimes superior to white.

Ellison's years in Jamaica, while harmful to his health, allow him to formulate a benevolent and gentle (white) masculinity in contrast to his first wife's unfeminine Jamaican meanness, on the one hand, and to a rebellious but restrainable slave population on the other. The scenes in England interweave with the scenes in the West Indies to define a manly national character, the gentlemanly version of "the British fair." Ellison's identity, carefully honed in Jamaica, contrasts to other masculinities in the characters Mr. Grantham, the industrious farmer; Mr. Allin, an extravagant wastrel; Mr. Blackburn, a learned but aged meritorious gentleman; young Blackburn, an insolent lover; and Lamont, Ellison's fellow traveller to Millenium Hall who thinks of women as "a race somewhat superior to monkeys; formed to amuse the other sex" (40). The greatest contrast, however, is to George's first cousin, Sir William Ellison of Dorsetshire, whom he lectures on kindness to laborers, on self-love, and social feeling. Sir William, a representative of old money and outdated values, opposes George's newer commercial philosophy and implicitly, his upstart brand of Englishness.

Sir William, a self-professed misogynist and eccentric, originally employed only male chambermaids, but when they broke his precious china, he succumbed to allowing women servants into his home: "And in every article his neatness and elegance exceeded even female delicacy; though had any thing feminine been brought into a parallel with him, the disgust he would have conceived might have converted him into a sloven" (45). His extreme fussiness places him among those male imitators of women, "dissipated, puerile, vain, and effeminate" (42) that, Ellison warns, trouble the nation. Mr. Ellison's peculiar brand of feminized – but not effeminate – masculinity is evidently superior. In a memorable display of Scott's keen satire, the narrator describes his purchase of a house whose "gardens were overrun with the rankest weeds; and as for the house, spiders had supplied the place of other inhabitants, and like good housewives, had hung every room with webs of their own weaving" (45). The spiders bear a telling resemblance to the first Mrs. Ellison in their capacity to weave tenacious silken threads of enslavement for their victims. The spiders must be eradicated, in spite of their being "so numerous a race, who had the rights of long posses- sion to plead. Incredible was the slaughter; thousands and ten thousands fell by the potent hand of a stout char-woman." In this case the spiders are the "race" (reminiscent of the class of Jamaican slave owners represented by the first Mrs. Ellison) that the charwoman wipes out. Ellison imports three married Negro couples, former slaves, to staff the new home. The comedy veils its heretical vision of insurrection. But Scott's idea of revolution does not seem to encompass the abolition of slavery or even an assumption of real equality since the blacks, having been released from slavery, are still in servitude; and Ellison's house, like his commercial Jamaican properties, is sustained through distanced but diligent black labor, dependent in spite of his benevolent protestations on an economy that values a difference of complexion.

Scott manages to create in Ellison an appealing man who maneuvers be- tween a nationally hybrid woman and a purer Englishwoman to establish his economic and social power through sentiment rather than violence or rapacity. She evidences cultural anxieties about race even as she renegotiates the social valances of complexion's palette, if not its economic investments. In *Sir George Ellison* Scott speculates about the extent to which sentimental men imbued with highly valued feminine qualities may be aligned with a set of increasingly institutionalized power relations that constitute "whiteness" and allow them, in spite of being men, to resemble "the British fair." The New World enables Ellison's exploration of this alternative version of manliness while still protecting his vested interests, and he returns to England to solidify and more fully articulate his newfound amalgama- tion and an original sort of manly character more appropriate to England than its colonies.[37]

IV

No single analytic of race, gender, or class is sufficient to explain these mutually constitutive categories in *Sir George Ellison*. Rather "complexion" in this period serves to isolate and exclude the human from the subhuman, the beautiful from the ugly, and the metropole from the periphery, as the concept of difference fluctuates between being perceived as an indelible indicator of intrinsic character or something more random and superficial. Complexion is the corporeal surface upon which these conjoined categories are negotiated, but not simply as racialized skin on which gender is im- posed, a sexualized bodily feature on which race is played out, or a class indicator which erases race and gender. Crucial to formulating a national aesthetic, coloring in its myriad and unpredictable manifestations is also a physical mark of the national character that makes whiteness emerge as part of Britain's imperial identity. Complexion calibrated from a standard of whiteness, then, becomes the exterior sign of interior merit as well as aesthetic value: it increasingly becomes a legible measure of beauty or ugliness, national character, health, social rank, economic and moral worth, even though its terms may, sometimes be puzzlingly reversed.

When abroad the British fair, like the first Mrs. Ellison, often take on the least desirable traits of the torrid environment. Some Englishmen recast color as a racial conundrum portraying white women's complexions as dull and lacking in luster in order to justify their turning to darker-skinned mistresses.[38] Aphra Behn, Eliza Haywood, Sarah Scott, and Elizabeth Montagu, like the abolitionist women who succeed them in the later eighteenth and early nineteenth centuries when pigmentation and other bodily features become the intractable differences that carry cultural meanings, variously negotiate the investments in the language of race. These features evolve into *the* difference of complexion that exemplifies the "race" of national character on which the political systems that undergird inequalities are based.

In short, as complexion's valence changes through time and migrates from place to place, what remains consistent is that the "British fair" possess the most highly valued difference of complexion. The brilliant Jamaican man, the green parrot, and the first Mrs. Ellison possess *the* difference of complexion which excludes them from being truly English. White women writing about race in the Enlightenment reveal that complexion and its indicators, essential and ephemeral, required critical negotiations of racial meanings, especially as they intersected with femininity. In the nineteenth century scientific racism elided differences into an increasingly rigidified division between black and white, but in the eighteenth century the relationships between costume and geography, pigmentation and the faculties of the mind, bodily features and character, and social privilege and "blood" remained inconsistent and uncertain, deemed to be both performative and foundational.

CHAPTER 6

Black women: why Imoinda turns white

The King of *Coramantien* had many beautiful *Black*-Wives; for most
certainly, there are Beauties that can charm of that Colour.

Aphra Behn, *Oroonoko*

I

An elusiveness about complexion is characteristic of the most compelling
representations of race in eighteenth-century literature including characters
such as Robinson Crusoe's Friday, Imoinda who first appears in Aphra
Behn's *Oroonoko*, and Yarico in love with the English seacaptain, Inkle.[1]
These popular characters deriving from various geographical origins are
most often women, recalling Alexander Pope's line from *Epistle to A Lady*
that women embodied "Matter too soft a lasting mark to bear."[2] "Blackness"
in the eighteenth century was of course used to characterize persons from the
Indies, the Americas, Africa, or the South Pacific; it was also applied to the
Irish as a mark of their Celtish origins, and more generally to the laboring
classes, especially coalminers and chimney sweeps. Yet it was not clear how
fundamental dark coloring might be. Aphra Behn's Imoinda in *Oroonoko*
(1688), for example, turns from black African to blanched European in
the story's dramatic versions by Thomas Southerne and other eighteenth-
century dramatists. Like her lover Oroonoko, Imoinda, "the beautiful black
Venus to our young Mars; as charming in her person as he, and of delicate
virtues," is possessed of Roman features rather incidentally located on an
ebony-colored body;[3] but in Southerne's tragedy *Oroonoko* (1695) based on
the novel and performed throughout the eighteenth century, Imoinda is
white, the daughter of a white European who visits Oroonoko's adoptive
father.

In some cases we can assign the racial muddles to historical accident and
in others to woefully inadequate geographical knowledge. For example,
contemporaries attacked Southerne for failing to portray Imoinda with

"an *Indian* Air, / . . . and Indian Hue"[4] (probably in the sense of her deriving from the East or West Indies) in an epilogue attributed to Congreve in the 1711 edition of *Oroonoko*:

> If they're of English growth, they'll bear't with patience:
> But save us from a Spouse of *Oroonokos* Nations!
> Then bless your Stars, you happy *London* wives,
> Who love at large, each day, yet keep your lives:
> Nor envy poor *Imoindas* doating blindness,
> Who thought her husband kill'd her out of kindness.
> Poor-Soul! She wanted some of our Town-breeding.
> Forgive this *Indians* fondness for her Spouse;
> Their Law no Christian liberty allows:[5]

The casual synthesis of Imoinda's being Indian, African, and white is completely typical of the period's discourses of racial thinking.

In another familiar tale involving racial transmutation, Yarico, victimized by the Englishman Inkle, appears as African in the multiple renderings of the story throughout the century. The Yarico of Richard Ligon's *True and Exact History of the Island of Barbados* (1657) is "of excellent shape and colour, for it was a pure bright bay," a naked reddish-brown shade usually applied to horses, while the reference drops out of Steele's version in *The Spectator* in which a finely clothed Indian Yarico whom Inkle sells to a Barbarian Merchant is charmed by his European complexion.[6] In *Yarico to Inkle An Epistle*, the heroine does not mention her color, but her naked beauty and subsequent sexual liaison with Inkle transform her lover's pale complexion into "native Bloom." Within the poetic lines of the Countess of Hereford's *The Story of Inkle and Yarrico* (1738), the Negro Yarico's attractive classical figure, only incidentally black, enraptures Inkle:[7]

> A *Negro* Virgin chanc'd to pass that way;
> He view'd her naked beauties with surprise,
> Her well proportion'd limbs and sprightly eyes!
> With his complexion and gay dress amaz'd,
> The artless Nymph upon the Stranger gaz'd.[8]

Yarico turns seamlessly from an Indian maiden to a Negro. Her designation as Negro signals her blackness rather than indicating any particular racial type and distinguishes her from the cannibals who eat Inkle's shipmates on the barbarous coast. The reprobate Inkle, falling into melancholy because he is not satisfied with the fortune he has gained through maritime adventures, prefers "*A thousand doating maids at home*" and abandons his "doating

Virgin" Yarico. Later in George Colman's play (1787) Yarico, "a good comely copper" but "quite dark" and "Black," portrays a shifting blend of Indian and Negro while her maid is clearly black and African.

An equally pliable heroine is the Sable Venus who appears in a print modeled after Botticelli's Venus in Bryan Edward's *The History of the British Colonies in the West Indies* (1794) (illustration 8) along with Isaac Teale's accompanying salacious ode. The lovely Aphrodite (known for her Asiatic origins in Greek and Roman mythology) rises in a vulvar oyster shell, a black pearl surfacing from the foam of the sea. The nearly naked goddess drives the reins for cherubs and sea creatures including the manfish Triton (a product of the union between Neptune and Salacia) whose blowing the shell trumpet announces the Sable Venus and embodies the anomalous offspring of a miscegenetic union. A bearded, crowned, and British flag-bearing Neptune gazes longingly at the black Venus as Cupid's arrow seems aimed at him while a whale spouts phallicly in the distance.[9] The barebreasted muscular black woman with cropped curly hair is guided by winged fish who carry her from Angola to the West Indies on an open-shell chariot in sharp contrast to the historical fact that such a voyage was most frequently taken in the bowels of a slave ship.

The poem is a variant on the Inkle and Yarico story in which the offspring resulting from the interracial union between the sable Venus and Neptune, disguised as a (white) seacaptain, is revered rather than sold, murdered, or orphaned: "Blest offspring of the warm embrace! / Fond ruler of the crisped race!"[10] While the Sable Venus does not actually change skin color within the poem, the naked African woman is understood to be quintessentially white but dyed black in a reversal of the familiar biblical trope of washing an Ethiop white. The goddess of love, "a beauty clad in sable dye," is at core a classical white goddess who playfully switches color and adopts a dark complexion merely to tease and test her lover:

> Then, playful Goddess! Cease to change,
> Nor in new beauties vainly range;
> Tho' whatsoe'er thy view,
> Try ev'ry form thou canst put on,
> I'll follow thee thro' ev'ry one;
> So staunch am I, so true.

Her black skin is an elaborate joke. Like the utopian narrative by Henry Neville, *The Isle of Pines*, in which all cats are famously grey in the dark, black and white women in the poem *The Sable Venus* are equally desired and desirous at night:

8 W. Grainger after Thomas Stothard, "The Voyage of the Sable Venus from Angola to
the West Indies," from Bryan Edwards, *The History, Civil and Commercial, of the
British Colonies in the West Indies: In Two Volumes* (1794). The Latin inscription to
Isaac Teale's accompanying poem reads in translation, "The white privet blossom is
left to fall, black whortle beries are picked."

The loveliest limbs her form compose,
Such as her sister VENUS chose,
In FLORENCE, where she's seen;
Both just alike, except the white,
No difference, no – none at night,
The beauteous dames between.[11]

The narrator's wanton sowing of European seed upon African slave women is perversely justified as his loyalty to the white goddess of love whose black skin is merely a disguise.

Joanna, the idealized mulatta mistress of John Gabriel Stedman in his *Narrative of a Five Years Expedition against the Revolted Negroes of Surinam* (1796), also does not literally change color but is variously described as black or olive. Stedman's "Surinam wife" (treated as married in her home territory but not legally recognized as such in England) is "Goddess like, modest, and sweet, her eyes reflecting an innate goodness . . . with Cheeks through which glow'd in spite of her olive Complexion, a beautiful tinge of vermillion when gazed upon – her nose was perfectly well formed rather small, her lips a little prominent which when she spoke discovered two regular rows of pearls as white as Mountain Snow – her hair was a dark brown – next to black, forming a beauteous Globe of small ringlets."[12] Joanna resembles earlier representations of women of color in being an amalgamation of the Indian and Negro maidens who cross in the representations of Imoinda and Yarico. Her status as slave, Surinam wife, or rejected lover depends on Stedman's whim.

In his narrative Stedman is at pains to provide dizzying distinctions operative in the greater Caribbean among quadroon (white and mulatto), mulatto (white and black), samboe (black and mulatto) and mestizo (white and quadroon). "Indians Mulatto's Negroes &c" (lvii), a frequent mantra in Stedman's narrative, are lumped together as servants or slaves and sexual partners, marriageable only in Surinam terms, as opposed to European matrons (xxxiii). These categories rankle against Stedman's attested utopian wish for universal harmony since "we all only differ in colour, but we are certainly created by the same hand and after the same mold" (316). Riveted by the sight of a young samboe woman and a quadroon he writes "that where the whole shapes are exposed to view, the features attract the smallest attention, while it is equally as true that the human figure of either sex, whether white, black, copper-colored, or olive, when naked particularly among the green or verdure, exhibits a very beautiful creature, to which the most splendid apparel cannot give any additional elegance" (248). He desires all women of these colors, all of whom blend in with the natural landscape as if they were camouflaged animals, even as he seeks to classify them.

Indigenous women, as Jennifer Morgan has pointed out, "bore an enormous symbolic burden as writers from Walter Raleigh to Edward Long employed them to mark metaphorically the symbiotic boundaries of European national identities and white supremacy";[13] and the fictions of Imoinda, Yarico, the Sable Venus, and Joanna underscore their power as catalysts for forming a white and English femininity in contrast to them. Each of these women is represented as a beautiful primitive, an oxymoron dissimilar from Hume's Jamaican man, a compelling and marvelous spectacle in spite of her complexion. The arbitrary and impermanent color of these women does not penetrate to their essence and can easily transmutate because it is merely superficial. Beautiful but sexually compromised and linked to more savage beings and to other species, each copper, black, or saffron figure reconciles incommensurable ideas; these women of varying complexions underplay difference within the categories of women of color in order to establish it more forcefully between white women and all women of color.[14]

Women of color in eighteenth-century England are seldom represented as possessing personhood or subjectivity, and a seemingly insurmountable difficulty in analyzing women and race in eighteenth-century England is the scant testimony from the women themselves. The only extant writing by black women writers comes from those who lived principally in America – Belinda's short "Petition of an African Slave, to the Legislature of Massachusetts" (1782) and the collected poems of Phillis Wheatley[15] – and the earliest full slave narrative written by a woman is *The History of Mary Prince, A West Indian Slave* (1831). Of critical importance in addressing issues of women and race in the period raised by this gap is to intuit, interrogate, and theorize this silence,[16] and here I begin by considering the cultural significance of Imoinda's transformation from black to white. As I have argued, in this historical period biological markers are not yet firmly fixed to nation or physiognomy, and the easy slippage from one color to another, from one place of origin to another, testifies on the one hand to an Enlightenment wish paradoxically to claim the inherent "whiteness" of all humankind and the inadequacy of pigmentation and physiognomic traits in revealing character; and on the other, the wish to formulate a philosophical basis for a racial thinking that could justify interracial libertinism, the slave trade, and an empire. The fictive women are simultaneously figured as being of indeterminate and incidental racial origin. Potential producers of hybrid children, they embody the fascination and fear of an imagined miscegenation without requiring the nation to grapple fully with its consequences and perhaps find ways to elude the encroaching reality. These slippery tales reflect and perpetrate profound cultural quandaries about color, complexion, national origin, and their relationship to gendered virtue.

II

Why then when her story migrates from fiction to theatre does the enslaved Imoinda turn white while her husband remains black throughout the eighteenth century? When Southerne revised Aphra Behn's novella *Oroonoko* just seven years later into the drama *Oroonoko; A Tragedy, in Five Acts* the black African heroine Imoinda is implausibly transformed into the daughter of the white warrior who commands Oroonoko's father's armies. The play also adds a comic and misogynist subplot. In Southerne's version an heroic stranger to Angola, the first white person whom Oroonoko had encountered, serves his father in war but dies from a poisoned dart intended for the young African prince. Oroonoko offers slaves as the spoils of war to Imoinda to atone for her father's death, and presents himself as a sacrifice before the woman whom he comes to regard as a white maiden goddess:

> But, when I saw her face,
> And heard her speak, I offer'd up myself
> To be the sacrifice. She bow'd and blush'd;
> I wonder'd and ador'd. The sacred pow'r,
> That hath subdu'd me, then inspir'd my tongue,
> Inclin'd her heart, and all our talk was love.
>
> (II.iii)

Southerne's decision to make Imoinda white and red, a fair woman capable of blushing and of having those blushes perceived on her white skin, is repeated in numerous versions produced on stage throughout the century including those by John Hawkesworth (1759), Francis Gentleman (1760), an anonymous playwright, and an adaptation by Dr. John Ferriar entitled *The Prince of Angola* (1788). Oroonoko, like his miscegenetic predecessor in *Othello*, was enormously attractive to eighteenth-century audiences. The tragedy, the second most frequently produced drama in the eighteenth-century theatre appearing each season from 1696 to 1801, becomes the locus of issues surrounding femininity, monstrosity, and miscegenation: "No play, with the exception of *Jane Shore*, seems to have been more popular in the eighteenth century."[17] This change has much to do with positing a white European femininity in opposition to the developing stereotypes of black womanhood such as Jezebel, Jemima, the mammy, and the tragic mulatta.[18]

Both black and white men wish to possess Southerne's white Imoinda (just as Yarico, the Sable Venus, and Joanna are the object of desire), and in various versions of the play she resists rape attempts by the African king and the Lieutenant Governor. Imoinda, at once a threat to white man and to white women, represents at least as ominous a figure as Oroonoko.

Since the color of complexion was an index to virtue by the eighteenth century, I am arguing, a black Imoinda could not easily represent a decorous and heroic femininity on stage. Another very important reason for Imoinda's color transformation is the material fact that no black woman had yet appeared on the eighteenth-century stage. A blackface white woman in a central serious dramatic role would have violated femininity in a way that another more familiar stage convention of disguise, crossdressing, did not.[19] In spite of Othello's prominence as a popular role, in early dramatic literature few female characters of color appear in a principal part, except perhaps Cleopatra whose supposedly dark complexion would explain her sensuality[20] (though the Egyptian queen was also portrayed as Greek). In *The Masque of Blacknesse* (1605) written at Anne of Denmark's request, which she performed with her aristocratic ladies at court, the white women paint themselves black to represent Father Niger's black daughters (nymphs from Niger) though they return to pearl-like whiteness in the sequel, *The Masque of Beauty* (1608). These waiting women contrasted with their sexually suspect white mistresses in much the same way that eighteenth-century ladies appeared more attractive and powerful in contrast to the black servant boys who were painted alongside them. Thus *The Masque of Blacknesse* offers the first known example of blackface pageantry in an English masque, as Kim Hall points out.[21] It is especially important to note that this inaugural staging of their faces as dark is located not just on women, but on the face and bodies of women actors, for the associations between a blackened femininity and acting persist into the Restoration. But the more common dramatic practice would have been that dark women characters such as those in Marston's *The Wonder of Women or the Tragedie of Sophonisba* (1606), Webster's *The White Devil* (1611–12), or Beaumont and Fletcher's *The Knight of Malta* (1616–18), performing on the public stage instead of at the court, were played by blackface boys.

Among the infrequent depictions of black women on the Restoration stage is John Crowne's masque *Calisto: or, The Chaste Nimph* (1675) in which four nymphs impersonate four corners of the world, including Europe, Africa, the East, and the Americas; and the dramatis personae distinctly lists "Two African Women or Blacks," played by English actresses Mrs. Butler and Mrs. Hunt.[22] The black women characters, complaining of having lost their white and red skin (surely an allusion to the actual whiteness of the actresses in blackface) after being exposed to the sun, wander the world in search of their lost beauty, and they may have appeared in blackface. In the play beauty is ultimately located in Diana's nymph Calisto, and her friend Nymphe whose color, class, and chastity contrast vividly to the group of Africans who carry their canopy. The African women happily relinquish their claims of beauty to the two nymphs represented by the daughters of James II, since their loss serves the cause of (white aristocratic) love. The play reinforces the idea that black women, possessing none of the attributes of ideal femininity, envy white women.

Blackness for these few early women actors on stage is performative and accidental rather than fundamental. Numbered among the scarce eighteenth-century darkish female characters in the early eighteenth century is also Zara, wife of the Moorish king in Congreve's *The Mourning Bride*, and a white actress who temporarily impersonates the Moor Jacinta, disguised in a veil rather than blackface in Pix's *Conquest of Spain* (1705). Typical of these plays is the Indian slave Zelaide in Pix's *The False Friend* (1699) who, though she attracts labels of blackness, appears white on stage; and Indian queens, signaled by feathers and animal skins rather than blackface, appear in several Restoration plays. Alterity in these instances was most probably conveyed through language and costume rather than paint until much later in the century when Yarico appears as a dark woman of various geographical origins, along with her black servant Wowski, in George Colman's version of the story.[23] Minor black characters on stage such as Cubba in William Macready, *The Irishman in London* (1797), a soft-spoken servant devoted to her mistress, acted more as liaisons between white women and white men than as sexual objects themselves.[24] Obviously disguised, their *features* remained European in spite of their painted skin, while later representations of black women such as the Sable Venus possess physiognomic features that are more characteristically African.[25] The competing images of Indian queens or Turkish sultanas, in demand on the Restoration stage, fade from eighteenth-century drama as the image of the black woman consistently sinks into the lower class and takes on a sensualized valence while the status of the problematic white woman, publicly and problematically displayed by actresses, dominates the stage.[26]

While it is certainly true that neither white women nor women of color appeared in the legitimate theatre before the Restoration, Englishwomen had participated in court entertainments, in public theatricality, in popular festival rituals, and in guild performances throughout the seventeenth century. Scholars are re-evaluating the abrupt closing of the theatres by the Puritans from 1642 to 1660 to include this history so that the initial appearance of a white woman on the English stage may be understood not so much as a startling break from the past but, as James Stokes writes, "the natural culmination of a cultural process that has been mostly obscured by the fierce battles between Puritans and others over the legitimacy of theatre itself."[27] Women had played female roles in France, Spain, and Italy as much as a century earlier than in England. While Catherine Coleman had acted as the veiled Ianthe in Davenant's *Siege of Rhodes* (1656), it is worthy of note that the first woman on the British stage after the theatres reopened very likely acted in the role of Desdemona in *The Moor of Venice* in 1660, a curious fact that is surely more than mere happenstance.[28] Margaret Hughes took the part with Thomas Killigrew's King's Company in *The Moor of Venice*, "a play which stood to gain a good deal in sexual sugges-tion from the presence of a female Desdemona,"[29] though it is possible that Hughes was only one among several actresses who early acted the role.

Another significant reason for Southerne's turning Imoinda white is to allege her similarity to white women in the public domain, especially ac-tresses and women writers like Behn, while her empowerment also evokes thoughts of similarly transforming African lands, commodities, and slaves into the properties of a white Albion. The Restoration audience see-ing Desdemona, or the early eighteenth-century audience witnessing a whitened Imoinda, would associate both heroines with the tropes that surround blackness without specific racialization. Desdemona conveys a universal (and thus European) femininity in her foolish passion to hear Othello's "round unvarnish'd" magical tales, just as Imoinda does when Oroonoko woos her. When Englishwomen first appear on stage, their sexual difference is all the more pronounced because their femininity is identified with *whiteness* in stark contrast to the principal man on stage, a white man in blackface. Yet being a woman on stage, even a white woman on stage, bears a tincture of contamination, a smudge of blackness. Because of the prejudice against actresses and the association with prostitutes, even the purest of white women may seem slightly tainted once she appears on the stage.

In Thomas Jordan's popular "A Prologue to introduce the first Woman that came to act on the Stage in the Tragedy, called The Moor of Venice" in *A Royal Arbour of Loyal Poesie* (1664) as well as the epilogue to *Othello*, we find clues to the connection between Desdemona – representing chaste but desiring white womanhood, murdered by black masculinity and victimized by white manhood in the person of Iago – and the first actress. An intruder who she dares to tread into the public domain, the Restoration actress is charged with sexual looseness just as Desdemona is unjustly accused of infidelity. In Jordan's risqué poem, "private" rhymes with the sexual innuendo of "drive at," and "Whore" rhymes with "Moor":

> 'Tis possible a vertuous woman may
> Abhor all sorts of looseness and yet play;
> Play on the Stage, where all eyes are upon her,
> Shall we count that a crime *France* calls an honour...
>
> And how d'ye like her, come what is 't ye drive at,
> She's the same thing in publick as in private;
> As far from being what you call a Whore,
> As *Desdemona* injur'd by the Moor?

A white actress on stage clarifies through spectacle that the color of proper femininity is white, while it also alludes to her compromised status as the wife of a Moor.

Aphra Behn's experiment in including a central black female character in the original *Oroonoko* thus seems ever more bold because of its rarity. By depicting multiracial and diverse others, Jacqueline Pearson argues, women playwrights such as Aphra Behn and Mary Pix cleared a public space which eventually abolitionist Englishwomen would fill to "make the antislavery movement possible, while at the same time by their disruption of binary oppositions they also facilitated the rich and multiple feminist discourses of the next century."[30] It seems more likely, however, that while Behn and Pix brought women of color to their fiction and drama, such spaces for opposition were tiny indeed when Behn's black Imoinda turns white almost immediately after mounting the public stage, and when Pix's characters of color on stage were actually white women in veiling or disguise. Establishing natural rights for white women is not the same thing as encouraging the emancipation of black women, and in fact the two activities often arose from contradictory impulses.

The eighteenth-century blanching of Behn's black heroine has received surprisingly little detailed analysis, and it deserves much more careful consideration. In all of the eighteenth-century dramatic versions of Behn's novella by Southerne, Ferriar, Gentleman, and the anonymous author, the unremarked spectacle of Imoinda's indelible whiteness would have contrasted visually to the blacked-up Oroonoko even as her intimacy with an enslaved black prince contaminates her virtuous femininity. Unlike Othello and Desdemona, the highborn black man and virtuous white woman in the eighteenth-century version are enslaved; Imoinda invites her own murder in the name of virtue, and Oroonoko prefers death to slavery. In both Shakespeare's *Othello* and Southerne's *Oroonoko* the heroic black man and the white woman, like their hybrid progeny, are eradicated by the conclusion. The play in its different versions eventually became a propaganda piece staged in the interests of abolition though the antislavery sentiments of the play are equivocal.

The most helpful commentary on these dilemmas has been Joseph Roach's argument that Imoinda's status as a white slave allows a closer comparison between women's oppression in marriage and slavery. Her whitening indicates the "relentless assimilation of African identity into European ideology" and the exile of the couple's "expendable excess" in order to prevent miscegenation. Margaret Ferguson in her study of the novella has shown the way that "a consolidation of Western female selfhood is predicated upon an 'othering' of the black woman"; but if this is the case, we might expect that Southerne's Imoinda would remain black on the stage since white women constituted perhaps half the audience at most, unless one imagines that male readers and audiences would also support that consolidation, or that the novel and play were intended primarily for female audiences.[31] Joyce Green MacDonald argues that eighteenth-century audiences would have tolerated a miscegenated *Oroonoko* more readily than one in which both of the lovers are black. Further she believes that Imoinda's blanching "helps to authorize white women's racial privilege and her chastity assists her silent assent to the operative racial fictions."[32] None of these critics, however, takes account of the importance of *white men's* attitudes toward *black men* as they are worked out through white women. In a significant way the plot is a negotiation between white men and black men over white women rather than about black women per se. I argue here and in subsequent chapters that both white male and white female subjectivities, peculiarly English masculinities and femininities, rest upon establishing black femaleness as distinctly different, and that making Imoinda white keeps black women at yet a further remove.

There are very few accounts of black women traveling from the East or West Indies, Africa or the South Pacific, real or imagined, to eighteenth-century England, and I want to pause to bring their shadowy presence to the light before looking more closely at Imoinda's whiteness. The black woman is deeply implicated in constructions of normative femininity as her spectral nature hovers over the eighteenth-century literature and theatre. In spite of black women's apparent invisibility, dark figures in Renaisance culture, Dympna Callaghan writes, are "the focal points for an extraordinarily dense system of signification,"[33] an observation that might be extended

9 Johann Zoffany, "Dido Elizabeth Belle, later Davinier, and Lady Elizabeth Murray, later Finch Hatton" (*c.* 1780).

to the eighteenth century as well. On stage and in life, black men over-whelmingly outnumbered black women living in England throughout most of the century. Further, the images of blacks in eighteenth-century art are most frequently males, perhaps because of the paucity of female mod-els or because artists were troubled about having such women in their studios.[34] English ladies of privilege posed for portraits, of course, along with black boys instead of pets such as lapdogs, and representing the sexes and races in this way confirms that racial hierarchy superceded patriarchy in this instance. Relationships between black and white women are only rarely figured in portraits. One unusual picture attributed to Zoffany de-picts Dido Elizabeth Belle, later Davinier, with Lady Elizabeth Murray, later Finch Hatton, niece to Lord Mansfield (the same Chief Justice who granted habeas corpus to all blacks in England) in whose home she was granted intermediate status between servant and family (illustration 9). In the portrait Dido, the mixed-race illegitimate daughter of Sir John Lindsay, exotically dressed in satin costume with Indian turban and ostrich feather and carrying tropical fruits, gestures toward her black cheek as if to contrast it to the white woman's face. The more prominent Elizabeth in the foreground is dressed in fashionable clothing, a garland of English flowers in her hair, and carrying an open book, as if she had been interrupted in pursuit of her leisurely reading activities by the smiling Dido.[35] Contrasting the learned with the exotic woman, the portait portrays their mutual affection while emphasizing their difference in status.

Pictures of "mixed" and "pure" black women in eighteenth-century England, supposed signs of the savage, sometimes functioned as satirical figures to expose the lack of civility in the culture that scorned them. A familiar boudoir scene from Restoration and eighteenth-century frontispiece illustrations is that of a woman lying in déshabillé on a heavily draped bed with an audience of men observing or even threatening her.[36] In one such representation Othello approaches his wife with pillow in hand ready to suffocate a partially nude Desdemona. William Hogarth's engraving *The Discovery* (1743) takes up the trope to reverse the power politics and transform the skin colors (illustration 10).[37] In that image the barebreasted black woman, perhaps a known bawd named Harriot whose black whores were in high demand, becomes a joke shared among white men when she is substituted for the white woman they expected to find in the boudoir, and the picture reverses a well-known engraving of the black Othello's discovery of a white Desdemona (illustration 11). The phrase beneath the picture, *Qui Color albus crat, nunc est contrarius albo* ("What was once white is now the opposite") suggests the gentleman's surprise when he discovers the practical joke.[38] Later the discovery scene became the occasion for a series of "black joke" cartoons, the term a derogatory reference to women's genitalia (illustration 12).[39] Among black women who became known in the eighteenth century is Harriot, a Guinean slave taken to England from Jamaica by a wealthy planter by whom she bore two children, became a brothel keeper in King's Place to support herself after her master died. Her alleged liaisons with aristocratic lovers are recounted in a thinly disguised pornographic account, *Les Sérails de Londres* (1801). The titillating narrative claims that her color was not always as engaging as "des belles filles d'Albion," but Harriot "was faithful to her master, full of care for his domestic needs, and exact in her accounts"; further, "she acquired a degree of politeness seldom found among Africans."[40] In the late eighteenth century and the early decades of the nineteenth century, other women such as prostitutes named "Black Moll" and "Sarah," the Barbados innkeeper

10 William Hogarth, "The Discovery" (1743). The engraving invokes a practical joke played on Highmore, manager of Drury Lane, and perhaps comprised a prank encouraged by the "Sublime Society of Beef Steaks."

Rachel Pringle caricatured by Thomas Rowlandson, the slave Grace Jones, William Stedman's "Surinam wife" Joanna, and finally the autobiographer Mary Prince testify to the slowly increasing visibility of black women in Britain and to their continuing eroticization, though for most of the century their small numbers made their appearance an unusual occurrence[41] (illustration 13). An Angolan hermaphrodite specifically combines darkness with monstrosity and aberrant sexuality, and is reduced to her unusual sexual parts in William Cheselden's *Anatomy of the Human Body* (reprinted in *A Treatise on Hermaphrodites*) where a picture of her genitalia is displayed in the name of science, not unlike the later more public exhibition of the Hottentot Venus.

Taking a particularly salacious delight in transculturated black women, a German visitor reports that he has observed numbers of blacks in London:

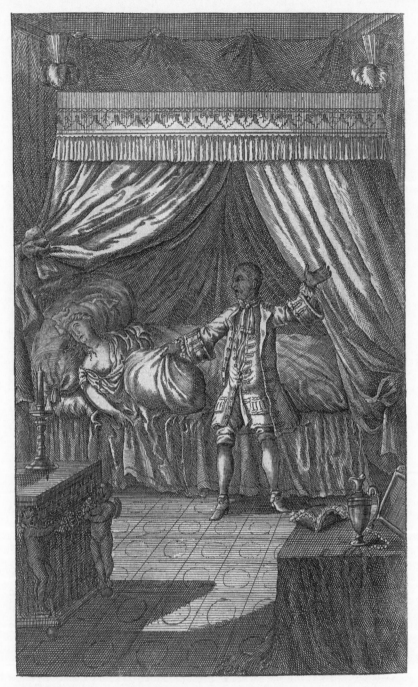

11 Frontispiece to *Othello*, Nicholas Rowe's *Works of Shakespeare* (1709), vol. v.

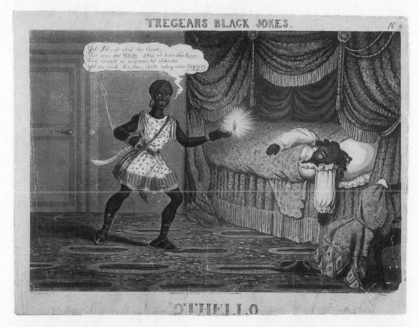

12 "Othello" from *Tregear's Black Jokes*, N: 9, published by G. S. Tregear 123 Cheapside (London W. Summers delt. Hunt sculpt. *c.* 1830s). The cartoon parodies Othello's speech in crude, racist dialect: "Yet I'll shed her blood; / Nor scar dat *Whiter Skin* ob hers dan *Snow*, / And *smoove* as *monumental alabaster*. / Yet she must die, else, she'll betray more *Niggers*."

"There are, in fact, such a quantity of Moors of both sexes in England that I have never seen as many before. Males and females frequently go out begging... The females wear European dress and there is nothing more diverting than to see them in mobs or caps of white stuff and with their black bosoms uncovered."[42] While this report hints that mulattoes abound, most suggest that perhaps as few as twenty per cent of blacks living in Britain were women. Advertisements offering African children for sale are plentiful, but they too principally describe boys. Among the actual black women of whom there is some record, criminal accounts show only three servants and a washerwoman, and there is little additional information concerning black women's occupations.[43]

That there was a scarcity of real black women in England also seems likely because only two black–black unions were recorded in the whole of the eighteenth century, one of which is Ignatius Sancho's marriage to his wife Anne. Even allowing for the fact that marriages between blacks probably

LAND STORES.

13 Thomas Rowlandson, *Land Stores*, Pl. 21 (1812). The posted paper states, "Voluntary Subscription for a Soldiers Widow the smallest donation will be gratefully received by Rachel Ram Part." The caricatured corpulent black woman (probably Rachel Pringle) seems to possess the phallic equipment the emaciated officer lacks.

were not regularly registered in parish records, it seems probable that the most common marriage, one to which the population would have become accustomed, would be that of a black man to a white Englishwoman. This kind of intermarriage would have been the rule until the early nineteenth century, though matters of status certainly skewed the statistics. Ignatius Sancho remained poor, regularly referring to his financial struggles and to himself as "a poor negroe" while Olaudah Equiano achieved wealth in his adopted country, England. Proudly tracing his lineage from the African elite, Equiano earned considerable money from promoting the nine editions of his autobiographical narrative,[44] and this distinction in class status may help to explain why Sancho marries a black woman and Equiano takes a white wife. The black woman in England and especially in London, then, is a *rara avis*, an unnerving sight.

Another reason for Imoinda's turning white, in addition to the scarcity of black women, is that there is no record of an East or West Indian, African, Aborigine, or Native American man or woman having performed in the English theatre before the nineteenth century. Ignatius Sancho had hopes of performing Othello and Oroonoko to become the first black actor on the London stage, but a persistent stammer apparently prevented the realization of his dream. Though Julius Soubise seemingly memorized passages for public declamation from *Othello* and *Richard III* (the Shakespearean dramas most evocative of race and deformity), Ira Aldridge, the "African Roscius," is the first known African male to perform in a starring role in 1834.[45] Bit parts for "slaves" or "Indians" may have been represented by people of color in pantomimes, and entertainers such as singers, drummers, and minstrels appeared in the street. In the 1780s black musicians, dressed as "Turks" and playing what came to be regarded as "Oriental" music, formed Janissary military percussion bands which may have appeared on stage. Though instrumental groups including violinists, horn players, and flautists were solely male, women may have sung or danced as amateur performers and accompanied singers on the harpsichord.[46] There is, however, no sighting of black women performing on the eighteenth-century stage with perhaps one exception. Late in the period the first woman of color may have acted in Lancashire as Polly, Macheath's moll in *Beggar's Opera*. (In the suppressed racialized continuation, the heroine Polly, having arrived in the West Indies crossdresses, saves the noble Indian Cawwawkee from pirates, and reunites with a blackface Macheath.) When Samuel Foote – who was about to interview the actress whose abilities had been much touted – learns that she is black, he allegedly responded, "*Oh! No matter . . . we will introduce the Roman fashion: the lady shall wear a* MASK." The commentator continues,

"Ridiculous as this circumstance may appear to the reader, I can assure him that I had it from Mr Foote himself. I could not help observing to my friend in the pit when *Macheath* addressed her with '*Pretty Polly, say*,' that 'it would have been more germain [sic] to the matter had he changed the phrase to SOOTY *Polly, say*.' I was informed that a few nights before, she had enacted *Juliet*, when doubtless her *Romeo* most feelingly recited,

> Her beauty hangs upon the cheek of night,
> Like a rich jewel in an Ethiop's ear.[47]

Of course Juliet was actually played by a crossdressed white boy in the Renaissance, and in the case of black Othello and white Desdemona, one actor was blackened by burnt cork and dark pigment, the other crossdressed and lead-painted as a white woman.[48] Juliet's blackness recalls *Othello* in its variation on starcrossed lovers as an interracial tragedy, and recent productions of *Romeo and Juliet* have sometimes portrayed the antagonism between the Montagus and the Capulets as a difference of complexion.

When white women actually appear on the Restoration stage, femininity continues to resonate with racial and other bodily differences. When John Jackson, manager of the Theatre Royal of Edinburgh, compares this nameless black woman's stage aspirations to a bear's trying to fly, or an audition by a deformed man or a deaf woman, he predictably aligns black femininity with anomaly. Black skin was clearly an insurmountable handicap in the theatre. The prologue to *Moor of Venice* cited earlier (8 December 1660) also imagines even white women's stage intrusion as grotesque display:

> Our women are defective, and so siz'd,
> You'd think they were some of the guard disguis'd,
> For to speak truth men act, that are between
> Forty and fifty, wenches of fifteen;
> With bones so large, and nerves so incompliant,
> When you call Desdemona, enter Giant.

Black and white women are both linked and distinguished from each other by their defects.

The spectacle of contingent blackness was first given visual representation in the medieval period and in court masques by draping diaphanous black fabric over the actors' extremities. Decorative black characters in such festivities lent an exotic Egyptian or Moorish element to the entertainment spectacle.[49] Soot was also sometimes rubbed on the skin to darken it. Black velvet apparently became the preferred fabric for racial disguise, remarkable for its depth of color, in the sixteenth century and later in the seventeenth century paint, black stockings, wigs, gloves, and masks were added.[50] In some versions of George Colman's production *Inkle and Yarico*, the heroine and her maid Wowski are dressed in animal skins – signifying closeness to the bestial – combined with other exotica. The "Indian" Yarico, dressed in skins and feathers, is "a good comely copper – quite dark but very elegant," while Wowski, marked simply by "Black skin, arms and legs," offers contrast as "an angel of a rather darker sort:"[51]

YARICO – White and colored striped muslin dress, with coloured feathers and ornaments, leopard's skin drapery across one shoulder, dark flesh-coloured stockings and arms, sandals, various coloured feathers in head, a quantity of coloured beads around the head, neck, wrists, arms, and ancles.
WOWSKI – Black skin, arms and legs, sandals, plain white dress with small skin hung across shoulder, beads, & c.[52]

These instructions do not offer sufficient detail to clarify whether the lighter Yarico blacks up her face. But a later notable Yarico, Frances Maria Kelly (1790–1882) in her 1833 memoir provides evidence that women's facial darkening, if not perhaps blackening, occurred in the early nineteenth century. Informed that she is to play Yarico, Kelly exclaims, "But I have no Dress for Yarico!" The theatre manager responds, "You shall have one. I have the materials in the house for a Leopard-skin dress..." She continues with her comic account:

Satisfied that a Leopard-skin mantel would look wildly simple and pretty enough over a plain white muslin dress, I was easy on the subject. In the evening I went to the Glass and carefully put on a Brown-Sherry complexion for Yarico. I was excessively African in my face and wanted only my promised mantel-piece.

Dressed in the nick of time, "The Lamps shewed me what a side-scene of an African I had been turned into – some 'mute unglorious' [a phrase drawn from Gray's 'Elegy in a Country Churchyard'] had painted me a hasty Leopard-skin on the spot, and I stood there a distemper'd Yarico" in contrast to the spotlessly white Inkle. "All went well 'till I had finished the Song (Wowski's properly, by the by) of 'White man don't leave me' when I flatter myself I made a very decided impression upon him – He could truly have exclaimed with Juliet: ''Tis not a set of features or complexion / The tincture of a Skin that I admire.' For, after embracing his Yarico, my Inkle shrunk back with nine and thirty black spots upon his bosom – and I found that I like melancholy had 'Marked him for my own.' "[53] This rich passage, introduced by Frances Kelly's adopting the persona of an Amazon (in order to speak on stage) and Othello (affecting to deliver his now familiar "round, unvarnish'd tale"), resonates with earlier productions in her insistence on the masquerade of race, and her ambivalent status signified by the warm painted tones of Yarico's complexion while appearing "excessively African" and singing the darker Wowski's part instead of her own. Plays with counterfeit blacks enact a cultural fantasy writ large that all blacks are really white, like the actors who play them, and they domesticate dark complexion through its imitation. Kelly's blacking up makes clear that it has become common practice by the 1820s.

Though Oroonoko and Othello blacked up, Southerne's Imoinda of course did not. Instead her vaguely African or Oriental garb carried the weight of marking spectacular difference. For European women in particular the cultural impetus to turn whiter, fairer, more porcelain, sets a standard of beauty, and the desirable direction of colorshifting is to lighten one's complexion. Imoinda's color transformation from black to white is, then, typical of the eighteenth-century theatre rather than the exception since black people did not appear in central roles. That black women were largely erased from the theatre of empire even as they figured critically in the lives of Jamaican planters and slaveowners, soldiers in the French and Indian War, traders with the East Indies, and voyagers to the Pacific Islands suggests that black women and their half-caste children, at least as much as white men's fear of the man of color, carried the power to unsettle colonial relations and narratives about them. After the Restoration when real women rather than crossdressed boys represented female characters, femininity plays a different yet still pivotal role in articulating race and effeminacy.

Thus, the first woman actor, the first Restoration role played by a woman, *and* the first woman to support herself by writing drama and fiction were white, but a whiteness linked to blackness. Southerne's Imoinda like Desdemona possesses a blackened whiteness that is exotic, erotically suspect, frivolous, and denigrated.[54] Both Imoinda and Desdemona in visual contrast to their black husbands, perform cultural work parallel to that of the white narrator in *Oroonoko*. These juxtapositions heighten their virtuous femininity and suggest its alignment with an intrinsically white and English nature as women. But Imoinda's white is also a blackened white, because she, like Aphra Behn's narrator and a whole country of Desdemonas, is seduced into romance with blackness. And, as I have argued, Imoinda turns white because no black actresses are recruited to the London stage until the nineteenth century, blackface for women was not common, and no central black parts exist for women comparable to Othello's or Oroonoko's roles until late in the century. Imoinda turns white because whiteness defines her sexual and racial difference, and thus her femininity.

III

When the female body appears on stage for the first time, only white bodies are culturally sanctioned as legitimate signifiers of femininity. On the Renaissance stage when white men and boys impersonated black men and women, femininity rather than actual women represents racial difference, as Karen Newman has argued, and it "plays a pivotal if problematic role in the articulation of race and sexuality."[55] Yet (white) femininity, though it can migrate from a female character to a crossdressed actor or actress, does not consistently serve as a trope for racial difference on the eighteenth-century stage. The real bodies of actresses interrupt this alignment between white men dressed as women signifying racial difference, and the plot in Southerne's *Oroonoko* separates into two stories, one featuring race and the other crossdressing, which do not inhabit the same dramatic space until the end of the play. This helps explain Southerne's addition of the misogynist comic plot to the tragic heroic love story of Imoinda and Oroonoko, as well as the uneasiness Hawkesworth and others felt about including it in their versions later in the century. The subplot in Southerne's play allows a compromised femininity to attach itself to a female body disguised as a male, and masculinity of a noble but sentimental and weakened sort to fix upon the black Oroonoko. These dramatic lines interconnect in various ways, most notably in the obstreperous crossdressed Charlotte Welldon's (perhaps Southerne's barb at Behn) abandoning her disguise as a man, and only then, having become a more proper Englishwoman, acting as an emissary of racial romance between the black man Oroonoko and the white woman Imoinda. Together Charlotte, the reconstituted feminine, and Imoinda, newly figured as a white woman by Southerne (though Congreve's epilogue describes her as "Indian"), discard two aspects central to Aphra Behn's novella, the central black woman figure and the love between a black African couple. Charlotte Welldon thus brings about the resolution of the play while separating herself from blackness.

The crossdressing subplot in Southerne's version of *Oroonoko* interplays with the main plot to reassure the audience that because sexual difference is as supple a category as changing one's clothes, perhaps race too involves mere costuming. The subplot, as foreign to Behn's novella as a white Imoinda, opens with the ribald speeches of Charlotte Welldon who, self-exiled in breeches to the plantations of America, seeks a husband and fortune by "marrying" a wealthy plantation-owning widow. Widow Lackitt satisfies the stereotype of the creolized English woman longing for a dark man while, bereft of heroic impulses, she is paired with the rambunctious

Charlotte. In traveling to the plantations of the New World in Southerne's *Oroonoko*, Charlotte and her sister Lucy escape from their commodification in London, where the women "like the rich silks ... are out of fashion a great while before they wear out" (1.i), into the freedom travel offers. The sisters hope that Surinam husbands, as plentiful as nature's bounty, will simply "drop into some woman's mouth: 'Tis but a little patience, spreading your apron in expectation, and one of 'em will fall into your lap at last" (1.ii). Charlotte in breeches courts the unsuspecting Widow Lackitt and eventually wins her in a mock marriage, and the widow's booby son Daniel marries Charlotte's silly sister. As the antithesis to feminine virtue (and thus to Imoinda), Charlotte is suitably paired with her "wife," the widow who is doubly identified with stinginess and with the lucrative slave trade. The Englishwomen find the slave mutiny headed by Oroonoko beneficial to their designs because they deflect attention from their money-grubbing shenanigans. In addition, the crossdressing plot allows parallels to be drawn between chattel slavery and the enslavement of white women to white men. Nevertheless, Charlotte and Lucy Welldon are subdued into ranges of femininity more appropriate than being swayed into romance with a black man; and the blackface character Oroonoko, like Othello, can murder a miscegenetic white woman while impersonating the black man who marries her. The play thus finally disavows white men's illicit passions for black and mixed-race women.

Southerne had earlier adapted Behn's fictions into two very successful plays, *Sir Anthony Love* (1690) and *The Fatal Marriage* (1694), and in *Oroonoko* he repeats the winning strategy while showing some anxiety about rewriting the productions of a woman writer.[56] The equivocal masculinity of the characters mimics his own fear about authorial emasculation. Daniel, the booby son, is stripped of his manliness by his mother and hints of incest: "I have no more manhood left in me already than there is, saving the mark, in one of my mother's old under-petticoats" (iv.i). They trade scurrilous insults as she beats him, and her "rod" becomes both a lash and a phallic symbol.

In the final act Charlotte Welldon reveals that Stanmore "has persuaded me into a woman again" (v.i). Once Charlotte, an "arrant woman" (v.i) like Behn herself, rejoins the feminine by dressing in petticoats, promising to marry Stanmore and becoming Oroonoko's go-between to Imoinda, the comic secondary story line folds back into the tragic one to connect the African woman and the Englishwomen through the black man:

BLANDFORD ...I know, the women too,
    Will join with me: 'Tis Oroonoko's cause,
    A lover's cause, a wretched woman's cause,
    That will become your intercession.
                   (v.ii)

As a woman of uncertain gender through much of the play, Charlotte intercedes to heal the rift between black man and white woman only after her heterosexual femininity is firmly reasserted. As long as Charlotte Welldon, dressing as a man to disrupt property laws, remains fractious and cunning, Oroonoko and the white males are potential allies in squelching her mischief. But once Charlotte is safely reintegrated into the colonial society and betrothed to Stanmore (rather than paired in breeches with Widow Lackitt), the bond between black and white men is broken, and Oroonoko becomes conveniently dispensable. Because the black woman is eradicated from Southerne's version of the play, the proper feminine – in the person of the white woman – is recovered from the cleavage between black heroine and white woman narrator which had complicated the earlier fictional version. Southerne focuses instead upon the connections between the women (Imoinda, Charlotte, Widow Lackitt, and Lucy) in their subservience to male authority. The threat of miscegenation is swept away by the death of the enslaved lovers, the white Imoinda and the black Oroonoko, as the threat the mixed-race slaves would have presented together is safely removed.

In eliminating the black woman from Behn's novella, Southerne concentrates instead on gender relations and evokes vague parallels between women's rights and slavery. Southerne's *Oroonoko* pays little overt regard to the protagonists' difference in color since their predicament as African slaves, black and white, is virtually identical. They bond through rank rather than complexion in spite of the spectacle of difference. Rather than opposing slavery in general, Southerne's *Oroonoko* and its several adaptations suggest the injustice of enslaving persons of rank. The laboring body of the slave woman is ignored; the slave's tortured body is reduced to Aboan's recounting of brutal beatings, and to the spectacle of Oroonoko staked and spread on the stage in the last act, rather than depicting the violence of his captors who castrate and mutilate him in the novel.

In addition, anxieties about the hybrid offspring in Imoinda's womb are displaced onto the slave trade rather than located in racial difference. The ostensible reason that she and her unborn child must die is because both mother and child will be enslaved, a fact Oroonoko cannot tolerate.

While it is true that "the other problem with women" is that they are reproductive vessels, it is a problem that is differently figured for white women and for black women,[57] and Southerne's *Oroonoko* provides the test case. White women give birth to those who control property and thus act as a conduit for those who inherit the birthright of a certain biological status. Black women, however, if they are enslaved, give birth to property, and their slave offspring inherit their mother's status. This makes for critical differences in black and white women's relation to slavery, just as their relationship to femininity diverges. The intricate relationships are further complicated because any maternalism a white woman might feel for a black slave woman is compromised and perhaps parodied in the slave's caring for the white woman's children. Turning Imoinda white also testifies to the power Southerne imaginatively exerts over Amazonian figures such as Behn, the white actresses and white women writers she represents, *and* over her black Imoinda.

As I have argued in the first section of this book, loving the seductive, monstrous black man is intertwined with a debased and defensive white femininity. A white slave, sexually desirable, a pregnant mother of a mixed-race child, and the embodiment of domestic virtue, Imoinda cannot sustain these contradictions as a character. To be truly feminine (white, heterosexual, passive, domestic, chaste, and of a certain status) is to possess tender feelings for the oppressed (the black, the enslaved, the laboring classes) and yet to remain distinct from them and superior to them. Consolidation of such a femininity paradoxically depends, then, on being enraptured by the monstrous and the black while recognizing one's difference.

In the later versions of *Oroonoko*, abolitionist sentiments are sometimes more pronounced, though whether slaves should be freed continues to be linked to the rank of the captives. In John Hawkesworth's adaptation of Southerne's play, performed at Drury Lane in 1759 (with David Garrick as Oroonoko and Susanna Maria Cibber as Imoinda), a freshly conceived first act gives voice to a crude racism, and it highlights the physical cruelty of the West Indian planters.[58] Though some critics have taken these changes to be an index to Hawkesworth's antislavery sentiments, they are more credibly ameliorist gestures. Omitting the subplot, Hawkesworth calls into question the cruelty of slavery and highlights class differences among those enslaved.[59] Oroonoko readily acknowledges that Africans, including his own father, were slavetraders. It is the slave status of Oroonoko's future royal son, not his mixed-race status, that concerns him, though of course the spectator witnesses a spectacle of counterfeit intermixture. Thus the matter of social status overrules every other consideration: "Shall the dear

babe, the eldest of my hopes, / Whom I begot a prince, be born a slave?"
(III.ii). The play promotes increased freedom for those few captives like
Imoinda and Oroonoko who are because of their rank judged the equal of
ten ordinary slaves.[60]

In relation to gender, however, Hawkesworth's changes have some important effects.[61] In omitting the playful subplot, the parallels between the
trade in women and the trade in slaves, the bonds between free and enslaved
white women (however vexed), and the commercial nature of plantation
owning as located specifically in the person of Widow Lackitt are left out.[62]
Imoinda, the locus of virtuous femininity, mourns the loss of her beloved
husband more than she laments her bondage, but the white heroine's fate
is "resolved" through Oroonoko:

> OROONOKO O! That we cou'd incorporate, be one,
>   [*Embracing her*]
>   One Body, as we have been long one Mind;
>   That, blended so, we might together mix,
>   And, losing thus our Being to the World,
>   Be only found to one another's Joys.
>   (Hawkesworth, v. Scene the last)

Because the play concludes with a spectacular death scene preceded by
the blackface male player and the white actress kissing and embracing, the
play hints *sub rosa* about blackness and intermarriage. If the eighteenth-
century audience felt any aversion to racial mixture, remembering at the
climactic moment of erotic encounter that both actors were actually white
would have lessened the visible effect of racial difference and heightened
the importance of bondage and class status.

When Elizabeth Inchbald chooses the text for her much-read collection
of eighteenth-century plays, she reinstates the crossdressing subplot and
ameliorist sympathies. For Inchbald *Oroonoko* strengthens the abolitionist
cause, and she famously comments about the slavetrading merchants of
Liverpool who would refuse its staging in that city. Drawing as well on her
feminist sympathies, Inchbald objects to the diminished role of Imoinda in
the play and criticizes the "repulsive qualities" in Southerne's subplot, deco-
rously changing Hawkesworth's version to erase the planters' low insults
that label Imoinda a "murrain" and "mongrel succabus" (a female demon
who has intercourse with sleeping men).[63] Yet in all of these eighteenth-
century dramatic versions of Behn's novella, even in Inchbald's edition,
Imoinda possesses a white complexion that is scarcely mentioned in the
course of the play.

The scene most frequently pictured in frontispieces accompanying the various eighteenth-century versions of the play is the climactic interracial embrace and death of the central characters in the last act. Imoinda, the African-born daughter of a European who died defending Oroonoko, debates the couple's fate while preparing to plunge a knife into her body. In some of the pictures Aboan, a rebellious fellow slave who has been murdered, lies prophetically at the couple's feet. A deeply affected Oroonoko, paralyzed with emotion, weeps over whether he should kill his wife in order that they can escape slavery or torture:

> I cannot, as I would, dispose of thee;
> And, as I ought, I dare not. Oh, Imoinda!
> My heart runs over, if my gushing eyes
> Betray a weakness which they never knew.
> (Southerne, Act v.iv)

She responds, "This dagger will instruct you," begging him to strike her. Finally, after a more highly charged deliberation, she stabs herself, and Oroonoko is inspired to his own suicide.

In Aphra Behn's original tale the female narrator shares Imoinda's enchantment with the black hero and implicitly competes with his black African wife for his attentions.[64] In Southerne's play the stabbing of Imoinda, unlike Othello's murder of his white wife, occurs at her own invitation, even at her insistence. These engravings offer highly varied visual representations of racial intermixture that is eventually evacuated of its potential threat since the married couple, and the mixed-race child the white woman is carrying, all die. Rather than destroying slavery, the miscegenetic pair dies, and the emblematic scene simultaneously displays their union and reassures the audience of their impending death. In turning now to these sometimes surprising engravings I want to emphasize two points: the couple's geographical origins are loosely and variously signaled, reiterating the flexibility of racial designation; and depictions of them often display a marked difference of complexion, even though the married couple may be similarly costumed. In many of the pictures a white Imoinda (as tall or taller than Oroonoko) seems to hold sway over a fainthearted darker man. The woman appears, if not to dominate, to hold her own with the noble savage next to her. She herself bears fewer signs of alterity or enslavement than he. Less primitive than her mate, she is occasionally dressed as a proper English lady.

Oroonoko's geographical origins are inconsistent. In the Edinburgh edition from 1774, Oroonoko is pictured as a dark-skinned Highlander in a forest-like setting (illustration 14). In this most stereotypically "savage" representation, he, recalling the Scottish Enlightenment four-stages theory, incorporates within his dress and physiognomy both Africa and the Highlands. The bearded, half-naked, and scowling hybrid African-Scots creature, set against a stormy sky, wears a low-slung furry loin cloth resembling a kilt, and a feather in his coonskin cap. He is consoled by a muse-like Imoinda draped in toga-like robes and barefoot, an Amazonian character who unveils only the right breast. The clawlike arm which she rests upon his shoulder is strangely piebald, as if to suggest her bestial affinity with the savage when she comes into contact with her lover. The very white Imoinda, slightly more prominently placed in the foreground and at the center, towers over the two black men. In spite of Oroonoko's fierce demeanor, his smaller stature and the lizard-like arm of Imoinda seem to infantilize him, and even to effeminate him. The signs of his primitivism, feathers and skins, accomplish the cultural work of erasing geographical boundaries in favor of aligning farflung civilizations that seem to share certain stages of development. Thus the Highland or Tahitian or Caribbean present re-enacts the European past, and the Scots are made to have affinities with the African slave.

In contrast, in the frontispiece to one of the editions of Hawkesworth's adaptation, a dark-skinned and bewigged Oroonoko is completely clothed in an English gentleman's attire, except for his hands and face, probably to make blacking up an easier task for the actor (illustration 15). Imoinda too is fashionably dressed with the barest hint of exoticism visible in the veil covering her hair. The dissonance between the couple's representation on the frontispiece and in the play is considerable since, surrounded by English foliage, neither resembles a slave in any way, and the African origins of the pair are completely effaced. Rather than Imoinda's holding the sword and entreating her partner to strike her, Oroonoko averts his face as he points the dagger toward her heart. Seemingly placid and less engaged, she raises a hand that appears to be almost protective of her mate, while Oroonoko's body posture indicates his reticence to murder her. The only suggestion of Imoinda's sexuality is that her legs are defined under the folds of her underskirt, but as one would expect of a decorous eighteenth century, there is no hint of the miscegenated offspring in her belly.

In these varied engravings, feathers and animal skins indicate a generalized otherness instead of a particular geographical region. In the 1791 edition of Southerne's play, the heroic couple are quite distinct from each

14 Frontispiece to Thomas Southerne, *Oroonoko, A Tragedy* (Edinburgh 1774).

15 Frontispiece to Thomas Southern[e] with alterations by John Hawkesworth, LL.D. "Mr. Savigny in the Character of Oroonoko" (1776), *Oroonoko, A Tragedy, As it is now Acted at the Theatre Royal in Drury-Lane.*

other in dress (illustration 16), and he exudes an air of being her servant rather than her husband. Imoinda is attired as an English maiden without any obvious sign of the exotic and, bending to peer at the dead Aboan, she does not touch Oroonoko. The black hero's feathered turban and a toga-like costume is at once reminiscent of a West Indian (a Carib) and an East Indian. In another production memorialized in the same 1791 edition, Mrs. Kemble as Imoinda appears alone with an English frock draped in a manner slightly reminiscent of a sari, though with petticoats (illustration 17). The large feather protruding from the turban and the ermine-spotted draping are synecdochical indicators of the heroine's exoticism. Standing in front of a bucolic European landscape, Imoinda lovingly extends her arms upon hearing her lost lover's voice. The epigram below the drawing reads, "There's something in that name, that voice, that face – / As I know myself, I cannot be mistaken." In both pictures, the sign of the other is figured most through the headdress. Her civilized whiteness is unquestionable.

In contrast, the erotically evocative picture accompanying an early nineteenth-century version of Southerne's play shows a very black Oroonoko with Roman features and princely circlet on his head. He grasps a very white Imoinda who aims a dagger at herself while leaning heavily onto Oroonoko's arm (illustration 18). Imoinda's sari-like clothing and veils mirror the Orientalized Oroonoko's luxurious ermine robes in the sumptuous setting reminiscent of *Roxalana* and other Turkish harem plays. Rather than standing very separately as they had in the eighteenth-century engravings, their entwined bodies imitate their sexual bond. The lower half of Imoinda's body stands between Oroonoko's leg so that their bodies seem to overlap, she with one leg, he with two. Each bears ankle bracelets evocative of slave chains. In all of these pictures, the pictorial representations of the couple exhibit the varieties of human types around the globe to show them as variously costumed and different from one other. In each case, however, Imoinda remains white and her status seems to equal or exceed Oroonoko's.

Finally, in the picture published in 1816 after the abolition of the slave trade, but before the abolition of slavery, both characters appear as half-nude slaves (illustration 19). In a tropical island clearing flanked by palms, river, and mountains, Imoinda looks both forceful and subservient. She kneels before Oroonoko who demurs with a hand to his face; her position in the foreground and her muscular body suggest womanly strength. The features that might be racialized are somewhat obscured, Oroonoko's by his hand, and Imoinda's by a shadow. Her nose, like Oroonoko's, appears sharp and aquiline, her body nearly as muscular as his, and her breasts bare

16 "Death is security for all our fears" (1791), Act v.3, Thomas Southerne's *Oroonoko,
Adapted for Theatrical Representation as performed at the Theatres-Royal, Drury-Lane and
Covent Garden. Regulated from the Prompt-Books, by Permission of the Managers.*

17 "Mrs. Kemble as Imoinda," *Oroonoko*, Act II.3 (1791), Thomas Southerne's *Oroonoko, Adapted for Theatrical Representation as performed at the Theatres-Royal, Drury-Lane and Covent-Garden. Regulated from the Prompt-Books, by Permission of the Managers.*

18 Frontispiece to *Oroonoko: A Tragedy in Five Acts*. – By Thomas Southern[e] (1825), Act v.4, vol. II in *The London Stage*.

but not fully exposed. Her hair, a feature which could be a more exact racial indicator, is hidden under a turban-like wrap, and like her husband she wears a generous loincloth. The couple's feet are each encircled by slave bracelets, doubled in Imoinda's case. Oroonoko casts a dark shadow. Though his sinewy dark figure with his tightly curled hair dominates the frame, his stance is hesitant in refusing the dagger which Imoinda offers, and her determination again overtakes Oronooko in this representation. The dagger she grasps is pointed at her heart, but because of its positioning, it also seems to be directed toward Oroonoko's middle, and it takes on a somewhat phallic fearsomeness. In the black and white engraving Imoinda's skin appears lighter than Oroonoko's but, as her status devolves into a lowly slave, it is darker than any of the eighteenth-century prints. The racially equivocal Imoinda, turning nearly full circle over a century later, begins again to resemble Behn's characterization.

What accounts for this merging of Imoinda's difference into Oroonoko's, and of the couple's various exotic costumings? These pictures certainly demonstrate the great geographic and racial suppleness of the story's multiple versions. Fears about miscegenation are never mentioned in Southerne's play or in its adaptations, and the play portrays the threat of the Lieutenant

OROONOKO.

IMOINDA   THIS DAGGER WILL INSTRUCT YOU
ACT V.   SCENE IV.

Painted by Howard.   Pub. by Longman & Co. 1816.   Engraved by C.Heath.

19 Frontispiece to Thomas Southern[e], *Oroonoko. A Tragedy, in Five Acts. As Performed at the Theatre Royal, Covent Garden* (1816).

Governor's potential rape of Imoinda, an unforgivable affront to her husband Oroonoko, as far exceeding her concerns about bearing a mixed-race child. Both she and Oroonoko speak only of the fact that the child would be enslaved. Miscegenation, at least between a black and a white slave, apparently did not inspire the fears and social concerns it was to carry until later in the nineteenth century though unquestionably the captivating visual spectacle of a mixed race couple must have drawn audiences to the theatre, and especially to the ineffable strangeness of a black man and a white woman embracing. Concerns about their hybrid union are thoroughly subordinated to the question of justifying the enslavement of nobility since, because the white Imoinda is a slave, captivity is clearly not confined to black Africans and an English audience might find that her captivity portends their own.

When the play is repeatedly, almost compulsively, produced during most of the eighteenth century, sexual relations between the races are treated as an unfamiliar, erotic curiosity. By the 1780s, however, as the movement for abolition began to gather force, the tide begins to turn toward thinking that such mixed-race couples were as gnawingly unnatural as their American cousins had already legislated them to be. In addition, in spite of the exciting depictions of pretended miscegenation between two white actors, Southerne's *Oroonoko* (like Shakespeare's *Othello*) makes clear that there is a mortal consequence to white women's caring for black men, even virtuous white women. The much-loved play exploring these explosive themes is coupled with reassurances that rebellious black men and the white women who love them both deserve the same tragic fate. The theatre of empire as represented in this play isolates a contact zone within the painted white actor's body but in that incorporation glosses over the bogus nature of the encounter between white and other. These diverse theatrical representations of Southerne's *Oroonoko*, representations over which the specter of black women tantalizingly and disquietingly hovered, helped negotiate attitudes toward the masquerade of race even as it remained an urgent matter to articulate the whiteness of femininity.

When Edmund Burke in *A Philosophical Enquiry into the Origin of Our Ideas of the Sublime and Beautiful* (1757) cites William Cheselden's account of a blind boy who miraculously regains his sight, he reports, "Among many remarkable particulars that attended his fair perceptions, and judgments on visual objects, Cheselden tells us, that the first time the boy saw a black object, it gave him great uneasiness; and that some time after, upon accidentally seeing a negro woman he was struck with great horror at the sight" (144). Behn's Imoinda lingers over Southerne's altered version and other performances throughout the period. Black women in the eighteenth century are not so much *absent* as they are a spectral *presence* that links desire with fear, dread, physical defect, and monstrosity. It matters immeasurably, I think, that though the first object that Burke's newly sighted boy sees is black, what he perceives is specifically a Negro *woman*, who, in being both dark and female, embodies the most horrific combination that he can imagine.[65] No wonder Imoinda turns white.

CHAPTER 7

Black men: Equiano, Sancho, and being a man

> I offer here the history of neither a saint, a hero, nor a tyrant.
>
> Olaudah Equiano, *The Interesting Narrative of the Life*
> *of Olaudah Equiano, or Gustavus Vassa, the African*

I

William Ansah Sesarakoo, son of John Corrente of Annamaboe (a black slave trader) and John Frederick, son of Chief Naimbanna from Sierra Leone, famously attended the performance of Southerne's *Oroonoko* at Covent Garden in 1749. Both African men, eventually ransomed and released into the hands of the Earl of Halifax, had been sold into slavery in violation of the understanding with Sesarakoo's father that they would be taken to England by a trader to be educated. Curiously enough, given what we have seen of the racial history of that play, the periodical press enlists the visitors in the cause of provoking abolitionist sentiments:

The seeing persons of their own colour on the stage, apparently in the same distress from which they had been so lately delivered, the tender interview between *Imoinda* and *Oroonoko*, who was betrayed by the treachery of a captain, his account of his sufferings, and the repeated abuse of his placability and confidence, strongly affected them, with that generous grief which pure nature always feels, and which art had not yet taught them to suppress; the young prince was so far overcome, that he was obliged to retire at the end of the fourth act. His companion remained, but wept the whole time; a circumstance which affected the audience yet more than the play, and doubled the tears which were shed for *Oroonoko* and *Imoinda*.[1]

Others have commented at length on this fascinating passage in the *Gentleman's Magazine*, but what has remained unremarked to my knowledge is that the "persons of his own colour" on stage would have included a blackface Oroonoko and the other counterfeit blackface slaves in the play, *not* Imoinda, who though she is enslaved in the tragedy is clearly portrayed as a white woman in Southerne's play. In short, if the observer's interpretation of the African visitors' response is somewhat accurate (it is not, of course, the direct testimony of the visitors), their sentiments were most likely inspired by the sufferings of the slave couple, blackface and white, rather than "seeing persons of their own colour on the stage." Further, it is noteworthy that neither the princes nor the commentator remark on the racial intermixture of the couple in the play.

In this incident, the two Africans of rank in the theatre audience are accorded sympathetic feelings which seem to signal their participation in human nature. As transculturated amalgams of African and English in that they affect sentimentality because they are not sufficiently sophisticated to disguise their "pure nature," the visitors are clearly princes capable of heroic emotion rather than simply ordinary slaves. In fact, the character Oroonoko himself remarks in the play that the injustice of slavery is much greater when a man of rank is involved. In sum, the commentator racializes the suffering, suggesting that it was spurred by mutual tenderness for those of the same complexion, while the tears of the visiting African princes may actually have been occasioned by their sympathizing most deeply with the injustice of slavery when it is perpetrated upon impavid people of high status.

This elision of the distinction between skin color and slavery, with scant attention paid to status, has as we have seen led to misinterpretations and misunderstandings of the history of the linkages among them. The description of the theatre scene for English consumption is further extended in William Dodd's two popular poems, "The *African* Prince, Now in *England*, To *Zara*, At his Father's Court" and "Zara, At the court of Anamaboe, to the African Prince now in England." These elegiac poems recount the apparently true story that the Prince, heroically torn between love and duty, reluctantly left Zara in Africa to pursue an English education in order to become a better ruler. Thrown into slavery and eventually ransomed, he alludes to seeing a moving production of *Oroonoko*. Eliding the differences between Africa and the Indies, East and West, he suggests that the hero and heroine in that play resemble him in being *Indian*:

> O! Zara, here, a story like my own,
> With mimic skill, in borrow'd names, was shown;
> An Indian chief, like me, by fraud betray'd,
> And partner in his woes an Indian maid,
> I can't recall the scenes, 'tis pain too great
> And, if recall'd, should shudder to relate.[2]

Of course, as we have noted earlier, the eighteenth century displays a remarkable casualness and apparent ignorance about the relationship of color to geography. In reference to Zara and the prince, "Indian" does not necessarily signify an Amerindian in the eighteenth century (though it most probably refers to an indigenous inhabitant of the West Indies), and most significantly it erases any difference in complexion between them. Neither one is the descendant of white Europeans or is a black African as in the case of Southerne's play. In order to make the characters on stage both seem to be "persons of their own colour" to the visiting African princes, Dodd also ignores the difference in complexion between Imoinda and Oroonoko in Southerne's play, seeming to revert to Behn's story, and the disparity between the actual Africans in the audience and their blackface representation on stage is forgotten. Even though Oroonoko and Imoinda were represented throughout the eighteenth century as being of differing complexions, miscegenation does not seem to be an issue for these commentators on the scene and the difference in color is actually forgotten, though we have no way of knowing for certain what the African prince and his companion may truly have thought.

The African visitors to the London stage and the Zara poems published following their visit suggest in England itself at midcentury a kind of cultural oblivion that forgives interracial love when the lovers share high rank or become proselytizing Christians. Zara's response similarly emphasizes the indignity of enslaving a prince. Playing Dido to her Aeneas, the tragic Zara is the one abandoned, whether deliberately and malevolently as in the case of Inkle and Yarico, or unwillingly as in the case of the African men who forsake their beloved women when they are forcibly enslaved.

The paired poems of racialized romance between two Africans, unlike the staple cultural fables of mixed race couples, do not simply replicate the expected patterns of interracial romance. As we have seen, the noble Negro in eighteenth-century literature is very rarely a woman: Imoinda turns white and Yarico shifts colors and places of origin. Femininity, so significant in determining the limits of the human, as I have argued, is contorted when the noble Negro is a woman. In fictions black women are often objects of the lascivious desires of white traders, but in the poems they are frequently represented as bereft lovers or wives pining away in their native country for their absent black lovers. A favorite plot involves the slave trade's interruption of the constant love between two Africans so that one is left behind, or they are sent to different plantations. Their love is threatened by a white man's villainy, or occasionally later in the century, by competition with another black man. Largely absent from fiction, and from the theatre except in a few representations in blackface, the black woman appears in the main as a tradeworthy sensual object in heroic poetry of the midcentury where she is paired with a black lover. In the poetry of "pseudo-Africa" she is present as a profoundly desirable woman who is worth struggling over to the death.[3] Much more than the noble native man, I suggest, she increasingly comes to represent the the sentimental locus of what is irretrievably lost to the slave – freedom, love, family, and his native country.

In Zara's lamentations, the African woman is an educated epistolary correspondent who embodies classical femininity *and* the feminization of the colonized territory plumbed by slavetraders. The virtuous and courageous Zara of Dodd's poems resembles Behn's black Imoinda and Southerne's white Imoinda more than the African/Indian Yarico, though her concern about competition from white Englishwomen echoes the Countess of Hereford's poem *The Story of Inkle and Yarico*. She fears that in spite of her lover's best intentions, the "blooming" rosy complexions of the English women will distract him from returning to her:

> But, that I know too well thy generous heart,
> One doubt, than all, more torment would impart:
> 'Tis this; in Britain's happy courts to shine,
> Amidst a thousand blooming maids, is thine –
> Art still thyself, incapable of wrong;
> No outward charm can captivate thy mind,
> Thy love is friendship heighten'd and refin'd.[4]

Zara, at the same time that she typifies the weeping, abandoned, and occasionally suicidal woman of popular interracial romance stories, is, more than her lover, an outsider unable to assimilate into England either as a slave or a free partner to an African man. Heroic virtue and sexual culpability are present together in this poetic heroine who, mocked for her grief over her lover by her own slaves, is ironically more sympathetically understood by the English than the Africans.

Like the drama, anti-slavery poetry counters assumptions that Africa produces degraded, brutal, and barbarous people, and it too particularly expresses concerns about enslaving black persons of the highest rank. Thomas Chatterton in his "Eclogues" (including "Narva and Mored," "The Death of Nicou," "Heccar and Gaira") and in "An African Song" (all written in 1770) present a romanticized version of the slavetrading continent.[5] Anticipating the lush and tumultuous magic of Coleridge's *Kubla Khan*,[6] the poems also recall the "Moorish fancy" that Shaftesbury had accused his countrymen of harboring. These poems are replete with the fantastic stuff of an imagined Africa, of macaws and elephants intermingled with elk and

fawns. Written by a poet who himself committed suicide, in "Narva and
Mored" and "Heccar and Gaira," the love stories of these African couples
descended from the gods also end tragically in their self-inflicted death,
though in the "Death of Nicou" an African warrior murders his sister's
abductor. The African warriors' actions reverberate with the loud and tumultuous streams, tempests, and whirlwinds of the African landscape. In
the poems the obscure and often inscrutable boundaries between teeming
nature and Africans blur in a sublime and horrific combination. Whether
an African princess or a servant, a black woman is often represented as the
tantalizing sexual object of a lascivious white man, like the Sable Venus,
but here dark panting virgins eagerly await their black lovers' return. The
idealized African woman at midcentury, portrayed as being at one with the
natural wild landscape and the sleek black animals native to the continent,
unequivocally inspires the passionate love of her fellow Africans in these
verses. Blackness, though sentimentality conveyed, would seem in these
poems not only to be incommensurable with a recognizable human form
but also distinct from a European femininity.

In Chatterton's steamy poem "An African Song" (in which the black
couple Narva and Mored also figure), the native man, "Swift as the wolf,
or hunted fawn" (662), resembles both a god and animals. Seeking "the
beauties of Mored," the skilled archer Narva pursues his beloved to a dark
retreat where she waits with impatient passion and "godlike charms" (663).
Their blackness is fetishized. He is "Black, as the glossy fruits which grow, /
Where Toyla's rapid waters flow" (662), and her face is as dark "as Toyla's
hidden cell (545). Mored, "the still sweeter flow'r," is simultaneously beautiful, dangerous, and at one with nature: "Black is that skin as winter's skies; /
Sparkling and bright those rolling eyes, / As is the venom'd snake" (663).
Similarly in Chatterton's ecologue on the same subject, Narva is characterized as exquisitely athletic: "Compact and firm," he is "completely
beauteous, as a summer's sun" (545). Death seems to be the only possible
conclusion, and Mored joins Narva in seeking "a watry grave" rather than
accepting slavery's confinement (545).

Black men are also pitted against white men in "Heccar and Gaira.
An African Eclogue." The warrior companions are united in their bloody
vengeance to fend off invading white men:

> Where the loud Tiger pawing in his rage
> Bids the black Archers of the wilds engage
> Stretch'd on the Sand two panting Warriors lay
> In all the burning Torments of the day...
>
> (433)

In this poem the indigenous men express powerful feelings for each other and for Cawna. Like Zara in the earlier poems, the black princess, captured among "a worthless train/In *common* slav'y drags the hated Chain" (435, italics added), does not deserve her fate because of her rank. The poem fixates on the African men's fury at her situation which leads them to seek legitimate revenge on the whites because they dared to capture a noblewoman, Gaira's beloved. Instead of representing the perfect English complexion, white and red here become ghostly "silver white" men caught in bloody torrents: "I'll strew the beaches with the mighty dead / And tinge the Lilly of their Features red" (435). The white slavetraders, tinged a "sick'ned Silver" are pallid in contrast to the bloody and majestic African warrior hunters. Cawna and her children are torn from the torrid landscape of which she seems to be a part:

> Cawna, O Cawna: deck'd in sable Charms
> What distant region holds thee from my arms
> Cawna the Pride of Afric's sultry Vales
> Soft, as the cooling Murmur of the Gales
> Majestic as the many color'd Snake
> Trailing his Glorys thro' the blossom'd brake
> Black as the glossy Rocks... (434)

In these poems written by a white Englishman, slavery is epitomized in the lament of the African man for his lost love, and Gaira's lovelorn cries woefully lament the misery that slavery occasions. Yet her femininity remains contested. When the noble savage is a female, her status as royalty is complicated because she is eroticized and shackled. This queenly African woman symbolizes the evils of slavery only as they may be gauged according to her class. As calls for abolition increase in the 1780s, the sacrificial noble black woman who had not yet appeared on stage in the century, in blackface or without, increasingly carries the cultural weight which makes her a sentimental symbol of the ruptures occasioned by slavery in poetry, fiction, and eventually in drama. Only toward the end of the eighteenth century does a European population that incarcerates its fellow human beings become alert to arguments for human rights regardless of rank, but the extent to which those sentiments extend to black women lingers on as a particularly fraught question.

II

Black men in the eighteenth century have certainly left more legible traces than black women. If the African woman represents the primitive past and the lost mother country in her most sentimental representations, what cultural metaphors adhere to black men in the eighteenth century? Oroonoko's partially classical, partially African physique, Roman nose, piercing eyes, and finely shaped mouth are of course reminiscent of the most elegant Greek and Roman statues, except for the blight of his color: "His face was not of that brown, rusty black which most of that nation are, but a perfect ebony, or polished jet... The whole proportion and air of his face was so noble, and exactly formed, that, *bating his colour*, there could be nothing in nature more beautiful, agreeable and handsome."[7] In addition, Oroonoko's greatness of soul, his civility and refinement, suggest that his ability to be a wise ruler equaled that of any European prince. These elements of physical and mental perfection testify to his humanity and to his manliness, both of which are at issue in the century which drew frequent facile parallels between Africans and parrots, monkeys, and lapdogs, and when the black male bodies most familiar to Europeans were either commodities to own or objects of spectacle.

Robinson Crusoe's Friday similarly embodies perfect symmetry and conveys "something very manly in his Face." His savagery is mitigated by "the Sweetness and Softness of an *European* in his Countenance too, especially when he smil'd."[8] Like Oroonoko, his features are distinguished from most blacks or negroes since his color is nearly indescribable – "not quite black, but very tawny" – and his well-shaped nose is small above thin lips. Again the combination of civility and barbarism incongruously yokes a European gentleness with an ostensibly generic manliness that seems untethered to geography, and yet tenuously connected to a distinctive coloring. It is difficult to conceive of a coherent black masculinity in the face of these popular representations, fractured as they are between the ugly and the perfectly formed, the savage and the princely, the soft and the manly. These fictional characters, and the real men who lived in their shadows, combine the highest status with the lowest rung on the chain of being, noble and slave, refined and fierce, tangled together in emblematic figurations which both replicate our understandings of British manhood in the period and threaten to expose the myths of a white masculinity still uneasy about its nationalist moorings.

It may seem somewhat odd to analyze issues of masculinity in Olaudah Equiano's *Interesting Narrative* (1789) and Ignatius Sancho's *Letters* (1782) which were published before abolition became law in England.[9] Both works were written, one might claim, when the question of the humanity of Africans superseded other issues, but it is my argument throughout this book that the nature of human beings is mutually constitutive with race and gender during this period. Equiano (1745?–97), Sancho (1729–80), and the other thousands of black men living in London, Bristol, and Liverpool in the later eighteenth century asserted their humanity regardless of social class against the overt and virulent racism of slavery's defenders such as Edward Long, author of *The History of Jamaica* (1774) and Philip Thicknesse in *A Year's Journey Through France, and Part of Spain* (1778) who did not believe that blacks are "in all respects human creatures" but are instead "men of a lower order."[10] Free blackmen in London and elsewhere faced a press teeming with racial hatreds in the midst of abolition debates. One treatise claimed that "the negro-race seems to be the farthest removed from the line of true cultivation of any of the human species; their defect of form and complexion being, I imagine, as strong an obstacle to their acquiring true taste (the product of mental cultivation) as any natural defect they may have in their intellectual faculties."[11] Unlike the fictional Oroonoko or the actual African princes who visited England, Equiano and Sancho could not easily claim a status sufficiently elevated to allow them to be treated deferentially in spite of their color and their geographical origins. A published review of Equiano's popular *Narrative* in *The Gentleman's Magazine* grudgingly acknowledges that he, unlike most men of his rank, deserved to be "on a par with the general mass of men in the *subordinate stations of civilized society*, and so prove[s] that there is no general rule without an exception."[12] The poem on the title page of *The Royal African: Or, Memoirs of the Young Prince of Annamaboe* testifies to the equality of all mankind and invokes Othello, Oroonoko, and Juba as justification for the belief that the visiting dignitary of the title, the black prince, demonstrates the universal truth that "human Nature is the same in all Countries, and under all Complexions."[13] In short, the literature of the period reflects that public consensus concerning the nature of actual African men had not yet jelled, and it vacillated erratically from pro-slavery racism, through benevolent amelioration bolstered by Enlightenment humanism, to abolitionist sentiments. The few standard dramatic and narrative fictions that portrayed black men carried cultural significance out of all proportion to the severely limited range of imagined masculinities they offered.

The cultural construction of black male subjectivity rests, according to W. E. B. DuBois' theory of "double consciousness," upon a simple if powerful bifurcation of possible identities, an oxymoronic opposition between being loyalties to nation or to negritude: "It is a peculiar sensation, this colour-consciousness, this sense of always looking at one's self through the eyes of others, of measuring one's soul by the tape of a world that looks on in amused contempt and pity. One ever feels his twoness... The history of the American Negro is the history of the strife, – this longing to attain self-conscious manhood, to merge his double self into a better and truer self."[14]

This influential theory is often invoked with reference to black manhood to characterize the impossibility of maintaining a coherent masculine subjectivity in the face of racism. The struggle to form a consistent identity as a black *man* in the later decades of the eighteenth century is less one of achieving an indigenous or national purity carved from the hybridity of being both African and Briton, but rather a more complex diasporic consciousness that is variously constituted across oceans and regions. Writing in a contemporary context, Seteney Shami argues, "Diaspora identities are constructed in motion and *along different lines than nation-states*. They affirm multiple attachments, deterritorialization, and cultural hybridity" (emphasis mine);[15] but transculturated identities – as evidenced by the African princes who were spectators of *Oroonoko* – had much earlier origins than the modern moment. The diasporic manner of thinking entails constituting oneself as located not simply on both sides of a border, but "in-between" geographical places and available identities including a repertory of cross-racial borrowings instead of a settled hybridity. Equiano and Sancho intermingle their British affiliations with African, Caribbean, and others before marginal, hyphenated, or even national designations were readily available to them. As Hazel Carby and other critics have recently pointed out, "Identities, like cultures, are negotiated not hermetically and in isolation, but in relation to others... and ... those identities shore up, respond to, and react against the cultures that the operating individuals identify with *and* against."[16] These and other black men, traveling on ships, in-between land sites, most often as slaves but sometimes as freed sailors, from Africa to the Caribbean, to North and South America, to India, the Antarctic, and of course to Europe, were among the first citizens of the world, though of course they did not possess the human rights accorded to others after the French and American Revolutions. The presence of black men in England paradoxically threatened an emerging national masculinity steeped in racism and homophobia even as they helped to shape its increasingly color-bound parameters.

Inevitably then, racialized expectations of masculinity in the period compete with black men's attempts to possess sufficient personal authority to shape their own destinies which were often elusive even after gaining or purchasing manumission. To enact a recognizable notion of black masculinity inevitably re-inscribed the racial fictions of popular culture even as black men resisted impersonating white men's versions of what a black man should be. I am arguing, then, that Equiano and Sancho generate original enactments of black manhood as newly freed black subjects in spite of functioning under the pall of characters such as Othello and Friday, of

visiting African princes and Oroonoko, and that both former slaves resist
being limited to the incompatible elements they are presumed to embody. In
particular, they refuse to allow virility, especially in relation to white women,
to stand as the primary measure of their person. Both Equiano and Sancho
seem acutely aware that British culture interprets black masculinity as conveniently distinct from white masculinity in order to subject black men to
unjust and inconsistent moral measures because of their complexion, and
thus to maintain their inequality.

If national identity at the end of the eighteenth century was largely
predicated on the assumptions of white metropolitan privileged men –
what Kathleen Wilson has called "a critical, objective, manly, and hence
white male subject"[17] – how then were former slaves like Equiano and
Sancho to locate a masculinity and a British identity which did not simply
replicate fictional stereotypes? How was a black man in England to shape
a masculinity when male sociability rested on imperialism, commerce, and
trade, the very trade to which he was subject and which made of him
a commodity? In the early eighteenth century large numbers of blacks
were kidnapped from Africa as boys and flaunted as prized young servants
who were ornaments to their masters and especially to their mistresses,
making especially vexing the problem of how a black *man*hood was to be
imagined and lived by a first generation of Africans who grew to maturity
in England.[18] It is the black boy rather than the black man who prevails
in English high culture of the period, a child who is converted to an *objet
d'art* and a status symbol who represents colonial wealth.[19] During the
early portion of *The Interesting Narrative of the Life of Olaudah Equiano, or
Gustavus Vassa, the African*, Equiano is, after all, narrating his childhood,
and to expect a mature masculinity to issue from the person described in
that portion of his autobiographical tale would be ludicrous.[20] Though the
status of black male servants attending women surely must have changed
rather abruptly after they had reached puberty, Equiano is baptized and
becomes a favorite of the eldest Miss Guerin. Much more than Sancho,
Olaudah Equiano has been interpreted as exemplifying the entire gendered
spectrum from a "mother's boy" (suspected of homosexual leanings) to a
manly warrior.[21]

Forged in part in the image of God, Equiano's manliness in his own account exudes the dignity, courage, and discipline of the Old Testament
prophets. Several recent critical assessments of Equiano imply that he
is exemplary of a rugged African masculinity made in the image of
such heroes. Folarin Shyllon, for example, found that Equiano "stood
uncompromisingly for black manhood, dignity, and freedom."[22] Paul

Edwards similarly thinks of the *Narrative* as depicting a universal epic quest for the lost father or mentor after Equiano was abducted from his family as a child,[23] since Equiano finds a master in Richard Baker and later is befriended by Daniel Queen who teaches him the Bible – and to dress hair. Closely attached to another father figure in Captain James Doran, Equiano occupies the posture of a black man who wields power over others when he becomes a "sable captain" who acts as a kind of "chieftain" (144) among the people for whom he is responsible. His connections to these and other older white Englishmen suggest an intense male bonding which either ignores color or covets adoption by a male authority. Equiano also presents himself as possessing a kind of muscular, sinuous masculinity which manifests itself in naval battles during the Seven Years' War as well as in his ability to withstand the mistreatment of slave owners and captains. Yet he also assumes a modest posture on the first page of his *Narrative* indicating that, though he counts himself among the most fortunate of slaves, he is no better than the common man, "neither a saint, a hero, nor a tyrant" (31).

Neither Equiano or Sancho emphasizes his manliness as a gendered characteristic, a fact worth remarking since England was increasingly constructing a manly national identity after the Seven Years' War. National fears about the loss of territory during the military conflict seemed to fuel British anxieties about metaphorical emasculation in the later eighteenth century. The *British* empire "was now represented as the antidote to aristocratic 'cultural treason' and effeteness, the bulwark and proving ground for the true national character and (middle class) potency and virtue."[24] Since a passion for liberty was synonymous with manliness, citizenship was also a function of maleness; Equiano, both the subject and object of empire, presents himself as a patriotic and active citizen who seeks to change national policy. He reports growing comfortable with English people and that he "relished their society and manners, wished to imbibe their spirit, and imitate their manners" (77), though he also gives vent to considerable ambivalence toward England's imperial vision. Well-versed in the doctrines of civic humanism, he shows a real cultural fluency in these principles when, as Adam Potkay has argued, in Equiano's early sketch of Ibo manners, he presents his native people not only as "the descendants of Abraham, but also as the true heirs of Cincinnatus – small farmers and militia-warriors, utterly unacquainted with the 'luxury' of modern Europe."[25] But he also reveals his social-class aspirations when, though thoroughly lacking the self-deprecatory quality of Sancho, Equiano is embarrassed by his poor horsemanship which would disqualify him from participating in the gentlemanly sport. Equiano's quandry is nothing less than the maddeningly puzzling conundrum of presenting in narrative a convincingly manly African who is *neither* noble nor savage, prince or slave, tragic hero or trickster, in spite of cultural expectations to the contrary, while at the same time demanding that he be accepted as a full citizen when the proper color of a citizen was unquestionably white.[26]

Equiano fully recognizes the economics of the British interest in Africa; and just as Wollstonecraft later claims that vindicating the rights of woman will snap the chains that bind men, Equiano argues that freeing slaves will benefit the British oppressors: "A commercial Intercourse with Africa opens an inexhaustible Source of Wealth to the manufacturing interests of Great Britain."[27] Equiano believes that slavery is an investment in an inhuman system of commerce, but that Africans would clearly benefit from the civilizing influences of British manufactures and culture, its "Fashions, Manners, Customs, &c.&c." (333). At times he even seems to disassociate England from the evils of slavery as when he vilifies the West Indies as a site of horror and inequity as distinct from the British Isles. Equiano demands "an humane and generous Treatment of *Negroes*, and indeed of all barbarous Nations in general, [and] that we must expect such Discoveries, as well as reap greater Advantages in Trade, than other nations." Abolition and its attention to slavery served partly as a distraction from other aspects of brutality on foreign shores as empire served to unify an English nationalism.[28]

While Equiano's heroic fighting in the Battle of Gibraltar (1759) and throughout the war offers him the opportunity to display his considerable fighting abilities – and he gains confidence when he knows that the ships he is sailing on will be entering the war (70) – the *Narrative* seems to me to give no hint of self-doubt in these matters of masculine prowess but only of the injustice with which he is treated.[29] The conventional rules of commerce do not apply to a man of Equiano's color since the money he earns can be withheld, his word refused to be accepted against a white man's, and by his own account he "suffered so many impositions in the commercial transactions in different parts of the world." Equiano's manliness is constantly compromised because his status as a freeman is not secure, though he never voices self-doubt about his reason and intelligence. As a black man he is, of course, an object of exchange rather than the possessor of property, and the idea of the unpredictability of exchange afforded to a black man is a regular refrain, "for, being a negro man, I could not oblige him to pay me" (128). A new, though illegal, slavery could be imposed at almost anytime, arbitrarily, no matter how high Equiano's own estimation of himself (220). Identity as a slave is, however, an assignation that Equiano never accepts as accurate, and he repeatedly and courageously asserts his humanity throughout the account of his life as he deals with the material reality of the status he refuses to accept.

In the ethnography which Equiano offers of his native Benin in the early pages of the *Narrative*, a portion heavily indebted to Benezet's travel accounts and perhaps entirely fictional as Equiano's life, he proudly presents his country's people as "warlike" (32). This is particularly pertinent to a discussion of manliness since during the later eighteenth century, Britons measured manhood in part by the willingness to serve in the military.[30] To be a warrior is not, however, necessarily synonymous with masculinity for an Ibo since according to his testimony, women too were warriors.[31] The manliness he describes as typical of his native people also incorporates artistic endeavors since he testifies that both sexes were dancers, singers, poets, and musicians, though the women as well as the men participate in military action throughout the African nations that Equiano visits. The rites of manhood, *ichi* or painful ritual scarification, however, were quite distinct from the requirements for women, and he reports that women and slaves ate separately from the men.

Oyeronke Oyewumi in particular has questioned the applicability of Western notions of gender, construed as unequal relations of power based on sexual characteristics, to West African societies (though her research concentrates on the Yoruba rather than the Ibo).[32] In fact Equiano would seem to be remarkably sensitive to these matters when he remarks that Ibo women joined the men in fighting and in tilling the soil, though their more typical occupations involved basket weaving, dyeing, sewing, and making earthen vessels. He does observe, however, that African women cultivate the crops while men fish and make canoes (26). Clearly the "head of family" is masculine, and the pipesmoking Creator whom the Ibos worship is referred to with masculine pronouns, as are the priests and healers of the tribe. Equiano boasts that in his Ibo tribe, scarification gave evidence of his father's extraordinary manliness, though later Equiano rejoices that he himself had not been similarly marked or had his teeth filed to points since those disfiguring features would have distinguished him as an exotic other in the non-African world (69). Like most European travel narratives which measure the level of civilization by the position of women, the *Narrative* seems eager to avoid accusations of Benin as primitive. At the same time, the typical division of labor between men and women, between public and the private spheres, generally characteristic of eighteenth-century Europe does not precisely correspond to that of eighteenth-century Africa, at least as Equiano reports it.

Equiano further maintains that the qualities of cleanliness, strength, beauty, and intelligence are universally distributed among his people without regard to gender. A distinction is made, however, regarding modesty: "Our women too were, in my eyes at least, uncommonly graceful, alert, and modest to a degree of bashfulness; nor do I remember to have ever heard of an instance of incontinence amongst them before marriage." All African woman are not the same, he is quick to add, and he remarks in disgust upon the lack of modesty in another tribe in another part of the continent to which he was taken (54). Thus the chastity of women is to be guarded, especially against enslaving men, even among warrior women. Similarly, he associates femininity with modesty, or its absence, when regarding the remarkably slender white women of Falmouth who seem to command less respect than other African women. Yet notably there is not a hint of misogyny or satire against women, white or black, in *The Interesting Narrative*, nor does Equiano's language reflect the common eighteenth-century associations of femininity with commerce and luxury. These are not the metaphors by which he lives or those by which he conceptualizes his life. His language is all politeness to "his kind patronesses, the Miss Guerins" (79) who recommend him as apprentice to a hairdresser, and to his former hostess in Guernsey and her daughter. Rather, Equiano's animus is reserved for the savage, brutal, and cannibalizing whites. Always aware of women and their fate from the screams of slave women in the ship's hold to their strife even while pregnant in the fields, for him the worst aspects of slavery are typified in the injustices done to black women including a cook whose jaw is cruelly muzzled with irons.

Other aspects of mid eighteenth-century British assumptions about black manhood are revealed unwittingly when the young Equiano confronts in close succession a white girl, white boys, and a black boy. Fearing being betrothed to a little white girl because such an obligation would take him away from his benevolent master, he reveals similar worries after a shipmate's daughter shows extraordinary attentiveness to him. In a wellworn phrase that echoes the trope of the Ethiop washed white, he documents becoming "mortified at the difference in our complexions" (69) when a white female playmate's face is made rosy with washing. The substitution he seems to desire is to possess for himself the red-and-white female beauty that is conventionally British. When Equiano longs to change his skin color, then, it is in relation to white womanhood, though he also wishes to escape from the compromisingly romantic potential of white femininity into male companionship.

Encounters with white femininity, even in children, create fears that he will be coerced into marriage; meetings with white boys lead to combat; and bonding with a black boy seems based on color in spite of his not recognizing its "naturalness," especially since he knows that there are differences among African nations.[33] Coerced by the ship's company into fighting as a spectacle for shipmates with a white boy on board ship, Equiano gains a bloody nose, though he defines it as "sport." On the Isle of Wight he famously encounters a black boy servant to a gentleman:

This boy having observed me from his master's house, was transported at the sight of one of his own countrymen, and ran to meet me with the utmost haste. I not knowing what he was about, turned a little out of his way at first, but to no purpose; he soon came close to me, and caught hold of me in his arms as if I had been his brother, though we had never seen each other before. (85)

Until he accepts the cultural force that demands they are brothers, Equiano does not recognize that sameness of complexion is supposed to be sufficient to bind boy to boy, man to man. Thus in the space of a few short pages, Equiano uncannily releases the culture's anxieties about black men in these consecutive vignettes. These incidents acculturate him to fabled ideas of Africanness, blackness, and black manliness while also reinforcing his own determinedly strong sense of self.

In sum, Equiano exemplifies the way that blackness, and in particular black maleness, artificially molds the incoherence of diverse African religions, customs, and tribes into a false unity through a perceived similarity of complexion. This fact becomes poignantly clear in Equiano's tale when others imagine that a young African woman must be his lost sister, though he immediately recognizes that the slave girl is from a different area of the Gold Coast. He seems proud of choosing his own countrymen when purchasing slaves for Doctor Charles Irving (205), again demonstrating that he is highly aware of the variations among African nations. It was, of course, politic for Equiano and Sancho to employ inaccurate and inexact epithets such as "Aethiopianus" or "unlettered African" as generic terms in order to draw together Ibos, Guineans, and other blacks in England who shared an interest in the abolition of slave trade. Equiano, for example, described the African slaves thrown alive into the ocean from the slave ship Zong as his countrymen; and as a leader in seeking justice, he talks of the Black Poor as "my countrymen" on several occasions. Sancho calls himself "an African" or a "Negur" (74) and refers to his "brother Moors" (75), yet when asked to write in behalf of a fellow black who is seeking a position, Sancho notes that sharing a similarity of color is not sufficient to merit a recommendation. His mocking self-description runs the national gamut in claiming French, African, and English influences on a "merry – chirping – white tooth'd – clean – tight – and light little fellow; – with a woolly pate – and face as dark as your humble; – and Guiney-born, and French-bred – the sulky gloom of Africa dispelled by Gallic vivacity – and that softened again with English sedateness" (60). Though color may constitute a politics, neither Sancho or Equiano conveys that the shade of complexion alone composes a predictable and consistent identity. The emergent European categories for racial identities in the later eighteenth century, more plastic and permeable than contemporary categories, do not provide sufficient variety to match the black men's understandings of difference.

A growing empire meant that various gendered and racial differences had to be integrated into the existing paradigms of "savage" or "exotic," and new ones had to be invented. Stereotypic blackness is often associated with hypersexualized virility, a fact which makes all the more curious Catherine Obianuju Acholonu's search for Equiano's African origins to argue that the historical Equiano may have been sold because he was insufficiently manly. The charge of "effeminacy" arises largely because, as the youngest son of seven children, he claims in his *Narrative* an unusually close relationship to his mother in Benin who lovingly tutored him. His inordinate fondness for her kept him close by her side at the market, when sleeping, and even during the forbidden period of menstruation. When describing the sublime pleasure of their visiting his grandmother's tomb together in the gloom of night, he becomes nostalgically euphoric. Equiano ignores, I am arguing, the conventional European gender restrictions that might label such behaviors as womanish or perversely feminine. Especially intimate with his sister with whom he was kidnapped, he laments that "the only comfort we had was in being in one another's arms all that night, and bathing each other with our tears" (47), encircled around the man who owned them. Seeking his sister throughout the narrative, he worries in an apostrophe that her innocence and virtue might have been trammeled. He also exhibits sentimental sympathy for the oppressed group of which he is a part, and he openly cries when Captain Doran, his master, refuses to take him to London. He reveals his intimacy with his mother and sister, his closeness with male friends on board ship, and other friends who were oblivious to color or sex, seemingly without embarrassment or elaborate protestations of manliness. Clearly then Equiano's autobiographical posture is often that of a public hero, an independent spirit and adventurer, who possesses a reassuringly secure masculinity which, in its lack of brutal aggressiveness and apparent asexuality, does not arouse white male anxieties or feminine libido.

It is difficult to ascertain the extent of Equiano's "effeminacy" as judged in eighteenth-century terms, especially since, as I have argued, the term was loaded with nationalist prejudices and implications. When Acholonu queries a native medicine man in contemporary Nigeria, as to whether a son's habit of following his mother so closely would have been considered excessively feminine, the shaman confirms that both parents would have been displeased by this behavior. Acholonu postulates, with the agreement of those she questions, that it was in fact Equiano's close adherence to his mother that would have led his family to send him away. She also provides strong hints of an impenetrable family secret that would explain Equiano's enslavement. Later she seems to reverse her conclusions, however, in indicating that though she "believed at first that Olaudah was singled out for sale because of his effeminate nature,"[34] she finally believes that Equiano was regarded fondly by his father and may have been sold by brothers or other relatives.

African princes might have been expected to be linked by social class with aristocratic corruption and its attendant luxury, most frequently figured as a troubling contaminant to British masculinity entering from France, the Mediterranean, or the East; but effeminacy was seldom associated with African men, in part perhaps because few Africans in Britain rose above the laboring classes and the poor, and as African princes they were instead linked with being military leaders. There is considerable evidence of increasing white apprehension about black male sexuality as greater numbers of freed slaves, largely male, enter Britain and develop some economic mobility, however limited it might be, in the later eighteenth century. In James Tobin's racist comments he argues that blacks are lazy, though it seems more likely that his comments could be interpreted as indicative of the high unemployment among former slaves in England: "did [Mr. Ramsay] ever meet with a ploughman, hedger, ditcher, mower, or reaper, in the country; or a black porter, or chairman, in London? On the contrary, I will be free to affirm, that out of the whole of this number, those who are not in livery are in rags; and such as are not servants, are thieves or mendicants."[35] Sancho, he claims, preferred being a servant to work until he became too obese for even that labor.

Equiano and Sancho are of course fully aware that the two most influential representations of the black man were the noble Africans Othello and Oroonoko, each of whom was married to a white woman. Like most African men in England in the eighteenth century, Equiano took a white English wife in spite of strong cultural objections to intermarriage and his own early association of whiteness with deformity (17).[36] In addition, as we have noted, Equiano negatively distinguishes white masculinity from black, in part by calling attention to the lack of morality of slaveowners and his inability to prevent their raping of innocent young slave girls. Equiano is quick to recognize the double standard for black men who are tortured and castrated for sex with white women, even prostitutes, "as if it were no crime in the whites to rob an innocent African girl of her virtue; but most heinous in a black man only to gratify a passion of nature, where the temptation was offered by one of a different colour, though that the most abandoned woman of her species" (104). Rather than alluding to the sexual characteristics of women slaves, he confines gender difference to their inequitable treatment to suggest that in the New World such issues rest on white men's perverse notions of their right to power rather than African men's respect for women's modesty. These arguments in behalf of a black male equality, and sometimes even their moral superiority to white men, are obviously intended to arouse abolitionist sentiments in Equiano's readers in claiming not only slavery's inhumanity, but that the color of virtue may indeed be black.

III

The character of Othello carried enormous cultural valence for all black men in the eighteenth century whether or not they married white women – and the majority did exactly that because of the relative scarcity of black women in England.[37] In the fifth edition of his *Narrative* published in 1792, the year of his marriage, Equiano ventriloquizes Othello's words to justify his action. Like the Shakespearean hero, he claims that love is the only witchcraft he applied in wooing a Desdemona (and perhaps inspiring Mungo Park's similar usage later), he protests that his "round unvarnished tale" (13), is a magical but "true" tale, and thus by analogy his autobiographical narrative becomes a love letter to the white feminized reader. In short, Equiano "becomes" Othello in order to sell his text even as he emphasizes his distance from the superstition and seduction inherent in the analogy.

Sancho too encountered the white mentality which could not distinguish between his person and that of the murderous dramatic former slave Othello. When *The Gentleman's Magazine* (January 1776) reprints Sancho's letter to Sterne urging his support of abolition, he is figured as possessing a white heart under a black exterior: "though black as Othello [he] has a heart as humanized as any of the fairest about St. James's."[38] Othello's words leap immediately to his consciousness as the prototypically tragic figure swayed by evil forces. When his friend John Meheux provides food and clothing in response to his petition, the weeping Sancho "quoted Othello, the fictional Moor whose life was wrecked by a planted handkerchief, and who, although 'unused to the melting mood,' wept at the sight of Desdemona's corpse. It is the shared experience of being black, socially buffeted and on the verge of ruination because of (a lack of) cloth that connects these two characters across the centuries" (59).[39] Yet Sancho's characteristic mode of dealing with entrenched cultural inscriptions is a sharp satiric humor finely attuned to the race and social class of the accuser. On another occasion Sancho is confronted by a rude white man who, thinking only of Shakespeare's tragic hero when seeing a black man, calls out "Smoke Othello!" William Stevenson reports that Sancho responded vehemently with "manly resentment" at being identified in such a manner: "'Aye, Sir, such Othellos you meet with but once in a century,' clapping his hand upon his goodly round paunch. 'Such Iagos as you, we meet with in every dirty passage. Proceed, Sir!'"[40] In this exchange Sancho calls attention to the incongruity of imagining a paunchy Othello and reflects racism back onto the white man by identifying him as a malevolent Iago-like creature. He is equally self-mocking in telling Meheux that he should choose more wisely than picking a blackamoor as a friend since all such "from Othello to Sancho the big – we are either foolish – or mulish – all – all without a single exception" (180). Such satire engages the offender at his level while demonstrating Sancho's superior trickster mode and his improvisational abilities to employ mimicry.[41] When hailed as Othello, Sancho thinks of Iago's trickery, and Equiano ponders cultural fears about miscegenation; each keeps Othello high in his consciousness, yet each resists too intimate an association with that identity.

Ignatius Sancho's letters date largely from the 1770s, a period of time when foppish effeminacy is tightly bound to foreign influences, and homophobia reigns. Soubise, whom Sancho counseled to live a more disciplined life (perhaps because Soubise's behavior led Sancho to remember his own sexual wanderings), lived for a time with persons of rank and became "one of the most conspicuous fops of the town."[42] Soubise was similarly haunted and taunted by the shadow of an Othello, this time imagined as a romance hero: "The duchess's maids [of the Duchess of Queensberry], who had little more to do than read novels, romances, and plays, lackadasically called him the young Othello,"[43] and when one of the maids brought charges of sexual advances against him, he was sent to Calcutta as a riding instructor. Having styled himself the *Black Prince*, his pretensions to high social status sparked his caricature as Mungo Macaroni, and Lady Mary Coke like other aristocratic women worried that his affectation of habits of the rich exceeded his station: "Why, Mrs. GAD, I'll tell you who he is: it is not Omiah [the Tahitian visitor to England Omai or Mai]; no, nor the Prince of – of – Oroonoko, who was here some years ago: – he is a Prince of Ana – Anna – madboe, who is come here to make peace or war with the *Premier*, and the rest of the great folks, for not having properly protected his father's Forts and Settlements. Remember the story of *Zanga* [in Edward Young's *Revenge*], and we must tremble." Mrs. Gad worries about the "dark design" she associates with any blackman, especially the vengeful Zanga, and she wonders whether he might turn out to be a Prince of France (like the hero of the Seven Years' War, for whom he most probably was named): "The name of S—se is known all over the world. He was a little tanned in the wars in Flanders; but our present Prince here has, if we are not much ill-informed, somewhat tarnished his reputation, if not his complexion, in the wars of VENUS, even in this Metropolis." She goes on to repeat the gossip of his having frequented the "nunneries" or houses of prostitution in King's Place because his constitution was full as warm as his complexion. The whores, regardless of his complexion, allegedly admired him, as Desdemona admired Othello, for "his manly *parts* and *abilities*." Soubise's antics are gleefully reported in order to confirm salacious expectations of black men and the attraction they hold for white women: "As to me, I acknowledge a Black man was always the favourite of my affections; and that I never yet saw either OROONOKO or OTHELLO without rapture" (349). Thus Soubise, even as the plaything of gentlewomen's maids, is supposed to resemble the universally applicable stereotypic black characters simply because of the resemblance in complexion.

Another African who leaves a written account, Ukawsaw Gronniosaw (James Albert), describes his falling in love with Betty, a silkweaver, while fearing that indulging his desire for her would repeat his unfortunate history with white women. Recounting their poverty and hunger, Gronniosaw talks of the unwillingness to bury his dead child in the Baptist churchyard or with the Quakers, perhaps because of his mixed-race status.[44] Unlike Equiano and Gronniosaw, Ignatius Sancho married a black woman, the West Indian Anne Osborne, apparently an unusual phenomenon in England in the eighteenth century, to curb his wildness and habituate himself to a wife whom he characterizes as "pretty well, pretty round, and pretty tame!" (38). Possibly Sancho had less access to potentially marriageable white women than Equiano because his lesser situation as a butler, grocer, and merchant would not have been commensurate with middling expectations. Still Sancho had no objection to intermarriage, though his Utopian vision of a raceless society is confined to the afterlife: "We will mix, my boy, with all countries, colours, faiths – see the countless multitudes of the first world – the myriads descended from the Ark – the Patriarchs – Sages – Prophets – and Heroes! My head turns round at the vast idea! We will mingle with them and untwist the vast chain of blessed Providence – which puzzles and baffles human understanding" (86). Sancho, driven by class concerns to support his large family, exhibits a certain class-conscious in suggesting that every wealthy person should willingly relinquish the family plate. There can be no pretence of African nobility here, and Sancho goes to the opposite extreme in condemning some of his race as "Blackamoor dunderheads" (182).

It is the appeal to sentimentality and its attendant social rank that most distinguishes Sancho from Equiano, a characteristic which has made him the object of criticism which would prefer to represent him as more manly.[45] His self-presentation as a man of sentiment is perhaps a kind of social reaching: "My soul melts at kindness – but the contrary – I own with shame – makes me almost a savage" (45). An admirer of Sir Charles Grandison, a man of sentiment and fashion, he also wants to separate himself from "the whole detail of eastern, effeminate foppery" characteristic of the British aristocracy, but he acknowledges his malleable character: "My fortitude (which is wove of very flimsy materials) too oft gives way in the rough and unfriendly jostles of life" (204). A review of the first edition of *Letters of the Late Ignatius Sancho* claims that the collection "presents to us the naked effusions of a negroe's heart, and shews it glowing with the finest philanthropy and the purest affections."[46] While this is an obvious appeal to readers who wish to engage in sentimentality, it also echoes a slave history in which slaves, ogled while stark naked, were chosen for their physical strength. According to Sancho, a viable masculinity includes evidencing sensibility to the slaves' sufferings, a view he shares with Ottabah Cugoano: "Every man of any sensibility, whether he be a Christian or an heathen, if he has any discernment at all, must think that for any men, or any class of men, to deal with their fellow-creatures as with the beasts of the field . . . that those men, that are the procurers and holders of slaves, are the greatest villains in the world."[47] He jauntily reveals his libertine streak and passion for gambling, yet he also insists that he is a family man. Jekyll's biographical sketch tidily commends his "domestic virtue," a phrase usually reserved for women (7).

Sancho signals in his frequent allusions to his color and to racial stereotypes his recognition that African authenticity is partially a performance doomed to predictable reviews even before its opening night.[48] He refers to himself as "a poor, thick-lipped son of Afric" (216) whose seven children, the Sanchonettes, were compared to little monkeys. At least one critic has argued that Sancho bore a "diseased psyche" that twisted him into believing he was the Caliban-like monster the society had assumed he was,[49] but alternatively we might regard Sancho as parodying himself or his children as dogs or monkeys precisely in order to insist on his humanity, and on his masculinity as well. Sancho's letters describing himself as "a coal-black, jolly African" (210) and a "Black-a-moor" (118) exhibit a playfulness and self-deprecating humor absent from Equiano. These references from the accomplished author and musician, friend of Sterne, and spokesperson for abolition are often tinged with an ironic recognition that such cultural designations are not strictly applicable.

Though Sancho mocks himself as fat, jolly, and ugly, he never impersonates or parodies the highly sexualized barbarian. More culturally adept than Equiano in adopting conventional attitudes toward women and the relationship between the sexes ("our sex are cowards" or "Time shrivels female faces" [65]), he mockingly reserves his right to demean the sex. On women's equality, he is fawningly chivalrous: "Could I new-model Nature – your sex should rule supreme – there should be no other ambition but that of pleasing ladies" (62). Sancho presents himself as erotically driven, guilty of an impossible relationship that leads to his ouster from a safe haven provided by his mistresses. The ostensible reason for his dismissal was a sexual offense, a mark of his virility that proved threatening to his chaste mistresses. According to Jekyll's biography, "Indignation, and the dread of constant reproach arising from the detection of an amour, infinitely criminal in the eyes of three Maiden Ladies, finally determined him to abandon the family."[50] But Jekyll's account is itself suspect, and it portrays Sancho – who documents his financial struggles – as luxuriating in the pleasures most often associated with aristocrats and nabobs. According to Jekyll, Sancho's passionate love of cards and women were inbred because of his geographical origins: "Freedom, riches, and leisure, naturally led a disposition of African texture into indulgences; and that which dissipated the mind of Ignatius completely drained the purse." Sancho positions himself clearly in opposition to "an effeminate gallimawfry" (48) and wants to participate in rescuing "this once manly and martial people from the silken slavery of foreign luxury and debauchery" (48). Here he firmly distances himself from the English, though elsewhere he identifies himself as a man of London rather than of the empire.

In sum, Sancho refuses to adopt an English masculinity based on commercial excess, or on foreign effeminacy, or even consistently as a man of feeling. When he speaks of the love for his country, he means England, though he signs a paper "Africanus" (114) and writes a set of dances called "Mungo's Delight," an obvious reference to the character in the popular operatic play by Charles Dibdin and Isaac Bickerstaffe, *The Padlock* (1768).[51] At a time when British manliness is most associated with economic man and imperial designs, Sancho – a grocer of a small shop in Westminster – wonders at the futility of the pursuit of commercial growth: "Trade is duller than ever I knew it – and money scarcer – foppery runs higher – and vanity stronger; – extravagance is the adored idol of this sweet town" (77). He cautions his friend Jack Wingrave to "despise poor paltry Europeans–titled–Nabobs" (129). The conquering British, he suggests, taught the natives of the East and West Indies bad behavior, not the opposite. He urges racial intermixture on Christian principles: "Blessed expiation of the Son of the most high God – who died for the sins of all – all – Jew, Turk, Infidel, Heretic; – fair – sallow – brown – tawney – black – and you – and I – and every son and daughter of Adam" (93), and he wants to knit the British empire together. Yet it was empire itself that demonstrated the limits of nationalist thinking, just as it was black masculinity that threatened to make British masculinity into a caricature of itself.

Equiano does not talk about himself as a sexual being with one rare exception after he is freed and wishes to go to London: "Some of the sable females, who formerly stood aloof, now began to relax, and appear less coy, but my heart was still fixed on London, where I hoped to be ere long" (138). For him sexuality involves white slaveowners brutally preying upon and ravaging African slave women when they "commit violent depredations on the chastity of the female slaves" (104) who thus disgrace themselves as Christians and as men. He does, however, speak openly (in response to James Tobin's racist writings in *The Public Advertiser*, 28 January 1788) about the irrationality of confining masculine desire to women of the same color, and about the hypocrisy of the forced, furtive liaisons between French planters and their black slaves. Equiano publicly questions the open resistance to the union of black men with white women, while the brutalizing of black women by white plantation owners is ignored.

Defined by its negation, black manhood meant *not* being a boy, *not* being a beast or monster, *not* being effeminate or a woman. Neither Sancho nor Equiano easily found a way to negotiate a black manhood that would avoid replicating the racial fictions of the pervasive representations of Othello and Oroonoko on the one hand, or the imperial white mercantilist man on the other. By the end of the century negative attitudes toward miscegenation and the fetishization of the sexual potency of black men had begun to coalesce and prevail. Being a (black) man involved skewing, twisting, and violating expectations based on the small but massively influential sampling of characters such as Friday, Zanga, Othello, and Oroonoko. Equiano and Sancho are remarkable in circumventing the monstrous racial fictions that erroneously and egregiously mapped the domestic and imperial regions of black masculinity to shape themselves instead into viable subjects who offered credible alternatives to reigning notions of white British manhood in the later eighteenth century. In a culture struggling to reconcile masculinity with sentiment while avoiding effeminacy, it was the very palpable presence of these real alternatives to national molds which made these black men the locus of fascination and pathos, at once both threatening and appealing to white women and white men alike.

CHAPTER 8

Black parts: racial counterfeit on stage

It does not alter the nature and quality of a man, whether he wears a black or a white coat, whether he puts it on or strips it off, he is still the same man. And so likewise, when a man comes to die, it makes no difference whether he was black or white, whether he was male or female, whether he was great or small, or whether he was old or young; none of these differences alter the essentiality of the man, any more than he had wore a black or a white coat and thrown it off for ever.

Quobna Ottobah Cugoano, *Thoughts and Sentiments on the Evil of Slavery*

I

Though Ignatius Sancho was born on a slave ship headed for the West Indies, he became extraordinarily accomplished as the first Afro-British playwright, theater critic, art critic, composer, and patron of the arts.[1] One "first" that Sancho did not manage to achieve was to become the first black actor on the British stage. Joseph Jekyll, Sancho's eighteenth-century biographer, suggests that the author "loved the theatre to such a point of enthusiasm, that his last shilling went to Drury-Lane, on Mr. Garrick's representation of Richard. He had been even induced to consider the stage as a resource in the hour of adversity, and his complexion suggested an offer to the manager of attempting Othello and Oroonoko; but a defective and incorrigible articulation rendered it abortive."[2] Jekyll does not seem to recognize the monumental significance of Sancho's aspiration, but the fact that the first African black did not appear on the British stage until Ira Aldridge's London debut in the early nineteenth century means that such a performance in the 1760s or 1770s would have been an unprecedented event in theatre history. That Aldridge chose to leave America and its all-black theatre troupe, the African Theatre, suggests that the history of black performance was very different in England from that of the New World. It appears, for example, that black actors in America were pushed aside to make way for blackface minstrel shows.[3] Aldridge's appearance on the stage coincided with the production of a sufficient number of roles for a black man to allow him to make a living as an actor in England.[4]

As we have seen throughout the eighteenth century the self-annihilating black heroes of Shakespeare's *Othello* and Southerne's *Oroonoko* continued to be presented on stage, and adaptations proliferated in the abolitionist years of the 1770s and beyond.[5] Continuing the analysis of racialized masculinity in the eighteenth century, this chapter turns from autobiographical writing to the dramatic repertory of black parts in the British theatre. The eighteenth-century stage provides a peculiar interlude between the all-white, all-male stage of Shakespeare and the appearance of the first black male actor in a patent theatre in 1833.[6] During that period white women appear on stage for the first time, frequently in breeches roles, and white male actors continue to appear in ever-increasing blackface parts.[7] The initial appearance of female bodies on the Restoration stage opened the possibility of a theatre career for women, stimulated the writing of cross-dressed roles, and at the same time clarified gender difference. In being crossdressed *women* for the first time after the Renaissance rather than boys in women's clothing, actresses were able to taunt audiences to imagine their heterosexual difference under men's clothing. Thus they performed difference and subjected it to regulation at the same time. The correlation between the represented black body and the actual black body was delayed by a full century and a half after white women had been admitted to the English stage. The popularity of black parts encouraged playwrights to invent appropriate roles as they had done in the case of breeches parts, but it seems likely that black characters acted by an actual black man also stabilized "race" – and in particular black masculinity – in a way that had not occurred before.

Ira Aldridge's appearance on the stage in England in October 1825 as Oroonoko in *The Revolt of Surinam, or A Slave's Revenge* at the Coburg (now the Old Vic), inspiring both devision and applause would have radically changed the theatrical scene. Aldridge, most probably born in New York of Senegalese Fulah ancestry, was known as "the African Roscius," although he could as easily have been termed an American. He first acted in the African Free School in New York. In order to describe the kinds of staged versions of black masculinity produced during the later eighteenth and the early nineteenth century, I will here examine several plays to illuminate further the complexities concerning the representation of black masculinity before the counterfeit black man, the blacked-up white in racial disguise, comes to coexist with the embodied black man on the early nineteenth-century

English stage. Aldridge performed admirably in numerous plays familiar to eighteenth-century audiences who were accustomed only to the greasepaint, lampblack, smeared cork, pomatum, and woolly-wigged caricatures of blackness of white English actors who affected nativism. (These actors would of course have been merely blackened Europeans rather than possessing distinctly African features.) Touring in the provincial theatres, his best-known roles were *The Ethiopian, or the Quadroon of the Mango Grove* (*The Slave*), Hassan in M. G. Lewis' *The Castle Spectre*, Zanga in Edward Young's *Revenge*, and Mungo in Isaac Bickerstaffe's *The Padlock*, all of which were parts written exclusively for black characters, though Aldridge also blanched himself for other roles in order to play, for example, a white-bearded, bewigged, and chalked King Lear, Macbeth, and Shylock (illustration 20). In the year that slavery was abolished in the British colonies, Aldridge's inaugural appearance at Covent Garden (one of two patent theatres) as Othello on 16 April 1833 received mixed reviews. After one more appearance, he acted instead in minor London theatres, Scotland, Ireland, Europe, and Russia until twenty-five years later.[8] Perhaps as early as 1838, performing as a black minstrel in a composite of his major roles, Aldridge competed with white minstrel shows which impersonated him and his fellow actors from the African Theatre.

In addition to the noble African blackface roles in the familiar tragedies *Oroonoko* and *Othello*, comic parts for blackfaced slaves, servants, or the working class such as *The Padlock*, *The Blackamoor Wash'd White*, and *Harlequin Mungo* became popular in the later eighteenth century. These plays, attended by visiting luminaries from around the emerging empire, presented dramatic figurings of black masculinity that vied with, and perhaps superseded, the real Indian kings and African princes occasionally reported to be in the audience, as well as the increasingly well-known Afro-British abolitionists Cugoano, Sancho, and Equiano. The plays provide, like minstrelsy, "the fetishized mark of genuineness...one big wink,"[9] to celebrate black male bodies by simulating them. Yet they also reduce actual blacks to sexualized stereotypes and occlude their slave labor. The tragedies, comedies, and pantomimes all deal with two major cultural fears which intensified in the later eighteenth century: that burgeoning numbers of free blacks arriving in the country would take the jobs of English domestics, and that mixing "races" brought contamination to a nation seeking a racialized identity distinctly different from its imperial territories.

If this public counterfeit of blackface defused the threat of black masculinity and helped regulate race relations in much the same way as American minstrelsy of the nineteenth century, then what difference does it

20 Ira Aldridge as Aaron in "Titus Andronicus" (1827). In addition to his roles as Othello and Oroonoko, Aldridge appeared as Aaron and as a whitened King Lear.

make when an embodied black male presence enters the theatre after slaves were finally emancipated in 1833 after the slave trade had ended in 1807? If "society has relied upon affirmations of masculinity to resolve social and political crises," as Hazel V. Carby suggests, does the appearance of the first black man on the English stage when slaves are freed negotiate this cultural turning point principally by replicating existing power relations?[10] How, we might ask, is black masculinity configured in a theater that is attempting to reconcile the anxieties of empire with its evolving national myths?

During the later eighteenth century when the British lost one empire and a second is not yet won, uncertainty and confusion are signaled by racial counterfeit. By figuring blackness in this way on the domestic home stage, the plays offer inchoate fictions that celebrate black masculinity while easing the path to continued dispossession of peoples and to exploitation in the empire. These plays, in spite of their being produced as the abolition movement gathers force, are not really anti-slavery dramas.[11] Black parts on the eighteenth-century stage occasionally serve the goals of abolition but more often, as this chapter argues, the parts heighten the contradictions surrounding race in an attempt to cleanse England of its racial impurities and reconcile itself to a slave history. Through an analysis of Aldridge's repertory, I examine here a nation's ability to distract itself from the violence perpetrated on the black male body, and from its uncertainties about human hierarchies through its investment in the public performance of a counterfeit black masculinity.

Blacking up in the eighteenth-century theatre, as I have argued in chapter 6, was almost exclusively masculine since very few women of color were represented in drama. The history of black men on the eighteenth-century stage is a very short history indeed since I know of no African male (or female) performers in the English theatre until Aldridge's appearance. Instead its history is one of blackface, of costume and disguise, other than the very few exceptions which record sightings of black performers at fairs and carnival gatherings. Blackface – white men pretending to be black men – emphasized performance as an important element of race; but in re-assuring the viewer that the actor was actually a white beneath the make-up, the practice also reflects elements of essentialism and racism. In becoming black, the white man can participate in the sublime thrill of blackness, yet in the very act of presenting it, of inhabiting it, he exerts some limited control over its effects. This impersonation of black men, more fluid than the binary of hybridity or miscegenation, establishes a border that W. T. Lhamon Jr. (following Mary Louise Pratt) has called a "contact zone" between cultures;[12] such an imaginative space encourages an irreverence about complexion's consequences that makes blackness appear to be both decorative and alien while also taming its effects.

There are a few recorded instances of black street performers during the period. In the late seventeenth century the account of the grocers' tribute in the Lord Mayor of London's pageant mentions a Negro boy holding exotic fruits and mounted on a camel. Another Negro is described as wearing a garland of feathers on his head, flanked by a goddess of plenty and by two West-Indian princes with three other Black-Moors, grotesquely dressed in bright silks and outlandish feathers, all of whom attend a black-faced king.[13] In the entertainments set forth by the company of drapers in the Lord Mayor's Procession for 1675, "two Negro's in Robes of Silver, girt about with skin-colour'd Scarffs, Crowned with Coronets of various colour'd Feathers" representing Strength and Concord parade through the streets of London.[14] It seems likely that these men were black impersonators adorned with exotic props rather than actual blacks since an observer comments that the imperial being in the grocers' pageant has "a Face black, and likewise his Neck and Arms, which are naked to the Elbows; on his Head a Crown of various coloured Feathers, a rope of Pearl about his Neck, Pendants in his Ears, short curl'd black wool-like-Hair, a Coat of several painted Feathers... Carnation Silk Stockings, and... Silver Buskins laced before."[15] Other accounts tell of two Negroes mounted on griphons dressed in "Indian" habits. On a later occasion, the *Daily Courant* (27 April 1704) remarks that a man called Penkethman, having rented out "a rope-dancing booth" in Brookfield Market Place, also spoke an epilogue from the back of an elephant "between Nine and Ten Foot High, arrived from Guinea, led upon the Stage by six blacks." Again it is not exactly clear whether these performers would have been Africans, though it seems most likely that these pageant performers were whites in black greasepaint.[16]

It is crucial to understanding the history of racial representation as well as abolition that the number of actual blacks visible in the streets of English towns continued to expand until it reached a conspicuous critical mass in the last two decades of the century. Observers suggest that black servants tended to congregate together, and that domestics of both sexes held fashionable gatherings in which they "supped, drank, and entertained themselves with dancing and music, consisting of violins, French horns, and other instruments, at a public-house in Fleet-street, till four in the morning. No Whites were allowed to be present, for all the performers were Blacks."[17] Among the centers of the black slave trade including Manchester, Liverpool, Birmingham, and Bristol, there must have been other private entertainments and assemblies as well. Freed blacks in England worked in the streets as buskers, sweepers, or beggars. Most of the slaves sold in London were children, but elite Africans had also sent their free young children to be educated in Europe: "By the 1780s there were always at least 50 African schoolchildren, girls as well as boys, in Liverpool and the villages around," many of whom were children of wealthy West Africans rather than slaves.[18] At the same time the number of blacks in the street started rising, the number of blackface roles in the theatre slowly increased even though Africans and East or West Indians themselves were not accepted as principal actors on the London stage.

When reading the plays rather than imagining their performances, it is easy to forget that black parts in eighteenth-century drama were enacted by white men. At the same time the racial markers are less an indicator of racial authenticity for blacks than a flexible masquerade that calls attention to itself and can shift according to the demands of the context.[19] The shift in those identities is particularly pronounced depending upon the genre of the play – the tragic emphasizing displaced noble princes and the comic portraying the lower classes, slaves and servants engaged in disruptive activities. Second, such plays allowed white men to inhabit the putative bodies of black men, to shape and mold the culture's perceptions of them, while simultaneously implying through racial simulation that race is ephemeral. The core beneath the racial counterfeit, and perhaps even the core of black men themselves, is imagined as "white." Third, these black parts also permitted white men to attempt an imagined interracial male bonding that could smooth over differences in rank and geographical origin.[20] These bonds between black and white men seem to surface especially at times of significant cultural shifts in race relations, as in the case of the later eighteenth century when England turned from slavery toward abolition. Finally, the male bonding between black and white men in these plays evokes both a homoerotic miscegenation and a misogynist racism that marginalizes white women and largely eradicates black women from the stage. These plays and others were critical in the formation of a national white masculinity, and important in unifying that masculinity as liberal white feminism and the discourse of human rights begins to gain a public voice.

Though Ignatius Sancho remained a member of the audience in the eighteenth-century theatre rather than a performer on stage, his life is reflective of major historical changes for black men and of the awful threat that they posed in the imaginations of white British men and women. Originally a servant to three Greenwich sisters, to the duke, and finally to heir to the Duke of Montagu's duchy (his widow's son-in-law), Sancho himself became an entrepreneur of sorts, opening a small grocery shop in Westminster in 1773 with the Duke of Montagu's assistance. As a young man, then, Sancho was typical in serving as a sign of white women's wealth, first as a commodity which was purchased and traded, and then as an unremunerated servant. As we have seen, portraits of aristocratic women in which young black male servants offer gifts in imitation of the black magi approaching the white madonna[21] testify not only to the ladies' pristine beauty in contrast to the African child, but also to their high rank as displayed through their connection to the commercial success of the empire.

Sancho's achievement, eventually becoming a producer of wealth in his own right, reflects the danger former slaves arriving in England posed since they could progress from being unpaid servants to competing with English domestic servants for paid employment. Though his letters were published only posthumously (1782), his writings were among the very first in England to voice antislavery sentiments.[22] As Sancho became better educated and more economically self-sufficient, he aspired to appear in the two most popular plays with black protagonists I have discussed throughout this book, Shakespeare's *Othello* and Southerne's *Oroonoko*. If Sancho had succeeded in mounting the boards, he would have afforded a stark reality to the interracial topic of both plays. His presence on stage would have granted some stability to racial categories and made less benign the assimilation of the other. The "defective articulation" which prevented the realization of his dream has sometimes been interpreted as stuttering, but it more likely can be attributed to his speaking with an inflection or dialect that reflected his origins and his very early years in New Granada. The ability to speak was often a critical issue in determining the relative humanity or bestiality of Africans. Further, the word "Hottentot," sometimes a broad synonym for any African in the eighteenth century, derives from the Dutch words for "stammer" and "stutter." In fact, "English and French medical literature still defines 'hottentotism' as a form of extreme stammering."[23]

Othello and *Oroonoko* continued to be presented in blackface throughout the century, and adaptations proliferated along with the increased consciousness of the cruelty of colonial slavery in the 1760s and 1770s. In fact, actors frequently debuted in tragic blackface roles, perhaps as a means of masking their features until the audience reception to the actors could be more fully gauged.[24] In addition to the familiar tragedies, comic blackfaced characters appeared most notably in Isaac Bickerstaffe's *The Padlock* (1768) and *The Blackamoor Wash'd White* (1776) written by Rev. Henry Bate. *The Blackamoor Wash'd White*, perhaps the first minstrel show, was booed from the stage after three performances and never performed again; but *The Padlock* was frequently revived, and the name of its blackfaced character

Mungo, originally a Scots name, enters the language as a synonym for a black man. The central male characters in these dramas were all acted by white men in blackface. These precursors to minstrelsy, I suggest, share minstrelsy's "mixed erotic economy of celebration and exploitation,"[25] as Eric Lott has put it, and show a white culture's fascination with black skin.

A critical view of minstrelsy now largely out of favor is that in robbing a culture to exploit it, blackface is simply a form of white dominance over blacks. In the two eighteenth-century comedies by Bickerstaffe and Bate we can see that the blackface characters certainly display some elements of cultural robbery – an exaggerated dialect, a performance of African dancing or singing – but the concept of such thievery is more accurately applied to the nineteenth century.[26] If not principally pillagers of a foreign territory, then what other functions do these blackface comic men absorb on the eighteenth-century stage? Lott remarks, "The blackface mask is less a repetition of power relations than a *signifier* for them – a distorted mirror, reflecting displacements and condensations and discontinuities between which and the social field there exist lags, unevennesses, multiple determinations."[27] This instability of meaning and its entangling with power relations requires much nuanced decoding when it is transposed to minstrelsy's prehistory where the fuzzy borders of "white" and "black," concepts still not fully articulated in culture, were being redrawn on stage. It seems likely that minstrelsy originated in the many songs and operettas staged between acts, including Ethiopian sketches, dialogues, burlesques and parodies that may have had roots in African culture.[28] Offering alternative representations to the dominant tragic images of the black prince and the noble savage, they racialize black men through cultural codes unavailable in the tragedies and make troubling issues such as miscegenation and slavery potentially risible, less horrifying, and at the same time more knotty.

Comic blackfaced actors appear most notably in *The Padlock* as well as Bate's *The Blackamoor Wash'd White*. Bate was the editor of *The Morning Post and Daily Advertiser* (1772–81)[29] and author of a popular pantomime that included African dancing, *Harlequin Mungo*. *The Blackamoor Wash'd White* is a two-act comic opera performed at Drury Lane in February 1776. Though the minstrel show was a nineteenth-century American "fiction about blacks that pleased its perpetrators,"[30] the blackface comedy in England which evolved a century before produced audience dissatisfaction. When the production was first mounted, reportedly it was loudly scorned: "Much hissing and Crying out no more no more!" The audience was temporarily appeased only to repeat the response the following night:

"as soon as they were quiet Mr G[arrick] told them that his Theatrical Life would be very Short and he should be glad to end it in peace – A man in the Pit said if you have a mind to die in Peace don't let this Farce be play'd again Mr Garrick was on and off the Stage several times nothing would content them."[31] The farce closed after three nights. It is not clear what exactly produced such a pronounced reaction, though the play was certainly unusual in its topic and approach. Perhaps the audience was simply providing a critical response to a weak script, but it may as likely have been rejecting the particular treatment of racial and class intermixture that the play advanced.

The Blackamoor Wash'd White deals with the cultural anxieties mentioned earlier – that increasing numbers of free blacks were spoiling the labor market for English domestics, and that their positions within an urban domestic space would hazard amalgamated unions. There is convincing evidence that when slaves first came to England their paltry wages might have merely amounted to shelter and clothing in exchange for their services, their devotion, and the display of themselves as part of their owner's wealth. Native-born English servants, however, were more likely to demand monetary remuneration, and even earlier in the century blacks had been legally prevented from gaining upward mobility and from competing with whites by serving as apprentices: "The Proclamation by the Lord Mayor of London...in September 1731...forbidding as it did the employment of blacks as apprentices in the city" was intended to prevent blacks from usurping jobs for white British among the working class.[32] Britain's Committee for the Relief of the Black Poor had convinced the British government to deport its black poor to Sierra Leone in the 1780s. *The Blackamoor Wash'd White* and *The Padlock* are poised between these two legal attempts to limit upward mobility for the poorest of Britain's immigrants. At the end of the Seven Years' War (1763) large numbers of the British military had returned home to find themselves in a sea of surplus labor. The surge of British soldiers seeking jobs corresponded in time to black servants' increased resistance to working without wages and produced a crisis not only in employment but also in white masculinity.

In a parody of the *Othello* plot, *The Blackamoor Wash'd White* explores the cultural confusions about sexual interaction between the races and explores the consequences of locating race in social class at a time when comic lowly black character begin to compete with the usual tragic ones. Blackface in the eighteenth century as well as in later minstrel shows invoked social class so forcefully that the genealogy of race also helps us track the formation of the working class. These blackface performers, for the first time comic, displayed in their competition with whites the troubles of the working class on stage.[33] Invoking the familiar tradition of washing the Ethiop white, the play comically proves that the blackamoor is after all only a masked and painted British soldier, and that white womanhood would not be sexually or racially threatened by black butlers, footmen, or valets.[34] Blacks were associated almost exclusively with the servant class and chastized in print for their alleged unwillingness to be employed in other capacities. But it is not completely clear in the play as to whether sexual intermixture, or unstable social class, is more troubling to the emerging consciousness of a middling class.

In *Blackamoor* the delusional Sir Oliver Oddfish, suspecting that his wife and daughter might be attracted to their white male servants, creates a moat around his estate and sacks his staff. While class issues appear right on the surface, conversations in the play about the labor of black servants in England help to distance the forced labor of Negro slaves in the colonies. The play sexualizes all male servants regardless of race because of their easy access to women in déshabillé and the boudoir, and it treats the difference in status between lady and attendant as irrelevant in the face of desire. As the play progresses, Sir Oliver Oddfish asks his nephew Grenville to replace the white servants with blacks, "a regiment of Blackamoor Devils," so that his womenfolk will be safer from sexual temptation.[35] The play mocks Oddfish's naiveté about the reputed sexuality of black men though the joke rests of course on the pretense of blackness – that a character in blackface, not an actual African, expresses desire for his daughter. Grenville coaxes his friend Frederic (played by Mr. Vernon) to disguise himself as the black Amoroso in order to court Sir Oliver's daughter Julia (played by famed Sarah Siddons, remarkable for her snowy complexion). That the disguise, a discarded masquerade costume, is readily available indicates the pervasiveness of racial impersonation in mid eighteenth-century culture. The use of dialect also distinguishes the blackface character, though Frederic worries about his ability to imitate adequately such defective artic-ulation. The comedy in *Blackamoor* rests in part on Frederic's speaking this dialect, one of the earliest examples of racialized speech, with genuflections to "massa," as well as offering the opportunity for disingenuous *double entendres*.

A taleteller like Othello, Frederic recounts the story of an Egyptian man who, like Sir Oliver, zealously hovers over the white and red fruit of his cherry tree, an obvious allusion to Julia's complexion. The tale is also vaguely linked to the garden of Eden in that a cherry tree substitutes for the fatal apple tree, and the blackened Frederic is likened to the devil. Sir Oliver is "blackened" too when, in an allusion to Othello, he puts a handkerchief over his head to spy on his wife whom he suspects of cuckolding him. The allegory allows for titillating allusions to a woman's sexual part, her cherry, ripe for picking. The comedy arises from averting an Othello-like tragedy; but since Othello is not really black, the sexual threat is merely a ruse, and the pretend "black" servant rises to become a white gentleman. To black up has been "the most fortunate metamorphosis of his life" since it has won him Sir Oliver's approval. In washing the blackamoor white, the comic opera offers cultural reassurance that white British men will not be contaminated by the threat of black servants, by miscegenated offspring, or by the working class. Blackface becomes a vehicle that allows a white man to win his beloved. This play underscores the way that class, like race, may be construed to be provisional and performative. Thus the theatrical practice incorporates strong elements of racism while it also brings to prominence the possibility of class mobility.

Though the character Frederic is not from the working class as later minstrels often were, the one white servant remaining, Jerry, gives voice to laborers' anxieties about black freemen and even East Indians taking English jobs: "Why surely the times are turn'd topsey turvey, that white Englishmen should give place to foreign Blacks." Fearing that "the Devils bastard" will "sculpt a body in one's sleep," the first act of the comic opera ends with a song because, though Frederic (Amoroso) pretends to be black and alien and working class, he turns out to be a white soldier. In short, black reassuringly proves to be white:

> Must a Christian man's son born & bred up,
>   By a *Negar* be flung in disgrace?
> Be asham'd for to hold his poor head up,
> 'Cause as how he has got a white face?
>   – No never mind it little *Jerry*,
>   Let your honest heart be merry;
>   British boys will still be right,
>   'Till they prove that *black is white*!

> M'hap the nabob, that brought the poor Creature
>   From Father, and Mother and all,
> Is himself of a Blackmoor nature,
>   Dark within as the tribe of Bengal!
>   – So never mind it, little *Jerry*,
>   Let your honest heart be merry;
>   *British Boys* will still be right,
>   'Till they prove that *black* is *white*!

A white man raised by a Negro servant need not be ashamed if *he* remains white, and he contrasts to the East or West Indian nabob who, in transporting the black to England, "Is himself of a Blackmoor nature in his heart if not his skin." In this play black *is* reassuringly white since Frederic blacks up and pretends to be a servant, and his essence remains white underneath.

The wish that blacks would prove to be white, that skin is merely a costume which can be discarded to reveal a white heart, soul, and core, is a constant theme of eighteenth-century representations that include black characters, a theme most famously articulated in William Blake's "Little Black Boy": "And I am black, but oh, my soul is white." In this comic opera being black is a whimsical habit to put on, a mere costume donned during the masquerade and easily removed, rather than a skin color or a geographical origin that has consequences in the real world. *The Blackamoor* introduces a precursor to American minstrelsy in a singing blackface trickster who engages in comic routines to contest the authority of a dominant, if easily duped, patriarch. In the concluding acts of the play the humor focuses on the grotesqueness of the blackened Frederic's courting the lovely white Julia. Their love scenes startle the audience while repeatedly reminding them that the disguised Frederic is truly white underneath, both as a character and as a man. The counterfeit black Frederic believes that turning color is less disgraceful than a change of heart. When he ironically asserts, "I think myself ev'ry bit as good a man as Massa Frederic," Sir Oliver rages infuriated, "Black or White's all one I see." Black and white men are united in Frederic: their masculinity and their sexual desire for a (white) woman erase any differences between them. The potential offspring of Julia and the black servant are only imagined to produce "a nest of Black-a-moor Devils hatch'd under his Roost" since the threat of miscegenation is feigned.

This play and others like it trifle with myriad connotations of "black," as if to suggest that the word itself carries hilarity. *The Blackamoor* also allows the characters unselfconsciously to utter racisms against the counterfeit black, including making allusions to a black mazzard (a wild cherry), ugly devil, blackey man, raven, magpie, Satan, and calling attention to "saucer" eyes. Like American minstrelsy in the nineteenth century which displays "the power of 'blackness' while deriding it,"[36] blackness and its performance in eighteenth-century England provoke white mirth. *The Blackamoor Wash'd White* displays racism in its full comic potential since the racial menace is completely obliterated by the play's end. The play washes Julia's lover white to erase the awful fear of blackness, even a counterfeit blackness, in both its racial and class meanings, as Africans and Indians (East and West) encroach on the British islands and move up the social ladder. The instability introduced by the intrusion of a blacked-up man on the stage and into a white woman's private space is evacuated of its threat. The play displays, toys with, and reduces the mystique of black masculinity. *The Blackamoor Wash'd White* evokes an eroticized lower-class black masculinity only to trivialize its power through lighthearted mockery as black man and white man are briefly melded together in the counterfeit protagonist. *Blackamoor* defers and postpones the shadow of miscegenation in spite of free blacks seeking employment after the war.

The black comic characters in this period are largely working-class servants, in contrast to the black male character of tragedy who is most frequently a princely African slave (or a former slave) whose captivity seems especially heinous because of his nobility. The comedy *Padlock*, like *Blackamoor Wash'd White* and *Harlequin Mungo*, centers on a black trickster who is a servant or slave. First performed very successfully at Drury Lane Theatre in 1768, *The Padlock* was among Aldridge's most frequently performed roles and his only comic part. It offered him an early minstrel role in which he sang and played the lute as the crafty slave of a West Indian planter.[37] The story involves an aging Don Diego who ponders marriage with his sixteen-year-old poverty-stricken ward Leonora who is in love with the young Leander. Padlocking Leonora and Mungo into his home to guard her purity in his absence, Don Diego tells of having "banish'd all that had the shadow of man, or male kind" (30), excluding Mungo from the category of humankind and ignoring his masculinity. Called an intoxicated slave, a drunken swab, and a monster, Mungo's status in the play is radically unstable since he also engages the audience's sympathy by siding with the young lovers. Leander, disguised as a disabled minstrel, even becomes Mungo's drinking partner. Mungo, calling himself "poor Negerman" (6), has no pretensions to nobility and complains of Diego's beatings on the grounds of human rights:

> Dear heart, what a terrible life am I led!
> A dog has a better that's shelter'd and fed:
> Night and day 'tis de same,
> My pain is dere game:
> Me wish to de Lord me was dead.
>
> Whate'er's to be done.
> Poor black must run;
> Mungo here, Mungo dere,
> Mungo every where;
> Above and below,

Sirrah come, Sirrah go,
Do so, and do so.
Oh! Oh!
Me wish to de Lord me was dead."
                    (Act 1.6.11)

Diego's cruelty is also in evidence on stage when he labels his servant "a lynx" and a "perverse animal." In contrast, Leander's story seems to lessen the savagery of Mungo's situation, deracialize it, and make it seem to be a condition common to the working class or the laboring poor. He laments, "I lived eleven years and three quarters upon cold water and the roots of the earth, without having a coat on my back, or laying my head on a pillow; an infidel bought me for a slave: he gave me the strappado on my shoulders, and the bastinado on the soles of my feet: now this infidel Turk had fifty-three wives, and one hundred twelve concubines" (1.8.13). Affecting to be a hobbled Barbary slave among the Moors and thus a kind of blackened white made more pitiful in his compromised state, Leander witnesses to *Turkish* barbarity, polygamy, and *white* slavery.

Like *The Blackamoor Wash'd White*, *The Padlock* is filled with masculine dominance and racialized violence. Diego's other servant, the ancient duenna Ursala, protests *her* mistreatment because of being a woman: "That men should rule our sex is meet, / But art, not force, must do the feat." Thus the play interestingly displaces enslavement and confinement onto women and onto white men rather than emphasizing black slavery. Yet it also displays a diminished black masculinity aligned with disability, white slavery, and passive white femininity to draw vague parallels among natural rights discourses of all sorts. White masculinity of a certain class is fortified by these comic dramatic representations, though giving voice to black masculinity in its actual embodied form as well as its counterfeit also sets up the possibility of resisting these equivocal ideas of blackness.

An anonymous one-act Christmas pantomime performed much later, *Furibond; or, Harlequin Negro* (1807), also focuses on a trickster character. Applauding the end of the slave trade, this comedy first performed at the Theatre Royal in Drury Lane follows the well-established harlequinade form with its sequential scenes of comic trickery.[38] In it a West Indian plantation owner, Sir Peevish Antique, is a collector of museum exotica who is about to return to England. His daughter Columbine resists Sir Peevish's plan to marry her to Furibond, a Caliban-like Jamaican enchanter who exercises his magic to pursue her to England and reappear as the Dandy Lover.

In the pantomime itself a serpent saves a grateful slave from angry pursuers. The serpent is miraculously transformed into the Fairy Benigna who grants the slave "the election of different characters." Lamenting his black complexion but refusing to be turned into a white Narcissus or a tyrant, the slave becomes instead Harlequin Negro through the machinations of the Fairy Benigna who asks "What, are thou weary of thy sable hue?" (287). The black-masked Harlequin (closely akin to theatre's corked blackface and the dark metallic mask of fencing we have seen in the picture of the Duchess of Queensberry) would of course typically be dressed in multicolored tights so little skin would be on display. (illustration 21). In that person he can alleviate the sufferings of slaves, an offer he cannot refuse. When he petitions the Fairy to free his fellow slaves, Britannia appears in the skies to grant the "manly" slave liberty, and the chains fall away from the captives.[39] *Furibond* thus incorporates a chorus which celebrates England as the home of liberty.

The entire pantomime is characterized by Harlequin's numerous magic tricks and transformations, some of which have little to do with the plot and are merely excuses for *trompe d'oeuil* in his pursuit of Columbine. Most relevant to my argument, however, are the scenes in which "black" is an inherently comic concept. *Harlequin* and other plays of the later decades are filled with specific references to the pejorative connotations of blackness to suggest that the word itself carries the uncomfortable humor expressed by embarrassed laughter. For example, a comic black female servant absconds with a basket laden with food, and the strokes of the Harlequin's magic sword turn a lottery bill into one for "shining japan blacking" (294). The Clown acting the part of a shoe-black applies the blacking to Furibond's white stocking. When a scuffle ensues, the Clown blackens Furibond's face, clothes, and legs in his disguise as "a Buck," a patronizing term for a young black man.

The attempt of Harlequin and Columbine to marry is thwarted by Furibond who kidnaps her to his reptilian cave. The Fairy finally intervenes to unite the lovers in a bejewelled palace on a beautiful silver lake. If we are to believe that Harlequin remains black (rather than stripping off his Harlequin costume to reveal an essential whiteness) when he marries Columbine, the resulting marriage is interracial. Still, the reason to contest the marriage is never explicitly complexion but rather Sir Peevish's initial preference for the enchanter Furibond. In spite of patriarchal slaveowners, an oppressive father, and the malignant power of Furibond's magic, the Fairy and Britannia prevail to unite the lovers. This pantomime is, then, in its comic revelry, a fulfillment of the potential intermarriage between black

21 "Harlequin Dr. Faustus in the Necromancer. Rich the Harlequin." The masked
and creolized harlequin evocatively resembles blackface characters on the
eighteenth-century stage.

servant and white master's daughter that was booed from the stage years
earlier in *A Blackamoor Wash'd White*. Yet the white man as harlequin is
more ambiguous than the white man as black servant. In fact, the original
complexion color of the black-masked Harlequin, another forerunner of
minstrelsy, is difficult to determine since his person benignly unites black

and white men. These comic plays make the ornamental nature of race the subject of ludicrous clowning and stage business. The performance of race is a laughing matter, blackness pliable and carnivalesque, and the easy union of black and white, especially black and white men, is a cause for rewriting national hymns to celebrate a masculinity that can simply incorporate black masculinity, making it curiously illegible.

II

The plays of the later decades of the eighteenth century and continuing into the nineteenth century increase the number of blackface roles played by white men. Late in the century, I am arguing, the masking and unmasking of black and white actors parallels and eventually substitutes for the confusion between geographical identities and hues – between Indian and African, between copper and mahogany – typical of the earlier period. White actors in blackface reassured their audiences that race is merely constructed and as easily removed as masking, washing, or smudging, to reveal an ineradicable whiteness within. Lacking a language and a cultural context for asserting that a black "heart"or "core" could be virtuous, some blacks submitted to the indignity of claiming they possessed white hearts under their black skins. Yet when Ottabah Cugoano (in the epigraph which introduces this chapter) argues for an "essential" man, the core of character and worth is devoid of color instead of unveiling white pith beneath the surface. For Cugoano men possess an essential humanity sans tincture rather than a black surface that can be removed to reveal an essential whiteness of the spirit (or a white surface which exposes a black base). Black greasepaint thus may have temporarily assuaged a culture's suspicions that "race" was ineradicable. The theatre at the end of the eighteenth century and into the early decades of the next century enacted the subtleties of these uncertainties in a series of plays which took up noble savagery, slavery, and intermarriage in ways that began to fix racial hierarchies to make them appear more readily identifiable.

The most frequently produced representations of the black man in the eighteenth-century British theatre, often played by Ira Aldridge, were of course the suicidal and self-destructive Othello and Oroonoko. The other two most significant were Zanga in Edward Young's *The Revenge* and Hassan in "Monk" Lewis' *The Castle Spectre*. The violence and rage of both these characters is mitigated by their sentimental capacities, and the justifiable nature of their heroic cause – loss of country, family, and love. Combining *Othello* and Aphra Behn's *Abdelazar, or the Moor's Revenge* (1671), *The*

Revenge, first coming to the stage in April 1721 at Drury Lane, was performed throughout the eighteenth century, and revived by Edward Kean in 1815.[40] Engaging in duplicity and deception to avenge his father's death, Zanga is a noble Moorish hero in the tradition of Othello and Oroonoko. He is, however, a richly mixed character, a fact that Elizabeth Inchbald recognizes when she asserts in her edition that the very act of performing Zanga's "high-sounding vengeance" required extraordinary courage: "This character is of such magnitude, and so unprotected by those which surround him, that few performers will undertake to represent it: a less number still have succeeded in braving the danger" (4).[41] Zanga is a fearsomely bold African who deserves to win justice, a remnant of an earlier model of black masculinity. Perhaps it was precisely this very mixture of nobility and savagery, of courage and sentiment, which made this role Aldridge's most popular one.

In the play the Moor Zanga vows revenge on Alonzo, the Spanish conqueror of Africa, for killing his father, King Abdallah. In the revenge plot to deprive the Spaniard of Leonora, Zanga allies himself with the reptilian Isabella. Driving Alonzo mad with jealousy, the Iago-like Zanga schemes to forge a letter and plant Don Carlos' picture in Leonora's bedroom. Her suspected adultery and subsequent murder again vaguely parallels Desdemona's story when Alonzo murders Don Carlos, believing him to be Leonora's love. Admitting to the diabolical plot, Zanga's final soliloquy heatedly charges that as an enslaved prince he was powerless to defend his father and his native country:

> Fall'n Christian, thou mistak'st my character,
> Look on me. Who am I? I know, thou say'st,
> The Moor, a slave, an abject, beaten slave:
> (Eternal woes to him that made me so!)
> But look again. Has six years cruel bondage
> Extinguished majesty so far, that nought
> Shines here to give an awe of one above thee?
> ... But, Oh! What,
> What were my wages! ...
> What was left to me,
> So highly born? No kingdom, but revenge.
>
> (v.ii)

In short the noble slave argues that, imprisoned and deprived of his father and his country, his only recourse was to wreak a pardonable revenge.

The Revenge makes untenable the potential linkages between black man and white, slave and colonizer, that were so prominent in the comedies.

Zanga's princely status justifies his revenge while avoiding any direct criticism of England's slave trade or arousing concerns about Othello-like
mixed-race liaisons. Amalgamation is not at issue, and the theme adds bite
to the *Othello* plot in making Zanga's revenge, the legitimate reprisal for
all Africans displaced from their country by Spain, representative of more
than a black man's jealousy. When Zanga was played by Ira Aldridge, the
antislavery message would have seemed especially powerful to the English
audience. On the other hand if Zanga were played by Edward Kean, as it
was in 1815, the black man's revenge might have appeared less terrifying since
the Moor was, after all, simply a painted white man whose enslavement
was only as permanent as the greasepaint on his skin.

Another frequently performed play in Aldridge's repertoire included *The
Castle Spectre* (1798), a Gothic melodrama by "Monk" Lewis which was
fashioned after Walpole's *Castle of Otranto*. The play features the usual sub-
terranean passages, ghostly apparitions, fratricide, terrorizing of women,
and resurrections of deceased family members characteristic of Gothic
fictions. Osmond is suspected of murdering his brother, Earl Reginald
(whose "ghost" wanders the castle) in order to become heir to Conway.
Though no major character is African, four attendants to the princi-
pals are "black," most prominently Hassan (Aldridge's role), as well as
Saib, Muley, and Alaric, all of whom forward Osmond's scheming. Like
Oroonoko and Zanga (and reminiscent of familiar tropes of ill-fated African
lovers), Hassan evokes the audience's compassion for his loss of country and
family:

I have been dragged from my native land, from a wife who was every thing to me,
to whom I was every thing! Twenty years have elapsed since these Christians tore
me away: they trampled upon my heart, mocked my despair, and, when in frantic
terms I raved of Samba, laughed, and wondered how a negro's soul could feel! In
that moment when the last point of Africa faded from my view, when as I stood on
the vessel's deck I felt that all I loved was to me lost for ever, in that bitter moment
did I banish humanity from my breast. I tore from my arm the bracelet of Samba's
hair, I gave to the sea the precious token, and, while the high waves swift bore it
from me, vowed aloud endless hatred to mankind. I have kept my oath, I *will* keep
it. (Act 1, 13)

Hassan's unrelenting anger at whites, and in particular at Christians who
tore his family asunder, is partially excused because of his capacity for strong
sentiment. He and his fellow avengers remain peripheral to the plot, though
their obvious victimization could be interpreted as justifying the return of
freed blacks to Africa rather than as an indictment of slavery which is not
mentioned in the play. Black parts in the eighteenth and early nineteenth

century display the deep ambivalence of a white England toward staging race in the theatre of empire.

The African hero Gambia in Thomas Morton's *The Slave* (1816) departs from Zanga in *The Revenge* and Hassan in *The Castle Spectre* in refusing to believe that slavery is the most deplorable state imaginable. Though the part was originally written for the actor William Macready, the singing role in the three-act musical set in Surinam was one of Aldridge's most popular ones.[42] Gambia charges outright that "there is a state worse than slavery – liberty engendered by treachery, nursed by rapine, and invigorated by cruelty" (314), since he is himself an enslaver of his fellow man, and the play is occasioned because of a slave rebellion which he does not fully support.

The Slave seems to question where a hybrid woman's loyalty should lie, with England or with Africa, and racial romance turns out to be a means of refining national loyalties. In love with the quadroon Zelinda, the fiery Gambia is given little hope of winning her though he saves her child from certain death. Captain Clifton, one of "Europe's cold sons" and a character remniscent of Inkle, is the father of her mixed-race child. Carried on the shoulders of the darker slaves when she marries the Captain in "An Indian Procession," Zelinda (played by a white woman and unlike Gambia given no direction to black up) is clearly treated as their superior. Gambia, proving his trustworthiness to the doubting Zelinda, magnanimously saves Clifton from the rebellious slaves. Gambia actually hands his beloved Zelinda over to Clifton, calling on the Englishman's patriotic fervor to encourage treating her well: "And, happy Briton, love her as well as I have done, and my Zelinda's – your Zelinda's virtues will be rewarded!"

In parodic contrast to Zelinda, the play introduces the wealthy super-annuated Dutch spinster Miss VonFrump, condemned to virginity but insistent on marrying in the colonies, even "tho' 'tis to one of my own black slaves." Sharpset, a notorious overseer on a sugar plantation, plots to marry her in order to gain a fortune. The zany subplot draws parallels between the "blackness" of money-grubbing hearts and the complexion of negroes. Promising to marry Sharpset, Miss VonFrump equates it with "a receipt for blanching the faces of the negroes, making black appear white." The Cockney Fogrum, the Yorkshire Samuel Sharpset, and the Scotsman Malcolm who sings songs of Loch Lomond and "the bonny North" all represent Britain in its various regions. British chauvinism extends to a duet between Malcolm and Zelinda who sing ridiculously of London's wonders including alabaster Venuses (in contrast to a black Venus), the Bank of London, and the Temple Bar. The distinction between

England and the Scottish Highlands collapses in that both seem to inspire romantic nostalgia for their homeland, though the British characters lack credibility and dignity.

In *The Slave* taking Africans into captivity turns out to be a contest of masculinity: "These fetters are too large – the forger of these bonds thought they were to control manly vigour." In a series of reversals, Clifton and Gambia, white man and black, become brothers whose bonds exceed Clifton's love for Zelinda: "If we are not brothers, let the white man blush that is alien to the blood that mantels in that noble breast" (353). After Clifton quells the rebellion with kindness, "The sword achieved much, but clemency more" (343), Zelinda willingly agrees to free Gambia (the slave in the title and his very name an African country) rather than herself. The black and white man are reconciled, and the quadroon woman does not mind remaining a slave so that the men can be together. Gambia will accompany Clifton as a free man while Zelinda willingly remains in Surinam, presumably with her child: "England! Shall I behold thee? Talk of fabled land, or magic power! But what land, that poet ever sung, or enchanter swayed, can equal that, which, when the Slave's foot touches, he becomes free!" (380). In turn Gambia arranges for Clifton's release from debtors' prison. In fact the African tutors the white man in civility.

The popularity of this play may be a partial explanation for the demise of the Inkle and Yarico story at the end of the eighteenth century. In that familiar cultural fable, as we have seen, an English sea captain mercilessly sells his pregnant mistress, variously African or American Indian, into slavery. Zelinda, unlike Yarico, embodies the hybridity within herself rather than shifting from one tinctured or geographical identity to another. At the moment of abolition, however, the freed black man – one without much sympathy for slave rebellion and one who heroically rejects the quadroon woman he loves – is encouraged to join hands in brotherhood with the white man. Both men desire her, yet both willingly relinquish her. Together they abandon the mixed-race woman and the hybrid child who provides all too public evidence of the white man's sexual desires. No longer a story of Inkle's misogyny and racism, the tale evolves into a tribute to the capacity of the black man to save the white man from himself. *The Slave* successfully desexualizes the black male as sexual competition and sentimentalizes him into a bleeding heart with little will of his own. Here as in *The Blackamoor Wash'd White* the relationship between black and white man may be interpreted homoerotically, though with a significant difference, since Gambia was sometimes played by a black actor.[43] *The Slave*, while offering an heroic part for Ira Aldridge and testifying to his humanity and his brotherhood with white men, justifies freeing the black man because even without his fetters he will continue to serve the white man – all the more crucial when an actual black man is playing the popular Gambia the Slave. In addition the play offers reassurance that the hybrid woman and her offspring will be appropriately abandoned and forgotten like Africa, slavery, and the miscegenation which she represents.

In another of Aldridge's parts, George Colman the Younger's *The Africans; or, War, Love and Duty*, the heroine Berissa, the daughter of an Islamic priest, is light, as is Sutta the maid, who insists that black is the handsomest color. Berissa's sexual virtue – like Desdemona's and Imoinda's – is tested, and like her lighter-colored predecessors, she remains chaste. In the play produced at the Haymarket 29 July 1808, a year after the slave trade had been abolished, the white man takes greater possession of the stage than the heroic black who remains loyal to the social ties which slavery had annihilated.[44] The sentimental hero Selico (Zeluco in the novel from which the play derives), a devout follower of Mahomet, plans to marry Berissa, but believing her to be dead, he sells himself into slavery to support his mother. Selico's legendary virtue arises from his ability to sort out their relative claims on him. Aldridge's certifiable blackness would have emphasized the importance of his color. Yet it is "the poor white man" (258) who is finally credited with saving Selico's mother. In the play the violence of slavery is largely diverted to a discussion of African upon African, Mandingo against Foulahs who were "yellow" rather than black, and apparently so light that the actors portraying them were not blackened by dark stockings or greasepaint. The Mandigo men – even Farulho who is called "mahogany holiness" – are depicted with black bodies, arms and legs, while all of the women, even the female slaves, remain white though decorated with exotic feathers and beads. At the same time the play turns tables on the white man to laud African virtue over European vice. The English slave and ivory merchants such as Grim, Marrowbone, Flayall, and Adamant are despicable lowlife creatures who possess all the worst traits of an Inkle. Mug, the crass white trader, for example, threatens to treat Sutta, the black woman for whom he professes a passion, as his slave. The power of the white man is compromised because of his base foolishness and his willingness to justify slavery's profits.[45] Sexualized because of her class as much as her race, Sutta wishes that the Cockney ivory-trading Mug's skin were "negro" to match his features. Mug is a buffoonish "chalk-face" (252) who was enslaved by "a trading blackamoor, a wooly old humbug" (254) and has taken on African features. Their lovesong duet mocks the difference in their complexions since she is "the jet feather'd raven," and he the "white swan" with black legs:

> Sutta: But I be Afric – I be Afric:
> Blacky man he be my delight, ah!
> Mug: And I'm a Cockney–I'm a Cockney:
> I love black when I can't get white, ah!
>   (236)

It is Sutta's *purchase* that Mug seeks rather than her love. The proof of an Englishness associated with whiteness, is benevolence and self-sacrifice. Yet the play levels the usual hierarchies in making the Africans and English equally dependent on commerce in a society in which money and people circulate rather than goods. Black and white men stage a national fiction of unity while the hybrid woman (a white actress) reminds the country of its vacillations by embodying the slave's loss of his African home and his embrace of English principles of liberty.

III

If masquerade is "both a displacement of empire and an embrace of it," and if it is "an almost erotic commingling with the alien"[46] that offers a celebration and adoration of otherness, it is also worth remembering that on the eighteenth-century stage the alien represented in racially fabricated masquerade is usually male. Racial counterfeit may be understood as the masculine counterpart to the bewitchingly flexible female characters in fiction and popular lore who vacillated in color and origin depending on the version of the story. Taking on a second skin in affecting to be a man of color and bearing witness to that impersonation diminishes the threat of black men by allowing white men to become one with the object of their oppression, rather than sexualizing them into submission as was more frequent with women of color. When the actor of African or Caribbean origin takes the stage, the white spectator freshly confronted the fictive nature of the performance of race while attaching blackness to a real body. The history of Aldridge's repertory and of other black parts in the theatre allows us to witness the masquerade of race as a spectacle which washes the *Englishman*, not the blackamoor, fundamentally and permanently white.

Hayden White's argument that the noble savage mocks or mimics Enlightenment's idealized view of the nobility of (European) humanity is, I think, incomplete.[47] While it is accurate to suggest that European culture seeks its origins in the aborigine or the native, and thus invents its own version of the noble savage to correspond with this flattering prehistory, there is extraordinary range in this invention, including the genre of its representation and the ways in which it is gender- and class-identified. As we have seen, the noble indigene, in addition to being virtuous and uncorrupt, is imagined as the monstrous and degenerate nemesis to the civilized. Both the noble and the ignoble Negro in these plays with blackface parts are manipulated to fortify a white and English masculinity when blackface, like minstrelsy, is enlisted for racist, misogynist, and class-related ends. Various blackface roles define blackness as noble *and* savage, as prince *and* slave, as heroic *and* comic, as white *and* black in blank verse *and* speaking dialect, as threatening to white women *and* forming a racial alliance against them. Yet racism's very uncertain boundaries in relation to other social issues makes tracking its labyrinthine workings difficult. Though sometimes transparent, racism also disguises itself in the clothes of class or gender privilege, and in impure and hybrid forms.

Once Aldridge took the stage (though blackface of course continues into contemporary times on stage and colorblind casting is an increasingly common practice), in an important way neither the Englishman *nor* the blackamoor could be washed white as convincingly.[48] What is then being staged is that unlike the case for whites, for blacks, race is not a performance which can be discarded. In fact, Aldridge's later performances in the 1860s as Othello made blatantly obvious the corporeality of "race"in a memoir by his Desdemona, Mrs. Madge Robertson (Kendal):

Mr. Ira Aldridge was a man who, being black, always picked out the fairest woman he could to play Desdemona with him, not because she was capable of acting but because she had a fair head. One of the great bits of 'business' that he used to do was where, in one of the scenes he had to say, 'Your hand, Desdemona,' he made a very great point of opening his hand and making you place yours in it, and the audience used to see the contrast. He always made a point of it and to a round of applause, how I do not know. It always struck me that he had some species of . . . real intelligence. Although a genuine black . . . the fairer you were the more obsequious he was to you.

When Aldridge staged the constructedness of race in his whiteface performance of blackness, at the same time he challenges the impermeability of *whiteness* by making *it* seem to be something that can wash off. Aldridge, like Equiano and Sancho before him, understands that color – if it is determined by corporeal elements – is at the crux of English culture in spite of white men's wish to make it appear to possess a contingent quality, and that whiteness cannot easily be transferred if one's complexion is dark. Once the white man in blackface – the simulated Other, the almost but not quite native – becomes instead a material presence, an actual body to deal with on the streets, in the parks, in the living museums of London, and on the stage – masqueraders no longer rushed to emulate aliens of color with such regular and studied pleasure.[49] In fact the public masquerade with its license for racial disguise largely disappeared in England about the time of the abolition of slavery. Instead, a new racial realism slowly makes a place for the first black actor whose dark skin and specifically African origins become a crucial part of his appeal on the English stage.[50] Freeing the slaves paradoxically exacerbated the racism that had fostered black slavery in England of the early nineteenth century, and abolishing the slave trade encouraged racism's evolution into newer, more modern, and more firmly fixed forms of credible fictions which the first black actor on the English stage took pains to exploit and to contest.

Coda: between races

In examining English cultural narratives, I have argued that emergent notions of normalcy locate racialized, anomalous, and wondrous beings, human and otherwise, in foreign parts and on cartographic margins. By the end of the eighteenth century that threat seems to move closer and closer to home. Women's depraved duplicity and men's excessive curiosity and effeminacy are, as we have seen, regularly blamed for the new social menaces impinging on the land, and white women frequently bear special responsibility for racial pollution because of their reputed lust for the inhabitants of other parts of the world. In a letter to Penelope Pennington on 19 June 1802, Hester Thrale gives voice to the irresolution that racial mingling arouses within England. With a mixture of fear and Christian resignation, she greets the shift that places racial issues firmly and visibly within the gardens, parks, and theatres of London: "Well!" writes Thrale, "I am really haunted by *black shadows*. Men of colour in the rank of gentlemen; a black Lady, cover'd with finery, in the Pit at the Opera, and tawny children playing in the Squares, – the gardens of the Squares I mean – with their Nurses, afford ample proofs of Hannah More and Mr. Wilberforce's success toward breaking down the *wall of separation*. Oh! How it falls on every side! And spreads its tumbling ruins on the world! Leaving all ranks, all customs, all colours, all religions *jumbled together*, till like the old craters of an exhausted volcano Time closes and covers with falacious green each ancient breach of distinction; preparing us for the moment when we shall be made *one fold under one Shepherd*, fulfilling the voice of prophecy."[1] Thrale seems troubled by the accession to rank of native peoples and at the visibility of mulatto children in public gathering places formerly reserved for the privileged English classes, and especially because geographic and spatial separation will no longer pertain. The crumbling wall of separation that Thrale describes is a border *within England* that had safely divided black from white, other from English, pagan and infidel from Christian, and especially the former slave or East Indian merchant from the genteel.

Such mingling is, of course, a threat to the definition of Englishness since these new inhabitants, or at least their children, may claim to be both black and British. As I have argued, the preservation of a particular racial stock depends upon maintaining a peculiarly English femininity and masculinity, "the white cheek of Europe," in spite of the entangling passions that leap the border. For Thrale, the ending of this divide leaves volcanic ash as its residue yet prophesies the loss of ancient distinctions. As such walls fall, however, "a falacious green" – a deceptive organic growth covering the ash – forecasts both an armageddon and a new, religiously sanctioned equality that the ambivalent Thrale finds frightening and haunting, even as she strains to accept it as providential.

This chapter returns to the issues with which I began – the difficulties posed for Europeans in defining and reassessing the limits of the human as voyagers encountered indigenous populations whose physique, attitudes, and customs were unfamiliar. Racial borders in England, I suggest, are both internal and external to the nation so that what matters about racial intimacy is not only who is involved, but equally, and perhaps more importantly, exactly *where* it occurs. Contact and intimacies between people of different "races" challenge rigid divisions and essentialisms at the same time that the very conceptualization of an incipient miscegenation reinforces those boundaries as fixed and oppositional. In other words, a clear dichotomy must be imagined (one Thrale apparently believes to exist) in order for it to be violated. Racism, as Stuart Hall has noted, "operates by constructing impassable symbolic boundaries between racially constituted categories, and its typically binary system of representation constantly marks and attempts to fix and naturalize the difference between belongingness and otherness." Rather than looking beyond race or ethnicity, to resist racial thinking Hall suggests that a new cultural politics "engages rather than suppresses *difference* and ... depends, in part on the cultural construction of new ethnic identities."[2] Racism has difficulty with the fluid identities and in-between spaces that create a venue where racial categories are negotiated. What Thrale worries about is internal borders which are crucially at issue at the turn into the nineteenth century as increased numbers of people of color intrude upon Britain. At the same time that legislation against interracial unions abounded in America dating from 1705 on, in England there were no such legal strictures during the century. As long as racial intimacy could be excluded from England's geographic shores, it could be treated with curiosity and relative nonchalance. But when internal borders are encroached upon by interracial couples and their children, the masquerade and spectacle of racial romance's "in-between" status metamorphosizes from spectacle to a matter of pressing importance. The shadows that haunt Thrale are real people.

Racial romance appears in novels of midcentury and later, as well as in poems such as Thomas Day's *Dying Negro*; in John Stedman's travel narrative of his Surinam marriage with Joanna; in the pantomime and poems about the South Pacific Omai who enthralled London women; and various dramas including Mariana Starke's *Sword of Peace* (1788) and *Widow of Malabar* (1791); Colman's *The Africans* (1808); and Thomas Morton's *The Slave* (1816), among many others. From varying perspectives, critics have argued that interracial romance in fiction, poetry, plays, and travel narratives embraces those who are being exploited in order to re-imagine the inequities and brutalities of empire as necessary and acceptable. Racial romance can indict the predicament of intermixture, but it can also query the cultural values that encourage or condemn interracial sex. The threat of romance sets up a means to refine national and geographical loyalties – to clarify Englishness vis-à-vis Africa, the South Pacific, India, and America; and it also affords a way to muddy the binary. It produces a zone of erasure, conversion, and accommodation in a liminal space between national boundaries that did not yet exist in the eighteenth century or existed only loosely. It sets up contingent identities described variously as "between civilizations" by James Clifford; as W. E. B. Dubois' "double consciousness," Gloria Anzaldúa's "borderlands" and "new mestiza consciousness," Lisa Lowe's hyphenated identities; or Homi Bhabha's "in-between spaces."[3] This alternative manner of thinking entails constituting couples as located not simply on each side of a border, but "in-between" geographical places and available identities, including a repertory of cross-racial borrowings rather than a settled hybridity. Representations of racial romance substitute binding affection for grappling with the hard realities of difference and substitute for ameliorating slavery, redefining resistance movements, obliterating empire's economic loss, and eradicating its contaminants. That marginal space of the in-between was, I think, largely imagined as elsewhere, outside of the boundaries of England, until the last decades of the eighteenth century when the impinging geographical urgency of transracial relations changes and fractures the perceived meanings of racial romance.

The paradigm of representing "the ideal of cultural harmony through romance" that Peter Hulme finds in the Pocahantas story, "always breaks down," according to Mary Louise Pratt's astute observation. "It is easy to see transracial love plots as imaginings in which European supremacy is guaranteed by affective and social bonding," she writes, "and in which romantic love rather than filial servitude or force guarantee the willful submission of the colonized."[4] But the failure of the paradigm of cultural harmony may also reveal the power differential between the sexes and the complications for women that interracial pregnancies and children bring. Each of the partners in racial romance – depending on rank, origin, and sex – experiences the effects of empire, and is differently constituted by it. Most critical to the early and mid eighteenth-century figurations of interracial romance, I am arguing, is the social rank of the darker partner, whether man or woman, though by the end of the century, interracial romance raises contradictions and hesitations no matter what the pairing of ranks may be. This threat of racial intermarriage was particularly pronounced in the years of abolitionist fervor. Ameliorist sentiments among the gentry were punctuated by the suspicion that blacks might presume to claim rank consonant with that which they possessed in their native lands or to develop unprecedented social mobility in England itself. Bluestocking Elizabeth Carter privately mused over the potential consequences of the presence of black visitors. Carter writes to Elizabeth Montagu on 12 June 1764, "Oh dear! I have read an article in the papers about the imprisoning a Negro, for calling himself an esquire. I am sadly afraid it is our Black Prince. It is surely a little hard if he is detained merely for this. I have never heard of any body being taken up for calling himself a scholar, or a critic, or a man of honor, and yet how many go about this world in unmolested possession of these titles, to which they have no better right, than our poor friend to his esquireship. Seriously, however, I shall be very sorry if he proves a cheat, that I recommended him to your notice, and procured for a rogue that protection for which so many honester people might have been the better."[5] Even princely rank granted elsewhere does not translate into English titles. Nobility, especially when applied to a "savage," seems to be a designation which the English reserved to assign particular individuals rather than a mobile status which an African visitor could dare to assume himself. Carter's concern about intermarriage in England translates into fear of class mobility for Africans, and thus for their children, as status continues to separate from inherited wealth and rank.

On the eighteenth-century stage, in poetry and in narrative, sexual in-termixture between "races" is far less troubling if the dark partner's rank is equal to or higher than the white partner. A dark beloved may be justified if he or she is noble, aristocratic, or characterized by European features or "blood," *and* if the beloved remains outside England. Such relation-ships extract labor, in Pratt's view, under the "mystique of reciprocity, or of equivalence between parties" and afford "some marginal or privileged space where relations of labor and property are suspended" – for example, in Stedman's narrative about his enslaved "Surinam wife" Joanna.[6] But this reading of interracial romance is inadequate if the romance ends tragically, or if the English or European involved in interracial romance is a woman so that the power differential in hybrid romances must indeed be taken into account.

The desire evoked by yet another divide, sexual difference, is to blame. As I have shown, eighteenth-century England was much occupied with Desdemona's longing for Othello and with parallel renderings in Southerne's *Oroonoko* where passion for the foreign is anchored to the white female and located within her longings. Native men especially inspire sexual desire, but at the same time they evidence characteristics that place them on the boundary between man and beast and return us to the alliance between anomaly and race. Frances Burney, for example, writes of the mutual admiration exchanged between the Tahitian Omai during his visit to England and several aristocratic women including Lady Townshend and Lady Craven. Burney promptly undercuts the attraction by mocking the way Omai's partial transculturation to an Englishman contrasts with his uncouth and barbaric speech to reflect the linguistic deprivation of his native culture: "To dumb shew he was probably familiar, the brevity and paucity of his own dialect making it necessarily a principal source of communication at Ulitea and at Otaheite."[7] Omai's allure is compromised by his inability to speak English properly, and like Othello's affinity to cannibals and Ignatius Sancho's stammer, these defects transform these native men into cross-bred, degenerate species.

The reverse of the enthralling appeal of alterity is, of course, repulsion and disgust, and there is considerable fear in the eighteenth century that, as Peter Stallybrass and Allon White have put it, "these low domains, apparently expelled as 'Other,' return as the object of nostalgia, longing and fascination."[8] The primitive, even in the person of the nobility, was also pervasively imagined to mock the dignity and distinctive qualities of humanity, and especially of European peoples. Observers nostalgically wish to possess the qualities of romanticized and exoticized others while at the same time to denigrate them as monstrous and corrosive. As Hayden White has recognized, European culture fetishized native peoples as both "monstrous forms of humanity" and the "quintessential objects of desire" to inhabitants of the larger world.[9] The black man shadows and deeply troubles the sociable gentleman, and he is also the disquieting object of libidinous European female appetite. But as we have seen, the "black" woman is often the antithesis of a proper femininity and, especially during the eighteenth century, rarely registers in literature as the object of *legitimate* reciprocal love from white men or from black men of a certain class unless they are confined to other shores.

As I have argued, two compelling stories of interracial intimacy in the period are Thomas Southerne's much produced revision of Aphra Behn's *Oroonoko*, and the multiple versions of *Inkle and Yarico* culminating in George Colman the younger's operatic play. These two stories mirror each other in that the sex of the darker partner is male in one and female in the other: the African Oroonoko and his white wife Imoinda in Southerne's play, and the dark maiden Yarico and English sea captain Inkle who appear most notably in the *Spectator* and in Colman's play.[10] In neither of these tangled nodes of racial romance is the woman empowered, whether she is white or dark. Imoinda willingly dies at her husband's hand, assisting him in thrusting the dagger into her breast; and in the versions up until the last-minute revisions to Colman's play changed the outcome, Yarico is cruelly sold into slavery along with her unborn hybrid child. An interracial romance in which both partners are of the same (non-noble) rank becomes more vexing during the century as social mobility for people of color in England increases when the slave trade ends. Racial intimacy is, however, for a large part of the century, principally imagined to be kept safely offshore.

The attitudes toward racial romance described in these cultural tales are various. As I have shown, in *Oroonoko* Southerne links the interracial central love story in the main plot between Oroonoko and Imoinda with a breeches-role subplot to juxtapose race and misogyny. In these earlier parables of mixed-race romance, the white feminine is uneasily reintegrated, the black feminine eradicated, and a tenuous bond is fashioned between black and white man. As feminist causes begin to congeal late in the century, the tie between black and white men becomes more critical to assert on behalf of abolition but also in the interest of clarifying what constitutes an appropriate femininity (illustration 22). Sexual difference contends with other differences to forge a strong, manly nation, and to gain cultural priority in the troubling new reality of an enlarged world filled with surprising and alien beings who increasingly intrude in England.

The dark woman of rank in later eighteenth-century poetry, drama, and fable comes to signify the English adventurer's sentimental indecisiveness regarding commerce and especially slavery; she is passionately desired and yet often considered to be expendable. As I have argued, the black woman is erased to bolster white femininity but haunts it. In Southerne's play white women's subservience to patriarchy bears affinities with male and female

Ye are the Children of one Father

22 Frontispiece to *Zimao, the African* (1800). A white child and a black child intertwine to figure as an emblem of brotherly love employed in the cause of abolition.

slaves' subjection to their master regardless of their race. The black woman simply disappears with only the shadow of Behn's courageous but compromised darker Imoinda haunting Southerne's revision. In this rendering of *Oroonoko* the threat of miscegenation is eliminated by the death of the enslaved lovers, the white Imoinda (and the hybrid child in her womb) and the black African Oroonoko. "Methinks I see the babe with infant hands / Pleading for life and begging to be born" (iv.ii), laments the dying Imoinda in Southerne's version. Alive the tragic couple represented no breach in rank since they shared significant stature, but their tragic deaths by suicide and murder as represented on stage positively and finally eliminate any threat to England itself.

In the case of the Inkle and Yarico stories, the woman is dark, and the man European. Yarico – represented as having various hues and origins – is abandoned by her English captain in a sentimental, if vexed, justification of colonial behavior which later in the century evolves into a sternly moral tale chastising the marauding English adventurer for disguising what is described as his black heart under a white skin. Blackness, then, defines a moral condition that can migrate to white bodies and escalate into greater evil within them. Inkle thus displays the ambivalence of an imperial nation to its colonization of Africa and the capture of its peoples by betraying his beloved. In these retellings of imperialism, the "nurturing native" woman ministers to the "beleaguered European traveler" (as Peter Hulme characterizes the tale) who in most versions until Colman's play loves her and leaves her.

As we have seen, the Inkle and Yarico story popularized in Steele's *Spectator* No. 11 reverses the pairing in Southerne's *Oroonoko* so that the male protagonist is white while the heroine derives variously from Africa, the Caribbean, or other parts of the Americas. In this context it is worth briefly revisiting one version of the fable. A "Mrs Weddell" was refused license to produce a dramatic version of *Incle and Yarico* printed in 1742, originally slated for Covent Garden but turned back for unexplained reasons.[11] Weddel's midcentury version, consistent with Steele's emphasis on Inkle's misogyny in selling her and her unborn child into slavery does not oppose slavery so much as it resists slavery's misogyny. The preface incorporates an early abolitionist plea for ignoring "*the casual Tincture of the Skin*" (6): "*however disagreeable this may be, methinks it should not prejudice the Minds of a wise People, and fond of Liberty, who consider all men as Denizens of the Earth's plenteous Blessings.*" Rather than being an Indian maiden, mulatto or copper colored, the regal heroine is clearly labeled African, a "*sable heroine*" *and* "*a native Black*" (6). Her virtue and social status combine to make her suitable for her native betrothed, Prince Satamano, until Incle, washing up on the shore, competes for her affection. (Apparently trading her virtue for silks, jewels, and the spoils of empire, she sails away to Jamaica with Incle.) Incle claims that he sells the pregnant Yarico because when they travel to Jamaica her native elevated status will not be recognized: "But to join Hands in Marriage with her would demean my Name, / Since her high Rank's unknown at this wide Distance, / And she without a Dow'r" (49). Exhausted from the physical labor of slavery, the pregnant Yarico succumbs. Again, place and rank are mutually constitutive. Yarico's status does not travel with her, though the Englishman Inkle's status would seem to be enhanced by travel. Finally Incle dies at the hand of the defender of another woman he double-crosses.

The eighteenth-century stage did not easily adjust to the idea of representing a black woman in a major role on the British stage, and as I have argued concerning Southerne's Imoinda, black actresses were virtually unknown in London. Weddel's play may have been refused by theatre censors because of its early portrayal of a black woman for whom there may have been no actresses willing to black up, and no theatre managers willing to risk presenting a problematic character whose skin color might mask her virtue. The idea of aligning virtue and innocence with black femininity, as we have seen, raised troubling incongruities, yet the dramatist here strongly implies that the story is applicable to *all* trusting virgins who succumb to men's duplicitous claims. Forecasting later treatments of complexion, the play reserves the usual metaphors to accuse white persons with low morals of being "black." Mrs. Weddel erases color difference among women, and in her rendition the mixed-race love story is a curiosity rather than a threat to racial purity.

Almost half a century later the most popular version of the *Spectator* story, George Colman's ballad opera *Inkle and Yarico* with music by Samuel Arnold, was initially staged at the Theatre Royal Haymarket in 1787, followed by a successful season at Covent Garden. It played constantly until 1800 and was performed in the imperial territories of Jamaica, Calcutta, and New York; it was revived at Covent Garden in 1790.[12] As Mrs. Weddell had done, Colman introduces a competitor to Yarico in Narcissa, daughter of the governor, Sir Christopher Curry, though Narcissa prefers Campley to Inkle who plans to sell Yarico to Sir Curry, Narcissa's father. After much soul-searching, and blaming his faulty upbringing on his father's mercenary ambitions for him, Yarico convinces Inkle to marry even though he is a flawed specimen of a man with his constant discussion of profit-taking and capturing slaves. Significantly there is no mention of a child, or of Yarico's loss of chastity; consequently, miscegenation is only threatened rather than enacted, and the black woman can be represented as exemplary of virtue.

When Colman writes his version of the play, he literally splits the identity of Yarico into two – a slightly lighter colored principal and a pipesmoking black female servant Wowski from a cannibal tribe.[13] Common to both the earlier Weddell play and the Colman play is the fact that they lack an ideal woman, an epitome of femininity against which to judge the black and the somewhat black women. Instead the frivolous white woman Narcissa further fractures the feminine beyond the doubling of the blackest licentious maid and the lighter-skinned pathetic virgin. By the time of Colman's play, deepest black in relation to women is more exactly class-coded, and the possibility of an enslaved black woman's rising to middle-class virtue (in the manner of, say, Samuel Richardson's *Pamela*) seems especially unlikely.

The servant Wowski is surely among the very first blackface women to play a significant role on the English stage, and that problem was at least on one occasion resolved by casting her as a child. The indelible quality of her face color is a joke about the makeup that the audience would certainly understand: "Blackamoor ladies, as you call 'em, are some of the very few, whose complexions never rub off!" (40). In the play the Cockney Trudge is as faithful to Wowski as Inkle is duplicitous to Yarico, but color difference gains new attention in century's final decades. Wowski, unlike Yarico, speaks a pidgin English and is a source of comedy. Though she marries Trudge on their way to Barbados, Wowski makes no pretense of being chaste after having had "a great many" lovers. Their difference in complexion is wittily exaggerated in light repartee and in song:

> TRUDGE Oh then turn about, my little tawny tight one!
> Don't you like me?
> WOWSKI Iss, you're like the snow!
> If you slight one. –
> TRUDGE Never, not for any white one;
> You are beautiful as any sloe.   (22)

Any concern about their intermingling is tempered because of their shared working-class status. When blackness is taken as a sign of low rank, skin color also becomes a visible and ineradicable marker of social location, and the inequality between partners is caricatured even as it remains offshore (illustration 23). This alignment of rank and color is increasingly significant as freed slaves enter the job market, and any claims to princely status in their home country meet the realities of blacks attempting to achieve a living wage in England and in their potential for social mobility.

Colman's play betrays an edgy racism, though at least one recent commentator has interpreted the slurs as the dramatist's satire against racial bigotry.[14] More likely the play reflects the unresolved tensions surrounding racial issues as blacks are incorporated within the English economy and culture. The natives in the wilds of America dance about in "black buff," and there are racialist allusions to a "gingy duke" and "inky commoner." The play indicates that white men should ogle white women rather than "hunting old hairy negroes" (12), and the white maid Patty calls Yarico "A Hotty-pot gentlewoman." The racist talk is safely located in the mouths of the cockney servant Trudge whose loyalties to his black wife are unwavering. Trudge mocks the idea of selling his "poor, dear, dingy wife" and accuses the "fair-trader" of having a face as black as an inkbottle to reflect his black heart: "Yes, all the fine men are like me: as different from your people as powder and ink, or paper and blacking" (29). But there is irony in the analogy because Trudge's social class is so lowly, and elsewhere Trudge praises Wowski's "pretty, ebony arms" in contrast to Inkle's detraction about Yarico. Unlike Weddell's play, Colman's popular *Inkle and Yarico* articulates concerns about interracial marriage, but its sentimental ending reasserts the paradigm of cultural concord.

Colman's *Inkle and Yarico*, set on the American mainland and then shifting to Barbados, marks an important change in English attitudes toward the hazard of racial impurity resulting from sexual contacts across race. At the end of the century with the push toward abolition, intermarriage within England becomes a real possibility rather than merely an imagined threat, but even its occurrence in a colonial land is troubling since mixed-race children are likely to emigrate to England. This intensified concern about miscegenation also parallels the demise of geographic vagaries as the exact classification becomes more acute within England itself. Once sexual intermixture becomes a greater peril after freed slaves became more prevalent and visible, figures varying in color and origin also become more consistent and legible. At the end of the century, the woman of color is not associated with or entitled to the femininity exemplified by her lighter counterpart.

While ending the British slave trade in the early nineteenth century made the play less exactly relevant to current interests,[15] the shift to a less benevolent view of miscegenation may also have figured equally importantly in the demise of the play's popularity. In this play Inkle is coached and "reformed" to forget commerce, renouncing his greed for profit, in the interests of Yarico, though originally in rehearsal the play was to end

23 James Gillray, "Wouski" (1788). Embracing in the hammock of Prince William Henry's ship returning to England from Jamaica, the Duke of Clarence and Wouski are exemplary of mixed-race and interclass offshore romance.

as in earlier versions with selling her into slavery. Inkle's reform is a last-minute revision that may have been the actor's suggestion. Colman's *Inkle and Yarico* voices concerns about miscegenation, but its ending legitimates the idea that attraction and sexual desire may take precedence over fears about interracial union. The entire company of characters determines to remain in Barbados, rather than returning to England. Miscegenation migrates into England, but the interracial pairing of Inkle and Yarico remains, for the time being, safely outside of the country. Finally, though these two enormously popular tables treat racial romance, neither inserts its effects into England itself.

In short, it was not until the later decades of the eighteenth century that the concern about interracial mixture became a more consistent topic of impassioned public debate in England, especially as the rank of the participants became more co-equal. From the 1760s through the 1780s West Indian travelers Philip Thicknesse and Edward Long had warned that miscegenation resembled crossing different species. Thicknesse worried, perhaps facetiously, about such mixed breeds resulting in being overrun with "Outang Europangs," and he claims that such unions are unnatural:

"London abounds with an incredible number of these black men, who have clubs to support those who are out of place, and every country town, nay in almost every village are to be seen a little race of mulattoes, mischievous as monkeys, and infinitely more dangerous. Linnaeus and many other authors of veracity assert, that the *Orang Outang*, or *Jocko* (for they are all the same species) can, and do converse together, and that they are so perfect, that it is impossible to say whether they are to be ranked as animals, or human creatures."[16] For Thicknesse such unions were thought to be illegal; and though "black may be...full as beautiful, as red, or white," he identifies Africans as "men of a lower order" who resemble the sterile mule, a mixed-species blend of horse and donkey.[17] James Tobin's assessment of such unions was equally repellent: "The great number of negroes at present in England, the strange partiality shewn for them by the lower orders of women, and the rapid increase of a dark and contaminated breed, are evils which have long been complained of, and call every day more loudly for enquiry and redress. – The lower ranks in Spain are avowedly debased, by their long intercourse with the Moors...and especially Portuguese."[18] In fact, the abolition movement paradoxically inspired discussions that laws similar to those against miscegenation in America ought to be passed in England, and writers in the nineteenth century increasingly associate the mulatto with defects and infertility.[19]

The pollution of mixed-race individuals extends to plays set in the East and West Indies. In Mariana Starke's *The Sword of Peace* (1788), for example, the Misses Moreton "barter English charms for Eastern gold" (Prologue), and resist the advances of the Resident, tainted by his stint administering India's Coromandel Coast. "I declare I wou'd as soon marry Tippoo Saib," scoffs Eliza Moreton (Act IV, p. 182). The uneven power relations between the two countries, resembling a marriage is, of course, not acknowledged. The half-caste Mrs. Tartar, "a vixen" and a "hag" is the dramatic equivalent to the creolized plantation-owning Mrs. Ellison in Sarah Scott's novel, *The History of Sir George Ellison*. Tartar, the daughter of a tallow chandler and a "black" Indian merchant's daughter and the wealthy widow of the son of an English basketmaker, is believed to be the instigator of a plot to poison the two Englishwomen. Her mixed-race status is the foil to proper English femininity. Complicating the orientalism of the plot is an abolition subplot. Jeffreys, himself a servant, sentimentally and beneficently purchases the black slave Caesar from his owner. When Caesar learns that he is free, Jeffreys offers to teach him to be an Englishman with whom, as an equal, he can dare to quarrel: "An Englishman...lives *where* he likes – *goes* where he likes – *stays* where he likes – *works* if he likes – lets it *alone*, if he likes – starves, if he likes – abuses who he likes – boxes who he likes – thinks what he likes – speaks what he *thinks* – for, damme, he fears nothing, and will face the devil... for a true-born Englishman, if he provokes him, damme, he'd knock his best friend's teeth down his throat, –... but never lifts his hand against the oppress'd." Being an Englishman – something ostensibly available to the freed slave – involves both class mobility and geographical mobility. The newly freed slave Caesar longs to travel to England where he can experience this kind of liberty.

According to the prologue of Starke's *The Widow of Malabar* (1791), the play is her "offspring" which invites an interpretation of the drama itself as the hybrid product of a union between England and India.[20] In this case the union of a Brahmin woman and English officer is represented as the natural result of England's occupation of India. Both of Starke's plays avow a broad humanity, "Whether their hue be tawny, black, or fair,"[21] but the interracial couples remain in India. Yet in Thomas Morton's *The Slave* (1816) the interracial child from Surinam is promised – but does not enact on stage – a home in England: "England! Shall I behold thee? Talk of fabled land, or magic power! But what land, that poet ever sung, or enchanter swayed, can equal that, which when the Slave's foot touches, he becomes free!" With abolition, this play celebrates England as a place of liberty that can tolerate an interracial couple, a captain and a quadroon slave whose worthiness is signaled by her lighter color rather than her rank, as well as their child; but the play equivocates by postponing the spectacle of absorption. The nation in the early nineteenth century is represented, as in *The Sword of Peace*, as the welcoming home of liberty, not the perpetrator of slavery.

In short, then, the eighteenth-century stage largely keeps intermarriage enticingly present but reassuringly distant, offering an isolated interlude between the seventeenth-century's versions of a Pocahantas who marries John Rolfe and the nineteenth-century's dramatic suggestion that intermarriage will become internal to England. Theatrical performances, differing from other genres, internalize the self as a benign other within its borders through racial counterfeit, yet they resist the dramatic portrayal of racial intimacy's effects and consequences. The concern about intermarriage in England in these representative texts expresses a fear of class mobility for freed Africans, creolized women, and nabobs in their potential to accrue goods, property, and status – and thus for their interracial children to invade London's gardens and parks.

Near the end of the century in a rejoinder to James Tobin, Olaudah Equiano registers the antagonism he confronted concerning his marriage to a white Englishwoman and the threat of anti-miscegenation laws. Arguing from monogenetic theory, Equiano transforms interracial love away from unbridled desire for the exotic into a human rights issue: "It is not sufficient for their bodies to be oppressed, but [must] their minds [be] also?" he writes. "If the mind of a black man conceives the passion of love for a fair female, he is to pine, languish, and even die, sooner than an intermarriage be allowed, merely because the complexion of the offspring should be tawney – A more foolish prejudice than this never warped a cultivated mind – for as no contamination of the virtues of the heart would result from the union, the mixture of colour could be of no consequence."[22] In fact, Equiano forecasts that an easy sexual commerce between the races would really decrease illicit behavior of white men toward black women. "Why not," he asks, "establish intermarriages at home, and in our Colonies[?] And encourage open, free, and generous love upon Nature's own wide and extensive plan, subservient only to moral rectitude, without distinction of the colour of a skin?" Reversing traditional arguments against intermarriage, Equiano – a Christian convert who enlists scripture rather than employing the language of interspecies or blood mixture – cites a biblical precedent that *blesses* intermarriage with strangers (the Israelite with the Ethiopian) or between nations. "Away then with your narrow impolitic notion of preventing by law what will be a national honour, national strength, and productive of national virtue – Intermarriages!" Such marriages in Equiano's impassioned argument are given divine sanction.

Countering the black man's figuration as a sexual threat, Equiano's vision transforms intermarriage into a material manifestation of national identity. For Thrale the issue is class. The black lady usurps the place of the Englishwoman of rank, and the tawny children, the offspring of the mis-cegenetic unions of black and white, nevertheless merit nurses. The black shadow harbored *within* the country, occupying a space within the borders, comes to signify by the turn into the nineteenth century both the promise of Enlightenment equality (exemplified in abolition) and the menace of impurity and degeneration (made more rigid in scientific racism) looming over imperial England. This geography of racial intimacy helps to explain plays and stagings that are at the same time antislavery yet pervaded by racial assumptions. What had previously seemed to be an exotic practice in-creasingly becomes a domestic one: racial intermixture – its borders violated intimately and privately, and yet so publicly manifested in tawny children – represents both at once. Alternatively we may see interracial intimacy and its in-between spaces as a means to loosen the division upon which colo-nialism is founded. As Equiano imagines, the mixed-race children are the liminal space made manifest, neither one nor the other, a public reminder of private desire struggling against labels of the illicit and illegitimate. The mixed-race babies invisible on stage in Imoinda's and Yarico's wombs enter the gardens and the parks of London to dwell with Hester Thrale and her friends.

The fear of racial amalgamation was certainly festering in England from the end of the seventeenth century. The strong aversion to the visual effects of an erotically entwined black and white couple within England was not the dominant view until differences of various kinds – including gender, sexuality, race, monstrosity, and geographical origin – began to cohere as they shift from lineage to a recognizable set of embodied characteristics. Dramatic adaptations of *Oroonoko* throughout the eighteenth century offered a sympathetic treatment of interracial love and a questioning of slavery coupled with reassurances that ungovernable black men and the easily duped white women who loved them both merited the same tragic fate. The change in popular taste occurs not simply because ending slavery meant that pro-abolitionist plays were no longer in demand. It also occurs, I think, because with abolition the threat of miscegenation became increasingly real rather than simulated, not easily mediated through paint and performance, and more exactly locatable in terms of geography and skin.

It has been the argument of this book that racial categories, closely aligned with anomaly, are highly adaptable within England in the eighteenth century, in spite of the pronounced and enormously significant rise of racial slavery in the New World and elsewhere. Physical differences that Europeans "discover" around the world are intimately connected with the formation of normative categories in relation especially to race, sex, and the limits of the human. "Race" had been staged as a geographically manipulable characteristic as easily changed as clothing and signaled by generalized exotica from the Americas, the Indies, or Oceania. The metropolitan bourgeoisie delights in its own transculturated performances and masquerades as it assimilates these differences in drama, fiction, poetry, and culture throughout the period. Similarly, a racialized, normative femininity and masculinity are also increasingly perceived, as we have seen, as less performative and more thoroughly physiognomic as they become yoked to more specific geographical locations.

The most vigorous attention to hybridity and mongrelization takes fire with the abolition of the slave trade in 1807 and with emancipation in 1833 to correspond to increasingly public attempts to clarify black inferiority. Safely relegated to the colonies, or reined in and distanced by the whimsy of blackface mimicry and masquerade costume through most of the century, racialized fears in England are, I suggest, most powerful and disturbing at its conclusion. The confusions of the imagination, often a simulated confusion, evolve into real social confusion.

By 1810 novelist Maria Edgeworth worries that a black man marrying a white woman will be thought scandalous, and upon hearing her father's objections she determines that it will give "the gentlemen the horrors" that a white female writer would seem to recommend intermarriage. Edgeworth had allowed the character Lucy, in earlier versions of her novel *Belinda*, to marry the black West Indian servant Juba but finally concludes that to assuage her father's fears, Lucy should marry Jackson instead.[23] For Charles Lamb writing in the early nineteenth century, however, the loathsome visual spectacle of the contrast in color between hero and heroine is paramount in evoking disgust, and he cannot put it aside in the interests of human rights: "I appeal to every one that has seen Othello played, whether he did not, on the contrary, sink Othello's mind in his colour; whether he did not find something extremely revolting in the courtship and wedded caresses of Othello and Desdemona; and whether the actual sight of the thing did not over-weigh all that beautiful compromise which we make in reading."[24] When Edward Kean, who had early acted the part of Omai, presented Othello as a "tawny Moor" or Arab in 1814,[25] there may well have been sighs of relief because the white Desdemona would no longer be paired with a white man playing a black African. The predominant class of visible blacks and other people of color began to shift from visiting African princes whose legitimate captivity was questionable to a plethora of freed slaves who possessed only minimal skills. The concerns that had in large part been confined to the colonies steadily creep into the English island.

As we have seen, the repertoire of human types is significantly gendered on a scale that ranges from the European white and red to the African sable Venus. Feminine defectiveness corresponds to the nascent discourse of racial typing, and this leads us to recall again Eve's prototypical defects, and Desdemona's fatal passion for the Moor whose tales seduce her into miscegenation and hint at the tawny children who would result from the union. Lord Monboddo recounts a much reprinted story of another wild girl, an Inuit child from Hudson's Bay blackened by West Indian slave-traders in order to allow her to pass as an African.[26] Shipwrecked upon the shores of France (along with an actual Negro girl who drops out of the narrative), she allegedly inspired those who first saw her to shout, "*Voilà le Diable!*" The savage white child, feeding on roots and raw game, lives as a weasel-like amphibious creature until she is captured and educated into gentility in a nunnery. Her life, lived at the limits of the human, extends beyond Eve's defective duplicity or Desdemona's fanciful romance to suggest an alternative narrative that would enable incorporating the untamable feminized primitive into civility through education and religious instruction. Neither course – following Desdemona (the personification of an England enthralled yet fearing the power and strangeness of its uncontrollable empire) in eloping with Othello as Shaftesbury cautioned against, or accepting the circumscription to proper sexual difference and sociability recommended for the Inuit girl – seems in its layered contradictions to allow for a national vision capacious enough to evade the newly congealing norms of the human. The appeal of the exotic, the anomalous, and the defective leads Desdemona to marry the monstrously jealous man, and to be tragically murdered in spite of her innocence. She, like the white Imoinda of Southerne's *Oroonoko*, exemplifies the special vulnerability that femininity, in its extremes between the ideal and the defective, exhibits when touched by a narrative of exotic wonders. In fact, of course, the multiple ways of being human undermine any single subject of modernity. White women's sexuality becomes the carefully guarded line between the infected and uninfected spaces of racial and cultural contagion as an intact normative femininity and a bolstered masculinity free of defect serve as signs of successfully fending off contaminating forms. The black shadow harbored now *within* the country, the potential pollution that blackness brings to that femininity, comes to signify the menace of impurity and degeneration looming over and within an increasingly imperial England in the long eighteenth century.

Notes

INTRODUCTION: MONSTROUS TALES

1 Colin Barnes, "Disability Studies: New or Not so New Directions?", *Disability and Society* 14.4 (1999): 577–80.

2 Tom Shakespeare and Nicholas Watson, "The Social Model of Disability: An Outdated Ideology?", in *Exploring Theories and Expanding Methodologies: Where We Are and Where We Need to Go*, ed. Sharon N. Barnart and Barbara M. Altman, vol. II (JAI, an imprint of Elsevier Science: London, 2001), p. 19.

3 Anthony Ashley Cooper, Third Earl of Shaftesbury, *Characteristics of Men, Manners, Opinions, Times* (Cambridge: Cambridge University Press, 1999), p. 151. All subsequent references are cited in parentheses in the text.

4 Clara Reeve, *The Progress of Romance* in *Bluestocking Feminism: Writings of the Bluestocking Circle, 1738–1785*, ed. Gary Kelly, 6 vols. (New York: Pickering and Chatto, 1999), vol. VI, pp. 169–264.

5 Reeve, *The Progress of Romance*, p. 171.

6 Robert Mack, ed. "Introduction," *Oriental Tales* (Oxford and New York: Oxford University Press, 1992), vii–xlix, argues this point.

7 David N. Livingstone and Charles W. J. Withers, ed. *Geography and Enlightenment* (Chicago: University of Chicago Press, 1999); and Jerry Brotton, *Trading Territories: Mapping the Early Modern World* (Ithaca: Cornell University Press, 1998).

8 The quotation is cited in the entry for the Duchess of Queensberry in *The Dictionary of National Biography*, vol. V, p. 1194.

9 See chapter 6 below.

10 *The Letters of Horace Walpole, Earl of Orford*, ed. Peter Cunningham, 9 vols. (London: Henry G. Bohn, 1861), vol. V, p. 477; and J. A. Home, Introduction, *The Letters and Journals of Lady Mary Coke*, 4 vols. (Facsimile 1970 of Kingsmead Reprints, Bath, 1889–96), vol. I, p. xliv.

11 M. Dorothy George, *Catalogue of Political and Personal Satires . . . in the British Museum* (London: British Museum, 1938), entry 5120, vol. V of XI, p. 120.

12 Johann Reinhold Forster, *Observations Made During A Voyage Round the World*, ed. Nicholas Thomas, Harriet Guest, and Michael Dettelbach (Honolulu: University of Hawai'i Press, 1996), p. 174. All subsequent references are cited in parentheses in the text.

13 *The Female Monster or, The Second Part of the World turn'd Topsy Turvey, A Satyr* (London 1705). See also *"Defects" : Engendering the Modern Body*, ed. Helen Deutsch and Felicity Nussbaum (Ann Arbor: University of Michigan Press, 2000).

14 P. J. Marshall and Glyndwr Williams, *The Great Map of Mankind: Perceptions of New Worlds in the Age of Enlightenment* (Cambridge: Harvard University Press, 1982), pp. 227–98.

15 See Andrew Curran and Patrick Graille, "The Faces of Eighteenth-Century Monstrosity," *Eighteenth-Century Life* 21 (May 1997): 1–15.

16 See Harriet Guest, "Looking at Women: Forster's Observations in the South Pacific," in Forster, *Observations*, xli–liv; and Sylvana Tomaselli, "The Enlightenment Debate on Women," *History Workshop* 20 (Autumn 1985): 101–24.

17 See Nicholas Thomas, " 'On the Varieties of the Human Species': Forster's Comparative Ethnology," in Forster, *Observations*, xxiii–xl.

18 James A. Boon, "Anthropology and Degeneration: Birds, Words, and Orangutans," *Degeneration: The Dark Side of Progress*, ed. J. Edward Chamberlin and Sander L. Gilman (New York: Columbia University Press, 1985), 24–28.

19 Margaret T. Hodgen, *Early Anthropology in the Sixteenth and Seventeenth Centuries* (Philadelphia: University of Pennsylvania Press, 1964), p. 259. For the implications of polygenetic theory in the nineteenth century, see Robert J. C. Young, *Colonial Desire: Hybridity in Theory, Culture and Race* (London: Routledge, 1995).

20 *The London Magazine* 64 (1775): 497.

21 For a brief description of this picture, see David Dabydeen, *Hogarth's Blacks: Images of Blacks in Eighteenth Century English Art* (Surrey: Dangaroo Press, 1985), p. 74.

22 Robert L. S. Cowley, *Hogarth's Marriage A-La-Mode* (Ithaca: Cornell University Press, 1983), pp. 83–99, and Judy Egerton, *Hogarth's "Marriage A-la-Mode"* (London: National Gallery Publication, 1997).

23 Felicity A. Nussbaum, *Torrid Zones: Maternity, Sexuality, and Empire in Eighteenth-Century English Narratives* (Baltimore: The Johns Hopkins University Press, 1995), and *"Defects,"* ed. Helen Deutsch and Felicity Nussbaum (Ann Arbor: University of Michigan Press, 2000). A sampling of recent writing on related topics includes Lorraine Daston and Katharine Park, *Wonders and the Order of Nature, 1150–1750* (New York: Zone Books, 1998); Harriet Ritvo, *The Platypus and the Mermaid and other Figments of the Classifying Imagination* (Cambridge: Harvard University Press, 1997); Lennard J. Davis, *Enforcing Normalcy: Disability, Deafness and the Body* (London: Verso, 1995); Dennis Todd, *Imagining Monsters: Miscreations of the Self in Eighteenth-Century England* (Chicago: University of Chicago Press, 1995); Marie-Hélène Huet, *Monstrous Imagination* (Cambridge: Harvard University Press, 1993); Joseph Roach, *Cities of the Dead: Circum-Atlantic Performance* (New York: Columbia University Press, 1996); Harriet Guest, *Small Change: Women, Learning, Patriotism, 1750–1810* (Chicago: University of Chicago Press, 2000); Laura Brown,

Fables of Modernity: Literature and Culture in the English Eighteenth Century (Ithaca: Cornell University Press, 2001); Jonathan Lamb, *Preserving the Self in the South Seas, 1680–1840* (Chicago: University of Chicago Press, 2001); Roxann Wheeler, *The Complexion of Race: Categories of Difference in Eighteenth-Century Culture* (Philadelphia: University of Pennsylvania Press, 2000); and Srinivas Aravamudan, *Tropicopolitans: Colonialism and Agency, 1688–1804* (Durham and London: Duke University Press, 1999).

1 FICTIONS OF DEFECT

1 *Female Rights Vindicated; or the Equality of the Sexes Morally and Physically proved*, By a Lady (London 1758), p. 115. Subsequent references cited in the text are to this edition. This is a later version of *Beauty's Triumph, Or, the Superiority of the Fair Sex invincibly proved*, 3 parts (London 1751). Also known as the "Sophia pamphlets", these and other translations of Poulain de la Barre's *De l'égalité des deux sexes* (1673), widely disseminated and regularly revised throughout the eighteenth century, typically included rhetorical contests between a misogynist and a feminist. It is uncertain how seriously the vindications, deriving from Catholic France but written by a Calvinist Poulain, were regarded in England. Their exaggerated nature suggests that they may have caricatured extreme views, though their egalitarian feminism and emphasis on reasoned religion might have mitigated the Catholicism. Poulain de la Barre became a convert to Calvinism. See Siep Stuurman, "From Feminism to Biblical Criticism: The Theological Trajectory of François Poulain de la Barre," *Eighteenth-Century Studies* 33 (2000): 367–82. In her letters Elizabeth Carter urgently inquires about the identity of the author of *Woman not inferior to man* (1739), perhaps suspecting an acquaintance. Subsequent references cited in the text are to these editions.

2 *Female Rights Vindicated*, p. 89. François Poulain (Poullain) de la Barre, *The Woman as Good as the Man Or, the Equality of Both Sexes*, trans. A. L., ed. Gerald M. MacLean (Detroit: Wayne State University Press, 1988) contends that women's brains are perfectly equal to men's: "Each [sex] was perfect in its kind; and they might ought both to be disposed, as they are at present: And all that depends on their particular Constitution, ought to be considered, as making a part of their Perfection. It is then without Reason, that some imagine, That *Women* are not so perfect as *Men*; and that they look upon that (in them) as a Defect, which is an essential Portion of their Sex; without the which, it would be useless for the end, for which it hath been formed; which begins and ceases with Fecundity, and which is destin'd for the most excellent use of the World; that is, to frame and nourish us in their Bellies," p. 131. (The author himself spelled his name both "Poulain" and "Poullain.")

3 Thomas Laqueur, *Making Sex: Body and Gender from the Greeks to Freud* (Cambridge: Harvard University Press, 1990) shows that women's internal organs were often imagined to be defective male appendages because they failed to descend.

4 *Beauty's Triumph, Or, the Superiority of the Fair Sex invincibly proved.* 3 parts (London 1751), p. 71. Part II is entitled "Being an ATTEMPT to refute SOPHIA's Arguments; And to probe the Natural Right of the Men to Sovereign Authority over the Other Sex," p. 96.

5 See Londa Schiebinger, *The Mind Has No Sex? Women in the Origins of Modern Science* (Cambridge: Harvard University Press, 1989), p. 203; and Bernard Albinus, *Tabulae sceleti et musculorum corporis humani* (Leiden, 1747).

6 For the concept of the prostitute as man-woman, see Felicity Nussbaum, *Torrid Zones: Maternity, Sexuality, and Empire in Eighteenth-Century English Narratives* (Baltimore: The Johns Hopkins University Press, 1995).

7 See especially Julia Epstein on the maternal power to deform fetuses in "Dangerous Wombs," in *Altered Conditions: Disease, Medicine, and Storytelling* (Routledge: New York, 1995), pp. 123–56: "Assigning responsibility for the horror of defective or malformed births affected inheritance, social organization. In a social system dependent on male lineage, it was more than just ideologically convenient to displace this responsibility onto the bodies and minds of women," p. 151.

8 *Orthopaedia: or, the Art of Correcting and Preventing Deformities in Children,* trans. from the French of M. Andry (London 1743), p. 29.

9 *Hebe; or, the Art of Preserving Beauty, and Correcting Deformity* (London 1786), pp. 13–14.

10 *Hebe,* pp. 13–14.

11 Aphra Behn, *The Works of Aphra Behn,* ed. Janet Todd, 7 vols. (Columbus: Ohio State University Press, 1995), vol. III, pp. 321–60. All subsequent references cited in the text are to this edition.

12 Janet Todd suggests that the fictional suitor calls to mind Thomas Dangerfield who participated in the Meal-Tub Plot, a Protestant attempt to counter the Popish Plot. Both the real and the fictional Dangerfield disguised themselves as Turks, *The Works of Aphra Behn,* vol. III, p. 336.

13 Ros Ballaster, *Seductive Forms: Women's Amatory Fiction from 1684 to 1740* (Oxford: Clarendon Press, 1992).

14 See *Eighteenth-Century Women Poets: An Oxford Anthology,* ed. Roger Lonsdale (Oxford: Oxford University Press, 1989), pp. 275–76.

15 Catherine Ingrassia, "Women Writing / Writing Women: Pope, Dulness, and 'Feminization' in the *Dunciad,*" *Eighteenth-Century Life* 14 (November 1990): 40–58, extends Pope's fears to men and interprets the *Dunciad* as "a symbolically emasculated man's personal and professional anxiety about the increasing power of creative and mercenary male and female writers."

16 Samuel Johnson, *Idler* 87 in *The Idler and The Adventurer,* ed. W. J. Bate, John M. Bullitt, and L. F. Powell, *The Yale Edition of the Works of Samuel Johnson* (New Haven: Yale University Press, 1963), vol. II, p. 272. As Addison writes in *Spectator* 434 (18 July 1712), "No Woman was to be married till she had killed her Man."

17 *Female Rights Vindicated,* p. 20. The Amazon's military heroics serve as a displacement of the cultural terror surrounding effeminacy and luxury; and as

Laura Brown has argued in *The Ends of Empire: Women and Ideology in Early Eighteenth-Century English Literature* (Ithaca: Cornell University Press, 1993), attributing violence to women helps men avoid acknowledging the violence of empire. The Amazon comes to represent both the native and the "alter ego of the male imperialist" at once, p. 131.

18 The reference to Semiramis also appears in John Bulwer, *Anthropometamorphosis: Man Transformed* (1650; London, 1653), p. 353. On the connections between ruling women and eunuchs, see especially Dympna Callaghan, "The Castrator's Song: Female Impersonation on the Early Modern Stage" in *Shakespeare Without Women: Representing Gender and Race on the Renaissance Stage* (London and New York: Routledge, 2000), pp. 49–74.

19 Callaghan, *Shakespeare Without Women*, noting a similar myth in Bulwer's *Anthropometamorphosis*, finds that the passage reveals a phallic logic that women, precisely because they do not have a penis and testicles, may castrate men without expecting retaliation. "In desiring men who are like herself, Semiramis implicitly presents . . . also the possibility of an erotic preference for a man devoid of the sexual use of his penis, a choice which threatens to make virility redundant," p. 29.

20 David Hume, "Of Love and Marriage," *Essays Moral, Political and Literary*, ed. Eugene F. Miller, revised edition (Indianapolis: Liberty Fund, 1987), p. 559. Hume's essay pleads for sexual equality and equanimity to heal the sexual division that derives from Jupiter's punishment of the prosperous Androgynes' rebellion.

21 Hume, "Of Love and Marriage," p. 559.

22 "Being an ATTEMPT to refute SOPHIA's Arguments; And to probe the Natural Right of the Men to Sovereign Authority over the Other Sex," *Beauty's Triumph, Or, the Superiority of the Fair Sex invincibly proved*, 3 parts (London 1751), Part II, p. 107.

23 *Eunuchism Display'd, Describing all the different Sorts of* Eunuchs; *the Esteem they have met with in the World, and how they came to be made so. Wherein principally is examin'd whether they are capable of Marriage, and if they ought to be suffer'd to enter into that State. . . ."* (London, 1718), p. 75.

24 According to Enid and Richard Peschel, "The Castrati in Opera," *Opera Quarterly* 4.4 (Winter 1986–87): 23, eunuchs' physical anomalies extended beyond the genitals. They "had subcutaneous fat localized to the hips, buttocks, and breasts, sometimes had fatty deposits on the lateral portions of the eyelids, had pale and oftentimes swollen and wrinkled skin, and possessed abnormally long arms and legs, resulting in what is technically called a 'eunuchoid appearance'" (27), cited in Beth Kowaleski-Wallace, "Shunning the Bearded Kiss: Castrati and the Definition of Female Sexuality," *Prose Studies* 15.2 (August 1992): 153–70, who emphasizes the non-phallic sexual threat that eunuchs represent. See also Jill Campbell, "'When Men Women Turn': Gender Reversals in Fielding's Plays," *The New Eighteenth Century: Theory/Politics/English Literature*, ed. Felicity Nussbaum and Laura Brown (New York and London: Methuen, 1987), pp. 62–83; and Yvonne Noble,

"Castrati, Balzac, and Barthes' *S/Z*," *Comparative Drama* 31.1 (1997/98): 28–41.

25 Kowaleski-Wallace, "Shunning the Bearded Kiss," pp. 163–67, discusses the close identification between Frances Burney as a woman writer and the castrato Pacchierotti, though she focuses on the social perceptions of mutilation rather than the analogies that defective organs inspire.

26 *Eunuchism Display'd*, p. 106.

27 Michael McKeon, *The Origins of the English Novel, 1600–1740* (Baltimore and London: The Johns Hopkins University Press, 1987), pp. 260–61.

28 Eliza Haywood, *Philidore and Placentia; or, L'Amour trop Delicat* in *Four Before Richardson: Selected English Novels, 1720–1727*, ed. W. H. McBurney (Lincoln: University of Nebraska Press, 1963), p. 162. All subsequent references in the text are to this edition.

29 Arithea's beauty is white and rosy, not at all resembling the darkness of the Orient.

30 For a convincing refutation of the attribution to Defoe, see Rodney Baine, *Daniel Defoe and the Supernatural* (Athens: University of Georgia Press, 1968) who believes that William Bond authored *The History* and *The Friendly Daemon*. Publisher Bond's *The Supernatural Philosopher: or, the Mysteries of Magick, In all its Branches, clearly Unfolded* (1728) appeared as a "second edition" to *The History*. This version, according to Baine, "reissued sheets of both of the 1720 editions . . . with a new title," p. 145.

31 Rodney Baine, *Daniel Defoe and the Supernatural*, p. 144.

32 Joseph Addison and Richard Steele, *The Spectator*, ed. Donald F. Bond, 5 vols. (Oxford: Oxford University Press, 1965), vol. IV, p. 512.

33 *The Weekly Medley*, 31 January–7 February 1719, is cited in Baine from the Bodleian microfilm record.

34 Georges Canguilhem, *The Normal and the Pathological* (1966), introduction by Michel Foucault, trans. Carolyn R. Fawcett (New York: Zone Books, 1989) remarks that "Between 1759, the date of the first appearance of the word *normal*, and 1834, the date of the first appearance of the word *normalized*, a normative class conquered the power to identify the function of social norms with its own uses and its own determination of content," p. 246.

35 Carl Linné [Linnaeus], *A General System of Nature, Through the Three Grand Kingdoms of Animals, Vegetables, and Minerals, Systematically Divided*, trans. William Turton MD, 7 volumes (London, 1802).

36 V. Y. Mudimbe, *The Invention of Africa: Gnosis, Philosophy, and the Order of Knowledge* (Bloomington: Indiana University Press, 1988), p. 71.

37 Charles W. Mills, *The Racial Contract* (Ithaca and New York: Cornell University Press, 1997), p. 41.

38 Jean-Jacques Rousseau, *Discourse on the Origins of Inequality (Second Discourse), Polemics, and Political Economy*, ed. Roger D. Masters and Christopher Kelly, trans. Judith R. Bush et al., in *The Collected Writings of Rousseau*, vol. III of 9 (Hanover and London: University Press of New England, 1992). Cited in Mills, *The Racial Contract*, p. 68.

39 Daniel Defoe, *The Life and Strange Surprizing Adventures of Robinson Crusoe of York, Mariner*, ed. J. Donald Crowley (Oxford: Oxford University Press, 1972), p. 142.

40 Kim Hall, *Things of Darkness: Economies of Race and Gender in Early Modern England* (Ithaca: Cornell University Press, 1995), p. 244.

41 Mills, *The Racial Contract*, p. 23.

42 Jean Coenrad Amman, *The Talking Deaf Man: or, A Method Proposed Whereby he who is Born Deaf, may learn to Speak* (1694), No. 357, English Linguistics 1500–1800 Series 3. Meston, England: Scholar Press, 1972.

43 James Burnet, Lord Monboddo, *Of the Origin and Progress of Language*, 2nd edn. (Edinburgh, 1774), vol. I, p. v.

44 George Sibscota, *The Deaf and Dumb Man's Discourse. Or A Treatise concerning those that are Born Deaf and Dumb, containing a Discovering of their knowledge or understanding; as also the Method they use, to manifest the sentiments of their Mind* (London, 1670), pp. 41–42.

45 *A New Relation of the Inner-Part of the Grand Seignor's Seraglio* (London 1677) notes that mutes in the seraglio communicated through sign language which functioned to avoid distracting the monarch with the sound of servants speaking.

46 Nicholas Mirzoeff, "Paper, Picture, Sign: Conversations Between the Deaf, the Hard of Hearing, and Others" in *"Defects": Engendering the Modern Body*, ed. Helen Deutsch and Felicity Nussbaum (Ann Arbor: University of Michigan Press, 2000), pp. 75–92. For the definitive work on the relationship between sign language and the aesthetic/visual arts in France, see Nicholas Mirzoeff, *Silent Poetry: Deafness, Sign, and Visual Culture in Modern France* (Princeton: Princeton University Press, 1995) who quotes Perier, one of Sicard's deputies as saying: "The Deaf-Mute is a savage, always close to ferocity and always on the point of becoming a monster," p. 62. Mirzoeff, *Silent Poetry*, also reports that anthropologists were encouraged "to learn sign language in order to communicate with the native peoples they encountered," p. 68.

47 According to Baine, *Daniel Defoe and the Supernatural*, information relevant to the parentage of Campbell's mother in Lapland was cribbed from Johannes Scheffer's *History of Lapland*, p. 150.

48 Rousseau, *Discourse on the Origins of Inequality (Second Discourse)*, writes that "There have been, and there perhaps still are, Nations of men of gigantic size; and apart from the fable of the Pygmies, which may well be only an exaggeration, it is known that the Laplanders, and above all the Greenlanders, are well below the size of man. It is even claimed that there are whole Peoples that have tails like quadrupeds," p. 80.

49 Oliver Goldsmith, *An History of the Earth, and Animate Nature*, 8 vols. (London, 1774), vol. II, p. 228.

50 Samuel Johnson, *A Journey to the Western Islands of Scotland*, ed. Mary Lascelles, *The Yale Edition of the Works of Samuel Johnson*, vol. IX (New Haven and London: Yale University Press, 1971), p. 107.

51 Mirzoeff, *Silent Poetry*, p. 75.

52 *The Secret Memoirs of the late Mr. Duncan Campbel[l]* is, I believe, inaccurately assumed to be a reprint of *The Friendly Daemon* (London, 1732).

53 See Baine, *Daniel Defoe and the Supernatural*.

54 Julia Epstein argues that within patriarchy, "women physically retreat... and can use only speech – the polite speech of self-command – to countermand violation," *The Iron Pen: Frances Burney and the Politics of Women's Writing* (Madison: University of Wisconsin Press, 1989), p. 149.

55 J. G. A. Pocock, *Virtue, Commerce, and History: Essays on Political Thought and History, Chiefly in the Eighteenth Century* (Cambridge: Cambridge University Press, 1985) was speaking more generally, but his insights could be applied to Campbell as the personification of "a society now living to an increasing degree by speculation and by credit" who possesses "the image of a secular and historical future." Fortunetelling exemplifies the way that "property... has ceased to be real and become not merely mobile but imaginary" and "what one owned was promises," pp. 98, 112, 113.

56 Midcentury brings the beginning of institutionalized special education according to Margaret A. Winzer, *The History of Special Education: From Isolation to Integration* (Washington, DC: Gallaudet University Press, 1993).

57 Stuart Sherman, *Telling Time: Clocks, Diaries, and English Diurnal Form, 1660–1785* (Chicago: University of Chicago Press, 1996), p. 207; and Martin Wechselblatt, "Finding Mr. Boswell: Rhetorical Authority and National Identity in Johnson's *A Journey to the Western Islands of Scotland*," *ELH* 60.1 (Spring 1993): 143.

58 Sherman, *Telling Time*, p. 197.

59 Ann Laura Stoler, *Race and the Education of Desire: Foucault's "History of Sexuality" and the Colonial Order of Things* (Durham: Duke University Press, 1995).

60 Rosemarie Garland Thomson, *Extraordinary Bodies: Figuring Physical Disability in American Culture and Literature* (New York: Columbia University Press, 1997).

61 Donna Haraway, "Ecco Homo, Ain't (Ar'n't) I a Woman, and Inappropriate/d Others: The Human in a Post-Humanist Landscape," in *Feminists Theorize the Political*, ed. Judith Butler and Joan W. Scott (New York and London: Routledge, 1992), pp. 86–100.

2 EFFEMINACY AND FEMININITY

1 On nationalism and gender, see Gerald Newman, *The Rise of English Nationalism: A Cultural History, 1740–1830* (London: Weidenfeld and Nicolson, 1987); Kathleen Wilson, *The Sense of the People: Politics, Culture and Imperialism in England, 1715–1785* (Cambridge: Cambridge University Press, 1995), pp. 185–205; and Linda Colley, *Britons: Forging the Nation, 1707–1837* (New Haven: Yale University Press, 1992).

2 Evidence for the evolution of a two-sex model in the eighteenth century, following the Renaissance assumption of a one-sex paradigm in which woman was simply an inferior version of a man, is most fully articulated in Thomas

Laqueur's *Making Sex: Body and Gender from the Greeks to Freud* (Cambridge: Harvard University Press, 1990). For an argument that emphasizes the dichotomy, see Michael McKeon, "Historicizing Patriarchy: The Emergence of Gender Difference in England, 1660–1760," *ECS* 28.3 (1995): 295–322. For a contrasting and more convincing view, see Amanda Vickery, "Golden Age to Separate Spheres: A Review of the Categories and Chronology of English Women's History," *Historical Journal* 36.2 (1993): 383–414.

3 For critical arguments that women writers after the 1740s turned from amatory fiction to sentimental domestic novels, see especially Ros Ballaster, *Seductive Forms: Women's Amatory Fiction from 1684 to 1740* (Oxford: Clarendon Press, 1992); Jane Spencer, *The Rise of the Woman Novelist from Aphra Behn to Jane Austen* (New York: Basil Blackwell, 1986); and Janet Todd, *The Sign of Angellica: Women, Writing and Fiction, 1660–1800* (London: Virago, 1989). For revisions to these ideas see, for example, Catherine Gallagher, *Nobody's Story: The Vanishing Acts of Women Writers in the Marketplace 1670–1820* (Berkeley: University of California Press, 1994) who examines the satiric inversions in Behn, Manley, Lennox, Burney, and Edgeworth which, she argues, paradoxically negate and redefine women's authorial property and public presence, though Gallagher also believes that midcentury brings a new moral seriousness and respectability to women's self-presentation, p. 147. Margaret Anne Doody, *The True Story of the Novel* (New Brunswick: Rutgers University Press, 1996) focuses especially on gendering the novel's reader, pp. 274–81.

4 Samuel Johnson, No. 115, Tuesday, 11 December 1753, *The Idler and the Adventurer*, ed. W. J. Bate, John M. Bullitt, and L. F. Powell, *The Yale Edition of the Works of Samuel Johnson* (New Haven and London: Yale University Press, 1963), vol. II, pp. 457–58. Jane Spencer argues that "at the same time as encouraging women to write, this [eighteenth-century] feminization of literature defined literature as a special category supposedly outside the political arena, with an influence on the world as indirect as women's was supposed to be" (p. xi), but political liberty did not easily translate into women's rights.

5 In ancient Ireland a little-known female satiric tradition was personified in the "dangerous enchanted" druidess who comprises at once a prophet, a poet, and a strategist capable of destroying her victims in battle. See Mary Claire Randolph, "Female Satirists of Ancient Ireland," *Southern Folklore Quarterly* 5.2 (June 1942): 75–87.

6 Most significant is Ros Ballaster, "Manl(e)y Forms: Sex and the Female Satirist," *Women, Texts, and Histories 1575–1760*, ed. Clare Brant and Diane Purkis (London and New York: Routledge, 1992), pp. 217–41, who finds that Delarivier Manley authorizes the *chronique scandaleuse* "as a peculiarly feminine form of satire" (p. 220) and develops a mixed genre satire that follows Varronian rather than Juvenalian or Horatian models.

7 See especially Catherine Gallagher's discussions of Aphra Behn, Delarivier Manley, and Charlotte Lennox who constructed "their authorial personae on a framework of commonplace insults" (p. 136) such as "whore" and "hack."

8 Fanny Burney, *Evelina or the History of a Young Lady's Entrance into the World*, ed. Edward A. Bloom and Lillian D. Bloom (Oxford: Oxford University Press, 1982), pp. 268–69.

9 Chloe Chard, "Effeminacy, Pleasure and the Classical Body," in *Femininity and Masculinity in Eighteenth-Century Art and Culture*, ed. Gill Perry and Michael Rossington (Manchester: Manchester University Press, 1994) notes, "Commentaries such as [John] Moore's ... present an admiration for male grace and beauty as dangerously effeminate by defining graceful male bodies as pleasing to women," p. 158.

10 See Jill Campbell, " 'When Men Women Turn': Gender Reversals in Fielding's Plays," in *The New Eighteenth Century: Theory/Politics/English Literature*, ed. Felicity Nussbaum and Laura Brown (New York and London: Methuen, 1987), pp. 62–83. On the performances of the *castrati*, see Curtis Price, Judith Milhous, and Robert D. Hume, *Italian Opera in Late Eighteenth-Century London*, vol. 1 of 2 (Oxford: Clarendon Press, 1995).

11 William Popple, *The Prompter*, No. 7 (4 December 1734), cited in Thomas McGeary, " 'Warbling Eunuchs': Opera, Gender, and Sexuality on the London Stage, 1705–1742," *Restoration and Eighteenth-Century Theatre Research* 7.1 (1992): 1–22. McGeary discusses Italian opera's threat to British masculinity and the attraction of Englishwomen to the *castrati*. See also Joseph R. Roach, "Power's Body: The Inscription of Morality as Style," in *Interpreting the Theatrical Past: Essays in the Historiography of Performance*, ed. Thomas Postlewait and Bruce A. McConachie (Iowa City: University of Iowa Press, 1989), pp. 99–118, 103, 105.

12 Peter J. Carlton, "The Mitigated Truth: Tom Jones's Double Heroism," *Studies in the Novel* 19 (1987): 407, discusses the shift in masculinity after the demise of the Jacobite hopes.

13 Sarah Fielding (1710–68), the third sister of Henry, lived with her brother to care for his motherless children between his marriages and was partially dependent on him for support. B. G. MacCarthy, *The Female Pen: Women Writers and Novelists 1621–1818* with a preface by Janet Todd (New York: New York University Press, 1994): "In its own day this work was adjudged a success, so much so, in fact, that it was ascribed to [Henry] Fielding" (p. 237).

14 Sarah Fielding, *The Adventures of David Simple,* ed. Malcolm Kelsall (Oxford and New York: Oxford University Press, 1987), p. 5. All subsequent references to this edition are cited in the text. Not completely generous to his sister, Henry Fielding chides Sarah for her want of learning while pointing out the "beauties of this little Work" (p. 6) though, according to Kelsall, she knew some Latin and was considered a bluestocking.

15 See Janet Todd, *The Sign of Angellica: Women, Writing and Fiction, 1660–1800* (New York: Columbia University Press, 1989), p. 164. The question of whether Fielding is feminist has been frequently discussed, and David Simple has been interpreted as "a man who rejects patriarchy, whose central beliefs are feminist and who is unable to effect his dreams because he is femininely virtuous to an extreme," in Carolyn Woodward, "Sarah Fielding's Self-Destructing Utopia,"

in *Living by the Pen: Early British Women Writers*, ed. Dale Spender (New York: Teachers College Press, 1992), pp. 65–81. Yet when David is rejected by Miss Nanny Johnson, he "repeated all the Satires he could remember on Women" (p. 39).

16 According to John Barrell in reference to painting, "comprehensiveness of vision and a 'penetration' ... are regarded in the late eighteenth century as characteristically or even exclusively masculine capabilities" in *The Birth of Pandora and the Divisions of Knowledge* (Philadelphia: University of Pennsylvania Press, 1992), p. 163. See also James Barry, *An Inquiry into the Real and Imaginary Obstructions to the Acquisition of the Arts in England* (London 1775).

17 Mary Wollstonecraft, *A Vindication of the Rights of Woman*, ed. Carol H. Poston (New York: W. W. Norton and Co., 1975).

18 Jayne Lewis contends, "It is only when women are able to break out of the [verse satire and misogynist] tradition, abandoning its stereotypes and stances in favor of a wider and more pliable perspective, that they may be said to write a satire of their own," "Compositions of Ill Nature: Women's Place in a Satiric Tradition," *Critical Matrix* 2.2 (1986): 31–69.

19 Sarah Fielding, *The History of the Countess of Dellwyn* (1759), 2 vols. in 1 (New York and London: Garland Publishing, Inc., 1974), vol. I, p. 260.

20 Ibid., vol. I, p. xx.

21 Ibid., vol. I, p. xliii.

22 Isabelle's narrative reiterates the cultural nationalism of the interpolated tale, "Leonora and the Unfortunate Jilt," in *Joseph Andrews*, a section that Sarah Fielding was rumored to have written. Leonora loses her lover Horatio because of a foolish flirtation with the modish aristocratic Parisian flatterer Bellarmine. See Gerald Newman, *The Rise of English Nationalism: A Cultural History, 1740–1830* (London: Weidenfeld and Nicolson, 1987), pp. 65–66.

23 See B. G. MacCarthy, *The Female Pen: Women Writers and Novelists 1621–1818* with a preface by Janet Todd (New York: New York University Press, 1994).

24 See Sara Gadeken, "Sarah Fielding and the Salic Law of Wit," *SEL 1500–1900* 42.3 (2002): 541–57. Euphemia in Clara Reeve, *The Progress of Romance*, in *Bluestocking Feminism: Writings of the Bluestocking Circle, 1738–1785*, ed. Gary Kelly (London: Pickering and Chatto, 1999), similarly associates the mercenary and narcissistic with effeminacy: "I would ask whether such a man is not more respectable, and more amiable, than a human being, wholly immersed in low, groveling, effeminate, or mercenary pursuits, without one grain of private virtue, or public spirit; whose only thoughts wishes and desires, are absorbed in a worthless self?" vol. VI, p. 208.

25 Martin Battestin discusses the evidence for incest in *Henry Fielding: A Life* with Ruthe R. Battestin (London: Routledge, 1989), pp. 27–30.

26 Margaret Doody, *The True Story of the Novel*, p. 292, emphasizes the domestic realist novel's exclusion of the foreign and its focus on the homeland as well as the home, but for the incursion of the exotic and savage into the novel, see Felicity Nussbaum, *Torrid Zones: Maternity, Sexuality, and Empire in Eighteenth-Century British Narratives* (Baltimore: The Johns Hopkins University Press, 1995).

27 George Ballard, *Memoirs of Several Ladies of Great Britain Who Have Been Celebrated for their Writings or Skill in the Learned Languages, Arts and Sciences* (1752), ed. Ruth Perry (Detroit: Wayne State University Press, 1985), p. 53.

28 On the increasingly popular female warrior motif in the later eighteenth century, see Dianne Dugaw, *Warrior Women and Popular Balladry 1650–1850* (Cambridge: Cambridge University Press, 1989). For a discussion of shifting gender roles in the family economy after 1750, see Bridget Hill, *Women, Work, and Sexual Politics in Eighteenth-Century England* (Oxford: Blackwell, 1989).

29 Jill Campbell, *Natural Masques: Gender and Identity in Fielding's Plays and Novels* (Stanford: Stanford University Press, 1995) brilliantly discusses *Tom Jones*, the female soldier, and gender-bending during the 1945 rebellion.

30 In the same year that Brown's *An Estimate of the Manners* was published, Garrick produced *The Male Coquette; or, Seventeen-Hundred Fifty-Seven* which satirized an effeminate heterosexual who attracts a cross-dressed lover.

31 John Brown, *An Estimate of the Manners and Principles of the Times* (London 1757).

32 J. G. A. Pocock, *Virtue, Commerce, and History: Essays on Political Thought and History, Chiefly in the Eighteenth Century* (Cambridge: Cambridge University Press, 1985) in a much-cited passage writes that when production and exchange "are given a new role in history, which is to refine the passions... there is a danger that they may render societies effeminate – a term whose recurrence ought not to be neglected," p. 114.

33 *Beauty's Triumph, Or, the Superiority of the Fair Sex invincibly proved*, 3 parts (London 1751), part II, p. 104.

34 Susan Staves, "A Few Kind Words for the Fop," *SEL* 22 (1982): 413–28, is correct, I think, in indicating that though the Restoration fop is effeminate, he is nevertheless presumed to be heterosexual.

35 Randolph Trumbach, "London Sodomites: Homosexual Behaviour and Western Culture in the 18th Century," *Journal of Social History* 11.1 (1977): 1–33; and "The Birth of the Queen: Sodomy and the Emergence of Gender Equality in Modern Culture, 1660–1750," *Hidden From History: Reclaiming the Gay and Lesbian Past*, ed. Martin Duberman, Martha Vicinus and George Chauncey, Jr. (New York: New American Library, 1989), pp. 129–40. Trumbach's assertion that the emergence of an exclusively homosexual identity leads to greater gender equality has appropriately been questioned. Though Trumbach argues that by the early eighteenth century, a fop or adult effeminate male was homosexual, evidence suggests that the fop's sexuality is much less fixed.

36 John Barrell, "'The Dangerous Goddess': Masculinity, Prestige, and the Aesthetic in Early Eighteenth-Century Britain," in *The Birth of Pandora and the Division of Knowledge* (Philadelphia: University of Pennsylvania Press, 1992), pp. 53–88.

37 See Chard, "Effeminacy, Pleasure and the Classical Body," pp. 142–61.

38 *Female Rights Vindicated; or the Equality of the Sexes Morally and Physically Proved*. By a Lady (London: Burnet, 1758), pp. 44–45. I thank Harriet Guest for calling this passage to my attention.

39 "She has besides dispossessed herself of that Awkward stiffness and effeminacy which so commonly attend the fair sex in breeches," *The Life of Mr. James Quin, Comedian* (London 1887), p. 40 (London 1766), and cited in Pat Rogers, "The Breeches Parts," *Sexuality in Eighteenth-Century Britain,* ed. Paul-Gabriel Boucé (Manchester: Manchester University Press, 1982), pp. 244–56; 248, 256.

40 Thomas A. King argues that the new eighteenth-century homosexual identity is figured by the moral bourgeois as aristocratic, or as an identity of excess and monstrosity. He suggests that the mollies' "self" was an escape from class alignment with the bourgeoisie in "Performing 'Akimbo': Queer Pride and Epistemological Prejudice," in *The Politics and Poetics of Camp,* ed. Moe Meyer (London and New York: Routledge, 1995), pp. 23–50.

41 *The Treasure: or Impartial Compendium* (London 1771), no. 3259: "There is indeed a kind of animal neither male nor female, a thing of the neuter gender, lately started up amongst us. It is called Macaroni. It talks without meaning... it eats without appetite... it wenches without passion," p. 75. The latter half of the eighteenth century, called "the golden age of male foppery in England," witnessed extraordinary luxury in the "Macaroni" style with its extreme fashion and enormous wigs throughout the 1770s, though I suggest that its potential threat to the national security then shifts the focus from fashion and sybarite pleasures to disease and degeneration.

42 James Boswell, *Boswell's London Journal, 1762–63,* ed. Frederick A. Pottle (New York: McGraw-Hill, 1952), p. 51. See Robert J. Allen, *The Clubs of Augustan London* (Hamden, Conn.: Archon Books, 1967), p. 149, and Walter Arnold, *The Life and Death of the Sublime Society of Beefsteaks* (London: Bradbury, Evans, and Co., 1871).

43 Edward Ward writes, "So far degenerated from all Masculine Deportment or Manly exercises that they [mollies] rather fancy themselves Women, imitating all the little Vanities that Custom has reconcil'd to the Female sex, affecting to speak, walk, tattle, curtsy, cry, scold, & mimick all manner of Effeminacy," *The Secret History of the Clubs; Particularly the Kit-Cat, Beef-stake, Vertuosos, Quacks, Knight of the Golden-fleece, Florists, Beaus & c.* (London, 1709), p. 28.

44 Performance theory contests the inner truth of sex versus "the illusion of an interior and organizing gender core" as Judith Butler has argued in *Gender Trouble* (New York: Routledge, 1990), p. 136. Though sex may be "performatively produced," performances themselves need to be historically contextualized and understood as subject to institutional and other hierarchies.

45 See Ananda Vital Rao, *A Minor Augustan, Being the Life and Works of George, Lord Lyttelton, 1709–1773* (Calcutta: The Book Company, 1934).

46 James Boswell, *The Life of Johnson,* ed. George Birkbeck Hill, rev. L. F. Powell, 6 vols. (Oxford: Clarendon Press, 1934–50), vol. IV, p. 73.

47 Hester Lynch Thrale Piozzi, *Anecdotes,* p. 160, cited in Boswell, *The Life of Johnson,* vol. III, p. 57 n.2.

48 Elizabeth Montagu to Elizabeth Carter, 17 [Oct.] [1765], Sandleford [Berks.], MO 3157. All subsequent references to the Montagu letters are from the Henry

E. Huntington Library, and I am grateful for permission to publish these selections.

49 Elizabeth D. Sklar writes, "English-language advocates sought to promote English as a language worthy of national pride, one that could be perceived, moreover, as competitive within an international linguistic community that had long held it in contempt. Representing English as a 'manly' language was a key strategy in this undertaking," "So Male a Speech: Linguistic Adequacy in Eighteenth-Century England," *American Speech* 64.4 (1989): 372–79, 373.

50 E. Montagu to Elizabeth Carter, 24 Oct. 1765 [Sandleford] [Berks.], MO 3158.

51 E. Montagu to Elizabeth Carter, 16 July 1766 [Sandleford] [Berks.], MO3148.

52 Elizabeth Eger, "Introduction," *Bluestocking Feminism: Writings of the Blue-stocking Circle, 1738–1785*, gen. ed. Gary Kelly, 6 vols. (London: Pickering and Chatto, 1999), vol. 1, p. lxxiii. Montagu's purpose is to establish, as Jonathan Kramnick has indicated, "an English literary tradition distinct from the classics," *Making the English Canon: Print Capitalism and the Cultural Past, 1700–1770* (Cambridge: Cambridge University Press, 1998).

53 See Eger, "Introduction," *Bluestocking Feminism*, and Kramnick, *Making the English Canon*.

54 E. Montagu to Carter, 21 October 1766 [Denton Hall, Northumberland], MO 3187.

55 E. Montagu to Henry Home, Lord Kames, 13 April 1767 in Eger, *Bluestocking Feminism*, vol. 1, p. 177.

56 On Johnson's manly prose as a reflection of character, see Felicity Nussbaum, *The Autobiographical Subject: Gender and Ideology* (Baltimore: The Johns Hopkins University Press, 1989), pp. 124–26.

57 E. Montagu to Elizabeth Carter, 20 [Nov.][1765], [London], MO 3162.

58 E. Montagu to Elizabeth Carter, [10] August 1765 [Berks.], MO 3150.

59 Frances Burney, *Evelina*, ed. Edward A. Bloom and Lillian D. Bloom (Oxford: Oxford University Press, 1982), p. 27.

60 E. Montagu to Henry Home, Lord Kames, 13 April 1767 in Eger, *Bluestocking Feminism*, vol. 1, pp. 174–75.

61 E. Montagu to George Lyttelton, 10 October 1760, Newcastle in Eger, *Bluestocking Feminism*, vol. 1, p. 159.

62 E. Montagu to Henry Home, Lord Kames, 13 April 1767 in Eger, *Bluestocking Feminism*, vol. 1, p. 177.

63 E. Montagu mentions the coalminers who "are litterally as black as coal" to Elizabeth Carter, 31 May 1766, Denton Hall, Northumberland, in Eger, *Bluestocking Feminism*, vol. 1, p. 169.

64 E. Montagu to Elizabeth Vesey, 1782, cited in *Mrs. Montagu, "Queen of the Blues": Her Letters and Friendships from 1762 to 1800*, ed. Reginald Blunt, 2 vols. (Boston and New York: Houghton Mifflin, 1923), vol. II, p. 162.

65 E. Montagu to Sir William Weller Pepys, 3 Nov. 1781, Hillstreet, in Blunt, vol. II, p. 157.

66 Montagu, *An Essay on the Writings & Genius of Shakespear* in Eger, *Bluestocking Feminism*, vol. 1, p. 112.

67 Montagu, *An Essay on the Writings & Genius of Shakespear,* vol. 1, p. 112.
68 Sarah Scott to E. Montagu [Jan. 1766], MO 5320.
69 E. Montagu to Sarah Scott [Oct.] [1765], Sandleford, MO 5831.
70 E. Montagu to Sarah Scott [26 Oct.] & 27 [1765], Sandleford, MO 5830.
71 E. Montagu to [William Pulteney, Earl of Bath], copies of letters dated 19 Oct. 1763, MO 4618.
72 E. Montagu to Sarah Scott [26 Oct.] & 27 Oct. [1765], Sandleford, MO 5830.
73 E. Montagu to Matthew Robinson [?10 Sept.] [1769], Suningwell, MO 4767, in Eger, *Bluestocking Feminism,* vol. 1, p. 185.
74 E. Montagu to Elizabeth Carter, 19 July 1766, Denton Hall, in Eger, *Bluestocking Feminism,* vol. 1, p. 170.
75 *Memoirs of the Life of Mrs Elizabeth Carter, with a new edition of her Poems; to Which are added, some Miscellaneous Essays and Prose, together with her Notes on the Bible,* ed. Montagu Pennington, 2 vols. 2nd edn. (London: Printed for F. C. and J. Rivington, 1808), p. 422.
76 David Garrick's poem celebrating Elizabeth Montagu appeared in *St James Chronicle* (January 1771), 24–26.
77 E. Montagu to Matthew Montagu, 9 June 1777.
78 E. Montagu, *An Essay on Shakespear* in Eger, *Bluestocking Feminism,* vol. 1, p. 102.
79 E. Montagu, *An Essay on Shakespear* in Eger, *Bluestocking Feminism,* vol. 1, p. 25.
80 While I have suggested a gendered distinction between the writings of Johnson and Montagu, Kramnick in *Making the English Canon,* argues that for both authors "masculine constancy is the agent of human permanence, depersonalized from the particulars of time and situation and abstracted into the eternal medium of print," p. 235.
81 Samuel Johnson, *The Adventurer* No. 115, Tuesday, 11 December 1753, vol. 11, pp. 457–58.

3 ODD WOMEN, MANGLED MEN

1 Madame D'Arblay [Frances Burney], *Memoirs of Doctor Burney,* 3 vols. (London: Edward Moon, 1832), vol. 11, pp. 262–63. John Doran, *A Lady of the Last Century (Mrs. Elizabeth Montagu): Illustrated in her Unpublished Letters; Collected and Arranged, with a Biographical Sketch, and a Chapter on Blue Stockings,* 2nd edn. (London 1873) ascribes the term's first usage to Montagu who in a letter to Dr. Monsey (March 1757) writes that Stillingfleet had "left off his old friends and his bluestockings, and is at operas and other gay assemblies every night," p. 20.
2 Madame D'Arblay, *Memoirs of Doctor Burney,* vol. 11, pp. 262–63.
3 N. William Wraxall, *Historical Memoirs of My Own Time* (1815; rpt. London: Kegan Paul 1904), pp. 84–85.
4 Madame D'Arblay, *Memoirs of Doctor Burney,* vol. 11, p. 276.
5 Ibid., vol. 11, p. 278.

6 Peter Clark, *British Clubs and Societies 1580–1800: The Origins of an Associational World* (Oxford: Clarendon Press, 2000), p. 198.

7 Among its membership were James Boswell, Edmund Burke, David Garrick, Edward Gibbon, Adam Smith, Joseph and Thomas Warton, Sir Joshua Reynolds, Joseph Banks, and Charles Burney, among others; the group met on Friday evenings. Boswell is surprisingly silent about the actual meetings of Johnson's club (*The Life of Johnson*, ed. George Birkbeck Hill, rev. L. F. Powell, 6 vols. [Oxford: Clarendon Press, 1934–50], vol. II, 345 n.5), partly because the biographer and his subject rarely attended the Club together.

8 For an argument of this nature concerning Mary Wollstonecraft, see Carol Kay, "Canon, Ideology, and Gender: Mary Wollstonecraft's Critique of Adam Smith," *American Journal of Political Science*, 15 (1986): 63–76.

9 Boswell, *Life of Johnson*, vol. III, p. 254.

10 Clark, *British Clubs and Societies*, p. 203.

11 Sylvia Harcstark Myers convincingly argues for this division in her definitive study, *The Bluestocking Circle: Women, Friendship, and the Life of the Mind in Eighteenth-Century England* (Oxford: Clarendon Press, 1990).

12 Madame D'Arblay [Frances Burney], *Memoirs of Doctor Burney*, vol. II, p. 263.

13 See Felicity Nussbaum, *The Autobiographical Subject: Gender and Ideology in Eighteenth-Century England* (Baltimore: Johns Hopkins University Press, 1989), pp. 102–26; and Michèle Cohen, "Manliness, Effeminacy and the French: Gender and the Construction of National Character in Eighteenth-Century England," in Tim Hitchcock and Michèle Cohen, eds., *English Masculinities 1660–1800* (London: Longman, 1999), pp. 44–61.

14 Elizabeth Montagu to Lord Lyttelton, 1770, Denton, in *Mrs. Montagu "Queen of the Blues": Her Letters and Friendships 1762–1800*, ed. Reginald Blunt, 2 vols. (Boston and New York: Houghton Mifflin Company), vol. I (1762–76), p. 240. All subsequent references to letters in this edition are cited in the text.

15 Elizabeth Montagu to Lord Lyttelton, 21 October [1760] MO 1403. For an illuminating discussion of these matters, see Harriet Guest, *Small Change: Women, Learning, Patriotism, 1750–1810* (Chicago: University of Chicago Press, 2000), and Elizabeth Eger, "Introduction," *Bluestocking Feminism: Writings of the Bluestocking Circle, 1738–1785*, ed. Gary Kelly, 6 vols. (London: Pickering and Chatto, 1999), vol. I, pp. lvii–lxxvii.

16 *Horace Walpole's Correspondence to the Rev. William Mason*, eds. W. S. Lewis, Grover Cronin, Jr., and Charles H. Bennett (New Haven: Yale University Press, 1955), vol. XXIX, part II, p. 97.

17 See especially Lawrence Klein, *Shaftesbury and the Culture of Politeness: Moral Discourse and Cultural Politics in Early Eighteenth-Century England* (Cambridge: Cambridge University Press, 1994).

18 Vicesimus Knox, "On the Present State of Conversation," *Essays Moral and Literary* (London 1784), vol. II, pp. 81–82.

19 Catherine Talbot, *Essays on Various Subjects*, No. 12, No. 164 (London 1772).

20 Deborah Heller, "Bluestocking Salons and the Public Sphere," *Eighteenth-Century Life* 22, ns 2 (May 1998): 59–82. I am much indebted to this fine essay.

21 James Boswell, *The Life of Johnson*, ed. George Birkbeck Hill, rev. L. F. Powell, 6 vols. (Oxford: Clarendon Press, 1934–50), vol. IV, p. III. Subsequent references are cited in the text.

22 Lawrence Klein, "Gender, Conversation and the Public Sphere in Early Eighteenth-Century England," *Textuality and sexuality: Reading theories and practices*, ed. Judith Still and Michael Warton (Manchester and NY: Manchester University Press, 1993), pp. 100–15.

23 J. Wheeler, "Reading and Other Recreations of Marylanders, 1700–1776," *Maryland Historical Magazine* 38 (1943): 44.

24 Elizabeth Montagu to Elizabeth Hardcocke [*c*. 1762], MO 6367.

25 E. Montagu to E. Vesey, 25 [Apr.][1763] [London], MO 3097.

26 E. Vesey to E. Carter, 2 Nov. 1744, cited in Clark, *British Clubs and Societies*, p. iii.

27 31 July 1765, ed. Pennington, *Series of Letters*, vol. III, p. 35.

28 E. Carter to E. Vesey, 2 Jan. 1765, in Rev. Montagu Pennington ed., *Series of Letters Between Mrs. Elizabeth Carter and Miss Catherine Talbot, from the Year 1741 to 1770: to which are added, Letters from Elizabeth Carter to Mrs. Vesey, between the Years 1763 and 1787, Four volumes printed in 3* (3rd edn London, 1819), vol. III, p. 30.

29 E. Carter to E. Vesey, 4 Dec. 1764, Pennington ed., *Series of Letters*, Deal, p. 28.

30 19 February 1766, Pennington ed., *Series of Letters*, vol. III, p. 50.

31 E. Montagu to S. Scott, January 1768, MO 5875.

32 E. Montagu to E. Carter, 15 May [1761], Ealing, Middlesex MO 3042.

33 E. Vesey to E. Carter, 2 Nov. 1744, Pennington ed., *Series of Letters*, p. iii.

34 E. Carter to E. Vesey, 20 June 1766, Pennington ed., *Series of Letters*, p. 61.

35 E. Montagu to E. Carter, 17 August 1765 Sandleford [Berks], MO 3151.

36 Heller, "Bluestocking Salons," p. 63.

37 Ibid., p. 70.

38 Wraxall, *Historical Memoirs*, p. 86. Heller cites a portion of this quotation and comments on its setting up an opposition between the universal masculine and the marked feminine.

39 Elizabeth Montagu to Lyttleton, 12 Aug. 1765 [10] Aug. 1765 [Sandleford] [Berks], MO 1440.

40 Madame D'Arblay [Frances Burney], *Memoirs of Doctor Burney*, vol. II, p. 262.

41 Elizabeth Montagu to Elizabeth Carter, 29 Sept. [1764], Sandleford [Berks], MO 3130.

42 Elizabeth Carter to Catherine Talbot, 11 April 1766 in Pennington ed., *A Series of Letters*, vol. III, p. 56.

43 Elizabeth Montagu to Elizabeth Carter, Fragment [*c*. 1765?], MO 3168.

44 Elizabeth Vesey to Elizabeth Montagu, 10 October [1766], MO 6278.

45 Hannah More, "The Bas Bleu: or, Conversation," in *The Works of Hannah More. A New Edition, in Eleven Volumes* (London: T. Cadell, 1830), vol. I, pp. 290–305. All subsequent references are cited in the text.

46 Cited from Frances Burney's diary (1783) in Reginald Blunt, "The Sylph," *The Edinburgh Review or Critical Journal*, 242 (October 1925): 364–79.

47 Madame D'Arblay, *Memoirs of Doctor Burney*, vol. II, pp. 265–66.

48 Sarah Scott to Elizabeth Montagu, 31 Aug. [1778], MO 5389.

49 Clara Reeve, *The Progress of Romance* in *Bluestocking Feminism: Writings of the Bluestocking Circle, 1738–1785*, 6 vols., ed. Gary Kelly (London: Pickering and Chatto, 1999), vol. VI, p. 235. All subsequent references to *Progress of Romance* will be cited in the text.

50 Lady Dorothy Bradshaigh to Samuel Richardson in Alan Dugald McKillop, *Samuel Richardson, Printer and Novelist* (Chapel Hill: University of North Carolina Press, 1936), p. 181.

51 Mary Granville Delany to Anne Granville Dewes, April 1760, *The Autobiography and Correspondence of Mary Granville, Mrs. Delany*, ed. Augusta Waddington Hall, Lady Llanover, 1st ser. 3 vols. (London 1861), vol. III, p. 588.

52 Elizabeth Montagu to Sarah Scott, 11 April 1765, in Blunt ed., *Mrs. Montagu "Queen of the Blues,"* vol. I, p. 188.

53 Elizabeth Montagu to Sarah Scott, April 1765, in Blunt ed., *Mrs. Montagu "Queen of the Blues,"* vol. I, p. 187.

54 Laurence Sterne, *The Life and Opinions of Tristram Shandy*, ed. Ian Campbell Ross (Oxford: Oxford University Press, 1983), VII. 25, p. 409. All subsequent references to this edition are cited in the text by volume, chapter, and page number.

55 Alan Dugald McKillop, *The Early Masters of English Fiction* (Lawrence: University of Kansas Press, 1956), p. 206.

56 Elizabeth Carter to Elizabeth Vesey, 17 April 1772, Pennington edn., *Series of Letters*, p. 186.

57 John Tosh, "The Old Adam and the New Man: Emerging Themes in the History of English Masculinities, 1750–1850," in Hitchcock and Cohen ed., *English Masculinities*, pp. 217–38.

58 See Tim Hitchcock and Michèle Cohen, "Introduction" in *English Masculinities*, for a convenient survey, pp. 1–22.

59 Lawrence Stone, *The Family, Sex, and Marriage in England 1500–1800* (London: Weidenfeld and Nicolson, 1977).

60 Carol Kay, *Political Constructions: Defoe, Richardson, and Sterne in Relation to Hobbes, Hume, and Burke* (Ithaca: Cornell University Press, 1988), pp. 205ff. Other critics have countered unconvincingly that Sterne critiques the Shandy men's contempt for women.

61 Martin Price, *To the Palace of Wisdom: Studies in Order and Energy from Dryden to Blake* (Carbondale: Southern Illinois University Press, 1964), pp. 321–22.

62 Boswell, *Life of Johnson*, vol. II, p. 449.

63 Carol Kay cites Hobbes' *Leviathan* I, 6, 125, in *Political Constructions*, p. 215.

64 *Mrs. Montagu "Queen of the Blues": Her Letters and Friendships from 1762 to 1800*, ed. Reginald Blunt, 2 vols. (Boston and New York: Houghton Mifflin Company, 1923), vol. I, p. 197.

4 SCARRED WOMEN

1 Mary Wollstonecraft, *A Vindication of the Rights of Woman*, ed. Carol H. Poston (New York: W. W. Norton, 1975), pp. 144, 37. All subsequent references cited in the text are to this edition.

2 "An Eccentric Lecture on the Art of Propagating the Human Species, and Producing a Numerous and Healthy Offspring," *The Rambler's Magazine; Or, the Annals of Gallantry, Glee, Pleasure, and the Bon ton* (January 1783), pp. 5–6.

3 Margaret T. Hodgen, *Early Anthropology in the Sixteenth and Seventeenth Centuries* (Philadelphia: University of Pennsylvania Press, 1964), p. 263.

4 James C. Riley, *The Eighteenth-Century Campaign to Avoid Disease* (New York: Macmillan, 1987), p. 115.

5 Robert Walker, MD, Fellow of the Royal College of Surgeons, *An Inquiry into the Smallpox, Medical and Political. Wherein A Successful method of Treating that Disease is Proposed, the Cause of Pits Explained, and the Method of their Prevention Pointed Out* (London, 1790), p. 456.

6 Derrick Baxby, "The Jenner Bicentenary: the Introduction and Early Distribution of Smallpox Vaccine," FEMS (Federation of European Micobiological Societies), *Immunology and Medical Microbiology* 16 (1996), 13. "An overall estimate that $\frac{1}{5}-\frac{1}{8}$ of smallpox patients died is generally accepted, although in some epidemics the mortality would be 50 per cent or higher. As an example of a typical epidemic in an English town we can take that in Chester in 1774, investigated by John Haygarth. The population was 14,713 and there were 1,202 cases of smallpox with 202 deaths. Thus about $\frac{1}{12}$ of the population were infected and $\frac{1}{6}$ of those died. All those dying were children. The fact that only $\frac{1}{12}$ of the population caught smallpox is due to the fact that almost everyone else had had it in previous epidemics," according to Peter Razzell, *Edward Jenner's Cowpox Vaccine: The History of A Medical Myth* (Firle, England: Caliban Books, 1977), p. 13.

7 See S. R. Duncan, S. Scott, and C. J. Duncan, "Modelling the Different Smallpox Epidemics in England," *Philosophical Transactions of the Royal Society, London* 346 (1994): 407–19, 407; Derrick Baxby, *Jenner's Smallpox Vaccine: The Riddle of Vaccinia Virus and its Origin* (London: Heinemann Educational Books, 1981), p. 12; and Harry Bloch, "Edward Jenner (1749–1823): The History and Effects of Smallpox, Inoculation, and Vaccination," *American Journal of Diseases of Children* 147 (July 1993): 772–74.

8 Walker, *An Inquiry into the Smallpox*, p. 488.

9 Baxby, "The Jenner Bicentenary," p. 9: "The introduction of vaccination was opposed by some variolators who saw the loss of a lucrative monopoly." Cowpox, a disease contracted from milking cows, offered some protection against smallpox. See also Edward Jenner, *An Inquiry into the Cause and Effects of Variolae Vaccinae* (London 1798).

10 See Jean Helvétius, M.D., *An Essay on the Animal Oeconomy. Together With Observations Upon the Smallpox*. Trans. from the French (London, 1723); and Robert Walker, *An Inquiry into the Smallpox*, pp. 393–99.

11 Helvitius, *An Essay on the Animal Oeconomy*, p. 219.

12 Annette Drew-Bear, *Painted Faces on the Renaissance Stage: The Moral Signifi- cance of Face-Painting Conventions* (Lewisburg: Bucknell University Press, 1994), p. 22.

13 Isobel Grundy offers a definitive account of the early literary history of in- oculation in "Medical Advance and Female Fame: Inoculation and its After- Effects," *Lumen* 13 (1994): 13–42. She writes, "It was opponents of the new practice who laid stress both on its oriental or Islamic origin and on its female associations... [to become identified] with 'a cultural and gender Other,'" p. 16. I am also indebted to Grundy's discussions of inoculation and smallpox in *Lady Mary Wortley Montagu: Comet of the Enlightenment* (Oxford: Oxford University Press, 1999).

14 Captain Watkin Tench, *A Narrative of the Expedition to Botany Bay and A Complete Account of the Settlement at Port Jackson*, ed. Tim Flannery (Melbourne: Text Publishing, 1996), p. 107.

15 Walker, *An Inquiry into the Smallpox*, p. 484.

16 See Adrienne Mayor, "The Nessus Shirt in the New World: Smallpox Blankets in History and Legend," *Journal of American Folklore* 108 (1995), 54–77. In 1763 Lord Amherst hatched a plan to exterminate Native Americans by giving them gifts of contaminated blankets taken from British soldiers who had died of the smallpox.

17 Walker, *An Inquiry into the Smallpox*, pp. 17–18.

18 Contrary to popular belief, Montagu's son was not the first Westerner to be inoculated in Turkey. See Grundy, "Medical Advance," p. 16.

19 William Wagstaffe, *A Letter to Dr. Freind; Shewing the Danger and Uncertainty of Inoculating the Small Pox* (London, 1722), pp. 5–6.

20 For the manuscript version of the account that was published in *The Flying Post* (September): 11–13, see Robert Halsband, "New Light on Lady Mary Wortley Montagu's Contribution to Inoculation," *Journal of the History of Medicine* 8 (October 1953): 401–02.

21 Lady Mary Wortley Montagu, "Plain Account of the Innoculating [sic] of the Small Pox by a Turkey Merchant," in *Essays and Poems and "Simplicity, A Comedy"*, ed. Robert Halsband and Isobel Grundy (Oxford: Clarendon Press, 1977), p. 96.

22 James Plumptre, *The Plague Stayed: A Scriptural View of Pestilence, Particularly of That Dreadful Pestilence the Small-Pox, With Consideration on the Cow-Pock; in Two Sermons, &c.* (London 1805), p. 2. Plumptre, a playwright and editor in addition to being a clergyman, was a brother of Anne Plumptre, author of *Some- thing New* (1801), a novel whose heroine is remarkably ugly. Bostonian minister Cotton Mather preached that smallpox was a scourge brought upon a sinful people and its pustules signs of error. See Rachel S. Stahle, "The Guilt-Heavy Theology of Cotton Mather," *Modern Theology* 5 (1 November 1997): 12–17.

23 James Plumptre, *The Plague Stayed*, p. 14.

24 Philip Rose, M.D. *An Essay on the Small-Pox; Whether natural, or inocu- lated. Shewing That by a New and Particular Method, the Dangerous Symptoms,*

and Fatal Consequences, in Either Sort, May Be Prevented, or Removed, and many Lives Saved. Wherein likewise All the OBJECTIONS *Brought Against* INOCULATION, *Are proved to Be both* Groundless *and* Ridiculous (London, 1724), p. 5.

25 Rose, *An Essay on the Small-Pox; Whether natural, or inoculated*, p. 7.

26 John Haygarth, *A Sketch of a Plan to Exterminate the Casual Small-Pox from Great Britain* (London, 1793), p. 497.

27 Dimsdale, *Thoughts on General and Partial Inoculations*, p. 67.

28 Henry Swinburne, *A Treatise of Spousal, or Matrimonial Contracts: Wherein All the Questions relating to that Subject Are ingeniously Debated and Resolved* (London, 1686). In the section "By what means Spousals are dissolved" the seventh case is "when as the one Party doth happen to be infected with some *foul Disease*, as *Leprosy*, or the *French-pox*, or to be afflicted with some notable deformity, as the loss of her Nose, or her Eye," p. 238.

29 Henry Jones Bath, *Inoculation; or, Beauty's Triumph; a Poem, in Two Cantos* (London 1768). Along with his six sons, Robert Sutton developed a flourishing inoculation business that included a fee that covered board for several weeks of recovery. From the 1760s until the 1780s, they opened innovative inoculation houses in which they could isolate patients. See David Van Zwanenbert, "The Suttons and the Business of Inoculation," *Medical History* 22 (1978): 71–82.

30 Jill Campbell, "Lady Mary Wortley Montagu and the 'Glass Revers'd' of Female Old Age," in *"Defects": Engendering the Modern Body*, ed. Helen Deutsch and Felicity Nussbaum (Ann Arbor: University of Michigan Press, 2000), pp. 213–51.

31 *The Spectator* No. 613, 5 vols. (29 October 1714), ed. Donald F. Bond (Oxford: Clarendon Press, 1965), vol. V, 97.

32 Walker, *An Inquiry into the Small-pox*, p. 399.

33 *The Spectator*, vol. III, 101, 102.

34 John Doran, *A Lady of the Last Century* (Boston: Francis A. Niccolls and Co., 1873), p. 17.

35 Sarah Scott, *A Description of Millenium Hall*, ed. Gary Kelly (Ontario: Broadview Press, 1995), p. 242.

36 Samuel Johnson, *The Rambler* No. 130, *The Yale Edition of the Works of Samuel Johnson*, ed. W. J. Bate and Albrecht B. Strauss (New Haven and London: Yale University Press, 1969), vol. IV, pp. 328–30.

37 Lady Mary Wortley Montagu, "Saturday: The Small Pox: Flavia," in *Essays and Poems and "Simplicity, A Comedy"*, ed. Robert Halsband and Isobel Grundy (Oxford: Clarendon Press, 1977), pp. 201–04. Jill Campbell, "Lady Mary Wortley Montagu," fruitfully considers connections between Flavia's smallpox scarring and the aging process in "Friday" and "Satturday." Campbell provides an exemplary instance of a woman's loss of beauty in Montagu's situation and expertly investigates the problem of how a woman is to claim selfhood when she does not recognize herself in the mirror or is terrified by the image she beholds.

38 John Whaley, *A Collection of Poems* (London 1732).

39 Roger Lonsdale, *Eighteenth-Century Women Poets: An Oxford Anthology* (Oxford: Oxford University Press, 1989), p. 226.

40 Cora Kaplan, "Afterword: Liberalism, Feminism, and Disability," in *"Defects:" Engendering the Modern Body*, ed. Helen Deutsch and Felicity Nussbaum (Ann Arbor: University of Michigan Press, 1999), pp. 303–18.

41 Introduction, Fanny Burney, *Camilla, or A Picture of Youth*, ed. Edward A. Bloom and Lillian D. Bloom (Oxford and New York: Oxford University Press, 1983). All subsequent references are cited in the text.

42 See *The Journals and Letters of Fanny Burney (Madame D'Arblay), 1791–1840*, ed. Joyce Hemlow, with Patricia Boutilier and Althea Douglas, 12 vols. (Oxford: Oxford University Press. 1972–), III.50.229; and Fanny Burney, *Camilla*, ed. Edward A. Bloom and Lillian D. Bloom (Oxford: Oxford University Press, 1983), p. 931 n.22.

43 According to Margaret Anne Doody, *Frances Burney: The Life in the Works* (Cambridge: Cambridge University Press, 1988), the final form of *Camilla* was not at all its original one, and it appears that Burney adds Eugenia at a fairly late stage. The final version "is a skeptical novel about the difficulty not only of making choices but of seeing the truth," p. 214. Deidre Shauna Lynch remarks on Eugenia's disfigurement as a result of "her very first excursion into the consumer economy," *The Economy of Character: Novels, Market Culture, and the Business of Inner Meaning* (Chicago: University of Chicago Press, 1998), p. 176.

44 Such assumptions are not limited to women, and they still persist. See, for example, Christopher Reeve's adamant declaration that he is *Still Me* (New York: Ballantine, 1999) after his spinal cord injury.

45 Kristina Straub, *Divided Fictions: Fanny Burney and Feminine Strategy* (Lexington: University of Kentucky Press, 1987) considers the issue of masculine carelessness, pp. 210ff.

46 Jacques-Mathieu Delpech (1777–1832) founded an institution for calisthenic treatment of scoliosis, spinal tuberculosis, and deformities of the back in Montpellier in 1825. The teeter-totter and the balance beam were among the remedies provided.

47 Charles Gold, *Oriental Drawings: Sketched Between the Years 1791 and 1798 [with descriptive text]* (London 1806).

48 Rosemarie Garland Thomson, *Extraordinary Bodies: Figuring Physical Disability in American Culture and Literature* (New York: Columbia University Press, 1997), p. 40, invents this term to distinguish and particularize what is assumed to be generic to human beings, though she does not, as I do, apply the term to a literary character. I am indebted throughout this discussion to Thomson's pathbreaking book.

49 See the definition for "guinea" in *The Oxford English Dictionary*.

50 Peter Fryer, *Staying Power: The History of Black People in Britain* (London: Pluto Press, 1984), "The Royal Adventurers included the king and queen, the queen mother, a prince, 3 dukes, 7 earls, a countess, 6 lords, and 25 knights. Aristocracy and gentry held about a quarter of the stock; the rest was snapped up by merchants and City men," p. 21.

51 The terms derive from Rosemarie Garland Thomson, *Extraordinary Bodies*, p. 29, though she does not apply them to *Camilla*.

52 Straub, *Divided Fictions*, pp. 210ff. argues that crossdressing is not critiqued in the novel, though men's authority is subject to question.

53 See Barbara Zonitch, *Familiar Violence: Gender and Social Upheaval in the Novels of Frances Burney* (Newark: University of Delaware Press, 1997), p. 95, for the way that subversive strategies are associated with the outspoken Mrs. Arlbery.

54 Margaret Doody, *Frances Burney*, notes that the name Camilla signifies Amazonian tendencies in Virgil (Chapter 7), and Eugenia of course becomes skilled in the classics. Dr. Marchmont turns the tables in enjoining "that the mind must itself be deformed that could dwell upon her personal defects" (2.13.149).

55 See especially Thomson, *Extraordinary Bodies*: "The history of begging is virtually synonymous with the history of disability," p. 35. For a significant counterview, see Brendan Gleeson, *Geographies of Disability* (London and New York: Routledge, 1999).

56 *An Enquiry Concerning the Principles of Taste, and of the Origin of our Ideas of Beauty* (London 1785) also connects blackness with mental deficiencies, pp. 26–27.

57 Kathleen Wilson, *The Island Race: Englishness, Empire and Gender in the Eighteenth Century* (London: Routledge 2003), notes that West Indian slave boys often performed Richard III in the Kingston streets, p. 166.

58 Margaret Doody, *Frances Burney*, pointing out that many illusions to *Othello* fill the novel, sees Edgar as a self-tormenting Othello-like character: "The constant ironic use throughout the novel of 'prove' and 'proof' and the delusions resulting from mad searches after shifting proofs can – and should – remind us of *Othello*," pp. 223–24. Beyond the scope of this book, Burney's *The Wanderer* (1814) richly complicates connections between the racial other, monstrosity, and femininity.

59 Patricia Parker, "Fantasies of 'Race' and 'Gender': Africa, *Othello* and bringing to light" in *Women, "Race," and Writing in the Early Modern Period*, ed. Margo Hendricks and Patricia Parker (London and NY: Routledge, 1994), pp. 84–100, 93.

60 Karen Newman, *Fashioning Femininity and English Renaissance Drama* (Chicago: University of Chicago Press), p. 75.

61 Kristina Straub, *Divided Fictions*, describes Camilla's fraught negotiation of the conventions of fashion and the economic disaster that results to show "the limits of the individual's ability to manipulate identity within the specific social and economic system depicted in the novel," p. 203. Deirdre Lynch argues that "animation is what separates her heroine from Indiana and Eugenia, neither of whom is really a character who moves or who develops," p. 184.

5 RACIAL FEMININITY

1 Folarin Shyllon, *Black People in Britain, 1555–1833* (London: Oxford University Press, 1977), p. 5. I am indebted to this important book, to the UCLA graduate students in my seminar, "Race and Gender in the Eighteenth Century," whose discussions contributed to this chapter, and to Roxann Wheeler.

2 David Theo Goldberg, *Racist Culture: Philosophy and the Politics of Meaning* (Oxford: Blackwell, 1993). See also Benedict Anderson, *Imagined Communities* (London: Verso, 1991).

3 Ann Laura Stoler, *Race and the Education of Desire: Foucault's "History of Sexuality" and the Colonial Order of Things* (Durham and London: Duke University Press, 1995), p. 27.

4 George L. Mosse, *Toward the Final Solution: A History of European Racism* (New York: Howard Fertig, 1978), p. xvi.

5 Michael Omi and Howard Winant, *Racial Formation in the United States: From the 1960s to the 1980s* (London: Routledge and Kegan Paul, 1986) emphasize the importance of recognizing that practices associated with racial meanings are politically charged and historically variable, pp. 76–79.

6 See Henry Louis Gates, Jr., "Critical Remarks," in *Anatomy of Racism*, ed. David Theo Goldberg (Minneapolis: University of Minnesota Press, 1990), p. 323.

7 Among such thinkers are Ann Laura Stoler, *Race and the Education of Desire*, and Paul Gilroy, *Against Race: Imagining Political Culture Beyond the Color Line* (Cambridge: Belknap Press of Harvard University Press, 2000).

8 David Hume, *Essays Moral, Political, and Literary*, ed. Eugene F. Miller, rev. edn. (Indianapolis: Liberty Fund, 1987), argues for Negroes' natural inferiority to whites: "Not to mention our colonies, there are NEGROE slaves dispersed all over EUROPE, of whom none ever discovered any symptoms of ingenuity; though low people, without education, will start up amongst us, and distinguish themselves in every profession. In JAMAICA, indeed they talk of one Negroe as a man of parts and learning; but it is likely he is admired for slender accomplishments, like a parrot, who speaks a few words plainly," p. 208. On the reference to Francis Williams, see *Unchained Voices: An Anthology of Black Authors in the English-Speaking World of the Eighteenth Century*, ed. Vincent Carretta (Lexington: University of Kentucky Press, 1996), pp. 72–76.

9 Richard Steele, *The Tatler* (Thursday, 2 November 1710), ed. Donald F. Bond, 3 vols. (Oxford: Clarendon Press, 1987), vol. III, p. 256.

10 *The Parrot. With a Compendium of the Times*. By the Authoress of *The Female Spectator* (London 1746), appeared in nine numbers from 2 August 1746 until 4 October 1746.

11 Carl Linnaeus, *A General System of Nature, through the Three Grand Kingdoms of Animals, Vegetables, and Minerals, Systematically Divided* ... translated by William Turton, MD, 7 vols. (London: Lackington, Allen, and Company, 1802), vol. I, p. 9. This first English translation of the multivolumed treatise is inexact and incomplete.

12 Lynn Thorndike, "De Complexionibus," *Isis* 49, Pt. 4 no. 158 (Dec. 1958): 398–408.

13 Mary Louise Pratt, *Imperial Eyes: Travel Writing and Transculturation* (London: Routledge, 1992), p. 32; and Winthrop Jordan, *White Over Black: American Attitudes Toward the Negro 1550–1812* (Chapel Hill: University of North Carolina Press), p. 221.

14 Charles W. J. Withers and David N. Livingstone, "Introduction: on Geography and Enlightenment" in *Geography and Enlightenment*, ed. David Livingstone and Charles W. J. Withers (Chicago: Chicago University Press, 1999), pp. 1–31, argue that geography begins in 1769 with the comparative work inspired by Cook's voyages to the Pacific.

15 Joseph Roach, *Cities of the Dead: Circum-Atlantic Performance* (New York: Columbia University Press, 1996), pp. 131, 156.

16 Nicholas Thomas, *In Oceania: Visions, Artifacts, Histories* (Durham and London: Duke University Press, 1997), pp. 93ff.

17 Elizabeth Montagu to Elizabeth Carter [1764] [?Nov. 25] [Bath] [Somerset], MO 3137. All subsequent references to the Montagu letters are from the Henry E. Huntington Library.

18 Terry Castle, *Masquerade and Civilization: The Carnivalesque in Eighteenth-Century English Culture and Fiction* (Stanford: Stanford University Press, 1988), pp. 60–61.

19 Aphra Behn, *Oroonoko, The Rover and Other Works*, ed. Janet Todd (London: Penguin, 1992), p. 76.

20 See Nicholas Thomas, *Entangled Objects: Exchange, Material Culture, and Colonialism in the Pacific* (Cambridge, MA: Harvard University Press, 1991), pp. 28, 144.

21 In the South Sea islands, Johann Reinhold Forster reports that "*Wainee-òu* and *Potatou* her husband, were so greedy after the possession of red parrots feathers, that having sold all the hogs, which they possibly could spare . . . they agreed to prostitute *Wainee-òu*, and she in consequence offered herself to Captain Cook, and appeared as a ready victim," Forster, *Observations Made during a Voyage Round the World*, ed. Nicholas Thomas, Harriet Guest, and Michael Dettelbach [Honolulu: University of Hawai'i Press, 1996], p. 243.

22 Moira Ferguson, *Subject to Others: British Women Writers and Colonial Slavery, 1670–1834* (London: Routledge, 1992) provides a useful introduction to the scope of Englishwomen's involvement in the abolitionist movement.

23 *Mrs. Montagu: "Queen of the Blues,"* ed. Reginald Blunt, 2 vols. (Boston: Houghton Mifflin, 1923), vol. 1, p. 187.

24 Sarah (Robinson) Scott to Elizabeth (Robinson) Montagu, 9 Feb. [1766] [Bath] [Somerset], MO 5321. Elizabeth Montagu, a subscriber to Equiano's first edition, voiced opposition to slavery in a letter to Sarah Scott, 16 Jan. [1788] [London], MO 5796, "I can with pleasure tell you that there is great reason to hope the slave trade will be abolish'd, such horrible accounts of the African Princes . . . & our usuage [sic] of the poor wretches we purchase, are now publishd, & in evry ones hands; that Mr Wilberforces application to Parliament on this subject can hardly fail of having a happy effect."

25 For differing views, see Eve W. Stoddard, "A Serious Proposal for Slavery Reform: Sarah Scott's *Sir George Ellison*," *Eighteenth-Century Studies*, 28.4 (1995): 379–96; Ferguson, *Subject to Others*, p. 104; and Markman Ellis, *The Politics of Sensibility: Race, Gender and Commerce in the Sentimental Novel* (Cambridge: Cambridge University Press, 1996).

26 The reference to Montagu's black subjects appears in Scott's letter 21 [July] 1766 [Denton Hall, Northumb.], MO 3177. Sarah (Robinson) Scott to Elizabeth (Robinson) Montagu 20 July [1766] [Sandleford] [Berks.], MO 5333.

27 Sarah (Robinson) Scott to Elizabeth (Robinson) Montagu [? July] [1766], [Sandleford] [Berks.], MO 5334.

28 Elizabeth (Robinson) Montagu to Sarah (Robinson) Scott, 17 July 1766 Denton [Hall] [Northumberland], MO 5840. James Grainger's *The Sugar Cane* (1764) encourages kindness to slaves but suggests that their fate is happier than that of Scottish mineworkers, and the poem may have influenced Scott.

29 Elizabeth (Robinson) Montagu to Sarah (Robinson) Scott, 3 March [1767], London, MO 5849.

30 For a fuller discussion, see Stoler, *Race and the Education of Desire*, p. 59. Benedict Anderson, *Imagined Communities* (London: Verso, 1983) also argues that racism begins with seventeenth-century aristocratic sympathies toward divine right rule.

31 Elizabeth (Robinson) Montagu to Sarah (Robinson) Scott, 10 July 1775.

32 Sarah (Robinson) Scott to Elizabeth (Robinson) Montagu, 13 May [1792], MO 5485. Upon Montagu's death the chimney sweeps issued an elegy of gratitude to her.

33 Johnson cites Milton's line: "Instead / Of spirits malign, a better race to bring / into their vacant room." Johnson gave no special attention to complexion as an indicator of race, though he does include an example under the word's second definition, "the color of the external parts of any body," from Addison's *Spectator* No. 262: "If I write any thing on a black Man, I run over in my Mind all the eminent persons in the Nation who are of that Complection."

34 Sarah Scott, *The History of Sir George Ellison*, ed. Betty Rizzo (Lexington: University of Kentucky Press, 1996), p. 10. All subsequent references to this text are cited parenthetically.

35 I am indebted to Harriet Guest for discussions about this point.

36 "Whiteness," writes Charles W. Mills in *The Racial Contract* (Ithaca: Cornell University, 1997), "is not really a color at all, but a set of power relations" (p. 127) among which, I would add, is social class.

37 Winthrop Jordan comments that it "was important, if incalculably so, that English discovery of black Africans came at a time when the accepted standard of ideal beauty was a fair complexion of rose and white," *White Over Black*, p. 9.

38 See, for example, John Gabriel Stedman, *Narrative of a Five Years Expedition Against the Revolted Negroes of Surinam*, ed. Richard Price and Sally Price (Baltimore and London: The Johns Hopkins University Press, 1988), p. 49, which unfavorably compares British women in Surinam to black, Indian, and mulatta women.

6 BLACK WOMEN

1 On Yarico, see Wylie Sypher, *Guinea's Captive Kings: British Anti-Slavery Literature of the 18th Century* (Chapel Hill: University of North Carolina Press, 1942), pp. 105ff.

2 Daniel Defoe's Friday in *Robinson Crusoe*, variously represented as Carib, African, and white, is the most significant male character of the eighteenth century who persistently changes color.

3 Aphra Behn, *Oroonoko, the Rover and Other Works*, ed. Janet Todd (London: Penguin, 1992), p. 81.

4 See Thomas Southerne, *Oroonoko*, ed. Maximillian E. Novak and David Stuart Rodes, *Oroonoko* (Lincoln: University of Nebraska Press, 1976), Introduction, p. xxxvii n.73 and Act II.ii.

5 Thomas Southerne, *Oroonoko* (London n.d.[1711]). Both "Indies" were best known through companies formed within two decades of each other (the East Indian Company in 1602 and the West India Company in 1621), though the reference may be to Native Americans on the American mainland.

6 Wylie Sypher observes that the anonymous "Story of Inkle and Yarico" in *London Magazine* (May 1734) "begins the confusion between the Indian Yarico and the Negress Yarico" because Yarico is African in that version. Sypher emphasizes the mythological qualities of "the Negro who is not a Negro," p. 131.

7 For various accounts of the story, see Lawrence Marsden Price, *Inkle and Yarico Album* (Berkeley: University of California Press, 1937) and Peter Hulme, *Colonial Encounters: Europe and the Native Caribbean 1492–1797* (London and New York: Methuen, 1986).

8 Price, *Inkle and Yarico Album*, p. 6.

9 Bryan Edwards, *The History, Civil and Commercial, of the British Colonies in the West Indies: In Two Volumes* (London: John Stockdale, 1794), vol. II, p. 32. *The Sable Venus: An Ode* was allegedly written in Jamaica in 1765. The picture, after a painting by Thomas Stothard, is "The Voyage of the Sable Venus, from Angola to the West Indies," engraved by W. Grainger. See also the illustrations of Caribbean women, some of which in Edwards are by Agostino Brunias. See Dian Kriz, "Marketing Mulatresses in the Paintings and Prints of Agostino Brunias," in *The Global Eighteenth Century*, ed. Felicity Nussbaum (Baltimore: The Johns Hopkins University Press, 2003).

10 *The Sable Venus: An Ode* (1794) in Edwards, *The History, Civil and Commercial, of the British Colonies*. The poem is described as "a performance of a deceased friend, in which the character of the sable and saffron beauties of the West Indies, and the folly of their paramours, are portrayed with the delicacy and dexterity of wit, and the fancy of elegance of genuine poetry," p. lxvii, p. 26.

11 *The Sable Venus: An Ode* (1794) in Edwards, *The History, Civil and Commercial, of the British Colonies*.

12 John Gabriel Stedman, *Narrative of a Five Years Expedition against the Revolted Negroes of Surinam*, ed. Richard Price and Sally Price (Baltimore and London: The Johns Hopkins University Press, 1988). Subsequent quotations from this edition are cited in the text.

13 Jennifer Morgan, " 'Women Could Suckle Over Their Shoulder': Male Travelers, Female Bodies, and the Gendering of Racial Ideology, 1500–1700," *William and Mary Quarterly* 54.1 Third Series (January 1997): 169; and Felicity Nussbaum, *Torrid Zones: Maternity, Sexuality, and Empire in Eighteenth-Century English Narratives* (Baltimore: Johns Hopkins University Press, 1995).

14 See Razia Aziz, "Feminism and the Challenge of Racism: Deviance or Difference?" in *Black British Feminism*, ed. Heidi Safia Mirza (London and New York: Routledge, 1997), p. 72.

15 For a convenient edition of Belinda's petition, see *Unchained Voices: An Anthology of Black Authors in the English-Speaking World of the 18th Century*, ed. Vincent Carretta (Lexington: University Press of Kentucky, 1996), pp. 142–44. Wheatley's work was published as *Poems on Various Subjects, Religious and Moral* (London 1773).

16 See, for example, Kim Hall, "Reading What Isn't There: 'Black' Studies in Early Modern England," *Stanford Humanities Review* 3.1 (Winter 1993): 23–33; and Jenny Sharpe, " 'Something Akin to Freedom': The Case of Mary Prince," *differences* 8.1 (1996): 31–56.

17 Sypher, *Guinea's Captive Kings*, p. 116. The play saw over three hundred performances during the century.

18 For later stereotypes of the black woman, see Diane Roberts, *The Myth of Aunt Jemima: Representations of Race and Region* (Routledge: London and New York, 1994).

19 *Memoir and Theatrical Career of Ira Aldridge, the African Roscius* (London 1849) reports that in America black actresses apparently appeared on stage at the turn into the nineteenth century, at least in black repertory companies. Ira Aldridge, the first black actor on the English stage, had acted the role of Rolla in Sheridan's *Pizarro* in the nineteenth century opposite a whitened heroine: "the gentle Cora was *very* black, requiring no small quantity of whiting, yellow ochre, and vermilion to bring her cheeks to the hue of roses and lilies."

20 Eldred Jones, *Othello's Countrymen: The African in English Renaissance Drama* (London: Oxford University Press, 1965). Shakespeare's *Antony and Cleopatra* was seldom produced in the late seventeenth or eighteenth centuries, though of course Dryden's *All for Love* was frequently staged.

21 Kim Hall, *Things of Darkness: Economies of Race and Gender in Early Modern England* (Ithaca: Cornell University Press, 1995), p. 130. Jacqueline Pearson, "Blacker than Hell Creates: Pix Rewrites *Othello*," in *Broken Boundaries: Women and Feminism in Restoration Drama*, ed. Katherine M. Quinsey (Lexington: University of Kentucky Press, 1996), pp. 13–30, argues that Pix makes white and black women equivalent in their "enslaved" condition.

22 John Crowne, *Calisto* in *The Dramatic Works of John Crowne*, vol. 1 (Edinburgh: William Paterson, 1873), pp. 219–342.

23 The Countess of Hertford and an anonymous poet recounted the tale of Yarico in several poems in the second and third decades of the century, a woman of color variously represented as Indian and African: "the Countess and Anon also allowed themselves to air problems faced by female contemporaries; they were among the few writers to afford black females any kind of subjectivity for at least fifty years" in Moira Ferguson, *Subject to Others: British Women Writers and Colonial Slavery, 1670–1834* (New York: Routledge, 1992), p. 73.

24 Elliot Tokson, *The Popular Image of the Black Man in English Drama 1550–1668* (Boston: G. K. Hall, 1982), p. 84.

25 When actresses such as Elizabeth Barry and Anne Bracegirdle were paired as bad and good women, Barry frequently took on the "darker woman" role while Bracegirdle always represented the pristine contrast. See Elizabeth Howe, *The First English Actresses: Women and Drama 1660–1700* (Cambridge: Cambridge University Press, 1992).

26 In Southerne, *Oroonoko*, the editors Novak and Rodes, p. xvi, note that Ramble, one of the speakers in *A Comparison between the Two Stages* (1702), responded to the mention of *Oroonoko* with "Oh! The Favourite of the Ladies."

27 James Stokes, "Women and Mimesis in Medieval and Renaissance Somerset (and Beyond)," *Comparative Drama* 27 (1993): 176–96; 189. See Katherine Romack, "Women's Representational Practice, 1642–60," unpublished dissertation, Syracuse University, 2000. Susan Wiseman, *Drama and Politics in the English Civil War* (Cambridge: Cambridge University Press, 1998) documents "a marked increase in the number of plays published by women," p. 96.

28 Dale B. J. Randall, *Winter Fruit: English Drama 1642–1660* (Lexington: University of Kentucky Press, 1995), pp. 173 and 178, suggests that the first woman on the public stage with a singing role rather than a speaking one may have been Catherine Coleman who rose from singing in the chorus to a primary singer in D'Avenant's *Siege of Rhodes* (1656), the first English opera and an incipient heroic play. Coleman was also perhaps the first acting woman as the veiled and chaste Ianthe, captive of the Turks, and her refusal to remove her covering in the first act creates "an interesting effect of appearing and yet not appearing." Though women did not appear in subsequent Davenant productions, apparently bowing to restrictions, the playwright is remarkable for introducing *cimmarones* or Moorish slaves brought to Peru by Spaniards in *The History of Sir Francis Drake*.

29 J. L. Styan, *Restoration Comedy in Performance* (Cambridge: Cambridge University Press, 1986), p. 90. Howe, *The First English Actresses*, does not mention Margaret Hughes's name. In one of Lely's paintings Hughes with one breast bared in Amazon fashion bears a striking resemblance to later pictures of Britannia. *Roscius Anglicanus, or an Historical Review of the Stage* (London 1708), ed. Judith Milhous and Robert D. Hume (London: The Society for Theatre Research, 1987), p. 19 n.55: "*Othello* (c. 1603–04) was performed at the Red Bull in the summer and early autumn of 1660 and at the Cockpit in Drury Lane in October. It was performed by the King's Company at Vere Street on 8 December 1660, with 'a Prologue to introduce the first Woman that came to Act on the Stage in the Tragedy, call'd *The Moor of Venice*.'" See Thomas Jordan, *A Royal Arbor of Loyal Poesie* (London: R. Wood for Eliz. Andrews, 1664), pp. 21–22. Which actress performed Desdemona in 1660 has been hotly debated, but unfortunately there is no definitive evidence. See Wilson, *All the King's Ladies*, pp. 5–8. Since Margaret Hughes seems to have joined the King's company in spring 1668 and left in 1670, the cast as given evidently belongs to the brief intervening period. A performance is recorded at Bridges Street on 6 February 1669.

30 Pearson, "Blacker than Hell Creates," pp. 13–30.

31 Joseph Roach, *Cities of the Dead: Circum-Atlantic Performance* (New York: Columbia University Press, 1996), pp. 153–59. In their edition of Southerne's *Oroonoko*, Maximillian Novak and David Rodes remark, "Surely Southerne's audience would have had little more difficulty admiring a beautiful African princess than a handsome African prince" (p. xxxvii n.73); Margaret Ferguson puzzles over the reason for the change in "News from the New World: Miscegenous Romance in Aphra Behn's *Oroonoko* and *The Widow Ranter*," *The Production of English Renaissance Culture*, ed. David Lee Miller, et al. (Ithaca: Cornell University Press, 1994), pp. 151–89; and Suvir Kaul notes, "The Restoration stage in any case seems not to have favored women in black face (though men played such roles), but to note this phenomenon is not to explain it," in "Reading Literary Symptoms: Colonial Pathologies and the *Oroonoko* Fictions of Behn, Southerne, and Hawkesworth," *Eighteenth-Century Life* 13.3 (November 1994): 80–96. Srinivas Aravamudan, *Tropicopolitans: Colonialism and Agency, 1688–1804* (Durham and London: Duke University Press, 1999), accusing critics of "imoindaism," believes that the play sets white women against black men and, of course, erases the black woman – but, he adds, turning Imoinda white "is shown to be a fruitless undertaking ultimately" because she is still perceived as other, p. 59. I argue instead that she is perceived as "both-and," a blackened white woman.

32 Joyce Green MacDonald, "The Disappearing African Woman: Imoinda in *Oroonoko* After Behn," *ELH* 66 (1999): 71–86.

33 Kim Hall, *Things of Darkness: Economies of Race and Gender in Early Modern England*, p. 141.

34 David Dabydeen, *Hogarth's Blacks: Images of Blacks in Eighteenth Century English Art* (Surrey: Dangaroo Press, 1985), p. 39, asks whether this was "because the black population in England, who were brought over to work, were overwhelmingly male, or was the white male artist nervous or guilty about depicting black women?" Both possibilities are likely.

35 See Reyahn King, "Ignatius Sancho and Portraits of the Black Élite," *Ignatius Sancho: An African Man of Letters* (London: National Portrait Gallery Publications, 1997), pp. 32–33; and G. Adams, "Dido Elizabeth Belle: A Black Girl at Kenwood," *Camden History Review* (1984).

36 Elizabeth Howe, *The First English Actresses: Women and Drama 1660–1700* (Cambridge: Cambridge University Press, 1992), pp. 38–39, discusses one such picture from Nicholas Rowe's edition of Shakespeare (1709).

37 For a discussion of associations between monstrosity, race, and sexuality see Sander Gilman, *Sexuality: An Illustrated History* (New York: John Wiley and Sons, 1989).

38 Dabydeen, *Hogarth's Blacks*, cites P. Thicknesse, *A Year's Journey through France and Part of Spain* (2nd edn., London 1788), vol. 1, p. 102, to remark that " 'black joke' was slang for the female sexual organs," p. 18. He also notes, "Moreover the very fact that Rakewell patronises a black whore is a measure of his degraded character for in the eighteenth century the taste for black women was seen as a squalid one," pp. 96–97.

39 A special thanks to Angela Rosenthal for sharing this picture with me.

40 *Les Sérails de Londres, ou Les Amusemens Nocturnes... et le Description des Courtisannes les plus célèbres*, 4 vols. in 2 (Paris [Londres] 1801), pp. 150–54, my translation. Ivan Bloch, *Sexual Life in England: Past and Present*, translated by William H. Forstern (London: Francis Aldor, 1938), cites this text, p. 130. See also Edward Scobie, *Black Britannia: A History of Blacks in Britain* (Chicago: Johnson Publishing Company Inc., 1972), p. 6, who discusses a Renaissance woman "Lucy Negro."

41 See F. O. Shyllon, *Black People in Britain 1555–1833* (London: Oxford University Press, 1974), pp. 210–29. The Rowlandson cartoon probably features Rachel Pringle, who in a picture by Thomas Rowlandson engraved by E. D. (1796) in the collection of Dudley P. K. Wood, also mentioned in Neville Connell, "Colonial life in the West Indies," *Antiques* 99 (May 1971): 732–77, is pictured as "a corpulent mulatto lady who ran a hotel in Bridgetown, Barbados." After her father William Lauder assaulted her, she ran away to Captain Pringle who set her up as hotelkeeper.

42 *London in 1710: from the Travels of Zacharias Conrad von Uffenbach*, trans. W. H. Quarrell and Margaret Mare (London: Faber and Faber, 1934), p. 88.

43 Norma Myers, *Reconstructing the Black Past: Blacks in Britain c. 1780–1830* (London: Frank Cass, 1996), pp. 74–78.

44 Ignatius Sancho, *Letters of the Late Ignatius Sancho, An African*, ed. Vincent Carretta (New York: Penguin, 1998), p. 109, and Olaudah Equiano, *The Interesting Narrative and Other Writings*, ed. Vincent Carretta (New York: Penguin, 1995).

45 Henry Angelo, *Reminiscences of Henry Angelo, With Memoirs of His Late Father* (London, 1828).

46 Jane Girdham, "Black Musicians in England: Ignatius Sancho and His Contemporaries," in *Ignatius Sancho: An African Man of Letters*, ed. Reyahn King et al. (London: National Portrait Gallery, 1997), pp. 116–24. Their leopard-skin mantels survive in the dress of modern military bands.

47 John Jackson, Ten Years Manager of the Theatre Royal of Edinburgh, *The History of the Scottish Stage From its First Establishment to the Present Time; with a Distinct Narrative of Some Recent Theatrical Transactions. The Whole Necessarily Interspersed wtih Memoirs of his own Life* (Edinburgh: Peter Hill and G. G. J. and J. Robinson, 1793), pp. 350–51.

48 Dympna Callaghan, *Shakespeare Without Women: Representing Gender and Race on the Renaissance Stage* (New York: Routledge, 1999). Callaghan's study of racial and gendered impersonation on the Renaissance stage, as well as the conference on Race in the Early Modern Period, University of California–Santa Cruz (May 1997) organized by Margo Hendricks, were important in shaping my work on the eighteenth-century stage.

49 Eldred Jones, *Othello's Countrymen: The African in English Renaissance Drama* (London: Oxford University Press, 1965), pp. 28–29.

50 Ruth Cowhig, "Blacks in English Renaissance Drama and the Role of Shakespeare's Othello," *The Black Presence in English Literature*, ed. David Dabydeen

(Manchester: Manchester University Press, 1985), p. 1. See also Jones, *Othello's Countrymen*, especially pp. 20–25.

51 Colman, *Inkle and Yarico*, p. 7.

52 George Colman, Esq., *Inkle and Yarico: An Opera, in Three Acts* (London 1787).

53 British Library MS 42920, ff. 120–210b. I am deeply grateful to Jenna Gibbs Boyer for generously sharing this passage with me. Kelly acted at Drury Lane (1800–06), and at the new Drury Lane from 10 October 1812 to 1848. She allegedly twice refused the poet Charles Lamb's marriage proposal.

54 Karen Newman, *Fashioning Femininity and English Renaissance Drama* (Chicago: University of Chicago Press, 1991) argues in relation to Shakespeare's *Othello*: "Femininity is not opposed to blackness and monstrosity, as are the binary opposites black and white, but identified with the monstrous in an identification that makes miscegenation doubly fearful. The play is structured around a cultural aporia, miscegenation" (p. 75).

55 For this argument concerning Desdemona, see Callaghan, *Shakespeare Without Women*.

56 Mary Vermillion, "Buried Heroism: Critiques of Female Authorship in Southerne's Adaptation of Behn's *Oroonoko*," *Restoration: Studies in Literary Culture 1660–1700* 16 (1992): 28–37.

57 Charlotte Sussman, "The Other Problem with Women: Reproduction and Slave Culture in Aphra Behn's *Oroonoko*," in *Rereading Aphra Behn: History, Theory and Criticism*, ed. Heidi Hutner (University of Virginia Press, 1993), pp. 212–31: "The narrator herself seems to side with the forces of romance in the conflict between love and rebellion; that is, she sides with the status quo of slave culture." Sussman does not mention that Southerne's Imoinda is white.

58 Thomas Southern[e] with alterations by John Hawkesworth, LL.D, *Oroonoko, A Tragedy, As It Is Now Acted at the Theatre Royal in Drury-Lane* (London 1759).

59 Francis Gentleman's version, *Oroonoko: or the Royal Slave. A Tragedy. Altered from Southerne* (Glasgow 1760) produced in Edinburgh in 1760 and followed by a run at Drury Lane in 1769–70, also omits the crossdressing subplot on the grounds that it was too licentious.

60 Suvir Kaul, "Reading Literary Symptoms: Colonial Pathologies and the *Oroonoko* Fictions of Behn, Southerne, and Hawkesworth," *Eighteenth-Century Life* 13.3 (November 1994): 80–96, helpfully discusses Hawkesworth's changes but with different emphases from mine. See J. R. Oldfield, " 'The Ties of Soft Humanity:' Slavery and Race in British Drama, 1760–1800," *HLQ* 56 (1993), 1–14.

61 In Hawkesworth the unscrupulous planters perniciously level the price for all the slaves and encourage breeding among them, while Oroonoko himself insists that he ranks higher than these common slaves (1.ii).

62 G. J. Finch, "Hawkesworth's Adaptation of Southerne's *Oroonoko*," *Restoration and 18th-Century Theatre Research* 16 (1977), 40–43. Hawkesworth adds six exchanges between Imoinda and the Lieutenant Governor.

63 Elizabeth Inchbald, *The British Theatre; or, a Collection of Plays, . . . by Mrs. Inchbald in 25 volumes* (London [1811–25]).

64 See the very full treatment of this issue in Margaret Ferguson, "Transmuting *Othello*: Aphra Behn's *Oroonoko*," *Cross-Cultural Performances: Differences in Women's Re-Visions of Shakespeare*, ed. Marianne Novy (Urbana: University of Illinois Press, 1993), pp. 14–49. Behn's narrator signals her sympathy with the plight of slaves of both sexes while also accentuating her superiority and her distance from personally engaging in the slave trade.

65 Without commenting on the gendering of pigmentation, Sara Suleri has noted that Burke begins to imagine a colonial sublimity linked with the heart of darkness, in *The Rhetoric of English India* (Chicago: University of Chicago Press, 1992), pp. 43–44.

7 BLACK MEN

1 Entry in *The Gentleman's Magazine* 19 (1749): 89–90. The prince was the probable subject of William Dodd, "The African Prince, now in England, to Zara at his father's court," and "Zara at the Court of Anamaboe, to the African Prince, When in England."

2 The often reprinted poems appear in *A Collection of Poems, In Four Volumes by Several Hands*, ed. Thomas Dodsley (London 1783), vol. IV, pp. 222–36, p. 229. Laura Brown, *Fables of Modernity: Literature and Culture in the English Eighteenth Century* (Ithaca and London: Cornell University Press, 2001) offers an enlightening discussion of the native prince, pp. 177–220.

3 Wylie Sypher, *Guinea's Captive Kings: British Anti-Slavery Literature of the 18th Century* (Chapel Hill: University of North Carolina Press, 1942), uses the phrase "pseudo-Africa," p. 131.

4 "Zara at the Court of Anamaboe, to the African Prince, When in England," in *A Collection of Poems*, IV, p. 235.

5 *The Complete Works of Thomas Chatterton*, ed. Donald S. Taylor with Benjamin B. Hoover, 2 vols. (Oxford: Clarendon Press, 1971), vol. I, pp. 432–35, 543–45, 590–93; 662–63. All subsequent references to these poems are cited parenthetically in the text.

6 See Wylie Sypher, "Chatterton's *African Ecologues* and the Deluge," *PMLA*, 54 (1939): 246–60.

7 Aphra Behn, *Oroonoko, The Rover and Other Works*, ed. Janet Todd (London: Penguin Books, 1992), pp. 80–81. I have added the italics.

8 Daniel Defoe, *The Life and Strange Surprizing Adventures of Robinson Crusoe, of York, Mariner*, ed. J. Donald Crowley (Oxford: Oxford University Press, 1972), p. 205.

9 Olaudah Equiano, *The Interesting Narrative and Other Writings*, ed. Vincent Carretta (New York: Penguin, 1995), and Ignatius Sancho, *Letters of the Late Ignatius Sancho, An African*, ed. Vincent Carretta (New York: Penguin, 1998). All subsequent quotations from these texts will be cited parenthetically.

10 Edward Long, *The History of Jamaica*, 3 vols. (London 1774), and Philip Thicknesse, *A Year's Journey Through France, and Part of Spain*, 2nd edn. with additions (London, 1778), vol. II, p. 102.

11 *An Enquiry Concerning the Principles of Taste, and of the Origin of our Ideas of Beauty* (London, 1785), p. 26.

12 Review of Olaudah Equiano's *Narrative, Gentleman's Magazine* 1 (June 1789): 539.

13 *The Royal African: Or, Memoirs of the Young Prince of Annamaboe* (London: c. 1749).

14 W. E. B. DuBois, *The Souls of Black Folk* (1903; rpt. New York: New American Library, 1982). Susan M. Marren sees the limitations of binary models and finds Equiano's conflict arises "between his commitment to speaking as an African for his fellow Africans and the necessity of speaking as white Englishman to make himself credible in eighteenth-century England," in "Between Slavery and Freedom: The Transgressive Self in Olaudah Equiano's Autobiography," *PMLA* 108 (1993): 104.

15 Seteney Shami, "Prehistories of Globalization: Circassian Identity in Motion," *Public Culture* 12.1 (2000): 178.

16 See Hazel Carby, "The Canon: Civil War and Reconstruction," *Michigan Quarterly Review* 28 (1989): 42–43, and *Race Men* (Cambridge: Harvard University Press, 1998), Charles W. Mills, *The Racial Contract* (Ithaca: Cornell University Press, 1997), and Nicholas Thomas, *In Oceania: Visions, Artifacts, Histories* (Durham: Duke University Press, 1997). Srinivas Aravamudan usefully coins the term "tropicopolitan" to describe the fictive colonized subject and the actual person who is both the "object of representation *and* agent of resistance," *Tropicopolitans: Colonialism and Agency, 1688–1804* (Durham and London: Duke University Press, 1999), p. 4.

17 Kathleen Wilson, "Citizenship, Empire, and Modernity in the English Provinces, c. 1720–1790," *Eighteenth-Century Studies* 29.1 (1995): 75.

18 See Gretchen Gerzina, *Black England: Life Before Emancipation* (London: John Murray, 1995), p. 53.

19 David Dabydeen, *Hogarth's Blacks: Images of Blacks in Eighteenth Century English Art* (Surrey: Dangaroo Press, 1985), pp. 87, 88.

20 Valerie Smith, *Self-Discovery and Authority in Afro-American Narrative* (Cambridge: Harvard University Press, 1987) helpfully interprets his slave narrative as a conflict between the "uninitiated, native" young African and the adult Christian convert.

21 Wilfred D. Samuels, "Disguised Voice in *The Interesting Narrative of Olaudah Equiano, or Gustavus Vassa, the African,*" *Black American Literature Forum* 19 (1985): 64–69; and Catherine Obianuju Acholonu, *The Igbo Roots of Olaudah Equiano* (Owerri, Nigeria: AFA Publications, 1989).

22 Folarin Shyllon, "Olaudah Equiano: Nigerian Abolitionist and First National Leader of Africans in Britain," *Journal of African Studies* 4 (1977): 433–51, 451.

23 Paul Edwards, "'Master' and 'Father' in Equiano's Interesting Narrative," *Slavery and Abolition* 11 (1990), 216–226; and Valerie Smith, *Self-Discovery and Authority in Afro-American Narrative.*

24 Wilson, "Citizenship, Empire, and Modernity," p. 85.

25 Adam Potkay, "Olaudah Equiano and the Art of Spiritual Autobiography," *Eighteenth-Century Studies* 27.4 (Summer 1994): 677–92.

26 Vincent Carretta, "Olaudah Equiano or Gustavus Vassa? New Light on an Eighteenth-Century Question of Identity," *Slavery and Abolition* 20.3 (2000): 96–106, argues that Equiano's African autobiographical account may be fictional since he was probably born in the Carolinas.

27 "Letter from Gustavus Vassa, Late Commissary for the African Settlement, to the Right Honourable Lord Hawkesbury," in Carretta, *Interesting Narrative*, p. 333.

28 Wilson, "Citizenship, Empire, and Modernity," pp. 69–96.

29 Wilfrid Samuels, "Disguised Voice," has argued that Equiano presents the Seven Years' War as "an avenue for regaining the power, valor, honor, and respect – in short, the humanity – of which he had been robbed by his abduction into slavery."

30 Linda Colley, *Britons: Forging the Nation 1707–1837* (New Haven and London: Yale University Press, 1992), pp. 283–320.

31 Katalin Orban, "Dominant and Submerged Discourses in *The Life of Olaudah Equiano (or Gustavus Vassa)*," *African American Review* 27.4 (1993): 655–64, confronts the stereotyping inherent in the claim that Equiano's heroic performance in the war is typical of African men: "One might want to ask whether all the heroes of the Seven Years' War epitomize the traditional African man."

32 See Oyeronke Oyewumi, *The Invention of Women: Making an African Sense of Western Gender Discourses* (Minneapolis: University of Minnesota Press, 1997). I would contend, however, that elements of uneven relations of power based on gender persist in Equiano's account.

33 Philip D. Morgan writes, "No single part of Africa, for example, supplied more than about thirty percent of arrivals to either Cuba, Barbados, Martinique, Guadeloupe, or the Danish islands," "The Early Caribbean in Atlantic Context, circa 1500–1800," in *The Global Eighteenth Century*, ed. Felicity A. Nussbaum (Baltimore: Johns Hopkins University Press, 2003).

34 Acholonu, *The Igbo Roots of Olaudah Equiano*, pp. 50, 90, 101.

35 [James Tobin], *Cursory Remarks Upon the Reverend Mr. Ramsay's Essay on the Treatment and Conversion of African Slaves in the Sugar Colonies* (London, 1785), p. 117. These comments though intended as racist incidentally reveal the difficulty freed slaves experienced in obtaining paid labor.

36 Equiano and his wife, Susanna Cullen, were parents to two mixed-race daughters, Anna Maria and Johanna.

37 Vincent Carretta notes that marriages in which both parties were African were extremely uncommon in eighteenth-century England in Ignatius Sancho, *Letters of the Late Ignatius Sancho*, p. 250 n.14.

38 Cited in Carretta, ed., Introduction to Sancho, *Letters*, p. xv.

39 Introduction to *Ignatius Sancho: An African Man of Letters*, ed. Reyahn King et al. (London: National Portrait Gallery, 1997), p. 9.

40 William Stevenson, 14 September 1814, in John Nichols, *Literary Anecdotes of the Eighteenth Century*, 9 vols. (London 1815), vol. VIII.

41 Homi Bhabha, "Of Mimicry and Man: The Ambivalence of Colonial Discourse," *October* 28 (1984): 125–33, is the classic text on the concept of mimicry as camouflage that "mimics the forms of authority at the point at which it deauthorizes them," p. 132.

42 Henry Charles William Angelo, *Reminiscences of Henry Angelo, with Memoirs of his late Father and Friends, including numerous anecdotes* (London: H. Colbourn, 1828), vol. I, p. 349.

43 Angelo, *Reminiscences*, vol. I, p. 347.

44 *Black Writers in Britain, 1760–1890*, eds. Paul Edwards and David Dabydeen (Edinburgh: Edinburgh University Press, 1991), pp. 18–20.

45 See Paul Edwards, "Introduction," in Ignatius Sancho, *Sancho's Letters, with Memoirs of his Life by Joseph Jekyll Esq. M.P.*, 5th edn (London: William Sancho, 1803) fascimile edition, ed. Paul Edwards (London: Dawsons, 1968), pp. 6–7, and Keith A. Sandiford, *Measuring the Moment: Strategies of Protest in Eighteenth-Century Afro-English Writing* (Selinsgrove: Susquehanna University Press, 1988), pp. 75–76, cited in Markman Ellis, *The Politics of Sensibility: Race, Gender and Commerce in the Sentimental Novel* (Cambridge: Cambridge University Press, 1996), p. 83. For these critics, sentimentality compromises Sancho's masculinity and associates him with the aristocratic, the foreign, and the effete.

46 Caryl Phillips, foreword to *Ignatius Sancho: An African Man of Letters*, ed. Reyahn King et al. (London: National Portrait Gallery, 1997).

47 Quobna Ottobah Cugoano, *Thoughts and Sentiments on the Evil of Slavery*, ed. Vincent Carretta (New York: Penguin Books, 1999), p. 25.

48 Though [Joseph Jekyll], "The Life of Ignatius Sancho," in *Letters of Ignatius Sancho* reports "it is during this period [after 1751] that he may briefly have taken up employment as an actor in Garrick's theatrical company," I am not aware of any other evidence to support this. See Edwards and Rewt, p. 2.

49 André Dommergues, "Ignatius Sancho (1729–80), the White-Masked African" in *The History and Historiography of Commonwealth Literature*, ed. Dieter Riemenschneider (Tübingen: Narr, 1983), p. 195.

50 See [Joseph Jekyll], "The Life of Ignatius Sancho," in *Letters of Ignatius Sancho*, p. 6.

51 Jane Girdham, "Black Musicians in England: Ignatius Sancho and his Contemporaries," in *Ignatius Sancho*, ed. King, pp. 115–24.

8 BLACK PARTS

1 Ignatius Sancho, *Letters of the Late Ignatius Sancho, An African*, ed. Vincent Carretta (New York: Penguin Books, 1998), back cover.

2 Sancho, *Letters of the Late Ignatius Sancho*, p. 7.

3 S. Foster Damon, "The Negro in Early American Songsters," *Papers of the Bibliographical Society of America* 28, pt. 2 (1934): p. 133, notes that the first dance by a black impersonator in America was on 14 April 1767. Lewis Hallam sang as Mungo in May 1769, and a "negress" singer appeared in 1839.

4 David Krasner, "Perspectives on American Minstrelsy," *Nineteenth Century Theatre* 27.2 (Winter 1999): 142, suggests that Aldridge left the American stage

because "race played a significant role in his lack of opportunities." The history of black actors in America deserves much more critical attention. Clifford Ashby tells of the likely presence of a black servant in a speaking role in "A Black Actor on the Eighteenth Century Boston Stage?" *Theatre Survey: The American Journal of Theatre History* 28.2 (1987): 101–2.

5 Among the blackface plays, operas, farces, and songs in America from 1716 to the mid nineteenth century (in addition to those in England) were 425 performances of *Othello* from its first performance in 1751, 101 of McCready's farce *The Irishman in London: The Happy African* beginning in 1793, and 66 performances of Bickerstaffe's *The Padlock* after 1769. Each of these was among the ten most frequently performed works. See Dale Cockrell, *Demons of Disorder: Early Blackface Minstrels and Their World* (Cambridge: Cambridge University Press, 1997), and James V. Hatch, *The Black Image on the American Stage: A Bibliography of Plays and Musicals, 1770–1970* (New York: DramaBook Specialists Publications, 1970).

6 See Herbert Marshall and Mildred Stock, *Ira Aldridge: The Negro Tragedian* (Carbondale: Southern Illinois University Press, 1968), pp. 37, 53. I have derived much information on Aldridge from this very useful biography.

7 But during these years when actual black men do not mount the boards and white women often act transgressively in breeches roles, the parts of black women are erased even when the story would seem to command their presence.

8 Aldridge's third performance at Covent Garden was cancelled, and he did not return to the London stage until 1858 after playing on the continent according to Herbert Marshall and Mildred Stock, *Ira Aldridge*, p. 133. He returned to the West End as Othello in 1865.

9 W. T. Lhamon, Jr., *Raising Cain: Blackface Performance from Jim Crow to Hip Hop* (Cambridge: Harvard University Press, 1998), p. 16.

10 Hazel V. Carby, *Race Men* (Cambridge: Harvard University Press, 1998), p. 37.

11 Here I agree with Wylie Sypher who states, "Strictly, there is no drama of anti-slavery; there are only a number of plays in which the Negro plays his part," *Guinea's Captive Kings: British Anti-Slavery Literature of the 18th Century* (Chapel Hill: University of North Carolina Press, 1942), p. 232. It is the nature of that "part" that this chapter investigates.

12 Lhamon, *Raising Cain: Blackface Performance from Jim Crow to Hip Hop*, p. 3.

13 Thomas Jordan, *London Triumphant: or, The City in Jollity and Splendour: Expressed in various Pageants, Shapes, Scenes, Speeches and Songs . . . for Sir Robert Hanson Knight, Lord Mayor of the City of London. At the Cost and Charges of the Worshipful Company of Grocers.* (London, 1672), p. 3.

14 Thomas Jordan, *The Triumphs of London, Performed on Friday, Octob. 29. 1675, for the Entertainment of the Right Honourable, and truly Noble Pattern of Prudence and Loyalty, Sir Joseph Sheldon Kt, Lord Mayor of the City of London . . . all set forth at the proper Costs and Charges of the Worshipful Company of Drapers* (London, 1675), p. 13.

15 Thomas Jordan, *London Triumphant*, p. 4.

16 Sybil Rosenfeld, *The Theatre of the London Fairs in the 18th Century* (Cambridge: Cambridge University Press, 1960), p. 110, quoted by Alfred Jackson, "London Playhouses, 1700–1705," *RES* 8 (1932): 301. The list of plates records, "From an engraving after a water colour, in *London Society* 1863, British Museum." "Drolls" are theatrical booths set up irregularly for the performance of a farce or a puppet show, or for lotteries or music.

17 *London Chronicle* xv/1116 (14–16 February 1764): 166, cited in Peter Fryer, *Staying Power: The History of Black People in Britain* (London: Pluto Press, 1984), p. 69. *The Servants Pocket-Book* (1761) remarks that black servants were known to "herd together," cited in J. Jean Hecht, *Continental and Colonial Servants in Eighteenth-Century England*, Smith College Studies in History, vol. 40 (Northampton, Mass., 1954), p. 18.

18 Fryer, *Staying Power*, p. 60.

19 Rachel Lee, " 'Faking, Dipping, Juking': (Asian) American Style as Cross-Racial Desire," Lecture at Center for the Study of Women, UCLA, December 1999, contrasts racial performance in Asian-American and African-American literature. I am very grateful for permission to consult this paper.

20 Robyn Wiegman, *American Anatomies: Theorizing Race and Gender* (Durham and London: Duke University Press, 1995), p. 126, writes evocatively, "The site for the nostalgic dream of bonding across incommensurate difference, while serving as the very signpost – the corporeal evidence – that sanctions, indeed reassures us, that the dream and its miscegenating potential remain impossibilities."

21 David Dabydeen, *Hogarth's Blacks: Images of Blacks in Eighteenth Century English Art* (Kingston-on-Thames, Surrey: Dangaroo Press, 1985), pp. 23–37.

22 See Ignatius Sancho, *Letters of the Late Ignatius Sancho, An African*, ed. Vincent Carretta (New York: Penguin Books, 1998).

23 When P. T. Barnum exhibited a macrocephalic African American as a man-monkey named "Zip, the What-is-it?", it was alleged to lack language. See the introduction to Bernth Lindfors, ed., *Africans on Stage: Studies in Ethnological Show Business* (Bloomington: Indiana University Press, 1999), p. ix, and Z. S. Strother, "Display of the Body Hottentot," p. 37.

24 Kristina Straub, *Sexual Suspects: Eighteenth-Century Players and Sexual Ideology* (Princeton: Princeton University Press, 1992), pp. 165–66. At least one actor, William Smith, a gentleman educated at Cambridge, stipulated that he would not appear in blackface.

25 Eric Lott, *Love and Theft: Blackface Minstrelsy and the American Working Class* (Oxford: Oxford University Press, 1993), p. 4.

26 David Dabydeen, *Hogarth's Blacks*, "There were representations of African dancing in many plays – Settle's *The Empress of Morocco*, Southerne's *Oroonoko*, D'Avenant's *The Playhouse To Be Let*, Foote's *The Patron* – as well as in pantomimes such as Bates's *Harlequin Mungo*," p. 50. George Colman the younger's *The Africans* is also ethnographically realist, presenting an imagined Africa with references to groundnuts and couscous, "broil'd ostrich" and "antelope's brisket," tigerskin robes and birds of paradise feathers.

27 Lott, *Love and Theft*, p. 8.

28 Eileen Southern, "Black Musicians and Early Ethiopian Minstrelsy," *Inside the Minstrel Mask*, ed. Annemarie Bean, James V. Hatch, and Brooks McNamara (Hanover, NH: Wesleyan University Press, 1996), pp. 43–63.

29 In Boswell's *Life* Samuel Johnson remarks that Bate, "associated with vice," is a man of courage but not virtue (cited in Carretta, *Equiano*, p. 289 n.2).

30 W. T. Lhamon, Jr., "Core is Less," *Reviews in American History* 27.4 (1999): 566.

31 *The London Stage 1660–1800*. Part 4; 1747–1776, ed. George Winchester Stone, Jr. (Carbondale: Southern Illinois University Press), 1960, pp. 1948–50.

32 Dabydeen, *Hogarth's Blacks*, p. 119. Folarin Shyllon, *Black People in Britain 1555–1833* (Oxford: Oxford University Press, 1977), p. 5, writes, "However rich they might be, such people objected to paying wages to English servants when there were black slaves available to work for nothing but food and clothing. So they brought their slaves here as personal and household servants."

33 Lott, *Love and Theft*, p. 69. This point about the nineteenth century is also, I am arguing, applicable to the eighteenth century.

34 Kim F. Hall, *Things of Darkness: Economies of Race and Gender in Early Modern England* (Ithaca: Cornell University Press, 1995) remarks, "The whitewashed Ethopian is a ubiquitous image in Renaissance literature, appearing often in emblem books and proverbs as a figure of the impossible," p. 115.

35 The play in Larpent MS 400 is cited in the Henry E. Huntington Library, San Marino, California.

36 Lott, *Love and Theft*, p. 26.

37 Isaac Bickerstaffe, *The Padlock, A Farce* (London, 1823). This edition in the William Andrews Clark Memorial Library is the only existing one which is faithfully marked with the stage business and stage directions, as it was performed at the Theatres Royal. There is a modern reprint in *Slavery, Abolition and Emancipation: Writings in the British Romantic Period*, ed. Jeffrey Cox (London: Pickering and Chatto, 1999), vol. v, pp. 73–108.

38 See the introduction to *Furibond; or Harlequin Negro* (London, 1808) in *Slavery, Abolition and Emancipation*, ed. Cox, vol. v, pp. 281–305. Subsequent citations are from this edition.

39 I have also consulted the British Library copy of *Furibond; or, Harlequin Negro. The Songs Choruses & c. With a description of the Pantomime. As Performed at the Theatre Royal, Drury-Lane*. Monday, December 28th 1807 (London, 1807), and Larpent LA 1553 in the Henry E. Huntington Library.

40 Marshall and Stock, *Ira Aldridge: The Negro Tragedian*, p. 70.

41 Edward Young, *The Revenge as performed at the Theatres-Royal Covent Garden and Drury Lane* in *The British Theatre; or, a Collection of Plays, . . . by Mrs. Inchbald in 25 volumes* (London: Longman, Hurst, Rees, Orme, and Brown [1811–25]), vol. XII.

42 Thomas Morton, *The Slave* (1816) in *Slavery, Abolition and Emancipation*, ed. Cox, vol. v, pp. 307–81.

43 Lott, *Love and Theft*, writes of nineteenth-century American minstrelsy, "There is evidence that performers and audiences also found in blackface, something closer to a homoerotic charge," p. 57.

44 George Colman the Younger, *The Africans; or War, Love and Duty* (1808) in *Slavery, Abolition and Emancipation*, ed. Cox, vol. v, pp. 221–80. Extending to thirty-one performances, the play derives from a French melodrama which was in turn translated into novel form in both languages.

45 But see Cox, ed. *Slavery, Abolition and Emancipation*, who suggests that the play condemns slavery, vol. v, pp. 221–22. Cox's argument is that "our notions of 'race' and 'colour' are as contingent, as constructed as the mask and make-up of the actors." On the contrary, even when the Harlequin dons a black mask the audience recognizes that he is essentially white at core.

46 Terry Castle, *Masquerade and Civilization: The Carnivalesque in Eighteenth-Century English Culture and Fiction* (Stanford: Stanford University Press, 1986).

47 Hayden White, "The Noble Savage Theme as Fetish," *Tropics of Discourse: Essays in Cultural Criticism* (Baltimore and London: The Johns Hopkins University Press, 1978), pp. 183–96.

48 Aldridge's appearance on stage is historically parallel to the increase in ethnographic shows such as the Hottentot Venus and of the European march toward scientific racism. See Z. S. Strother, "Display of the Body Hottentot," *Africans on Stage: Studies in Ethnological Show Business*, ed. Bernth Lindfors (Bloomington: Indiana University Press, 1999), pp. 1–61.

49 The phrase "almost the same, but not white" appears in Homi Bhabha's classic essay, "Of Mimicry and Man: The Ambivalence of Colonial Discourse," *October* 28 (1984): 125–33. I have obviously altered the meaning of Bhabha's phrase.

50 Though I cannot here pursue the many reasons for this shift, I will simply note that in the subcontinent of India, "The wearing of Indian dress in public functions by employees of the [East India] Company was officially banned in 1830." Bernard S. Cohn, *Colonialism and its Forms of Knowledge: The British in India* (Princeton: Princeton University Press, 1996), p. 112.

CODA: BETWEEN RACES

1 Mrs. Hester Lynch (Salusbury) Thrale, *The Letters of Mrs. Thrale*, ed. R. Brimley Johnson (New York: Dial Press, 1926), pp. 143–44.

2 Stuart Hall, "New Ethnicities," *Stuart Hall: Critical Dialogues in Cultural Studies*, ed. David Morley and Kuan-Hsing Chen (London: Routledge, 1996), p. 445.

3 See especially Walter D. Mignolo, *Local Histories / Global Designs: Coloniality, Subaltern Knowledges, and Border Thinking* (Princeton: Princeton University Press, 2000), and Gloria Anzaldúa, *Borderlands / La frontera: The New Mestiza* (San Francisco: Spinsters/Aunt Lute, 1987); James Clifford, *Routes: Travel and Translation in the Late Twentieth Century* (Cambridge: Harvard University Press, 1997); Homi Bhabha, ed., *Nation and Narration* (London: Routledge, 1990); W. E. B. DuBois, *The Souls of Black Folk* (1903; rpt. New York: New American

Library, 1982); and Lisa Lowe, *Immigrant Acts: On Asian American Cultural Politics* (Duke University Press, 1996).

4 Peter Hulme, *Colonial Encounters: Europe and the Native Caribbean 1492–1797* (London: Routledge, 1986), p. 141; and Mary Louise Pratt, *Imperial Eyes: Travel Writing and Transculturation* (London: Routledge, 1992), pp. 86–107, 97.

5 *Letters from Mrs. Elizabeth Carter to Mrs. Montagu, Between the Years 1755 and 1800*, ed. Rev. Montagu Pennington, 3 volumes (London: F. C. and J. Rivington, 1817), 12 June 1764, vol. I, p. 222. The Black Prince may have been the same Julius Soubise befriended by the Duchess of Queensberry though it is unlikely because the "Prince" reputedly married an heiress instead of withdrawing in disgrace to India as did Soubise.

6 Pratt, *Imperial Eyes*, p. 6.

7 Frances Burney (Madame d'Arblay), *Memoirs of Doctor Burney*, 3 vols. (London: Edward Moxon, 1832), vol. II, p. 8. Burney follows James Burnet, Lord Monboddo, *Of the Origin and Progress of Language* 2nd edn., vol. IV (Edinburgh, 1774), pp. 6–7, who believed all indigenous languages were barbarous and defective.

8 Peter Stallybrass and Allon White, *The Politics and Poetics of Transgression* (Ithaca: Cornell University Press, 1986), pp. 5 and 91.

9 Hayden White, "The Noble Savage Theme as Fetish," *Tropics of Discourse: Essays in Cultural Criticism* (Baltimore: The Johns Hopkins University Press, 1978), p. 194.

10 Oroonoko offers Imoinda slaves as the spoils of battle when her father dies defending him.

11 See Frank Felsenstein, ed., *English Trader, Indian Maid: Representing Gender, Race, and Slavery in the New World* (Baltimore and London: The Johns Hopkins University Press, 1999), p. 167. I am indebted to this helpful history of the *Inkle and Yarico* versions, though my conclusions differ somewhat. Felsenstein labels Weddell's drama "portentous and turgid," but Jeffrey Cox finds the play sufficiently interesting to include it in his recent edition of slavery and abolition plays. See also Lawrence Marsden Price, *Inkle and Yarico Album* (Berkeley: University of California Press, 1937).

12 Felsenstein, ed. *English Trader, Indian Maid*, pp. 167–68.

13 George Colman, *Inkle and Yarico: An Opera, in Three Acts*, Cumberland's British Theatre (London: n.d. [1827]), vol. III, pp. 1–54. All subsequent references to this edition are cited parenthetically in the text.

14 Felsenstein ed., *English Trader, Indian Maid*, pp. 18–27.

15 Ibid., believes the end of the slave trade brought the loss of interest in the play since it "took away at a stroke what had been become the story's most topical component," p. 27.

16 *A Year's Journey through France, and Part of Spain. By Philip Thicknesse, esq.* 2nd edn. with additions (London, 1778), vol. II, p. 108.

17 Thicknesse, *A Year's Journey through France, and Part of Spain*, vol. II, p. 102.

18 James Tobin, *Cursory Remarks Upon the Reverend Mr. Ramsay's Essay on the Treatment and Conversion of African Slaves in the Sugar Colonies* (1785), p. 118.

19 Robert J. C. Young, *Colonial Desire: Hybridity in Theory, Culture and Race* (London: Routledge, 1995), p. 8.
20 Mariana Starke, *The Widow of Malabar, A Tragedy in Three Acts*, 3rd edn. (London, 1791).
21 Starke, *The Widow of Malabar*, p. 14.
22 Olaudah Equiano, "To J[ames] T[obin] Esq; Author of the BOOKS called CURSORY REMARKS & REJOINDER," *The Public Advertiser* (28 January 1788) in Olaudah Equiano, *The Interesting Narrative and other Writings*, ed. Vincent Carretta (Penguin: New York, 1995), Appendix E. Subsequent quotations are from the text.
23 Marilyn Butler, *Maria Edgeworth: A Literary Biography* (Oxford: Clarendon Press, 1972), Appendix C, p. 495.
24 Charles Lamb, *The Works of Charles Lamb*, 2 vols. (London: C. and J. Ollier, 1818), vol. II, pp. 1–36.
25 Ruth Cowhig, "Blacks in English Renaissance Drama and the Role of Shakespeare's Othello," *The Black Presence in English Literature*, ed. David Dabydeen (Manchester: Manchester University Press, 1985), p. 16.
26 James Burnet, Lord Monboddo, *Of the Origin and Progress of Language*, 6 vols. (Edinburgh 1774), vol. I, pp. 193–94. See also *Account of a Most Surprizing Savage Girl... translated from the French* (Glasgow 1799).

Bibliography

Account of a Most Surprizing Savage Girl... translated from the French. Glasgow, 1799.

Acholonu, Catherine Obianuju. *The Igbo Roots of Olaudah Equiano.* Owerri, Nigeria: AFA Publications, 1989.

Adams, G. "Dido Elizabeth Belle: A Black Girl at Kenwood." *Camden History Review* (1984).

Addison, Joseph, and Richard Steele. *The Spectator.* Ed. Donald F. Bond. 5 vols. Oxford: Oxford University Press, 1965.

Albinus, Bernard. *Tabulae sceleti et musculorum corporis humani.* Leiden, 1747.

Allen, Robert J. *The Clubs of Augustan London.* Hamden, Conn.: Archon Books, 1967.

Amman, Jean Coenrad. *The Talking Deaf Man: or, A Method Proposed Whereby he who is Born Deaf, may learn to Speak.* 1694. No. 357 *English Linguistics 1500–1800.* Series 3. Meston, England: Scholar Press, Limited, 1972.

Anderson, Benedict. *Imagined Communities.* London: Verso, 1991.

Angelo, Henry Charles William. *Reminiscences of Henry Angelo, With Memoirs of His Late Father and friends, including numerous original anecdotes.* 2 vols. London: H. Colburn, 1828.

Anzaldúa, Gloria. *Borderlands/La frontera: The New Mestiza.* San Francisco: SpinsterAunt Lute, 1987.

Aravamudan, Srinivas. *Tropicopolitans: Colonialism and Agency, 1688–1804.* Durham and London: Duke University Press, 1999.

Arnold, Walter. *The Life and Death of the Sublime Society of Beefsteaks.* London: Bradbury, Evans, and Co., 1871.

Ashby, Clifford. "A Black Actor on the Eighteenth Century Boston Stage?" *Theatre Survey: The American Journal Theatre History* 28. 2 (1987): 101–2.

Aziz, Razia. "Feminism and the Challenge of Racism: Deviance or Difference?" In *Black British Feminism*, ed. Heidi Safia Mirza, 70–77. London and New York: Routledge, 1997.

Baine, Rodney. *Daniel Defoe and the Supernatural.* Athens: University of Georgia Press, 1968.

Ballard, George. *Memoirs of Several Ladies of Great Britain Who Have Been Celebrated for Their Writings or Skill in the Learned Languages, Arts and Sciences.* 1752. Ed. Ruth Perry. Detroit: Wayne State University Press, 1985.

Ballaster, Ros. "Manl(e)y Forms: Sex and the Female Satirist." In *Women, Texts, and Histories 1575–1760*, ed. Clare Brant and Diane Purkis, 217–41. New York and London: Routledge, 1992.

Seductive Forms: Women's Amatory Fiction from 1684 to 1740. Oxford: Clarendon Press, 1992.

Barnes, Colin. "Disability Studies: New or Not so New Directions?" *Disability and Society* 14.4 (1999): 577–80.

Barre, François Poulain (Poullain) de la. *The Woman as Good as the Man Or, The Equality of Both Sexes*. Trans. A. L. Ed. Gerald M. MacLean. Detroit: Wayne State University Press, 1988.

De l'égalité des deux sexes. Paris: 1673.

Barrell, John. *The Birth of Pandora and the Division of Knowledge*. Philadelphia: University of Pennsylvania Press, 1992.

Barry, James. *An Inquiry into the Real and Imaginary Obstructions to the Acquisition of the Arts in England*. London, 1775.

Bath, Henry Jones. *Inoculation; or, Beauty's Triumph; a Poem*. London, 1768.

Battestin, Martin, with Ruthe R. Battestin. *Henry Fielding: A Life*. London: Routledge, 1989.

Baxby, Derrick. "The Jenner Bicentenary: the Introduction and Early Distribution of Smallpox Vaccine," FEMS (Federation of European Microbiological Societies). *Immunology and Medical Microbiology* 16 (1996).

Jenner's Smallpox Vaccine: The Riddle of Vaccinia Virus and Its Origin. London: Heinemann Educational Books, 1981.

Beauty's Triumph, Or, the Superiority of the Fair Sex invincibly proved, 3 parts. London, 1751.

Behn, Aphra. *Oroonoko, The Rover and Other Works*. Ed. Janet Todd. London: Penguin, 1992.

The Works of Aphra Behn. Ed. Janet Todd. 7 vols. Columbus: Ohio State University Press, 1995.

Bhabha, Homi. "Of Mimicry and Man: The Ambivalence of Colonial Discourse." *October* 28 (1984): 125–33.

Nation and Narration. London: Routledge, 1990.

Bickerstaffe, Isaac. *The Padlock, A Farce*. London, 1823.

Biddulph, Violet. *Kitty, Duchess of Queensberry*. London: Ivor Nicholson and Watson, 1935.

Bloch, Harry. "Edward Jenner (1749–1823): The History and Effects of Smallpox, Inoculation, and Vaccination." *AJDC* 147 (July 1993): 772–74.

Bloch, Ivan. *Sexual Life in England: Past and Present*. Trans. William H. Forstern. London: Francis Aldor, 1938.

Blunt, Reginald, ed. *Mrs. Montagu, "Queen of the Blues": Her Letters and Friendships From 1762 to 1800*. 2 vols. Boston and New York: Houghton Mifflin, 1923.

"The Sylph." *The Edinburgh Review or Critical Journal* 242 (October 1925): 364–79.

Boon, James A. "Anthropology and Degeneration: Birds, Words, and Orangutans." In *Degeneration: The Dark Side of Progress*, ed. J. Edward Chamberlin and Sander L. Gilman, 24–48 (New York: Columbia University Press, 1985).

Boswell, James. *Boswell's London Journal.* Ed. Frederick A. Pottle. New York: McGraw-Hill, 1952.

The Life of Johnson. Ed. George Birkbeck Hill, rev. L. F. Powell. 6 vols. Oxford: Clarendon Press, 1934–50.

Brotton, Jerry. *Trading Territories: Mapping the Early Modern World.* Ithaca: Cornell University Press, 1998.

Brown, John. *An Estimate of the Manners and Principles of the Times.* London, 1757.

Brown, Laura. *The Ends of Empire: Women and Ideology in Early Eighteenth-Century English Literature.* Ithaca: Cornell University Press, 1993.

Fables of Modernity: Literature and Culture in the English Eighteenth Century. Ithaca: Cornell University Press, 2001.

Bulwer, John. *Anthropometamorphosis: Man Transformed.* London, 1653.

Burke, Edmund. *A Philosophical Inquiry into the Sublime and Beautiful.* London, 1757.

Burnet, James, Lord Monboddo. *Of the Origin and Progress of Language.* 2nd edn. 6 vols. Edinburgh, 1774.

Burney, Fanny. *Camilla, or A Picture of Youth.* Ed. Edward A. Bloom and Lillian D. Bloom. Oxford and New York: Oxford University Press, 1983.

Evelina or the History of a Young Lady's Entrance into the World. Ed. Edward A. Bloom and Lillian D. Bloom. Oxford: Oxford University Press, 1982.

The Journals and Letters of Fanny Burney (Madame D'Arblay), 1791–1840. Ed. Joyce Hemlow, with Patricia Boutilier and Althea Douglas. 12 vols. Oxford: Oxford University Press, 1972–84.

[Burney, Fanny] Madame D'Arblay. *Memoirs of Doctor Burney.* 3 vols. London: Edward Moxon, 1832.

Butler, Judith. *Gender Trouble.* New York: Routledge, 1990.

Butler, Marilyn. *Maria Edgeworth: A Literary Biography.* Oxford: Clarendon Press, 1972.

Callaghan, Dympna. *Shakespeare Without Women: Representing Gender and Race on the Renaissance Stage.* London and New York: Routledge, 2000.

Campbell, Jill. *Natural Masques: Gender and Identity in Fielding's Plays and Novels.* Stanford: Stanford University Press, 1995.

" 'When Men Women Turn': Gender Reversals in Fielding's Plays." In *The New Eighteenth Century: Theory/Politics/English Literature*, ed. Felicity Nussbaum and Laura Brown, 62–83. New York and London: Methuen, 1987.

Campbell, R. *The London Tradesman.* London, 1747.

Canguilhem, Georges. *The Normal and the Pathological.* Introduction by Michel Foucault, trans. Carolyn R. Fawcett. 1966. New York: Zone Books, 1989.

Carby, Hazel. "The Canon: Civil War and Reconstruction." *Michigan Quarterly Review* 28 (1989): 35–43.

Race Men. Cambridge: Harvard University Press, 1998.

Carlton, Peter J. "The Mitigated Truth: Tom Jones's Double Heroism." *Studies in the Novel* 19 (1987): 397–409.

Carretta, Vincent. "Olaudah Equiano or Gustavus Vassa? New Light on an Eighteenth-Century Question of Identity." *Slavery and Abolition* 20. 3 (2000): 96–106.

ed. *Unchained Voices: An Anthology of Black Authors in the English-Speaking World of the Eighteenth Century*. Lexington: University Press of Kentucky, 1996.

Castle, Terry. *Masquerade and Civilization: The Carnivalesque in Eighteenth-Century English Culture and Fiction*. Stanford: Stanford University Press, 1986.

Chard, Chloe. "Effeminacy, Pleasure and the Classical Body." In *Femininity and Masculinity in Eighteenth-Century Art and Culture*, ed. Gill Perry and Michael Rossington, 142–61. Manchester: Manchester University Press, 1994.

Chatterton, Thomas. *The Complete Works of Thomas Chatterton*. Ed. Donald S. Taylor with Benjamin B. Hoover. 2 vols. Oxford: Clarendon Press, 1971.

Clark, Peter. *British Clubs and Societies 1580–1800: The Origins of an Associational World*. Oxford: Clarendon Press, 2000.

Clifford, James. *Routes: Travel and Translation in the late Twentieth Century*. Cambridge: Harvard University Press, 1997.

Cockrell, Dale. *Demons of Disorder: Early Blackface Minstrels and Their World*. Cambridge: Cambridge University Press, 1997.

Cohn, Bernard S. *Colonialism and Its Forms of Knowledge: The British in India*. Princeton: Princeton University Press, 1996.

Colley, Linda. *Britons: Forging the Nation, 1707–1837*. New Haven: Yale University Press, 1992.

Colman the Younger, George. *Inkle and Yarico: An Opera, in Three Acts*. Vol. III of *Cumberland's British Theatre*. 48 vols. London: n.d. [1827].

Inkle and Yarico: An Opera, in Three Acts. London, 1787.

The Africans; or War, Love and Duty (London 1808). In *Slavery, Abolition and Emancipation*, vol. 5, ed. Jeffrey Cox. 10 vols.

Connell, Neville. "Colonial Life in the West Indies." *Antiques* 99 (1971): 732–77.

Cook, G. D. "Dr. William Woodville (1752–1805) and the St. Pancras Smallpox Hospital." *Journal of Medical Biography* 4 (1996): 71–78.

Cooper, Anthony Ashley, Third Earl of Shaftsbury. *Characteristics of Men, Manners, Opinions, Times*. Cambridge: Cambridge University Press, 1999.

Cowhig, Ruth. "Blacks in English Renaissance Drama and the Role of Shakespeare's *Othello*." In *The Black Presence in English Literature*, ed. David Dabydeen, 1–25. Manchester: Manchester University Press, 1985.

Cowley, Robert L. S. *Hogarth's Marriage A-La-Mode*. Ithaca: Cornell University Press, 1983.

Cox, Jeffrey, ed. *Slavery, Abolition and Emancipation: Writings in the British Romantic Period*. 10 vols. London: Pickering and Chatto, 1999.

Crowne, John. *Calisto*. Vol. I. In *The Dramatic Works, with Prefatory Memoir and notes*. 4 vols. Edinburgh: William Paterson, 1873.

Cugoano, Quobna Ottobah. *Thoughts and Sentiments on the Evil of Slavery*, ed. Vincent Carretta. New York: Penguin Books, 1999.

Cunningham, Peter, ed. *The Letters of Horace Walpole, Earl of Orford*. 9 vols. London: Henry G. Bohn, 1861.

Curran, Andrew and Patrick Graille. "The Faces of Eighteenth-Century Monstrosity," *Eighteenth-Century Life* 21 (May 1997): 1–15.

Dabydeen, David. *Hogarth's Blacks: Images of Blacks in Eighteenth Century English Art*. Kingston-on-Thames, Surrey: Dangaroo Press, 1985.

Damon, S. Foster. "The Negro in Early American Songsters." *Papers of the Bibliographical Society of America*. 28, Pt. 2 (1934): 132–63.

Daston, Lorraine, and Katharine Park. *Wonders and the Order of Nature, 1150–1750*. New York: Zone Books, 1998.

Davis, Lennard J. *Enforcing Normalcy: Disability, Deafness and the Body*. London: Verso, 1995.

Day, Thomas. *The Dying Negro, A Poetical Epistle Supposed to be written by a black, (Who lately shot himself on board a vessel in the river Thames); to his intended Wife*. London, 1773.

Defoe, Daniel. *The Life and Strange Surprizing Adventures of Robinson Crusoe of York, Mariner*. Ed. J. Donald Crowley. Oxford: Oxford University Press, 1972.

Deutsch, Helen, and Felicity Nussbaum, eds. *"Defects": Engendering the Modern Body*. Ann Arbor: University of Michigan Press, 2000.

Dimsdale, Thomas. *Thoughts on General and Partial Inoculations. Containing a Translation of Two Treatises written when the Author was at Petersburg, and published there... also Outlines of Two Plans: One, for the general Inoculation of the Poor in small Towns and Villages. The other, for the general Inoculation of the Poor in London, and other populous Places*. London, 1776.

Dodd, William. "The African Prince, now in England, to Zara at his Father's Court." In *A Collection of Poems*. Ed. Thomas Dodsley. 4 vols. London, 1783. IV, 222–30.

"Zara at the Court of Anamaboe, to the African Prince when in England." In *A Collection of Poems*. Ed. Thomas Dodsley. 4 vols. London, 1783. IV, 230–36.

Dodsley, Thomas, ed. *A Collection of Poems, In Four Volumes by Several Hands*. 4 vols. London, 1783.

Dommergues, André. "Ignatius Sancho (1729–80), the White-Masked African." In *The History and Historiography of Commonwealth Literature*, ed. Dieter Riemenschneider. Tübingen: Narr, 1983.

Doody, Margaret Anne. *Frances Burney: The Life in the Works*. Cambridge: Cambridge University Press, 1988.

The True Story of the Novel. New Brunswick: Rutgers University Press, 1996.

Doran, John. *A Lady of the Last Century (Mrs. Elizabeth Montagu): Illustrated in Her Unpublished Letters; Collected and Arranged, With a Biographical Sketch, and a Chapter on Blue Stockings*. Boston: Francis A. Niccolls and Co., 1873.

Drew-Bear, Annette. *Painted Faces on the Renaissance Stage: The Moral Significance of Face-Painting Conventions*. Lewisburg: Bucknell University Press, 1994.

DuBois, W. E. B. *The Souls of Black Folk*. 1903. Rpt. New York: New American Library, 1982.

Dugaw, Dianne. *Warrior Women and Popular Balladry 1650–1850*. Cambridge: Cambridge University Press, 1989.

Duncan, S. R., S. Scott, and C. J. Duncan. "Modelling the Different Smallpox Epidemics in England." *Philosophical Transactions of the Royal Society, London* 346 (1994): 407–19.

"An Eccentric Lecture on the Art of Propagating the Human Species, and Producing a Numerous and Healthy Offspring." *The Rambler's Magazine; Or, the Annals of Gallantry, Glee, Pleasure, and the Bon ton* (January 1783): 5–6.

Edwards, Bryan. *The History, Civil and Commercial, of the British Colonies in the West Indies: In Two Volumes.* London: John Stockdale, 1794.

Edwards, Paul. " 'Master' and 'Father' in Equiano's Interesting Narrative." *Slavery and Abolition* 11 (1990): 216–26.

Edwards, Paul and David Dabydeen, eds. *Black Writers in Britain, 1760–1890.* Edinburgh: Edinburgh University Press, 1991.

Edwards, Paul and Polly Rewt, eds. *The Letters of Ignatius Sancho.* Edinburgh: Edinburgh University Press, 1994.

Egerton, Judy. *Hogarth's "Marriage A-la-Mode."* London: National Gallery Publication, 1997.

Ellis, Markman. *The Politics of Sensibility: Race, Gender and Commerce in the Sentimental Novel.* Cambridge: Cambridge University Press, 1996.

An Enquiry Concerning the Principles of Taste, and of the Origin of our Ideas of Beauty. London, 1785.

Epstein, Julia. *Altered Conditions: Disease, Medicine, and Storytelling.* New York: Routledge, 1995.

The Iron Pen: Frances Burney and the Politics of Women's Writing. Madison: University of Wisconsin Press, 1989.

Equiano, Olaudah. *The Interesting Narrative and Other Writings.* Ed. Vincent Carretta. New York: Penguin, 1995.

Eunuchism Display'd, Describing All the Different Sorts of Eunuchs; the Esteem they have met with in the World, and how they came to be made so. Wherein principally Is examin'd whether they are capable of Marriage, and if they ought to be suffer'd to enter into that State... London, 1718.

Fahrner, Robert. "A Reassessment of Garrick's *The Male Coquette: or, Seventeen-Hundred* As Veiled Discourse." *Eighteenth-Century Life* 17 (November 1993): 1–13.

Felsenstein, Frank, ed. *English Trader, Indian Maid: Representing Gender, Race, and Slavery in the New World.* Baltimore and London: The Johns Hopkins University Press, 1999.

The Female Monster or, The Second Part of The World Turn'd Topsy Turvey, A Satyr. London, 1705.

Female Rights Vindicated; or the Equality of the Sexes Morally and Physically Proved. London, 1758.

Ferguson, Margaret. "News From the New World: Miscegenous Romance in Aphra Behn's *Oroonoko* and *The Widow Ranter.*" In *The Production of English Renaissance Culture*, ed. David Lee Miller et al., 151–89. Ithaca: Cornell University Press, 1994.

"Transmuting *Othello*: Aphra Behn's *Oroonoko*." In *Cross-Cultural Performances: Differences in Women's Re-Visions of Shakespeare*, ed. Marianne Novy, 14–49. Urbana: University of Illinois Press, 1993.

Ferguson, Moira. *Subject to Others: British Women Writers and Colonial Slavery, 1670–1834*. London: Routledge, 1992.

Fielding, Sarah. *The Adventures of David Simple*. Ed. Malcolm Kelsall. Oxford and New York: Oxford University Press, 1987.

——. *The History of the Countess of Dellwyn*. 2 vols. in 1. 1759. Rpt. New York and London: Garland Publishing, Inc., 1974.

Finch, G. J. "Hawkesworth's Adaptation of Southerne's *Oroonoko*." *Restoration and 18th-Century Theatre Research* 16 (1977): 40–43.

Foster, George. *A Voyage Round the World*. Ed. Nicholas Thomas and Oliver Berghof. 2 vols. Honolulu, HI: University of Hawai'i Press, 2000.

Forster, Johann Reinhold. *Observations Made During a Voyage Round the World*. Ed. Nicholas Thomas, Harriet Guest, and Michael Dettelbach. Honolulu, HI: University of Hawai'i Press, 1996.

The Friendly Daemon. London, 1732.

Fryer, Peter. *Staying Power: The History of Black People in Britain*. London: Pluto Press, 1984.

Furibond; or, Harlequin Negro. The Songs Choruses & c. With a description of the Pantomime. As Performed at the Theatre Royal, Drury-Lane. Larpent Collection, Henry E. Huntington Library.

Gadeken, Sara. "Sarah Fielding and the Salic Law of Wit," *Studies in English Literature, 1500–1900*. 42.3 (2002): 541–57.

Gallagher, Catherine. *Nobody's Story: The Vanishing Acts of Women Writers in the Marketplace 1670–1820*. Berkeley: University of California Press, 1994.

Gates, Henry Louis, Jr. "Critical Remarks." In *Anatomy of Racism*, ed. David Theo Goldberg, 319–29. Minneapolis: University of Minnesota Press, 1990.

Gautier, Gary. "Henry and Sarah Fielding on Romance and Sensibility." *Novel* 31. 2 (1998): 195–214.

Gentleman, Francis. *Oroonoko: or the Royal Slave. A Tragedy. Altered from Southerne*. Glasgow, 1760.

George, M. Dorothy. *Catalogue of Political and Personal Satires... in the British Museum*. 11 vols. London: British Museum, 1938.

Gerzina, Gretchen. *Black England: Life Before Emancipation*. London: John Murray, 1995.

Gilman, Sander. *Sexuality: An Illustrated History*. New York: John Wiley and Sons, 1989.

Gilroy, Paul. *Against Race: Imagining Political Culture Beyond the Color Line*. Cambridge: Belknap Press of Harvard University Press, 2000.

Girdham, Jane. "Black Musicians in England: Ignatius Sancho and his Contemporaries." In *Ignatius Sancho: An African Man of Letters*, ed. Reyahn King, 116–24. London: National Portrait Gallery, 1997.

Gleeson, Brendan. *Geographies of Disability*. London and New York: Routledge, 1999.

Gold, Charles. *Oriental Drawings: Sketched Between the Years 1791 and 1798 [with descriptive text]*. London, 1806.

Goldberg, David Theo. *Racist Culture: Philosophy and the Politics of Meaning*. Oxford: Blackwell, 1993.

Goldsmith, Oliver. *An History of the Earth, and Animate Nature*. 8 vols. London, 1774.

Grundy, Isobel. *Lady Mary Wortley Montagu: Comet of the Enlightenment*. Oxford: Oxford University Press, 1999.

"Medical Advance and Female Fame: Inoculation and Its After-Effects." *Lumen* 13 (1994): 13–42.

Guest, Harriet. *Small Change: Women, Learning, Patriotism, 1750–1810*. Chicago: University of Chicago Press, 2000.

Hall, Kim. "Reading What Isn't There: 'Black' Studies in Early Modern England." *Stanford Humanities Review* 3. 1 (Winter 1993): 23–33.

Things of Darkness: Economies of Race and Gender in Early Modern England. Ithaca: Cornell University Press, 1995.

Hall, Stuart. "New Ethnicities." In *Stuart Hall: Critical Dialogues in Cultural Studies*, ed. David Morley and Kuan-Hsing Chen, 441–449. London: Routledge, 1996.

Halsband, Robert. "New Light on Lady Mary Wortley Montagu's Contribution to Inoculation." *Journal of the History of Medicine* 8 (1953): 401–02.

Haraway, Donna. "Ecco Homo, Ain't (Ar'n't) I a Woman, and Inappropriate/d Others: the Human in a Post-Humanist Landscape." In *Feminists Theorize the Political*, ed. Judith Butler and Joan W. Scott. New York and London: Routledge, 1992.

Hatch, James V. *The Black Image on the American Stage: A Bibliography of Plays and Musicals, 1770–1970*. New York: DramaBook Specialists Publications, 1970.

Hay, William. *Deformity: An Essay*. London, 1754.

Haygarth, John. *A Sketch of a Plan to Exterminate the Casual Small-Pox from Great Britain*. London, 1793.

Haywood, Eliza. *The Adventures of Eovaai*. London, 1736.

The History of Jemmy and Jenny Jessamy. 3 vols. London, 1753.

The Parrot. With a Compendium of the Times. By the Authoress of *The Female Spectator*. London, 1746.

Philidore and Placentia; or, L'Amour Trop Delicat. In *Four Before Richardson: Selected English Novels, 1720–1727*, ed. W. H. McBurney. Lincoln: University of Nebraska Press, 1963.

Hebe; or, the Art of Preserving Beauty, and Correcting Deformity. London, 1786.

Hecht, J. Jean. *Continental and Colonial Servants in Eighteenth-Century England*. Vol. 40 of Smith College Studies in History. Northampton, Mass., 1954.

Heller, Deborah. "Bluestocking Salons and the Public Sphere." *Eighteenth-Century Life* 22 ns. 2 (1998): 59–82.

Helvétius, Jean, M.D. *An Essay on the Animal Oeconomy. Together With Observations Upon the Smallpox*. Trans. from the French. London, 1723.

Hill, Bridget. *Women, Work, and Sexual Politics in Eighteenth-Century England*. Oxford: Blackwell, 1989.

Hillary, William, M.D. *A Rational and Mechanical Essay on the Small-Pox*. London, 1735.

Hitchcock, Tim, and Michèle Cohen, ed. *English Masculinities 1660–1800*. London: Longman, 1999.

Hogden, Margaret T. *Early Anthropology in the Sixteenth and Seventeenth Centuries*. Philadelphia: University of Pennsylvania Press, 1964.

Home, J. A., ed., *The Letters and Journals of Lady Mary Coke*. Facsimile 1970 of Kingsmead Reprints. 4 vols. Bath, 1889–1996.

Howe, Elizabeth. *The First English Actresses: Women and Drama 1660–1700*. Cambridge: Cambridge University Press, 1992.

Hudson, Nicholas. "From 'Nation' to 'Race': The Origin of Racial Classification in Eighteenth-Century Thought." *Eighteenth-Century Studies* 29. 3 (1996): 247–64.

Huet, Marie-Hélène. *Monstrous Imagination*. Cambridge: Harvard University Press, 1993.

Hulme, Peter. *Colonial Encounters: Europe and the Native Caribbean 1492–1797*. London and New York: Methuen, 1986.

Hume, David. *Essays Moral, Political and Literary*. Ed. Eugene F. Miller. Revised edition. Indianapolis: Liberty Fund, 1987.

Inchbald, Elizabeth. *The British Theatre; or, a Collection of Plays, which are acted at the Theatres Royal, Drury-Lane, Covent-Garden, and Haymarket ... with biographical and critical remarks by Mrs. Inchbald; in 25 volumes*. London: Longman, Hurst, Rees, Orme, and Brown [1811–25].

Ingrassia, Catherine. "Women Writing/Writing Women: Pope, Dulness, and 'Feminization' in the *Dunciad*." *Eighteenth-Century Life* 14 (November 1990): 40–58.

Isaac Lord Bishop of Worcester. *Sermon Preached Before His Grace, John Duke of Marlborough, President ... Hospital for the Small-Pox, and for Inoculation, at the Parish Church of St Andrew Holborn, Thurs. March 5, 1752*. London, 1752.

Jackson, Alfred. "London Playhouses, 1700–1705." *RES* 8 (1932): 291–302.

Jackson, John, Ten Years Manager of the Theatre Royal of Edinburgh. *The History of the Scottish Stage From Its First Establishment to the Present Time; with a Distinct Narrative of Some Recent Theatrical Transactions. The Whole Necessarily Interspersed With Memoirs of His Own Life*. Edinburgh: Peter Hill and G. G. J. and J. Robinson, 1793.

Jenner, Edward. *An Inquiry into the Cause and Effects of Variolae Vaccinae*. London, 1798.

Johnson, Samuel. *The Idler and The Adventurer*. Ed. W. J. Bate, John M. Bullitt, and L. F. Powell. vol. 2 of *The Yale Edition of the Works of Samuel Johnson*. Ed. W. J. Bate and Albrecht B. Strauss. 16 vols. New Haven: Yale University Press, 1963.

A Journey to the Western Islands of Scotland. Ed. Mary Lascelles. Vol. ix of *The Yale Edition of the Works of Samuel Johnson*. Ed. W. J. Bate and Albrecht B. Strauss. 16 vols. New Haven and London: Yale University Press, 1971.

The Rambler. Ed. W. J. Bate and Albrecht B. Strauss. Vol. IV of *The Yale Edition of the Works of Samuel Johnson*. 16 vols. New Haven and London: Yale University Press, 1963.

Jones, Ann Rosalind, and Peter Stallybrass. "Fetishizing Gender: Constructing the Hermaphrodite in Renaissance Europe." In *The Cultural Politics of Gender Ambiguity*, ed. Julia Epstein, and Kristina Straub, 80–111. New York: Routledge, 1991.

Jones, Eldred. *Othello's Countrymen: The African in English Renaissance Drama*. London: Oxford University Press, 1965.

Jordan, Thomas. *London Triumphant: or, The City in Jollity and Splendour: Expressed in Various Pageants, Shapes, Scenes, Speeches and Songs . . . for Sir Robert Hanson Knight, Lord Mayor of the City of London. At the Cost and Charges of the Worshipful Company of Grocers*. London, 1672.

A Royal Arbor of Loyal Poesie. London: R. Wood for Eliz. Andrews, 1664.

The Triumphs of London, Performed on Friday, Octob. 29. 1675, for the Entertainment of the Right Honorable, and Truly Noble Pattern of Prudence and Loyalty, Sir Joseph Sheldon Kt, Lord Mayor of the City of London . . . all set forth at the proper Costs and Charges of the Worshipful Company of Drapers. London, 1675.

Jordan, Winthrop. *White Over Black: American Attitudes Toward the Negro 1550–1812*. Chapel Hill: University of North Carolina Press, 1968.

Kaul, Suvir. "Reading Literary Symptoms: Colonial Pathologies and the *Oroonoko* Fictions of Behn, Southerne, and Hawkesworth." *Eighteenth-Century Life* 13. 3 (November 1994): 80–96.

Kay, Carol. *Political Constructions: Defoe, Richardson and Sterne in Relation to Hobbes, Hume, and Burke*. Ithaca: Cornell University Press, 1988.

"Canon, Ideology, and Gender: Mary Wollstonecraft's Critique of Adam Smith." *American Journal of Political Science* 15 (1986): 63–76.

Kelly, Gary, ed. *Bluestocking Feminism: Writings of the Bluestocking Circle, 1738–1785*. 6 vols. London: Pickering and Chatto, 1999.

King, Reyahn et al., eds. *Ignatius Sancho: An African Man of Letters*. London: National Portrait Gallery Publications, 1997.

King, Thomas A. "Performing 'Akimbo': Queer Pride and Epistemological Prejudice." In *The Politics and Poetics of Camp*, ed. Moe Meyer, 23–50. London and New York: Routledge, 1995.

Kiple, Kenneth F. *Plague, Pox, and Pestilence*. London: Weidenfeld and Nicolson, 1997.

Klein, Lawrence. *Shaftesbury and the Culture of Politeness: Moral Discourse and Cultural Politics in Early Eighteenth-Century England*. Cambridge: Cambridge University Press, 1994.

Knox, Vicesimus. "On the Present State of Conversation." In Vol. II of *Essays Moral and Literary*, 81–82. 2 vols. London, 1784.

Kowaleski-Wallace, Beth. "Shunning the Bearded Kiss: Castrati and the Definition of Female Sexuality." *Prose Studies* 15. 2 (August 1992): 153–70.

Kramnick, Jonathan. *Making the English Canon: Print Capitalism and the Cultural Past, 1700–1770*. Cambridge: Cambridge University Press, 1998.

Krasner, David. "Perspectives on American Minstrelsy." *Nineteenth Century Theatre* 27. 2 (1999): 137–51.

Lamb, Charles. *The Works of Charles Lamb*. 2 vols. London: C. and J. Ollier, 1818.

Lamb, Jonathan. *Preserving the Self in the South Seas, 1680–1840*. Chicago: University of Chicago Press, 2001.

Laqueur, Thomas. *Making Sex: Body and Gender From the Greeks to Freud*. Cambridge: Harvard University Press, 1990.

Lawrence, Errol. "Just Plain Common-Sense: the 'Roots' of Racism." In *The Empire Strikes Back: Race and Racism in 70s Britain*. Centre for Contemporary Cultural Studies. London: Hutchinson, 1982.

Lee, Rachel. " 'Faking, Dipping, Juking': (Asian) American Style As Cross-Racial Desire." Lecture at Center for the Study of Women, UCLA, December 1999.

Lewis, Jayne. "Compositions of Ill Nature: Women's Place in a Satiric Tradition." *Critical Matrix* 2.2 (1986): 31–69.

Lewis, W. S., Grover Cranin, Jr., and Charles H. Bennett, eds. *Horace Walpole's Correspondence to the Rev. William Mason*. Vol. 28–29. 1955. *The Yale Edition of Horace Walpole's Correspondence*. 48 vols. New Haven: Yale University Press, 1937–1985.

Lhamon, W. T., Jr. "Core Is Less." *Reviews in American History* 27.4 (1999): 566–71. *Raising Cain: Blackface Performance From Jim Crow to Hip Hop*. Cambridge: Harvard University Press, 1998.

The Life of Mr. James Quin, Comedian. London: Reader, 1887.

Lindfors, Bernth, ed. *Africans on Stage: Studies in Ethnological Show Business*. Bloomington: Indiana University Press, 1999.

Linnaeus, Carl. *A General System of Nature, Through the Three Grand Kingdoms of Animals, Vegetables, and Minerals, Systematically Divided*. Trans. William Turton, MD 7 vols. London: Lackington, Allen, and Company, 1802.

Livingstone, David N. and Charles W. J. Withers, eds. *Geography and Enlightenment*. Chicago: University of Chicago Press, 1999.

Long, Edward. *The History of Jamaica*. 3 vols. London, 1774.

Lonsdale, Roger, ed. *Eighteenth-Century Women Poets: An Oxford Anthology*. Oxford: Oxford University Press, 1989.

Lott, Eric. *Love and Theft: Blackface Minstrelsy and the American Working Class*. Oxford: Oxford University Press, 1993.

Lowe, Lisa. *Immigrant Acts: On Asian American Cultural Politics*. Durham: Duke University Press, 1996.

Lynch, Deirdre Shauna. *The Economy of Character: Novels, Market Culture, and the Business of Inner Meaning*. Chicago: University of Chicago Press, 1998.

MacCarthy, B. G. *The Female Pen: Women Writers and Novelists 1621–1818*. With a preface by Janet Todd. New York: New York University Press, 1994.

MacDonald, Joyce Green. "The Disappearing African Woman: Imoinda in *Oroonoko* After Behn." *ELH* 66 (1999): 71–86.

McGeary, Thomas. " 'Warbling Eunuchs': Opera, Gender, and Sexuality on the London Stage, 1705–1742." *Restoration and Eighteenth-Century Theatre Research* 7, no. 1 (1992): 1–22.

McKeon, Michael. "Historicizing Patriarchy: The Emergence of Gender Difference in England, 1660–1760." *ECS* 28.3 (1995): 295–322.

The Origins of the English Novel, 1660–1740. Baltimore and London: The Johns Hopkins University Press, 1987.

McKillop, Alan Dugald. *The Early Masters of English Fiction*. Lawrence: University of Kansas Press, 1956.

Samuel Richardson, Printer and Novelist. Chapel Hill: University of North Carolina Press, 1936.

Mack, Robert, ed. *Oriental Tales*. Oxford and New York: Oxford University Press, 1992.

Maitland, Charles. *Account of Inoculating the Smallpox Vindicated*. 2nd edn. London, 1723.

Marren, Susan M. "Between Slavery and Freedom: The Transgressive Self in Olaudah Equiano's Autobiography." *PMLA* 108 (1993): 94–105.

Marshall, Herbert, and Mildred Stock. *Ira Aldridge: The Negro Tragedian*. Carbondale: Southern Illinois University Press, 1968.

Marshall, P. J., and Glyndwr Williams. *The Great Map of Mankind: Perceptions of New Worlds in the Age of Enlightenment*. Cambridge: Harvard University Press, 1982.

Mayor, Adrienne. "The Nessus Shirt in the New World: Smallpox Blankets in History and Legend." *Journal of American Folklore* 108 (1995): 54–77.

Memoir and Theatrical Career of Ira Aldridge, the African Roscius. London, 1849.

Mignolo, Walter. *Local Histories / Global Designs: Coloniality, Subaltern Knowledge, and Border Making*. Princeton: Princeton University Press, 2000.

Mills, Charles W. *The Racial Contract*. Ithaca and New York: Cornell University Press, 1997.

Mirzoeff, Nicholas. *Silent Poetry: Deafness, Sign, and Visual Culture in Modern France*. Princeton: Princeton University Press, 1995.

Montagu, Lady Mary Wortley. *Essays and Poems and "Simplicity, A Comedy"*. Ed. Robert Halsband and Isobel Grundy. Oxford: Clarendon Press, 1977.

More, Hannah. "The Bas Bleu: or, Conversation." In *The Works of Hannah More. A New Edition, in Eleven Volumes*, 1: 290–305. London: T. Cadell, 1830.

Morgan, Jennifer. " 'Women Could Suckle Over Their Shoulder': Male Travelers, Female Bodies, and the Gendering of Racial Ideology, 1550–1700." *William and Mary Quarterly* 54. 1, Third Series (1997): 167–92.

Mosse, George L. *Toward the Final Solution: A History of European Racism*. New York: Howard Fertig, 1978.

Mudimbe, V. Y. *The Invention of Africa: Gnosis, Philosophy, and the Order of Knowledge*. Bloomington: Indiana University Press, 1988.

Myers, Norma. *Reconstructing the Black Past: Blacks in Britain c. 1780–1830*. London: Frank Cass, 1996.

Myers, Sylvia Harcstark. *The Bluestocking Circle: Women, Friendship, and the Life of the Mind in Eighteenth-Century England*. Oxford: Clarendon Press, 1990.

A New Relation of the Inner-Part of the Grand Seignor's Seraglio. London, 1677.

Newman, Gerald. *The Rise of English Nationalism: A Cultural History, 1740–1830*. London: Weidenfeld and Nicholson, 1987.

Newman, Karen. *Fashioning Femininity and English Renaissance Drama*. Chicago: University of Chicago Press, 1991.

Nichols, John. *Literary Anecdotes of the Eighteenth Century*. 9 vols. London, 1815.

Noble, Yvonne. "Castrati, Balzac, and Barthes' *S/Z*." *Comparative Drama* 31.1 (1997/98): 28–41.

Nussbaum, Felicity. *The Autobiographical Subject: Gender and Ideology*. Baltimore: The Johns Hopkins University Press, 1982.

   Torrid Zones: Maternity, Sexuality, and Empire in Eighteenth-Century English Narratives. Baltimore: The Johns Hopkins University Press, 1995.

   ed. *The Global Eighteenth Century*. Baltimore: The Johns Hopkins University Press, 2003.

Oldfield, J. R. " 'The Ties of Soft Humanity': Slavery and Race in British Drama, 1760–1800," *HLQ* 56 (1993): 1–14.

Omi, Michael, and Howard Winant. *Racial Formation in the United States: From the 1960s to the 1980s*. London: Routledge & Kegan Paul, 1986.

Orban, Katalin. "Dominant and Submerged Discourses in *The Life of Olaudah Equiano (or Gustavus Vassa)*." *African American Review* 27. 4 (1993): 655–64.

Orthopaedia: or, the Art of Correcting and Preventing Deformities in Children. Trans. from the French of M. Andry. London, 1743.

Oyewumi, Oyeronke. *The Invention of Women: Making an African Sense of Western Gender Discourses*. Minneapolis: University of Minnesota Press, 1997.

Parker, Patricia. "Fantasies of 'Race' and 'Gender': Africa, *Othello* and Bringing to Light." In *Women, "Race," and Writing in the Early Modern Period*, ed. Margo Hendricks and Patricia Parker, 84–100. London and New York: Routledge, 1994.

Pearson, Jacqueline. "Blacker than Hell Creates: Pix Rewrites *Othello*." In *Broken Boundaries: Women and Feminism in Restoration Drama*, ed. Katherine M. Quinsey, 13–30. Lexington: University of Kentucky Press, 1996.

Pennington, Rev. Montagu, ed. *Letters From Mrs. Elizabeth Carter to Mrs. Montagu, Between the Years 1755 and 1800*. 3 vols. London: F. D. and J. Rivington, 1817.

   Memoirs of the Life of Mrs Elizabeth Carter, With a New Edition of Her Poems; to Which Are Added, Some Miscellaneous Essays and Prose, Together With Her Notes on the Bible, 2nd edn. 2 vols. London: Printed for F. C. and J. Rivington, 1808.

   Series of Letters Between Mrs. Elizabeth Carter and Miss Catherine Talbot, from the Year 1741 to 1770: to which are added, Letters from Mrs. Elizabeth Carter to Mrs. Vesey, Between the Years 1763 and 1787, Four Volumes Printed in 3. 3rd edn. London, 1819.

Peschel, Enid and Richard. "The Castrati in Opera." *Opera Quarterly* 4.4 (Winter 1986–87): 21–38.

Piozzi, Hester Lynch. *Anecdotes of the Late Samuel Johnson: During the Last Twenty Years of his Life*. 4th edn. London 1786.

Plumptre, James. *The Plague Stayed: A Scriptural View of Pestilence, Particularly of That Dreadful Pestilence the Small-Pox, With Consideration on the Cow-Pock; in Two Sermons, &c.* London, 1805.

Pocock, J. G. A. *Virtue, Commerce, and History: Essays on Political Thought and History, Chiefly in the Eighteenth Century.* Cambridge: Cambridge University Press, 1985.

Popple, William. *The Prompter.* No. 7 (4 December 1734).

Potkay, Adam. "Olaudah Equiano and the Art of Spiritual Autobiography." *Eighteenth-Century Studies* 27. 4 (Summer 1994): 677–92.

Poullain de La Barre, François. *The Woman as Good as the Man Or, the Equality of Both Sexes.* Trans. A. L., ed. Gerald M. MacLean. Detroit: Wayne State University Press, 1988.

Pratt, Mary Louise. *Imperial Eyes: Travel Writing and Transculturation.* London: Routledge, 1992.

The Pretty Gentleman; or, Softness of Manners Vindicated. Ed. Edmund Goldsmid. 1747. Edinburgh: Privately printed, 1885.

Price, Curtis, Judith Milhous, and Robert D. Hume. *Italian Opera in Late Eighteenth-Century London.* 2 vols. Oxford: Clarendon Press, 1995.

Price, Lawrence Marsden. *Inkle and Yarico Album.* Berkeley: University of California Press, 1937.

Price, Martin. *To the Palace of Wisdom: Studies in Order and Energy From Dryden to Blake.* Carbondale: Southern Illinois University Press, 1964.

Rackin, Phyllis. "Historical Difference/Sexual Difference." In *Privileging Gender in Early Modern England*, ed. Jean R. Brink. *Sixteenth-Century Essays and Studies* 23 (1993): 37–63.

Randall, Dale B. J. *Winter Fruit: English Drama 1642–1660.* Lexington: University of Kentucky Press, 1995.

Randolph, Mary Claire. "Female Satirists of Ancient Ireland." *Southern Folklore Quarterly* 5. 2 (June 1942): 75–87.

Rao, Ananda Vital. *A Minor Augustan, Being the Life and Works of George, Lord Lyttelton, 1709–1773.* Calcutta: The Book Company, 1934.

Razzell, Peter. *Edward Jenner's Cowpox Vaccine: The History of A Medical Myth.* Firle, England: Caliban Books, 1977.

Reeve, Christopher. *Still Me.* New York: Ballantine, 1999.

Reeve, Clara. *The Progress of Romance.* Vol. 6 in *Bluestocking Femininism: Writings of the Bluestocking Circle, 1738–1785*, ed. Gary Kelly, 6 vols. New York, Pickering and Chatto, 1999.

Review of Olaudah Equiano's *Narrative. Gentleman's Magazine* 1 (June 1789): 539.

Riley, James C. *The Eighteenth-Century Campaign to Avoid Disease.* New York: St. Martin's Press, 1987.

Ritvo, Harriet. *The Platypus and the Mermaid and Other Figments of the Classifying Imagination.* Cambridge: Harvard University Press, 1997.

Roach, Joseph. *Cities of the Dead: Circum-Atlantic Performance.* New York: Columbia University Press, 1996.

"Power's Body: The Inscription of Morality As Style." In *Interpreting the Theatrical Past: Essays in the Historiography of Performance*, ed. Thomas Postlewait, and Bruce McConachie, 99–118. Iowa City: University of Iowa Press, 1989.

Roberts, Diane. *The Myth of Aunt Jemima: Representations of Race and Region*. London and New York: Routledge, 1994.

Rogers, Pat. "The Breeches Parts." In *Sexuality in Eighteenth-Century Britain*, ed. Paul-Gabriel Boucé, 244–56. Manchester: Manchester University Press, 1982.

Romack, Katherine. "Women's Representational Practice, 1642–60." Diss., Syracuse University, 2000.

Roscius Anglicanus, or an Historical Review of the Stage. London, 1708. Ed. Judith Milhous and Robert D. Hume. London: The Society for Theatre Research, 1987.

Rose, Philip, M.D. *An Essay on the Small-Pox; Whether natural, or inoculated. Shewing That by a New and Particular Method, the Dangerous Symptoms, and Fatal Consequences, in Either Sort, May Be Prevented, or Removed, and many Lives Saved. Wherein likewise All the OBJECTIONS Brought Against INOCULATION, Are proved to Be Both* Groundless *and* Ridiculous. London, 1724.

Rosenfeld, Sybil. *The Theatre of the London Fairs in the 18th Century*. Cambridge: Cambridge University Press, 1960.

Rousseau, Jean-Jacques. *Discourse on the Origins of Inequality (Second Discourse), Polemics, and Political Economy*. Vol. iii of *The Collected Writings of Rousseau*, ed. Roger D. Masters and Christopher Kelly, trans. Judith R. Bush et al. 9 vols. Hanover and London: University Press of New England, 1992.

The Royal African: Or, Memoirs of the Young Prince of Annamaboe. London, *c.* 1749.

Samuels, Wilfred D. "Disguised Voice in *The Interesting Narrative of Olaudah Equiano, or Gustavus Vassa, the African*." *Black American Literature Forum* 19 (1985): 64–69.

Sancho, Ignatius. *Letters of the Late Ignatius Sancho, An African*. Ed. Vincent Carretta. New York: Penguin, 1998.

Sancho's Letters, With Memoirs of His Life by Joseph Jekyll Esq. M.P. 5th edn. London: William Sancho, 1803. Facsimile edition. Ed. Paul Edwards. London: Dawsons, 1968.

Sandiford, Keith A. *Measuring the Moment: Strategies of Protest in Eighteenth-Century Afro-English Writing*. Selinsgrove: Susquehanna University Press, 1988.

Schiebinger, Londa. *The Mind Has No Sex? Women in the Origins of Modern Science*. Cambridge: Harvard University Press, 1989.

Scobie, Edward. *Black Britannia: A History of Blacks in Britain*. Chicago: Johnson Publishing Company, Inc., 1972.

Scott, Sarah. *A Description of Millenium Hall*. Ed. Gary Kelly. Ontario: Broadview Press, 1995.

The History of Sir George Ellison. Ed. Betty Rizzo. Lexington: University of Kentucky, 1996.

Les Sérails de Londres, ou Les Amusemens Nocturnes... et le Description des Courtisannes les plus célèbres. 4 vols. in 2. Paris [Londres], 1801.

Shakespeare, Tom and Nicholas Watson. "The Social Model of Disability: An Outdated Ideology?" In *Exploring Theories and Expanding Methologies: Where We Are and Where We Need to Go*, ed. Sharon N. Barnart and Barbara M. Altman. 2 vols. JAI: London, 2001.

Shami, Seteney. "Prehistories of Globilization: Circassian Identity in Motion." *Public Culture* 12. 1 (2000): 177–204.

Shapiro, Susan C. " 'Yon Plumed Dandebrat': Male 'Effeminacy' in English Satire and Criticism." *RES* 39, no. 155 (1988): 400–12.

Sharpe, Jenny. " 'Something Akin to Freedom': The Case of Mary Prince." *Differences* 8. 1 (1996): 31–56.

Sherman, Stuart. *Telling Time: Clocks, Diaries, and English Diurnal Form, 1660–1785.* Chicago: University of Chicago Press, 1996.

Shyllon, Folarin. *Black People in Britain, 1555–1833.* London: Oxford University Press, 1977.

"Olaudah Equiano: Nigerian Abolitionist and First National Leader of Africans in Britain." *Journal of African Studies* 4 (1977): 433–51.

Sibscota, George. *The Deaf and Dumb Man's Discourse. Or a Treatise concerning those that are Born Deaf and Dumb, containing a Discovering of their knowledge or understanding; as also the Method they use, to manifest the sentiments of their Mind.* London, 1670.

Sklar, Elizabeth D. "So Male a Speech: Linguistic Adequacy in Eighteenth-Century England." *American Speech* 64. 4 (1989): 372–79.

Smith, Valerie. *Self-Discovery and Authority in Afro-American Narrative.* Cambridge: Harvard University Press, 1987.

Southern, Eileen. "Black Musicians and Early Ethiopian Minstrelsy." In *Inside the Minstrel Mask*, ed. Annemarie Bean, James V. Hatch, Brooks McNamara, 43–63. Hanover, NH : Wesleyan University Press, 1996.

Southern[e], Thomas. *Oroonoko. A Tragedy, in Five Acts. As Performed at the Theatre Royal, Covent Garden.* London: Longman, Hurst, Rees, and Orme, 1816.

Oroonoko. Ed. Maximillian E. Novak, and David Stuart Rodes. Lincoln: University of Nebraska Press, 1976.

Oroonoko, A Tragedy. Edinburgh, 1774.

Oroonoko, A Tragedy, As It Is Now Acted at the Theatre Royal in Drury-Lane. London, 1775.

Oroonoko, Adapted for Theatrical Representation As Performed at the Theatres-Royal, Drury-Lane and Covent-Garden. Regulated From the Prompt-Books, by Permission of the Managers. London, 1791.

Oroonoko, A Tragedy, As it is now Acted at the Theatre Royal in Drury Lane. With alterations by John Hawkesworth, LL.D. London, 1759.

Spencer, Jane. *The Rise of the Woman Novelist from Aphra Behn to Jane Austen.* New York: Basil Blackwell, 1986.

Stahle, Rachel S. "The Guilt-Heavy Theology of Cotton Mather." *Modern Theology* 5 (1997): 12–17.

Stallybrass, Peter, and Allon White. *The Politics and Poetics of Transgression.* Ithaca: Cornell University Press, 1986.

Starke, Mariana. *The Widow of Malabar, A Tragedy in Three Acts.* 3rd edn. London, 1791.

Staves, Susan. "A Few Kind Words for the Fop." *SEL* 22 (1982): 413–28.

" 'The Liberty of a She-Subject of England': Rights Rhetoric and the Female Thucydides." *Cardozo Studies in Law and Literature* 1. 2 (1989): 161–83.

Stedman, John Gabriel. *Narrative of a Five Years Expedition Against the Revolted Negroes of Surinam.* Ed. Richard Price and Sally Price. Baltimore and London: The Johns Hopkins University Press, 1988.

Steele, Richard. *The Tatler.* Ed. Donald F. Bond. 3 vols. Oxford: Clarendon Press, 1987.

Sterne, Lawrence. *The Life and Opinions of Tristram Shandy.* Ed. Ian Campbell Ross. Oxford: Oxford University Press, 1983.

Still, Judith and Michael Warton, ed. *Textuality and Sexuality: Reading Theories and Practices.* Manchester and New York: Manchester University Press, 1993.

Stoddard, Eve W. "A Serious Proposal for Slavery Reform: Sarah Scott's *Sir George Ellison.*" *Eighteenth-Century Studies* 28. 4 (1995): 379–96.

Stokes, James. "Women and Mimesis in Medieval and Renaissance Somerset (and Beyond)." *Comparative Drama* 27 (1993): 176–96.

Stoler, Ann Laura. *Race and the Education of Desire: Foucault's "History of Sexuality" and the Colonial Order of Things.* Durham: Duke University Press, 1995.

Stone, George Winchester, Jr., ed. 2 vols. Pt. 4, *1747–1776* of *The London Stage 1660–1800; a calendar of plays, entertainments & afterpieces, together with casts, box-receipts and contemporary comment.* Carbondale: Southern Illinois University Press, 1960–1968.

Stone, Lawrence. *The Family, Sex, and Marriage 1500–1800.* London: Weidenfeld and Nicolson, 1977.

Straub, Kristina. *Divided Fictions: Fanny Burney and Feminine Strategy.* Lexington: University of Kentucky Press, 1987.

Sexual Suspects: Eighteenth-Century Players and Sexual Ideology. Princeton: Princeton University Press , 1992.

Stuurman, Siep. "From Feminism to Biblical Criticism: The Theological Trajectory of François Poulain de la Barre." *Eighteenth-Century Studies* 33 (2000): 367–82.

Styan, J. L. *Restoration Comedy in Performance.* Cambridge: Cambridge University Press, 1986.

Suleri, Sara. *The Rhetoric of English India.* Chicago: University of Chicago Press, 1992.

Sussman, Charlotte. "The Other Problem with Women: Reproduction and Slave Culture in Aphra Behn's *Oroonoko.*" In *Rereading Aphra Behn: History, Theory and Criticism,* ed. Heidi Hutner, 212–31. Charlottesville: University of Virginia Press, 1993.

Swinburne, Henry. *A Treatise of Spousal, or Matrimonial Contracts: Wherein All the Questions relating to that Subject Are ingeniously Debated and Resolved.* London, 1686.

Sypher, Wylie. "Chatterton's *African Ecologues* and the Deluge." *PMLA* 54 (1939): 246–60.

Guinea's Captive Kings: British Anti-Slavery Literature of the 18th Century. Chapel Hill: University of North Carolina Press, 1942.

Talbot, Catherine. *Essays on Various Subjects* 2 vols. London, 1772.

Tench, Captain Watkin. *A Narrative Expedition to Botany Bay and A Complete Account of the Settlement at Port Jackson.* Ed. Tim Flannery. Melbourne: Text Publishing, 1996.

Thicknesse, Philip. *A Year's Journey Through France and Part of Spain.* 2nd edn. 2 vols. London, 1788.

Thomas, Nicholas. *Entangled Objects: Exchange, Material Culture, and Colonialism in the Pacific.* Cambridge: Harvard University Press, 1991.

In Oceania: Visions, Artifacts, Histories. Durham and London: Duke University Press, 1997.

Thompson, E. P. *Customs in Common.* New York: The New Press, 1991.

Thomson, Rosemarie Garland. *Extraordinary Bodies: Figuring Physical Disability in American Culture and Literature.* New York: Columbia University Press, 1997.

Thorndike, Lynn. "De Complexionibus." *Isis* 49, Pt. 4, no. 158 (December 1958): 398–408.

Thrale, Mrs. Hester Lynch (Salusbury). *The Letters of Mrs. Thrale.* Ed. R. Brimley Johnson. New York: Dial Press, 1926.

Tobin, James. *Cursory Remarks Upon the Reverend Mr. Ramsay's Essay on the Treatment and Conversion of African Slaves in the Sugar Colonies.* London, 1785.

Todd, Dennis. *Imagining Monsters: Miscreations of the Self in Eighteenth-Century England.* Chicago: University of Chicago Press, 1995.

Todd, Janet. *The Sign of Angellica: Women, Writing and Fiction, 1660–1800.* London: Virago, 1989.

Tokson, Elliot. *The Popular Image of the Black Man in English Drama 1550–1668.* Boston: G.K. Hall, 1982.

Tomaselli, Sylvana. "The Enlightenment Debate on Women." *History Workshop* 20 (Autumn 1985): 101–24.

The Treasure: or Impartial Compendium, no. 3259. London, 1771.

Trumbach, Randolph. "The Birth of the Queen: Sodomy and the Emergence of Gender Equality in Modern Culture, 1660–1750." In *Hidden From History: Reclaiming the Gay and Lesbian Past*, ed. Martin Duberman, Martha Vicinus, and George Chauncey Jr., 129–40. New York: New American Library, 1989.

"London Sodomites: Homosexual Behaviour and Western Culture in the 18th Century." *Journal of Social History* 11. 1 (1977): 1–33.

Uffenbach, Zacharias Conrad von. *London in 1710: From the Travels of Zacharias Conrad Von Uffenbach.* Trans. W. H. Quarrell and Margaret Mare. London: Faber and Faber, 1934.

Van Zwanenbert, David. "The Suttons and the Business of Inoculation." *Medical History* 22 (1978): 71–82.

Vermillion, Mary. "Buried Heroism: Critiques of Female Authorship in Southerne's Adaptation of Behn's *Oroonoko*." *Restoration Studies in Literary Culture 1660–1700* 16 (1992): 28–37.

Vickery, Amanda. "Golden Age to Separate Spheres: A Review of the Categories and Chronology of English Women's History." *Historical Journal* 36. 2 (1993): 383–414.

Waddington, Lady Llanover Hall, ed. *The Autobiography and Correspondence of Mary Granville, Mrs. Delany*. 1st ser. 3 vols. London: R. Bentley, 1861.

Wagstaffe, William. *A Letter to Dr. Freind; Shewing the Danger and Uncertainty of Inoculating the Small Pox*. London, 1722.

Walker, Robert, M.D., Fellow of the Royal College of Surgeons. *An Inquiry into the Smallpox, Medical and Political. Wherein A Successful Method of Treating That Disease Is Proposed, the Cause of Pits Explained, and the Method of Their Prevention Pointed Out*. London, 1790.

Ward, Edward. *The Secret History of the Clubs; Particularly the Kit-Cat, Beef-stake, Vertuosos, Quacks, Knight of the Golden-Fleece, Florists, Beaus & c.* London, 1709.

Watts, Sheldon. "The African Connection." In *Epidemics and History: Disease, Power and Imperialism*, 109–14. New Haven: Yale University Press, 1997.

Wechselblatt, Martin. "Finding Mr. Boswell: Rhetorical Authority and National Identity in Johnson's *A Journey to the Western Islands of Scotland*." *ELH* 60.1 (Spring 1993): 117–48.

Whaley, John. *A Collection of Poems*. London, 1732.

Wheatley, Phillis. *Poems on Various Subjects, Religious and Moral*. London, 1773.

Wheeler, J. "Reading and Other Recreations of Marylanders, 1700–1776." *Maryland Historical Magazine* 38 (1943).

Wheeler, Roxann. *The Complexion of Race: Categories of Difference in Eighteenth-Century Culture*. Philadelphia: University of Pennsylvania Press, 2000.

White, Hayden. "The Noble Savage Theme as Fetish." In *Tropics of Discourse: Essays in Cultural Criticism*, 183–96. Baltimore and London: The Johns Hopkins University Press, 1978.

Wiegman, Robyn. *American Anatomies: Theorizing Race and Gender*. Durham and London: Duke University Press, 1995.

Wilson, Kathleen. "Citizenship, Empire, and Modernity in the English Provinces, c. 1720–1790." *Eighteenth-Century Studies* 29, no. 1 (1995): 69–96.

The Island Race: Englishness, Empire and Gender in the Eighteenth Century. London: Routledge, 2003.

The Sense of the People: Politics, Culture and Imperialism in England, 1715–1785. Cambridge: Cambridge University Press, 1995.

Winzer, Margaret A. *The History of Special Education: From Isolation to Integration*. Washington, DC: Gallaudet University Press, 1993.

Wiseman, Susan. *Drama and Politics in the English Civil War*. Cambridge: Cambridge University Press, 1998.

Wollstonecraft, Mary. *A Vindication of the Rights of Woman.* Ed. Carol H. Poston.
  New York: W. W. Norton, 1975.
Woman Not Inferior to Man. London, 1739.
Woodward, Carolyn. "Sarah Fielding's Self-Destructing Utopia." In *Living By the
  Pen: Early British Women Writers*, ed. Dale Spender, 65–81. New York: Teachers
  College Press, 1992.
Wraxall, N. William. *Historical Memoirs of My Own Time.* 1815. Rpt. London:
  Kegan Paul, 1904.
Young, Edward, *The Revenge as performed at the Theatres-Royal Covent Garden and
  Drury Lane* in *The British Theatre: or, a Collection of Plays, . . . by Mrs. Inchbald
  in 25 volumes* (London: Longman, Hurst, Rees, Orme and Brown, 1811–25),
  vol. XII.
Young, Robert J. C. *Colonial Desire: Hybridity in Theory, Culture and Race.* London:
  Routledge, 1995.
Zonitch, Barbara. *Familiar Violence: Gender and Social Upheaval in the Novels of
  Frances Burney.* Newark: University of Delaware Press, 1997.
Zwanenbert, David van. "The Suttons and the Business of Inoculation." *Medical
  History* 22 (1978): 71–82.

Index

Note: Page references in italics indicate illustrations and their captions.

Montagu, Elizabeth Robinson (*cont.*)
 and complexion 150
 and deformity 78
 and degeneration 110
 Essay on Shakespeare 73, 74, 75, 78–81, 89
 and "feminalities" 75, 89
 and Johnson 18, 60–61, 73–82, 89
 and Lyttelton 73–74, 77, 100
 as philanthropist 143, 144–45
 and racial impersonation 140–41
 and smallpox 118
 and Sterne's *Tristram Shandy* 101–02, 107–08
Montagu, George Brudenell, 4th Earl of Cardigan and Duke of 219
Montagu, Lady Mary Wortley
 "A Plain Account of the Inoculating of the Small Pox" 114
 and Pope 78
 as satirist 61
 "Satturday: The Small Pox" 18, 119–20, 124, 126
 and smallpox 114, 119
The Moor of Venice 156–70
More, Hannah
 as Bluestocking 87, 96–97, 99
 and racial mixing 239
 and racialized femininity 142
Morgan, Jennifer 156
The Morning Post and Daily Advertiser 221
Morton, Thomas, *The Slave* 233–35, 241, 252
Mosse, George L. 136
Mr. Campbell's Packet 39
Mudimbe, V. Y. 42
mulattoes and mulattas 20, 155, 157, 167, 251
Mungo, as nickname 6–8, 9, 211, 221
musicians, black 169
muteness 28–30, 43–44
 see also Campbell, Duncan

nationalism *see* identity, national
Neville, Henry, *The Isle of Pines* 153
Newman, Ken 130
nominalism, cultural 136
normality 1, 41, 55, 56, 72
 and gender 27
 and the other 110, 239
 and whiteness 172
novel, English
 as domestic 86
 and racial romance 241
 smallpox in 116
 for women 100–01
 see also Behn, Aphra; Burney, Frances; Haywood, Eliza; Scott, Sarah; Sterne, Laurence
novelty, and *Tristram Sandy* 108

oddity
 and Campbell 40
 and Johnson 76, 105
 in *Tristram Shandy* 84–85, 102, 103–08
 see also anomaly; monstrosity; primitiveness
Omai (Tahitian) 208, 243, 255
Omi, Michael and Winant, Howard 136
ornamentation 77, 78, 81, 94–95
 and difference 18, 142, 143, 198, 230
Orthopaedia: or, the Art of Correcting and Preventing Deformities in Children 25, 26
Osborne, Anne (wife of Equiano Sancho) 167, 208
Othello *see* Shakespeare, William, *Othello*
other
 and abnormality 41, 44, 243–44
 and the exotic 3, 94–95, 110, 140, 182, 236
 and the self 162
Oyewumi, Oyeronke 201

The Padlock see Bickerstaffe, Isaac
pantomime 169, 221, 227–30, 241
Park, Mungo, *Travels in the Interior Districts of Africa* 4, 206
The Parrot 42, 137–38
parrots
 and race 137–38, 195
 and speech 42–43, 136–37
patriarchy 228
 and economic values 123
 and race 163, 225, 228, 244
 and satire 68
patriotism
 female 12, 68, 79
 male 87, 233
Pearson, Jacqueline 161
Pepys, Sir William Weller 85
perversity, sexual
 and Amazons 33
 and women writers 60
philanthropy
 and class 127, 143–45
 and gender 86
Pickering, Priscilla Pointon 30
Pilkington, Laetitia
 Memoirs 59
 as satirist 61
Pix, Mary
 Conquest of Spain 159
 The False Friend 159
 and women of color 161
Plumptre, James 114–15, 119
poetry
 anti-slavery 192–94
 and racial romance 190–94, 241, 242

venereal disease *see* disease
Vesey, Agmondesham 95
Vesey, Elizabeth
  as anomaly 99
  as Bluestocking 85, 87, 96
    correspondence 17, 91, 92, 93, 96, 99, 100
    and gatherings 95–99
  and deafness 97–99
  depression 93, 100
  and Sterne 100
  and withdrawal from public life 91
violence
  racialized 20, 124, 227, 235
  see also cruelty
virtue
  and beauty 27, 118
  and complexion 116, 157, 158, 161, 206, 230,
    233, 235, 248
  and defect 130
  female 12, 25, 59, 71, 90, 172, 174, 176,
    177
  male 62, 72, 86
  skin color 247
Voltaire, F. M. A. de 75, 79, 80, 81, 83

Wagstaffe, William 114
Walker, Sir Robert 111, 113, 118
Walpole, Horace
  and Bluestockings 74, 88, 96
  The Castle of Otranto 232
  and Soubise 7
war
  and masculinity 201
  and national identity 84, 111, 199
  see also Seven Years' War
Webster, John, *The White Devil* 158
Weddell, Mrs. 246–47, 249
Weekly Medley 39
West Indies
  and skin color 155–56, 182, 190
  and slavery 135, 143, 176, 200
  see also Jamaica
Whaley, John 120
Wheatley, Phillis 156
White, Hayden 236, 243
whiteness 36, 156, 177
  and character 138, 140
  and civilization 182
  and deformity 206
  essential 230, 237
  and femininity 160, 161, 172, 175, 187
  and national identity 149, 150
  as norm 172
  and performance of race 236
Wilberforce, William 239

Williams, Anna 73
Williams, Francis 136
Wilson, Kathleen 198
wit
  and masculinity 72, 101, 107
  and satire 63, 64–66, 82
Woffington, Peg (actress) 71
Wollstonecraft, Mary
  and degeneracy 109–10
  and effeminacy and retardation 25, 109
  and femininity 62, 142
  Vindication of the Rights of Woman 20, 109–10,
    131, 200
womb, as defective 23, 25, 28, 33, 38, 108
women
  black
    in England 162–69, 188, 206
    eroticization 165, 191
    and human rights 194
    as satirical figures 164
    as slaves 202
    on stage *see* actresses
  commodification 141–42, 174
  as defective *see* defect, femininity as
    disabled 17, 25, 28–30
  effects of smallpox 18
  and fencing 8
  and national identity 81
  as pinnacle of human species 10–11
  in private sphere 59, 60, 91, 201
  in public sphere *see* public sphere 87
  as talkative 42
  trade in 141–42
  and travel narratives 4, 5–6
  and virtue 11–12, 25, 59, 71
  see also actresses; Bluestockings;
    empowerment; femininity
Woodville, William 115
working classes
  and competition from blacks 222, 224
  and degeneration 111
  and femininity 130
  and race 222, 224, 225–26, 227
  and smallpox 115
Wraxall, N. William 94, 99
writers, female
  as Amazons 59, 68, 79, 80, 176
  black 156
  as Bluestockings 87
  as British 68
  and Campbell 38, 39, 41
  and cult of domesticity 59–60, 68
  and defect 17, 27, 30, 120
  and effeminacy 61–67
  and friendship 18, 65–66, 91–94